The Ten Lost Tribes

The Ten Lost Tribes

A World History

ZVI BEN-DOR BENITE

OXFORD
UNIVERSITY PRESS

2009

OXFORD
UNIVERSITY PRESS

Oxford University Press, Inc., publishes works that further
Oxford University's objective of excellence
in research, scholarship, and education.

Oxford   New York
Auckland   Cape Town   Dar es Salaam   Hong Kong   Karachi
Kuala Lumpur   Madrid   Melbourne   Mexico City   Nairobi
New Delhi   Shanghai   Taipei   Toronto

With offices in
Argentina   Austria   Brazil   Chile   Czech Republic   France   Greece
Guatemala   Hungary   Italy   Japan   Poland   Portugal   Singapore
South Korea   Switzerland   Thailand   Turkey   Ukraine   Vietnam

Published by Oxford University Press, Inc.
198 Madison Avenue, New York, New York 10016

www.oup.com

Oxford is a registered trademark of Oxford University Press

Library of Congress Cataloging-in-Publication Data
Ben-Dor Benite, Zvi.
    The ten lost tribes : a world history / Zvi Ben-Dor Benite.
        p. cm.
    Includes bibliographical references.
    ISBN 978-0-19-530733-7
    1. Lost tribes of Israel.   2. Jews—History.   3. Jewish diaspora—History.   I. Title.
    DS131.B35 2009
    909'.04924—dc22   2009001739

9 8 7 6 5 4 3 2 1

Printed in the United States of America
on acid-free paper

For Zvi Salih,

Sassoon Ghazal,

and Miriam b. Samra,

of blessed memory,

and Salha b. Lulu,

my grandparents

Acknowledgments

The idea of writing a world history of the ten lost tribes was born during two conversations I had in the summer of 2004, one with Avner Ben-Zaken and another with David Myers. I thank them both. Eugene Sheppard, Center for Exilic Studies, always thought it was a good idea to write about exile. I thank him for his encouragement. I have never met Professor Tudor Parfitt, but his scholarship on the ten tribes convinced me that a history of things lost is not only possible, but is also an exciting adventure. I received further encouragement from Jerry Bentley, who was patient enough to spend time with me when I simply seized him during the annual meeting of the American Historical Association in January 2005. His work in the field of world history has always been a source of inspiration for me. At New York University, I have benefited immensely from the friendship of Joanna Waley-Cohen. A senior colleague in my own core field of Qing China, Joanna patiently listened to my never-ending monologues about the ten tribes and was a friend in many other ways besides. Many conversations with Luke Fleming helped me to think more clearly about some of the issues. My friend Jay Furman's sustained interest in the book for two whole years was a special source of encouragement. I thank all of them for their enthusiasm.

Writing a world history takes the author in many directions where, in my case, I found helpful and friendly colleagues. I was lucky to have the occasional ear of and receive tips from (among many others) Gil Anidjar, Nicola Di Cosmo, Simo Parpola, Haggai Ram, and Elchanan Reiner. Elchanan, who always knows where to find the most elusive sources, helped me to obtain copies of several rare documents used in this book and helped with the translation of few crucial passages in Yiddish. My colleagues at NYU's history department, Kostis Smyrlis and Yanni Kotsonis, helped to clarify the meaning of specific words in Greek. Edward Sullivan, dean of humanities at NYU, took hours of his busy time to help me find ways into sixteenth-century Spanish history. Above all, I am profoundly indebted to Amnon Raz-Krakotzkin for the thoughtful care, unparalleled generosity, and unflagging support with which he engaged with this book, which in many ways is written in dialogue with his thought. I cannot thank Amnon enough for all that I learned and gained from him. For me, Amnon truly embodies what Confucius means when he says that a scholar should be both "earnest and keen amongst friends."

A faculty fellowship at the Remarque Institute at NYU helped me start writing in the spring of 2006. I thank its director, Professor Tony Judt, for his support and friendship. The staff of the Remarque Institute, particularly Jennifer Ren, was very helpful with many technical aspects of this book's production. Jair Kessler, assistant director of the institute, gave immense and relentless support at critical stages. I am deeply grateful to her.

I am also grateful to Dr. Marcel and Deborah (Dvorah) van den Broecke of *Cartographica Neerlandica* (www.orteliusmaps.com) for their kindness and for allowing me to use Abraham Ortelius's maps. They also provided good quality scans of them. I also thank Rolf Stein (www.classicalgraphics.de), who provided a scan of Sebastian Münster's woodblock of Asia and permitted me to use it here. Adam Hirschberg, rights and permissions associate at Cambridge University Press, was prompt in allowing me to reproduce a map of the Assyrian and Babylonian empires. My friend Yigal Nizri helped with preparing the images and was always happy to help me to get books I could not reach.

Christopher Wheeler at Oxford University Press (UK) supported this book from the start and was kind enough to put me in touch with my editor at the press in New York, Cynthia Read, who was supportive—and most important of all—very patient and understanding throughout. I am deeply grateful for Read's support at critical moments. Justin Tackett, editorial assistant at the press, with whom I corresponded endlessly, has been a paragon of good-humored efficiency. I also thank the readers whom Oxford recruited to comment on my book: they provided important correctives and, no less important, encouragement.

I could not have written this book without it having at least some impact on my family. Special thanks go to my sister-in-law, Meital Ben-Dor. My daughters, Sophia, Lulu, and Cora, made this book better by making sure I didn't think about it *all* the time. Katherine, my friend in and for life, is difficult to thank in my own words for her unrelenting love and support so I choose to quote to her Mevlana Rumi, who writes, "We love: that's why life is full of so many wonderful gifts."

I cannot say, like some other contemporary scholars of the ten lost tribes, that I have always dreamed about them. I am not personally connected to this study in such a long-standing way. But at some point while writing this book, I was reminded of what I always knew: that I am personally connected to the city of Nineveh, capital of the Assyrian Empire, the polity responsible for the ten tribes' exile. Over fifty years ago, the Jewish community of the Iraqi city of Mosul—site of the ancient city of Nineveh—was uprooted. Since then, images of the ancient capital of Assyria often mix with memories of the modern city left behind. The journal of the Mosuli community in Israel, where many of its elders publish memoirs and poems written in beautiful Arabic, is called *Minhat Ashur* (Tribute of Assyria). I grew up dreaming of Mosul, not so long ago the home of Muslims, Christians, and Jews, and the city where my parents were born and grew up. Mosul is also the place where my grandparents, Sassoon Ghazal and Miriam bint Samra, Zvi Salih and Salha bint Lulu (who always reminds me that she is actually from Baghdad), met and lived. I dedicate this book to them.

Contents

A Note on Transliterations

As this book is intended for a varied community of readers and
scholars and draws on sources in a variety of languages, I have
tried my best to simplify the complexity of the transliteration of
non-Latin languages. There are a few citations that are transliterated
with Akkadian words that include the sign š (representing the
Semitic letter *shin*), which I replace with *sh* for the sake of ease
(as in *Aššur/Ashur*). The Japanese and Chinese in the book follow
the conventions of Hepburn romanization (commonly referred to
as *rōmaji*) and the pinyin transliteration system. More important, for
Arabic and Hebrew, I have kept only the diacritics of *ayn/ayin* (as in
'ilm/da'at) and *alif/alef* (as in Qur'an/*Miqra'ot*). For biblical names,
I use the familiar transliterations, hence Reuben and not Re'uven,
Zebulun and not Zevulun, Issachar and not Issaschar. In many
cases, early modern English, Spanish, and Italian texts included
spellings that today would seem nonconventional (e.g., "neer" for
near); I have left them as they were written. I tried to represent
the original language of certain phrases and terms as much as
I could, without making it too difficult on the eyes. Hence, in
many cases, the original language appears in the endnotes.

The Ten Lost Tribes

Introduction

Ten Lost Tribes
and Their Places

Upon retiring from professional life, Avigdor Shahan, a prolific writer, historian, and educator, embarked on the greatest journey of his life: following in the footsteps of the ten lost tribes. The ensuing voyage culminated in a book, *El 'Ever ha-Sambatyon* (Towards the Sambatyon), which is half a history of the tribes and half a travelogue for which Shahan had a deeply personal impetus. As he explains:

> I was eight years old [in 1940] when our teacher at the traditional Jewish school told us with trembling voice about the exile of the ten tribes: Reuben, Shimon, Zebulun, Yissachar, Dan, Gad, Asher, Naphtali, Ephraim, and Manasseh—by the kings of Assyria and their cruel soldiers. He described the formidable river they crossed in their wanderings, the *Sambatyon;* and the fearsome mountains of darkness behind which they disappeared. He told us about that great country where they live a life of freedom and liberty; the commanders of their armies alert and ready, their swords sparkling, and their legions ordered in columns behind their banners and flags.

The young pupils, children of the Jewish quarter of Komarov, Romania, listened with "breathless anticipation." Finally, one of them exclaimed, "Why don't we send messengers to let them know about our misery?"

"Indeed, throughout the generations many messengers set out towards the tribes," the teacher answered solemnly. "[T]hese messengers climbed high mountains and wandered in desolate deserts, but their traces were also lost."

That very day, Shahan and two young friends, Moishe'le and Leibe'le, set out themselves in search of the ten tribes. They decided that the nearby Dniester River was in fact the Sambatyon. They undertook to leave Komarov, but never got to cross even the limits of its Jewish quarter. A large black dog standing at its edge frightened them back home.[1]

Just one year later, in September 1941, the Jews of Komarov went on their own terrible march. Following the Nazi invasion of the Soviet Union, Romanian soldiers deported Komarov's Jews to Transnistria, a mass death zone created by the occupying forces across the Dniester.[2] Shahan recalls how his friend Moishe'le likened the Romanian soldiers leading the forced march to the ancient Assyrian military that had so cruelly deported the ten tribes. Growing frantic, the boy fled the ragtag column of marchers, and ran for the Dniester—the "Sambatyon." As he had the year before, Moishe'le wanted to seek the help of the ten tribes, which he imaged to be on its far bank. He never reached them; a soldier murdered him beside the river. Shahan later learned that Romanian soldiers had also killed his other friend, Leibe'le, by drowning him in the Dniester. Of his own experiences during the march and the war, Shahan does not tell. Many years later, Shahan wrote: "I have remembered the dreamers and the visionaries who throughout generations have set out searching for them. I remembered Moishe'le and Leibe'le also, who marched towards the ten tribes until they died without reaching them."[3] Indeed, these are powerful memories about millennia-old powerful visions and dreams.

The book that you hold in your hands is about the messengers, visionaries, and dreamers who over the centuries have searched for the lost tribes— through scholarship and travel, through both scientific and religious means. *The Ten Lost Tribes* is particularly concerned with the speculation that has evolved over the past two millennia over the precise identity and location of the ten lost tribes. Where and who "today"—that is, at any given moment of asking—are the descendants of the Israelite kingdom deported by the Assyrians? The question of the ten tribes emerged from the very beginning as a geographical problem. Adolf (Adolphe) Neubauer (1831–1907), an early scholar of the tribes, put it pithily: his collection of tribes-related documents bears the simple title "Where Are the Ten Tribes?"[4]

Why have so many different people searched untiringly for the ten lost tribes for such a long time? The answer is at once simple and profound: because they are lost. One of this book's central arguments is that the lostness represented by the ten tribes is, in Western historical consciousness, one of the most acute and oldest known instances of loss still "alive" today. This is because it is also globe spanning in nature—closely related to the world's spatial, temporal, and human dimensions. The ten tribes are not merely a random group of people who disappeared following the destruction of their homes. They are permanent exiles, a missing limb from the body of the "people of Israel," lost to Jews and Christians alike. The history of this question—the multiple contexts and frames in which it was posed and the multiple answers that have been given—together constitute nothing less than a map of the world and a world history. The tribes have been a marker for defining the world, laying out the *oikoumene*—the known inhabited world—at any given moment in world history. In this regard, this book is a history of the absent, the missing—that which becomes present when expressed as lost.

The ten tribes are lost *to* and lost *from* the world in converging ways, corresponding to the three meanings of the word "world": the world as "all humanity" (as in *tout le monde*), the world as the physical face of the earth, and the world as temporality (as in "end of the world").[5] The peculiar way in which the ten tribes were removed from the world—from its space, times, and humanity—is, as we shall see, one of the main thrusts at work in the various attempts at positioning and locating the ten tribes on earth.

This peculiar condition of lostness corresponds with the main features of the ten tribes. They are described as superhuman or as "off-human" (outside humanity); placed at the edges of the earth or beyond its boundaries (beyond its physical borders); and associated with the end of the time, the end of the world. This threefold condition is what makes the lostness of the ten tribes so acute and so rich. This is the first and main reason that this book is a "world history" of the ten lost tribes.

Those asking the question, throughout history and today, make up a huge and by no means homogeneous group. Avigdor Shahan understood himself to be a link in a long chain of previous seekers. The famous Jewish traveler Benjamin of Tudela (fl. twelfth century) came close, or so he thought, to finding the tribes somewhere in Asia. The seventeenth-century Jesuit missionary and scholar Diego Andrés Rocha (1607–1688) was "certain" that the tribes were in South America.[6] The Irish nobleman Lord Edward Kingsborough (1795–1837) lost his fortune looking for them in pre-Columbian Mexican art. He died, age forty-two, in the Dublin Debtor's Prison, but his passion left us with a codex of Mesoamerican arts in nine massive volumes.[7] The Scots missionary Nicholas McLeod (fl. 1868–1889) spent decades in Japan and Korea, searching for the true Israelites. He wrote Japanese history as a history of the ten tribes in the Japanese isles.[8] The European nobleman Alexander Beaufort Grimaldi (b. 1839) thought some of the tribes were in Scotland and constituted its royalty.[9] The reverend and scholar Charles Forster (d. 1871) used ancient Assyrian, Babylonian, and Persian monuments as keys to identifying the lost tribes in Asia.[10] Joseph Wolff (1795–1862), a convert son of a rabbi from Bavaria, won fame as a globe-trotting British missionary and Orientalist and spent many dangerous decades in Central Asia searching for the tribes. Enslaved in the Caucasus, he once walked naked 900 kilometers through Central Asia looking for the tribes.[11] Wolff's son Sir Henry Drummond Wolff, appointed to be the British delegate to Tehran in 1888, organized several expeditions to find the tribes. In an indication of the excitement the quest for the tribes generated in Victorian England, scores of Londoners donated £10 apiece for young Wolff's expeditions. His approach to Lord Palmerston (1784–1865), asking for the £10 contribution, produced a classic Palmerston-ism: famous for his scathing wit, Palmerston declared, "I will give you £100 if you will [simply] lose the remaining two!"[12]

Lord Palmerston's disdain for tribe searchers is itself a reflection of the craze the phenomenon had generated in his day. Everyone, it seemed, was on the hunt. Across the Atlantic, Rabbi Uziel Haga of Boston convinced President William McKinley (1843–1901) to allow him to tag along with the U.S. forces sent to suppress the Boxer Rebellion in China, just so he could look for the tribes there.[13] On the Continent, politicians, scholars, and clergy alike pondered their whereabouts; just one example is the German diplomat and Orientalist Friedrich Rosen (1865–1935), who toured the Middle East, Africa, and East Asia, debating the likelihood of an encounter with some of the long-lost exiles.[14]

These travelers, and many others discussed in this book, were not roaming the world within a cultural vacuum, nor without intelligence. Over the course of 2,000 years, Jews, Christians of various denominations, and, to a lesser extent, Muslims had used the tribes as a point of reference, tying historical develop-ments to their exile and return. Clerics, theologians, missionaries, biblical and Qur'anic commentators and exegetes—all were concerned with the simple question: where are the ten tribes? Such late antique historians as Flavius Josephus (37–c. 100) had similarly speculated on the tribes' whereabouts. From early modernity on, geographers, cartographers, ethnographers, linguists, and, most recently, geneticists and natural scientists joined the growing circle of tribal scholars and seekers.[15] Together, they have created an impressive edifice of ten tribes "knowledge," with imbricated pieces of information, lore, and "fact" resting one upon another, which can be found among anthropological, mytho-logical, and even sci-fi literature. The Library of Congress demarcates a sizable special category for books related to the lost tribes. One can find many volumes about them on the shelves, next to books on the Samaritans, an *existing* ethnic group whose origins are traceable, according to their own traditions, back to peoples deported *to* Palestine by the Assyrians after the latter supposedly emptied the Israelite kingdom.

The ongoing debate and speculation about the location of the ten tribes and the active search for them are this book's pivot. This book is, paradoxically, a history of a nonexistent place, a place conjured into being only through its designation as a tribal home. It is a history of places with meanings charged or transformed by the designation that they were home to a specific group of people. Thus, while this volume proceeds more or less in chronological order, the story leaps from one location on the surface of the earth to another, following the ten tribes' appearances. Changes, shifts, and expansions in world geographical knowledge have relocated the tribes from one place to another to yet another. Searchers for the tribes have accompanied this changing world geography with adjusted, updated, increasingly "scientific" speculation as to the tribes' whereabouts. No sooner were new terrains discovered than were the tribes relocated to them in the seekers' calculations in an ongoing process of accommodating the earth's physical geography to the ten tribes' story.

Speculation over the location of the tribes has been in close dialogue with scientific, geographic knowledge, upon which tribe seekers—travelers and scholars alike—have drawn and to which in turn they have contributed. New geographic discoveries inspired new speculation and further accommodation. One can picture this geographic dialogue as a layer of writings spreading across the world's map, at times prompting geographic expansion and at others feeding off of it. This ongoing process in a way constituted a history of the world, one based not on what was in it, but on what was supposed to be in it.

Another key component to the history of the search for the lost tribes is the numerous cases of identifications of various ethnic groups all over the world as descendants of the tribes. Already in 1903, Albert Hyamson (1875–1954), a prolific English Jewish intellectual, declared that "no race has escaped the honour, or the suspicion, of being descended from" the ten tribes.[16] Today, more than a century later, various groups around the world, from the Zebulunites in Japan, to various African-American groups in the United States, to Latin American indigenous peoples, claim that they are the descendants of one all of the tribes.[17] Claims of ten tribes descent played a role in the imperial pansions of Spain, Portugal, and, chiefly, Britain.

At least three royal houses—those of England, Scotland, and Japan—are said by some to be descendants of ten tribes royals.[18] Some have come to believe that the ten tribes are the most distinguished race among humanity—"God's covenant race."[19] Political claims regarding the ten tribes status of various groups have been made since the early modern period, attaching themselves to real and imagined peoples from, literally, A to Z. The Afghans (both Pashtuns and Phathans), Armenians, Berbers, Celts, Eskimos, Estonians, Finns, Ibos, Laps, Lembas, Mayans, Native North Americans, Scythians, Tartars, and Zulus, among many more, have been variously claimed as the descendants of the long-lost tribes. In earlier periods, such religious movements or groups as the ancient Christian Nestorians and the medieval Muslim Almohads were attached to the story of the ten tribes; their claims are replicated in modernity in the instance of the Mormons.[20] In sum, in the words of one modern observer, "traces of the Tribes are popping up all over!"[21]

The histories and stories of the various contemporary claimants in different places of the world have become over the years a topic well researched by both professional and amateur scholars. The story of the ten lost tribes "was invoked by colonial powers and missionaries in their efforts to remake the histories of indigenous peoples, and is the basis for continuing efforts to locate descendants of the missing ten tribes."[22] That is to say, the ten tribes story is present among the many other features that meet, clash, and intersect in colonial "contact zones"—locations "of colonial encounters, the space in which peoples geographically and historically separated come into contact with each other." The ten tribes are to a certain extent also present in some instances of "autoethnographic expression"—"instances in which colonized subjects undertake to represent themselves in ways that *engage with* the colonizer's own terms."[23]

These observations still leave the question of why the ten tribes story is so powerful and globe spanning in nature. While they might explain ongoing efforts to locate the tribes, they do not explain how and why these efforts began. As Hyamson states, "The total absence of all evidence of their fate has cleared the ground for innumerable theories." In fact, he says, "with the beginning of their captivity [the ten tribes] seem to have passed from human knowledge, and the mystery of the lost tribes has almost from that day to this been the lodestone that has attracted and bewildered students of many races and varied beliefs."[24] How has this total lack of evidence created such a huge edifice of related knowledge? The relationship between loss and knowledge is a central concern of this book.

Introducing the History of the Ten Tribes: Prophecy Complements History

Sociologist Stanford Lyman observed that "the ten tribes of Israel have been lost from—and lost to—conventional modes of secular temporal historiography."[25] This observation is a central challenge inspiring this book. Indeed, the first comprehensive book dedicated exclusively to the *history* of the tribes appeared only in the early modern period and drew exclusively on scripture. In 1683, Herman Witsius (1636–1708), a professor of divinity at Leiden, published *Dekaphylon: Sive De Decem Tribubus Israelis*.[26] Witsius was a reform theologian and Hebraist.[27] Certainly not the first to discuss the tribes, Witsius *was* the first systematically to discuss what he considered their history, an approach derived from his methodologies for reading theology and its derivation from the Bible.

Witsius took pains to explain his study's organization and made particular reference to his method. The history of the tribes, he explained, falls into four periods: the tribes existed, they disappeared, they exist somewhere right now, they shall return. This underlying framework of loss and redemption is applicable whether the source in question is Jewish or Christian—indeed, whether the source is religious or secular. Witsius's corresponding periodization was:

1. the time before their deportation and their departure for exile
2. during the Babylonian captivity of the Jews
3. after the Jews' return to Zion and during the Second Temple
4. the time of their restoration with the rest of Israel and their restitution in latter days[28]

Strikingly, the only portion of Witsius's history that corresponds with actual historical time is the first—deportation and exile. The second and third periods correspond with the "present" time of the tribes' history, about which we have no concrete information, during which we have no connection with the tribes, and which has not yet ended. The fourth and final period corresponds with prophecy, with the preordained future of the tribes. In this formulation—shared by the majority of ten tribes seekers—fully three-quarters of the ten tribes' "history" is invisible history, for which we have no evidence.

Witsius was well aware that most of his history lacked corroboration, and he relied on prophecies or fleeting allusions to the ten tribes in the Old and New Testaments. Witsius addressed this head-on with his view of the complementary relationship between history and prophecy (*prophetiae respondet historia*).[29] The history of the tribes is made of two corresponding layers, the "historical" (in the biblical context) and the prophetic. Both layers enjoy the same status as "truth," and the absence of either renders this history incomplete. This argument stands as an imperative for understanding the theological platform upon which the search for the lost tribes has long rested. This link between history and prophecy generates the tension that feeds the story told in this book.

A digest of the biblical narrative that serves as the historical kernel lying behind the story of the tribes is in order. Derived mainly from the first and second books of Kings, the story has been universally regarded by ten tribes seekers as historical truth. Of course, nearly two centuries of probing biblical criticism and contested biblical archaeology have taught us nothing if not that the biblical narrative cannot be treated as a chronological history narrating the past as it happened. Indeed, in the case of the biblical narrative with which we're concerned here, it is important to bear in mind that at least the first part of the actual (as opposed to the prophetic) history of the ten tribes story (the first book of Kings, which tells the story of the united kingdom created by David and its split into two under his grandson) is considered by biblical scholars to be almost entirely fictional. The second part, found in 2 Kings (which covers the history of the two kingdoms and the deportations of the Israelites), is thought to have been heavily edited and full of interpolations. Nevertheless, for the purposes of this book, it is imperative that we follow the biblical narrative as it tells the story. For this is the truth of the tribes as their various seekers have understood it.

In the beginning, there was one unified kingdom under the great kings, David and Solomon, in the land of Israel, home of the twelve tribes, who had descended from the third patriarch, Jacob. Things were good under Solomon and the kingdom enjoyed prosperity and many years of peace. However, as Solomon aged, he began to sin. He married foreign women and worshipped their gods. He even built altars for these gods in Jerusalem, next to the temple he himself had built for the Lord God. As a result, God becomes angry with him and sends his messenger Ahijah the Shilonite to a "mighty man of valor" from the tribe of Ephraim, Jeroboam, son of Nebat. He is to lead the Ephraimites out of the kingdom and tear it into two.

As the biblical account has it, on his way out of Jerusalem, Jeroboam encounters Ahijah, who in a dramatic gesture tears his own new garment into twelve pieces. He then turns to Jeroboam: "take thee ten pieces: for thus saith the Lord, the God of Israel, Behold, I will rend the kingdom out of the hand of Solomon, and will give ten tribes to thee." Ahijah explains that one tribe, Judah, will remain in the hands of the Davidic house, "for my servant David's sake and for Jerusalem's sake, the city that I have chosen out of all the tribes of Israel." The prophet soon repeats this message, again speaking of God's plan to divide up the united Davidic kingdom: "But I will take the kingdom out of his son's hand and will give unto thee even ten tribes" (1 Kings 11:30–36).

This prophecy is the first mention in the biblical narrative of the "ten tribes"—indeed, it coins the term, which appears nowhere else in the Hebrew

Bible or the New Testament. Here, it appears twice within a few verse chooses a man specifically from the tribe of Ephraim for the job of lead ten tribes. Ephraim and Manasseh, sons of Jacob's most beloved lo: Joseph, receive a deathbed blessing from the patriarch. Like Judah, they belong in the category of "blessed tribes." But while both of them are blessed, in a significant dramatic gesture, Jacob crosses his arms and places his *right* (indicating greater blessing) hand on the head of his youngest grandson— Ephraim.

Ahijah's prophecy quickly becomes reality. Solomon's son and successor, Rehoboam, is far less smart than his father and grandfather. He rules tyrannically and foolishly and abuses the dominion over the rest of the tribes given to the tribe of Judah. Schisms and unrest spread among the people of the kingdom. Armed with God's promise, Jeroboam rebels and leads his tribe of Ephraim to secede from the united Davidic kingdom, creating a separate dominion in the northern part of the Holy Land. Nine other tribes follow him, and the Ephraimite monarchy becomes the kingdom of Israel, home of the ten tribes. The great united kingdom of Israel no longer exists. Instead, there are the smaller Israel and Judah. The new Israelite kingdom controls an expanse of land from a point only a few kilometers north of Jerusalem to the mountains of Lebanon. In the south, the house of David remains with only two tribes, Judah and its smaller neighbor, Benjamin, and with the temple in Jerusalem, which is still the cultural and religious center of all twelve tribes.

But the story does not end there. Fearing that the people of the new secessionist kingdom might revert to Judah's dominion when they go to worship in Jerusalem, Jeroboam decides to build a new center for worship within the boundaries of his own domain. The Bible tells us that he "took two calves of gold" and said to the people: "It is too much for you to go up to Jerusalem: behold thy gods, O Israel, which brought thee up out of the land of Egypt" (1 Kings 12:28). Jeroboam's political and cultural shrewdness proves to be a grave error with everlasting consequences. Worshipping the two calves is the "original sin" of the ten tribes, and it never leaves them. (Witsius calls the episode the "separation of the tribes from the House of the Lord.")[30]

In a typical burst of wrath, God vows to destroy not only the clan of Jeroboam, but his entire kingdom. The same Ahijah the Shilonite delivers another horrifying prophecy: "For the Lord shall smite Israel as a reed is shaken in the water and he shall root up Israel out of this good land which he gave to their fathers and shall scatter them beyond the river because they have made their graves provoking the Lord to anger" (1 Kings 14:15). This banishment from the divine domain, perhaps a historical recasting and transposition of the story of the expulsion from Eden, is crucial in the later formulations of the tribes' location. It would come to be understood as expulsion from the inhabited civilized world.

In the wake of Ahijah's prophecy, the Israelite kingdom is plunged into 200 years of political turbulence that culminate in its destruction. The house of Jeroboam falls first, and the kingdom sees many dynasties rise and fall. None

CAPTIVITY OF THE TEN TRIBES.
2 Kings 17 : 9-18.
IF THOU SEEK HIM, HE WILL BE FOUND OF THEE ; BUT
IF THOU FORSAKE HIM, HE WILL CAST THEE
OFF FOREVER.

FIGURE 1.1. "Captivity of the Tribes," *Little People's Lesson Pictures (LPLP),*
The American Sunday-School Union, Sept. 18, 1898. Courtesy Zvi Ben-Dor Benite

of the kings removes the golden calves that had made God so angry. On the contrary, they begin worshipping even more foreign gods. The country continues to suffer from chronic political instability. Israel's end finally comes when the Assyrian Empire, the "Rod of God," as the prophet Isaiah so loved to call it, conquers Israel and deports its people. The biblical narrative laconically reports, "In the ninth year of Hoshea, the king of Assyria took Samaria and carried Israel away into Assyria and placed them in Halah and in Habor by the river of Gozan and in the cities of the Medes" (2 Kings 17:6).

The authors of 2 Kings hasten to remind the reader why it all happened: because Israel had sinned against God and deserted him. "Therefore the Lord was very angry with Israel and removed them out of his sight; there was none left but the tribe of Judah only" (2 Kings 17:18). The episode concludes with a summary of the deportation and its ongoing status: "the Lord removed Israel out of his sight, as he had said by all his servants the prophets. So was Israel carried away out of their own land to Assyria unto this day" (2 Kings 17:23).

A "Little People's Lesson" picture, produced by the American Sunday-School Union in 1898, depicts this horrible moment clearly (see figure 1.1). On the back of the card were nine related vital points that the children could learn. Item 9 on the list asks: "How did he [God] punish them?" The answer: "Removed all from his sight." How to write the history (and the geography) of what was "removed from God's sight" is a question with which many featured in this study have struggled.

Fantasies and Fantastic Literature

The fascination with the tribes has generated, alongside ostensibly nonfictional, scholarly studies, a massive body of fictional literature and folktale. In this literature, the tribes appear in various ways, most often as formidable warriors of the sort Shahan's teacher described. One particularly popular motif derives from the centuries-old portrayal of the tribes as superhuman beings of extraordinary physical proportions, possessed of incredible abilities. This theme owes a lot to apocalyptic and millenarian texts that depict the tribes as a mass of great warriors accompanying the return of the Messiah or the arrival of the Antichrist. A common early modern interpretation of their role during the latter days is found, for instance, in the physician John Floyer's (1649–1734) systematic exposition of the "return of ten tribes at last" that accompanies or precedes, among other things, "the burning of the world, and the resurrection of the body."[31]

The tale Shahan heard as a child displays the main features of the ten tribes as imagined over centuries: martial, strong, always ready to show up or to be found, never coming, and intimately connected to apocalyptic and messianic visions dating back to the Middle Ages.[32] Such rumors were not exclusive to Jews. Christians and Muslims, too, subscribed to them. And over time, an array of peoples who were identified as being the tribes came to subscribe to them as well.

The ten lost tribes story also lies behind a distinct genre of Indiana Jones-type adventure fiction, on the rise since the early twentieth century. A good instance is *Quest for the Lost Tribes,* a film by Simcha Jacobovici and Elliott Halpern, one of the first in a career that has also produced a film on the lost tomb of Jesus.[33] While not a focus of this book, some other examples are illuminating. In one instance, Mark Lee's 1998 *The Lost Tribe,* an expedition comprising a relief worker, an anthropologist, a "black shaman," and an American journalist searches for the tribes in contemporary war-torn Africa, encountering a variety of adventures and misadventures along the way.[34] Somtow Suchairtkul, in his 1988 sci-fi novel, *The Aquiliad: Aquila in the New World,* imagines a Roman Empire that has expanded globally thanks to the invention of steam power. The fictional Romans arrive in America, where they experience a series of troublesome encounters—with Bigfoot, with space aliens, with a time-traveler, and of course, with the ten lost tribes.[35]

The origins of this specific literary *topos* lie in the nineteenth century. In some cases, the ten tribes served to promote a utopian social or religious order. In 1901, Father Thomas McGrady, a Catholic socialist priest from Kentucky, situated a historical/utopian novel in "New Israel," a "trans-arctic" kingdom founded by the ten tribes, which had struggled against tyranny during Jeroboam's time.[36] In another "arctic" novel from 1903, the Mormon *Trip to the North Pole,* a boat leaving San Francisco on April 16, 1879, drifts off course; its sailors find themselves at the North Pole, where they find a mysterious kingdom inhabited by the lost tribes, which "were sent to the Northwestern part of Asia, and from there sent into the North Country." The young widow of King Manasherous (a clear allusion to the biblical Manasseh) rules. Her husband had been murdered by the evil Captain Shenakeribous (an allusion to Sennacherib, the Assyrian king who laid siege to Jerusalem in 701 BCE), who serves as the story's villain. One Joe B. Lothare, a youth serving on the boat, is the main hero and narrator. He immediately suspects that these are the lost tribes and turns into a sort of anthropologist, whose main source of ethnographic information is the Bible: "I refer to my Bible to investigate if perchance this not be the Ten Tribes of Israel and I shall at least call them so, from all these Bible readings and also on account of other information."[37] The adventure ends with Lothare not only learning Hebrew, but also affirming his faith in Christ, whose truth emerges through the biblical readings that accompany the boy's search for the identity of his hosts—who turn out to be good, upstanding, decent Christians.

It was not only the fictional Lothare who stumbled on adventure and spiritual experiences. The book's author, Otte Julius Swanson Lindelof (b. 1852) of Salt Lake City, a Mormon, tells us that he himself had learned of the story when, on a visit to a village in "Northern Europe," he encountered a dying man to whom he administered the last rites. In "his last moment," Lindelof claims, this man had given him Lothare's records.[38] Thus, this allegorical fairy tale is presented at one and the same time as a novel and as a truthful account, ripe with the suggestion that the lost tribes might be there still, waiting to be rediscovered.

Jewish tradition has generated a vast number of stories and folktales revolving around the theme of the lost tribes. One example is the famous nineteenth-century fictional traveler Binyamin the Third, whose travels took him to "those distant islands beyond the mountains of darkness" where the tribes were thought to live. A Tunisian Jewish folktale tells of one figure, "a merchant and a scholar," en route from Portugal to India, who was captured by "almost naked dark skinned men" after a shipwreck threw him into the sea. After "three days of drifting," he was tossed up on the shore of an unknown island. The strange inhabitants were "almost like the negroes" and armed with bows and arrows. The Jewish castaway, certain that "these cannibals" were going to eat him, began to cry out the Shema' Yisra'el—the opening words of the centerpiece of Jewish prayer. Upon hearing him, all the men around him joined in, completing the prayer. The men turned out—surprise!—to be members of two of the ten lost tribes. Soon thereafter, they all assemble in the local synagogue. The guest beseechingly asks the local king if the time has come for the lost tribes to come out of hiding and rescue their Jewish brethren. The king, dressed in his prayer shawl, prays for an answer from the Almighty. Eventually he reports, weeping, that the "time of redemption has not yet arrived."

Another tale tells of a Jew whose goat used to disappear mysteriously into the woods every Sabbath night. One week, the Jew decided to follow as it went "deeper and deeper into the forest" that lay outside his village. Suddenly, the man saw "a very tall man . . . as tall as Goliath . . . coming towards him." By now, of course, we know the end of the story: sure enough, after a few scary moments, the giant turns out to be a "ten triber," who congratulates the Jew for being so "righteous" that he could accomplish the impossible task of finding him, "for we are the Ten Tribes and this is the land beyond the

Sambatyon River." The giant invites the Jew to spend the Sabbath with "the Ten Tribes." After the Sabbath ended, "the giant threw him into the air" and the Jew found himself instantly across the river, where his loyal goat was waiting to lead him home. Similar stories from the Muslim tradition tell of the discovery of the ten tribes en route to Arabia; there, they are presented as the protectors of Muslims on pilgrimage to Mecca.[39]

While the characteristics of the tribes differ from tale to tale, in all such stories they are annoyingly, tauntingly elusive. The tribes are at once distant and very close. Only the bravest and cleverest can find them, yet once found, they are revealed to have been right next door all along. This simultaneous proximity and distance is mirrored in their appearance, which is both alien and familiar. They may be almost naked and armed with bows and arrows, yet they pray in the synagogue wrapped in their *talith*. They live in the North Pole, isolated for millennia, but they are good Christians. At issue here, in part, of course, is the question of (ethnic, racial, and religious) purity. The lost tribes hold out the promise that, while we, the seekers, may be degenerate, may be far removed from the true greatness of our origins, the tribes, in their isolation, remain pure.

Against the millennia-old backdrop of the frustrating, fruitless, and tantalizing quest for these lost ancestors, the contemporary American Jewish poet Chana Bloch, for one, has tried to cool the fantasies of ten tribes seekers, pouring cold water on the supposed mystery of their location and suggesting that perhaps the time has come to let the lost tribes disappear once and for all, this time from our minds and imaginations: "What happened to the ten lost tribes / is no great mystery: / they found work, married, grew smaller, / started to look like the natives / in a landscape nobody chose. / Soon you couldn't have picked them out of a crowd."[40]

Bloch's lovely poem, perhaps deliberately, misses the point. The tribes are the tribes precisely because they are identifiable as such—indeed, because it was thelogically preordained that they *will be identified as such*.

The Ten Tribes as a Theological Loophole on Earth

"Theology has its 'Lost tribes of Israel,' history has its 'lost arts,' and Johnson County [Iowa] has its lost record," mused the county's historian: the treasury records from the years 1859–1861 had disappeared.[41] The rather inelegant relationship between the lost tribes and the word "theology" in this sentence seems bizarre, but there is lot of truth in it. The undying fountain from which the ten lost tribes draw their mystery and allure is their theological significance and the theological anxieties they generate.[42] Their absence is (differently) significant for Jews and Christians alike, and its theological implications are many.[43]

Any discussion of the tribes and the searches which they've inspired must begin with the scriptural foundations of their story: the biblical narratives that provide the history of the tribes and the prophecies understood to relate to them. Theology—in the sense of both the application of doctrine and dogma to reality, and more so as a set of tools designed for the interpretation and shaping of reality according to the word of God—guides the search, informs it, and shapes it. The power of the tribes as a mystery, unlike, say, the myth of the lost Excalibur, owes its persistence to the authority of the biblical narrative—the ur-text of the tribes' story.

The biblical narrative not only describes the tribes' history "as it happened." It also lays out the present and future of the lost tribes as read into the various biblical prophecies concerning them. Moreover, biblical authority plays a crucial role in the history of searches for the tribes. For centuries, the Bible was seen as proof of the facticity of the ten tribes' story, and the validity of the related biblical prophecies remained beyond doubt throughout most of the history discussed here. For many, it is beyond doubt even today. The theological referents of the story of the ten lost tribes is taken as evidentiary, and the Bible provides recourse to "facts"—a feature of ten-tribes-ism that bridges the supposed divide between the religious and secular realms. For centuries, to talk of the ten tribes was to talk theologically, but it was also to talk scientifically and factually—and for many, it still is.

Similarly, the sense of loss is embedded in the historical core of the story. The ten tribes fleetingly appear in the biblical narrative only to disappear definitively from it thereafter. The story begins with the tearing apart of a whole people into two, vividly and viscerally echoed in the tearing of Jeroboam's robe, and continues with the deportation of one part to somewhere else. How are the pieces to be put back together? The sense of loss that pervades the story derives not so much from any termination of the tribes, but rather from their ongoing—but unreachable—existence. This, then, is the true and most wrenching loss of the story—the history of this unknown-but-known and missing people, which is unfolding in a distant-but-close and unfound place. As the history of the remaining children of Israel, the people of Judah, unfolds, unfolding silently alongside it is the ever-present if unknown history of the missing tribes. The river that must be crossed is the river that divides those parallel histories.

The people of Judah fared only slightly better in comparison to their brethren from the north. They also went into exile—the Babylonian captivity—in 586 BCE. However, the Judahite exiles do not disappear from the Bible itself. While we never hear from the ten tribes after their deportation, the period of the Babylonian captivity is present, loud and clear, in the biblical narrative. In this sense, the Babylonian captivity highlights the disappearance of those other, earlier exiles. Where did *they* go, and what became of *their* story?

Against the backdrop of destruction and exile, prophecy provided an element of consolation. And it was not simply those expelled during the Babylonian exile, but those of the earlier exile, too, who were promised resolution. The biblical prophets admonish the people for their sins but also promise them return and restitution at some point in the future. All of the great prophets—Isaiah, Jeremiah, Ezekiel—promise an end to exile. They emphasize that God will not leave forgotten *any* of the scattered exiles.[44]

The prophet Jeremiah, for example, declares (31:7): "Behold I will bring them from the North Country and gather them from the coasts of the earth." (Here, we find the inspiration for Lindelof's North Pole.) Ezekiel (37:15–22) elaborates on how God shall reunite Judah and Ephraim again. The Lord "will take the children of Israel from among the heathen whither they be gone and will gather them on every side and bring them into their own land . . . and they shall be no more two nations neither shall they be divided into two kingdoms any more at all." Most famously, the prophet Isaiah declares in one of his famous latter-days visions: "And it shall come to pass in that day that the great trumpet shall be blown and they shall come which were ready to perish in the land of Assyria and the outcasts in the land of Egypt and shall worship the Lord in the holy mount at Jerusalem" (Isaiah 27:13).

Here, Isaiah coins a conceit that has become central to the ten tribes quest. They are, as the Hebrew has it, "lost in Assyria." The translators of the King James Version render the Hebrew *ovdim* (lost, pl.) as "ready to perish," implying (imminent) destruction—another meaning of the word "lost." The Vulgate, however, retains the geographical dimension of that loss: qui perditi fuerant de terra Assyriorum, "those lost *from* the land of Assyria" (how the original "in Assyria" turned into the Vulgate's "from Assyria" becomes clearer later in this book). Speaking of this, Rashi, the great eleventh-century biblical commentator and exegete, wrote, "Because they were dispersed in a distant land beyond the River Sambatyon, he [Isaiah] called them *lost [ovdim]*." This understanding of *ovdim,* which emerged as dominant, suggests at once a past and a present state and provides a glimpse of an ongoing present in which the lost tribes are still lost, but still present (and hence "ready to perish" in King James and not "perished"). The tribes are lost twice over—once as a collective torn away from the body of Israel and a second time as a group physically lost in the wilderness of exile.

Yet absence is just another layer of this loss laid upon loss. More important is the promise of return, which has yet to be fulfilled. Here is the pivot that turns past history into prophecy, into predictive history. Fatefully, the prophets also provide an image of the future. They tell how a unified crowd, represent-ing *all* twelve tribes, shall worship in Jerusalem at some future point. This future moment will mark the end of the tearing of the ten tribes from the people and land of Israel.

Quite miraculously, in the last decades of the sixth century BCE, not long after the fall of Judah, the exiles did in fact return to build the House of God in Jerusalem. However, the returnees came only from the tribes of Judah and Benjamin—the exiles in Babylon. The ten tribes did not return. The book of Ezra tells us, "Then rose up the chief of the fathers of Judah and Benjamin, and the priests, and the Levites, with all them whose spirit God had raised, to go up to build the house of the Lord which is in Jerusalem" (Ezra 1:5). The other ten tribes never resurfaced throughout the long years after the return from the Babylonian captivity and the restoration of the temple in Jerusalem. As one nineteenth-century tribes fan put it, "the records of the Scriptures, which include the return of the Jews from Babylon [2 Chronicles 36:21–23; Zechariah 7:5], declare most emphatically, that though the Jews had returned from the Babylonish [*sic*] captivity the Ten Tribes had not."[45]

Not returning was the tribes' third and most profound loss. It opened "a huge wound that does not heal," as one rabbi put it over a century ago.[46] With the other two tribes returned, the loss of the remaining ten seemed greater still. This rabbi was not alone. Barbara Simon, an early nineteenth-century tribes scholar, discovered the anonymous scribbling of a student in the margins of a Christian theology book dealing with the tribes: "Judah returned:—but where was Ephraim still? / Where are the lost ten of Jacob's race? / Roam they through distant deserts wilds and vast / Without home or resting place. / Is theirs the fettered captive's hopeless doom? / Find they no refuge but the silent tomb?"[47]

The palpable sense of loss here can be likened to that of a family searching for a long-lost loved one. Even a dead body in a grave would be better than nothing, no knowledge at all, of what ultimately befell them. What torments the seekers is the idea that the tribes are out there still, lost, wandering, and unknown.

To understand the hole created when the tribes did not return, one must recognize the promise of return as the main legacy of the Babylonian captivity. Israel Yuval has commented on the centrality of the Babylonian captivity in Jewish and Christian historical consciousness.[48] He convincingly argues that this has framed the ways in which the dispersal of the Jews came to be seen as the product of an exile, specifically as the effect of the Roman exile of the Judeans. We know that there was *no* mass deportation after 70 CE, when Titus took Jerusalem and destroyed the Second Temple. Furthermore, we know that significant Jewish communities existed outside the region well before its conquest and destruction by the Romans. In short, the dispersal of the Jews, even in ancient times, was connected to an array of factors, none of them clearly exilic. Yet, as Yuval shows, the traumas of the loss of independence and the destruction of the temple that came with the Romans were collectively described as a third "event," a grand expulsion that subsumed everything else under the term "exile." Yuval shows how this process took place in the long centuries after the destruction of the temple, reaching completion during medieval times. He invokes the emergence of this narrative of exile as the quintessential example of the power of the Babylonian chapter as a frame and as prefiguring for subsequent events in Jewish history. The sequence of events surrounding the Babylonian captivity as the Bible describes it—destruction, exile, and return—was superimposed on the Roman episode, which came to be understood in later generations as reenacting the same pattern.

Similarly, albeit for different purposes and in different ways, Christian theology also processed the loss of Judea and the temple into a story of exile. After Augustine, Christian theology held that "[e]xile [as dispersal], not [as] loss of political sovereignty, was the punishment for the crucifixion."[49] As Yuval concludes, superimposing the parameters of the Babylonian captivity onto the Roman story is the basis for the centrality of the notion of return in both Christian and Jewish traditions: "An old concept of historical time, shared by Christians and Jews, helped create a justification for—an understanding of the necessity of—the Jewish return to Zion."[50] When the Roman occupation of Jerusalem in 70 CE becomes an exile story, a happy ending is implied—fulfilled in the case of the Babylonian captivity, but yet to come in the case of the Roman exile. Thus, "conceiving of the destruction of the Second Temple as the beginning of a new exile made it possible for the Jews to turn their historical time into messianic time."[51] In the wake of the Babylonian captivity, the story of the ten tribes is transformed in several ways. First, the return that ended the Babylonian captivity accentuates the fact that the ten tribes did not return and enhances the sense of lostness associated with them. At the same time, the myth of return makes the question of the complete return (for the Jews, now from the Roman exile) a much more urgent issue. If the Jewish return to Zion is yet to be fulfilled, what of the return of the rest of the children of Israel, the ten tribes? No return is complete until *all* of the tribes return. Syllogistically, if the tribes are bound to return *someday*, that means that they are *somewhere* on earth *right now*. This basic logic is exemplified by the standard interpretation of the biblical verse telling us that the tribes are somewhere in their place of exile "to this day" (2 Kings 17:23). According to this interpretation, this phrase refers not to the specific moment when it was written, but to (any) day of reading. This implies a sort of continuous present condition of being lost, but not completely lost. Paradoxically, the lostness is mitigated by the text's insistence on the ongoing knowledge of the ongoing existence of the lost tribes.

Like the stories and folktales we have seen, 2 Kings hints at the ambiguous worldliness of the missing tribes, lost but findable, distant but close, unreachable but available. The guarantee that they exist is as important as the fact that they are lost. Adam Rutherford, a strong proponent of the notion that Britain, the "Greatest of all World Empires," is made up of the ten tribes, wrote in 1934: "The ultimate re-union of the House of Israel and the House of Judah is repeatedly prophesied in the Bible (e.g., Jer. 3:18; Jer. 31:27–31; Ezek. 37:15–23). But how can Israel and Judah be re-united if Israel is non-existent or not identifiable?" Note that "identifying" and "finding" are analogous in Rutherford's phrasing. But more important, to deny the existence of the tribes is tantamount to blasphemy. Rutherford explains: "The idea that the above prophesies . . . are not only unfulfilled, but impossible of fulfillment owing to Ephraim-Israel having 'disappeared' has proved to be one of the principle [sic] causes of modern infidelity." Rutherford identifies "such noted infidels as Thomas Paine and David Hume."[52] Paine actually debated the existence of the tribes with the famous Elias Boudinot, the lawyer and statesman who presided over the Continental Congress, and with the Jewish theologian David Levi (1742–1801).[53] During the so-called Age of Reason, the tribes were deployed as a tool for proving biblical truth in a rational and scientific way. It is impossible to prove or to find scientifically accepted evidence for distant past events such as the law giving at Mount Sinai. One could, however, validate scripture by finding the tribes. The ten tribes' story was provable according to the parameters set by modern rational science. This made them a very tempting topic for debate during the period. It also made the search for them more feverish.

A variety of concerns, then, were attached to the specifically locative dimensions of the story of the ten lost tribes. Yet no less important, though less self-evident, are its temporal, chronological dimensions. These have already been alluded to in the predictive, messianic/apocalyptic framework, which foretells the return of the lost tribes, in either a dreadful or a paradisiacal future moment. As we have seen, the ten tribes belong in the messianic package; all the prophets lump their return together with the other signs of the end of time. If the central question about the ten lost tribes has long been: where are they? then the central question concerning the messianic age is:

when will it happen? An untold number of thinkers have undertaken to answer that question.

The integration of the ten tribes into the messianic/apocalyptic narrative fuses a spatial framework with a temporal one. The discovery and subsequent return of the ten lost tribes as an expected apocalyptic, prophetic event brings geography and space together with history and time. Moreover, the insistent worldliness of the tribes, the avowal that they are here among us, somewhere on earth, creates within the messianic/apocalyptic schema a sort of loophole by suggesting that at least one aspect of the messianic age may be with us already. Access to the messianic age is as easy as finding the lost tribes. All one has to do to set the promised end times in motion is to find the tribes and bring them home—a much more worldly, almost masterable task compared to what one has to do in order to bring the Messiah himself. Rutherford fretted, "how can Israel and Judah be re-united if Israel is non-existent or not identifiable?" The question's happy obverse is: how can the prophetic messianic age not come if Israel and Judah are reunited?

This dimension of the abiding fascination with the ten lost tribes is related to what Moshe Idel and others term "natural redemption," that is, a redemption that takes place not after or beyond, but *within* history.[54] The tale of the man's wandering goat, which leads him to the tribes; the novelistic account of the boat that drifts off course to the North Pole; Somtow's Roman steam-driven, world-conquering boats—all entertain the possibility of a wrinkle in space, a strange step across the map that will suddenly, instantly, unexpectedly lead to the ten lost tribes. The geographic dimensions of the story render redemption accessible and worldly, in Idel's terms, "natural." This aspect of the tribes' lostness, in particular, inspired many travelers to search for them. And it is this aspect in particular that has made the subject of the ten tribes compatible with modernity and rationality, rather than weakened by them. So it is, for instance, that with the appearance of modern sea navigation, making leaps in space more and more plausible, a new round of ten tribes mania burst forth, just as other developments and discoveries had spurred it on at other times. It is also this dimension of the redemptive narrative offered by the myth of the lost tribes, the natural dimension, that has allowed it to endure right down to the present day, woven into the national narratives of more than one contemporary polity.

The lostness of the ten tribes is thus both loaded with and derived from an acute theological anxiety created by this loophole. Stanford Lyman aptly described the tribes as presenting an "existential controversy and epistemological conundrum."[55] Unlike other prophetic/messianic conundrums, however, the solution of this one does not call for esoteric practice, but rather its opposite.

Thus, the theological quest has often become a political one. As historian Amnon Raz-Krakotzkin has shown, in the modern period interpretations of the notion of exile, in both Jewish and in Christian circles, have often given rise to political theologies or theologically based politics.[56] The ten tribes' exile is an integral, if not always salient, feature of many of these, most potently in Britain, the United States, and the state of Israel.

History and Loss, History of Loss

Theological anxiety is a chief dimension of the history told in this book. Another is loss itself. Put in the simplest words, a sense of loss is the experience of knowing that something is no longer present. How is the historian to write the history of a lost entity, the lostness of which is experiential and subjective?

One example is Sumathi Ramaswamy's groundbreaking study, *The Lost Land of Lemuria*, which contends that loss is a "category of knowledge."[57] Lemuria is a "land that is declared to have once existed but that is no more," which was thought to lie in the Indian Ocean.[58] Lemuria has been a preoccupation through the modern period and particularly since the 1800s. A sort of Tamil Atlantis, it supposedly vanished at some point in the Paleolithic era. Long ago above the ocean's surface, Lemuria in some unclear but clearly catastrophic manner disappeared suddenly beneath the waves. Lemuria has long existed in Tamil myth, but during modern times received renewed interest as a panoply of searchers began to look for its traces. As Ramaswamy shows, scientists, cartographers, geographers, and historians, along with occultists and individuals who could be best understood simply as romanticist scholars, Indian as well as English, engaged in intense speculation as to Lemuria's whereabouts, its catastrophic end, its possible connection to the origins of humanity, and its general significance in world history and geography. Ramaswamy calls these endeavors *labors of loss*—"those disciplinary practices, interpretive acts, and narrative moves which declare something as lost, only to 'find' them through modernity's knowledge protocols, the very act of discovery and naming constituting the originary loss."[59] Labors of loss produce knowledge. And this book offers a history of the knowledge that the loss of the tribes produced, a knowledge that further nourished the sense of loss itself. It is a study of the labors of loss around the ten tribes. As Ramaswamy argues, focusing on the "productive potentiality of the rich structure of [the] sentiment of loss" allows us to write about it "without too hastily reducing [it] to a pathology."[60]

The search for the ten tribes has provoked nothing if not anger and pathologizing. In their lostness, the tribes share the basic quality that attaches itself to other losses: Lemuria, Atlantis, the kingdom of Ophir, El Dorado, the Holy Grail, aliens from outer space, Prester John, Noah's Ark, the lost ark of the covenant—even the lost records of Iowa's Johnson County. These are often dismissed as legendary, as mythic, or as "noble lies," concern with them understood, at least tacitly, as pathology or, at best, as a sort of parlor pastime.

The ten lost tribes have long invited such dismissals. Chief among them is Allen Godbey's monumental 1930 study, *The Lost Tribes a Myth: Suggestions towards Rewriting Hebrew History,* which took issue with the proliferation of ethnographies suggesting or "proving" the claims that one or another ethnic group was a lost tribe. Godbey's 800 pages refuted the work of ethnologists and anthropologists of all sorts who claimed to have discovered the lost tribes in various corners of the earth, or to have identified traces of Jewish ritual in the practices of certain ethnic groups. More hostile still was archaeologist Robert Wauchope, who in 1962 published *Lost Tribes & Sunken Continents: Myth and Method in the Study of American Indians.* "Charlatan, clod and scholars alike— [most] have shared . . . attitudes and personality traits that give them as a group, a certain identity. . . . [W]hat theories are these that so capture imagination and fierce allegiance, and what sort of man [is] so obsessed with mystic and religious interpretations."[61] Yet often, outright dismissal of the tribes brings to the fore the history of the labors of loss surrounding them. In a way, Wauchope and Godbey have in fact paved the way for this study, by struggling to find the meeting point of academic study and the various forms of "labors of loss" represented by the predecessors they find vexing.

The Geographical Theology of the Ten Lost Tribes

Suppose an extensive continent, a new world, should have been recently discovered, north east of Media, and at the distance of a year and half's journey from thence, inhabited by people whose religion is pure Theism.
                              —Barbara Simon, *Hope of Israel* (1829)

Where are the ten lost tribes? There is a strong complementary relationship between theology and geography. Theological considerations frame the tribes' condition of simultaneous lostness and findability. The place of exile, while difficult to find, is real—it is somewhere on earth, a real, if occluded, geographic terrain. The possibility, indeed promise, that the tribes will be found is encoded in biblical prophecy. The prophets place the tribes beyond human *reach*, but not completely beyond our *control*—after all, our scripture says that, one day, they shall return. Even to say that the tribes are beyond our reach is a form of locating them.

The quality of being locatable is dual. On the one hand, there is the possibility of finding the tribes by physically searching: exploration, navigation, travels. On the other, there is the possibility of locating them through study, deduction, and sleuthing—placing them on the map, as it were. The locatibility of the tribes marks the interface of theological and geographical knowledge, what might broadly be termed religious and scientific modes of thought. The most basic version of this was the identification and mapping of the concrete locations identified in the biblical *ur*-text. Where, for instance, nineteenth-century tribalists wondered, was the "River Gozan," alluded to in 2 Kings 17:6? Could it be the Ganges? The river's location (in the generic "east"), along with its vaguely similar name, were at play here. (More recently, the Gozan has been identified by other seekers as the Volga.)[62] Similar were painstaking attempts to identify specific named groups as the ten tribes, in light of prophecies that described them as "scattered among the nations" (Joel 3:2 and passim). Somewhat more sophisticated were attempts to pinpoint the "islands of the sea" mentioned by the prophets. Were they the Canaries? The British isles? Other attempts—like the Romanian child Shahan's—rested on the knowledge that the tribes were to be found behind "the mountains of darkness" and across the River "Sambatyon." Countless candidates emerged, with one mountain range or river giving way to the next as each possibility was exhausted in turn.

These fabled locales merit attention not only as the settings for fantastical tales of adventure and travel, but also as geography. Ramaswamy's key term, "fabulous geography," the product of "the process of thinking imaginatively— and enchantingly—about places not actually present or existing," is clearly at play in the placing of the ten lost tribes.[63] But while the lost land of Lemuria is a place no one has seen, nor ever shall see, the lands inhabited by the lost tribes are defined by the opposite: their resolute and inevitable findability as dictated by theological concerns. The putative locations of the ten lost tribes are understood by the seekers as real, actual; and their geography is at once fantastical and literal. The fabulous geography of the ten lost tribes is the geography of territories as yet unfound, constantly examined, tested, and interpreted against theologically guided parameters. In the enduring search for the lost tribes, theology and geography work in tandem, mutually inform each other, and produce knowledge that is a fusion of the two. This geographical theology is the product of theologically implied mappings of territory, through imagination, attempted empirical verification, and the accommodation of prophecy. The search is an exercise in thinking theologically about geography.

Roberto Rusconi, editor of Christopher Columbus's *Book of Prophecies*—a collection of biblical prophecies that Columbus annotated between his third and fourth voyages—comments that, as his "eschatological awareness" matured, Columbus sought to find "a historic and theological context in which he could locate his geographical discoveries."[64] The principle applies to other bodies of knowledge as well. Central are Columbus's attempts "to locate his geographical discoveries within a historic and theological context." The discoveries carried for Columbus a theological meaning because they took place not only in a specific moment in time, but also in a special geographic location. Columbus was thinking theologically about geography. Geographical theology provides a mechanism for charting the evolution of the labors of loss connected to the lost tribes over a long span of time. We will see that, up until the early modern period, labors of the tribes' loss consisted almost exclusively of locating the tribes at a fixed but unreachable spot upon the earth. All of the unseen places "beyond the Sambatyon" were candidates in this process. Geographical imagination and place making were at play, but not simple enchanted thinking. Serious theological considerations were at work.

During the early modern period, as the world's geography became both ontologically and epistemologically destabilized, geographical theology did not disappear. It did, however, acquire and develop new meanings and tools in the search for the tribes. During the age of discovery, the possibility of finding the tribes became more and more real. Again, the rise of modernity with all of its signature trappings—science, rational thought, technology, navigation—increasingly fostered the search for the tribes, its techniques deployed in the service of finding them, accounting for their dispersion across the globe, and paving the way for their ostensible repatriation.

Scholar of religion Mircea Eliade famously argued that, "for religious man, space is not homogeneous; he experiences interruptions, breaks in it; some parts of it are qualitatively different from others."[65] Geographical theology is a spatial parallel; the topography it produces is nonhomogeneous. But its objective is not to transform space into specifically sacred space. Instead, it aims at interpreting space and *spatial* (as opposed to temporal) events according to theological considerations.

The exile of the lost tribes; the exile of the remaining tribes under the Romans; migrations, displacements, transformations of terrains; and, above all, the discovery of new lands—all of these spatial events created an uneven *topos* that would be made smooth only with the repatriation of the tribes. The coming of the Messiah, the second coming of Jesus—apocalyptic events—were brought, through the search for the ten lost tribes, into a spatial as well as temporal domain.

The geographical theology that operates in this book belongs in the realm of what geographer John K. Wright called *geosophy*: a form of knowledge that "extends far beyond the core area of scientific geographical knowledge or of geographical knowledge as otherwise systematized by geographers."[66] This opens the door to thinking creatively about geography and theology or religion. I am not, of course, the first to observe that, as one writer has put it, in "ancient and modern times alike, theology and geography have often been closely related studies because they meet at crucial points of human curiosity."[67] This relationship is already suggested in Immanuel Kant's conceptualization of "theological geography," that is, "the distribution of religions" on earth.[68] Speaking of various definitions of geography, Kant put this term to use in describing different religions in varying geographical contexts.[69] An important dimension of geo-ethnographic inquiries about the ten tribes has been the meticulous examination of indigenous peoples' religious customs in an attempt to trace them back to an "Israelite source." The geography of the ten lost tribes as it emanated from centuries of discussion as to their location also relates closely to the practice of *geographia sacra*—an early modern, biblically based antiquarianism that eventually gave way to scientific geography. Sacred geography was also "a geography that is global in scope and founded on the Holy Scriptures."[70]

Yet, the potential salvation that was encrypted in the search for the tribes itself distinguishes the geographical theology presented here from Kant's theological geography and sacred geography. *Geographia sacra* contained elements of this messianic promise, but theological geography did not. Sacred geographers were intensely interested, for example, in the location of the earthly paradise. But, as one of the sacred geographers admitted in 1630, "knowing where the Terrestrial Paradise was located is not necessary for salvation."[71] In sharp contrast, knowing where the ten tribes reside is arguably the sine qua non of salvation, be it spiritual or political. This is not to say that finding the tribes was sufficient for salvation. Rather, finding the tribes had redemptive possibilities attached to it. It was at once one of the signs of and the preconditions for redemption.

In this important regard, the numerous attempts to identify Great Britain as the "isles of the sea" mentioned in Isaiah were not an exercise in sacred geography. The positive identification of Great Britain with the lost tribes was an explicit instance of geographical theology, linked as it was to the potential for salvation, in turn providing the underpinnings for a political theology that justified—mandated—imperial expansion. Personal pursuits no less than national and imperial ones were driven by the specifically redemptive promise of the search for the lost tribes. When Uziel Haga, who sought McKinley's permission to travel to China, set out with his "soul . . . yearning" to make a "new covenant" with the "children of the Ten Tribes,"[72] he was engaged in his own form of geographical theology. Haga, the righteous Jew and his goat, the British Empire—all set out not just to find the tribes, but to find (or bring) salvation. Moishe'le's tragic, desperate attempt to cross the Dniester/Sambat-yon and call upon the tribes to rescue the Jews of Komarov is but the most vivid and crushing example.

Theology has guided both travel and abstract thinking about geography. In his messianic opus *Netzah Israel* (Eternity of Israel), Rabbi Juda Loew (Maharal) of Prague (c. 1525–1609) had geography uppermost in his mind in thinking about the ten tribes:

> And there are people who say that the learned men of the gentiles wrote [mapped] each and every place in every inhabited location on earth, and [they say that] there is no place not written in their books, and that they know of every [location on earth], and that there is no place known as [the location of] the Ten Tribes. However, there is no proof for that claim, and their mouths utter nonsense, because it is very possible that there is a place on earth that they do not know of, because it is disconnected from civilization by mountains etc. Here, only recently they found a place that they call in their language "new world," of which they did not know before. And so, just as they did not know about this new world, it is possible that they do not know of other worlds.[73]

In the context of rapidly changing world geography and ever more destabilized sacred geography, this was unassailable logic. If a whole new world could be discovered, why not one new small place, tucked away behind mountains or across an unknown river? Maharal is sanguine in the face of a new world geography, one far different from that described by scripture. What is unacceptable, to his mind, is not that the world may not look as we have long thought, but the idea that this newly mapped world has no room within it for the ten lost tribes. It is evident that Maharal is well abreast of the geographical discoveries of his day, fully informed of the new scientific proof they represent.[74] What he rejects, decidedly and angrily, is that this new mapping might lead to the abandonment of the notion that the tribes are out there. A doubt about the ten tribes is tantamount to uncertainty about the messianic vision as a whole. This same logic persists for diehards down to the present day. Perhaps, some now argue, the tribes are in a real world we have yet to discover, on a different planet or in a distant galaxy.

Maharal's conclusion was not only logical. It also proved correct, up to a point. Since his time, other new, albeit smaller, worlds have indeed been discovered. At a deeper level, though, Maharal's desire, common in the literature, is to rescue the question of the ten lost tribes and their location from the hands of cartographers. This replicates the very condition of the tribes' exile as first described in the Bible: at once close to hand and set at a remove. By Maharal's logic, the thing that stands as the most incontrovertible evidence of the tribes' existence is the very fact that they are lost. Their very hiddenness is the basis of the promise that they shall be found. Thus, the tribes constantly recede beyond the horizon, just beyond our grasp. Maharal effectively immunizes the tribes from any such further threat: who cares if the entire world is mapped? Another new world can always be discovered, scientific facts can always be rewritten, the map redrawn, on and on, ad infinitum. Here, Maharal reveals the dynamism of geographical theology, its ability to accommodate ever-greater spatial shifts, its infinite capacity for accommodating nonhomogeneous space. Indeed, this relentless dynamism and infinite ability to accommodate all new evidence is arguably the most consistent characteristic of the theological encounter with temporal events.

Maharal's insistence that other worlds will be found brings to mind historian Amos Funkenstein's observation that eschatology tends "to postpone the end of history indefinitely into the future" so that the "embarrassment" caused by the failure to predict the "First (for the Jews) or Second Coming (for the Christians)" is avoided.[75] Maharal postpones not only a moment in history indefinitely into the future but also, and more important, a moment in the ongoing process of revealing the world's geography.

The Ten Lost Tribes as World History

In 1652, the theologian Thomas Thorowgood wrote that the lost tribes were "a nation lost in the world." This marked the first time that the tribes' location in "the world" had been so explicitly designated. The world is, after all, the quintessentially "mundane" and "worldly" space. Yet at the same time, it is the world that is home to the most otherworldly of peoples, the lost tribes. In *Islands of the Mind: How the Human Imagination Created the Atlantic World*, John Gillis devotes a chapter, "Worlds of Loss," to a discussion of the perpetual quest for "secret islands," a leitmotif in Atlantic (and other) histories. This quest continues "despite the fact that the world is now mapped in the minutest detail."[76] The perpetuity of the quest is, for Gillis, testimony that the "island of the mind is not just a passive contemplation. It has been an incentive to action, an agent of history."[77] Similarly, the case of Lemuria demonstrates the power and vitality of the geography of what is not visible, a *topos* that escapes "the hegemony of the real and the visible."[78] These works suggest a new way to write world history. Absences, they propose, are vital to our understanding of the visible and present world.

Arif Dirlik observes that a "fundamental problem with World History as a historical genre is an inability to define its boundaries."[79] The boundaries of the world are too elusive. Loss presents itself as a useful vehicle for world historical inquiry in at least two important respects. First is the fact that loss (or, otherwise put, spatial absence), since it is not real and visible, allows for the easy transcendence of boundaries. The second utility of the concept rests on the paradoxical fact of its being the obverse referent for the actual, physical, visible world. It can be taken as that world's complementary image.

This leads us to the second spatial problem inherent in world history—not that of defining spaces *within* the world, but grasping and defining the space that is the world itself, an entity that claims in its very name all-encompassment, a goal beyond the reach of any history or historian. What, in thinking of an entire world, is that world's point of reference? Might it not be this world's counterpart, a lost world, its photographic negative? "Lost-world" histories help us to "perform" world history more fully by offering us the "view from nowhere,"[80] a look at the world as at once "seen from nowhere" and from anywhere.[81] They offer a way to see how the *oikoumene*, the known world, makes itself present through its laboring over and around that which is known but absent—here, the ten lost tribes.

In the case of the ten lost tribes, it is a lost ethnos—a category that denotes both a human group and a geography—that encompasses the geographic and mythical loss so evocatively described by Ramaswamy and Gillis. Its discovery, reconstitution, and repatriation are understood as vital—indeed, definitive—steps on the path to making the world whole, complete. Here, it is not only a geographic *topos* that is at issue—a lost island, or continent. It is also a human landscape—of races, nations, and human origins. The labors of loss surrounding the ten tribes—lost in the past, continuously present, to be found in the future—present themselves ultimately as speculation about the world itself, its geography and humanity, its borders, limits, and ends. Indeed, in the centuries-long hunt for the lost tribes, the unit of analysis, always, has been the world as a whole. The geographical theology involved in the search for the tribes always has had as its ultimate frame of reference the world. It is always global in scale. The pattern is classically world historical—while having the world as a whole as the "ultimate frame of reference,"[82] the seekers of the lost tribes, like the world historian herself, never really cover the entirety of the world at one go. The focus on a subset, framed by a whole world, is a defining characteristic of world history and of ten-tribes-ism alike. *The Ten Lost Tribes*, too, like the seekers it describes, has the world as its ultimate frame of reference, but this book is a history of only some of the world's parts.

With the world as its ultimate frame of reference, *The Ten Lost Tribes* moves from the pivotal locations of the story of the ten tribes—ancient Israel and Assyria, Judah and Babylon, Judea and Palestine under the Romans—outward, following the ever-widening radius within which knowledge of the ten tribes was generated. Rome and the Mediterranean, Portugal, Spain, the Netherlands, Great Britain, and, finally, the United States and Israel—each in turn has become a potent *topos* in the quest. The motion in this book follows the literal movement of the seekers of the tribes, the constant recalibration of the location the tribes were thought to occupy, and the ever-elusive, ever-receding quality of the tribes themselves. This book tracks the emergence in different world locations of ten tribes knowledge and, as such, is a sequence that reflects shifts in the (largely Western) understanding of the notion of a political and cultural center. As each site in turn became the new hub for the global dissemination of knowledge, it became in turn the center for a new wave of ten tribes speculation, study, and investigation. This study proceeds chronologically, albeit with frequent forays into different times, from the moment a group of people was indeed deported from the capital of the Ephraimite kingdom during the eighth century BCE up to the relatively recent moment when another group of people was "repatriated" to the very same place.

I

Assyrian Tributes

I besieged and conquered Samerina.
I took as booty 27,290 people who lived there.
I gathered 50 chariots from them.
And I taught the rest [of the deportees] their skills.
I set my governor over them, and
I imposed upon them the [same] tribute as the previous king.
                    —Sargon II, king of Assyria, cited in Younger,
                        "Deportations of the Israelites"

Thus, the Assyrian king Sargon II (r. 722–705 BCE) summarized his successful campaign against the kingdom of Israel, which had existed for nearly two centuries.[1] Sargon, not the first Assyrian ruler to wage war against Israel, had managed to conquer its capital, Samaria (Samerina), deported a number of its inhabitants, and turned what was left of it into another Assyrian province.[2] The event marked a high point in Assyrian history; by the end of the eighth century, the Assyrian Empire was a world power, "a colossus: the largest and most complex political structure the ancient Near East had known up to its period."[3] The capture and destruction of Samaria was certainly a moment to remember. Contemporary scholars summed it up with brutal brevity: "It was all over. Two stormy centuries had come to a catastrophic end."[4] This chapter discusses the context and circumstances within which the Israelite kingdom was destroyed and some of its people deported—the ur-text for the subsequent millennia of searching for them. More important, it presents and analyzes the ways in which these defeats and losses were theologized and belabored in the biblical narrative describing the events.

The initial context for the tribes' story and tradition was the Assyrian imperial one and the *oikoumene* that derived from it. It was within this context that the tribes were deported, and it was into this *oikoumene* that their loss was written. The story of Assyrian ascendancy, conquest, and dominance was most potently, from the biblical perspective, the context within which the fate of the Israelite kingdom was sealed, interpreted, and written. This history takes two basic forms: the first is made up of the concrete events of war and deportation, and the second of the overlay of biblical embroidery upon them. The biblical authors' ideological/theological agenda is exposed in the manner in which the events were recorded and interpreted. In approaching the biblical sources, which are inexhaustible, I will limit my discussion mostly to the books of 2 Kings, Hosea, Amos, and Isaiah. These texts set the parameters of the ten tribes story and the prophecies attached to it as they were followed by later biblical texts— such as Chronicles, Jeremiah, and Ezekiel—and by much-later searchers alike. By scholarly consensus, the time of the writing of these four books places them closest in time to the actual events of the late eighth century BCE.

My aim is not so much to reconstruct a historical reality as to identify several key moments, initial phases of labors of loss, as it were, in the development of the historical deportations from a past event into an ongoing story of exile and loss. These are not moments in a diachronic history, but they identify and outline the core components and parameters of the ten lost tribes' story as they were handed down to later readers. The biblical narrative matters less as a chronology of past events than as a living blueprint used in endless interpretations as circumstances changed. But bear in mind that this distinction is not one that would have held meaning during much of the history discussed in this book, when the historicity of the narrative in all its forms was scarcely called into question.

Assyrian Deportations

Sargon's war with the Israelite kingdom was a chapter in a series of Assyrian campaigns against it and other neighboring kingdoms over several decades. The first Assyrian ruler to make a significant appearance on the eastern shores of the Mediterranean was Tiglath-pileser III (r. 745–727), who marked the beginning of a new era in Assyrian history, launching several campaigns against the empire's western neighbors.[5] In the wake of these early Assyrian forays, Israel, a relatively prosperous kingdom in the northern part of Palestine, entered a long turbulent period. It became at first a vassal of the expanding empire, but soon lost a number of its territories to direct Assyrian rule. In a subsequent offensive, Tiglath-pileser's successor, Shalmaneser V (r. 727–722), apparently besieged Israel's capital, Samaria, but as he died shortly thereafter, the campaign retreated. While the biblical narrative tells of mass deportations following Shalmaneser's campaign (2 Kings 17:1–6), it is not clear whether there actually were any.[6] The third and final blow came in 720, when Shalmaneser's successor, Sargon II, captured the city and brought the end of the kingdom.[7]

In the wake of his 733–732 campaign, which destroyed the kingdom of Aram Damascus (house of Haza'el) and annexed parts of Israel, Tiglath-pileser III wrote, "I carried off [to] Assyria the land of Bit Humria [Israel]... [its] auxiliary [army]... all its people, [I killed] Pekah, their king, and I installed Hoshea [as king] over them. I received from them 10 talents of gold, X talents of silver, [with their property] and [I car]ried them [to Assyria]."[8]

Israel barely survived these attacks and saw its rival northern neighbor and onetime ally in the wars against the Assyrians, Aram Damascus, annexed and entirely swallowed up by the empire. In 2 Kings 16:10, we learn that the Aramean king, Rezin, the last king of the house of Haza'el, was executed and Damascus's people deported to a place known as "Kir."[9] In the same Assyrian inscription, Tiglath-pileser comments on the event, boasting, "I annexed to Assyria the en[tire] wide land of [Bit Hazai]li."[10]

Sargon II, the Assyrian king who completed the destruction of Israel, was equally boastful about his triumphs. Fortunately, the inscriptions detailing his success are better preserved than those of his predecessor. Another inscription discussing Sargon's war against Samaria tells a fuller story than the one offered above:

> [The inhabitants of Sa]merina, who agreed [and plotted] with a king
> [hostile to] me, not to endure servitude and not to bring tribute to
> Assyria and who did battle, I fought against them with the power of
> the great gods, my lords.
> I counted as spoil 27,280 people, together with their chariots, and
> gods, in which they trusted.
> I formed a unit with 200 of [their] chariots for my royal force.
> I settled the rest of them in the midst of Assyria.
> I repopulated Samerina more than before.
> I brought into it people from countries conquered by my hands.
> I appointed my commissioner as governor over them.
> And I counted them as Assyrians.[11]

As in the earlier case, the biblical narrative provides a similar account: the king of Assyria deported the people of Samaria, settled them in Assyria, and brought others "in place of the Israelites" (2 Kings 17:6, 23–24). Soon, they were assimilated. Thus, the three major campaigns against Israel were followed by two significant deportations, the first under Tiglath-pileser III and the second under Sargon II. However, it is quite evident that the Assyrians did not totally depopulate Israel. Thousands, possibly tens of thousands, of people were deported in each episode, but by no means was the entire Israelite population "carried away." Scholars estimate that the population of the entire area of Palestine at the time was about 400,000 people, the majority of them resident in the kingdom of Israel.[12] The overall demographic impact of these specific deportations alone was thus not massive, even if we take the numbers quoted in the Assyrian inscriptions as accurate. The fact that, after the destruction of Israel, three other Assyrian kings—Sennacherib (r. 705–681), Esarhaddon (r. 681–669), and Ashurbanipal (r. 669–627)—also deported people from Palestine, albeit in much smaller numbers, is surely one factor contributing to the sense that the devastation was more complete than it was. Whatever their numeric scope, it is clear that the psychological effect of the deportations was long lasting. As one scholar puts it, "One thing is certain: the impact of these two kings' policies was felt for many generations to come."[13]

Biblical authors were very familiar with this form of forced migration. It had repeatedly changed the demographic makeup of the region. Not only were there deportations *from* Palestine. There were also forced migrations *to* the land. Famously, the biblical narrative tells us that, after the final destruction of Samaria, the Assyrian king "brought men from Babylon, and from Cuthah, and from Ava, and from Hamath, and from Sepharvaim, and placed them in the cities of Samaria instead of the children of Israel: and they possessed Samaria, and dwelt in the cities thereof" (2 Kings 17:24). The account has an Assyrian equivalent, presented as Sargon's own narration, which recounts the acculturation of divergent groups within the newly conquered Assyrian territory: "The people of the four [quarters], of foreign tongue and divergent speech, inhabitants of mountain and plain, all whom the Light of the gods, the lord of all, shepherded, whom I had carried off with my powerful scepter by the command of Assyria, my lord—I made them of one mouth."[14]

The relentless Sargon also tells of another deportation to Palestine he carried out, involving peoples from the most distant southern borders of the empire: "I defeated [the tribes of] Thamud, Ibadidi, Marsimani, and Hayapa, the far-off Arabs, who are dwelling in the desert.... I removed [them] and in Samaria I caused them to dwell." Moreover, in 716, Sargon is known to have brought another group of people "from the countries of the east."[15] Additional

Assyrian deportations to Palestine are recounted in the book of Ezra, in which there are two instances of groups of people claiming to have been brought to Palestine by Esarhaddon and Ashurbanipal. In the latter case, the people in question unequivocally identify themselves as the "Dinaites, the Apharsath-chites, the Tarpelites, the Apharsites, the Archevites, the Babylonians, the Susanchites, the Dehavites, and the Elamites. And the rest of the nations whom the great and noble Asnapper [Ashurbanipal] brought over, and set in the cities of Samaria, and the rest that are on this side [of] the river, and at such a time" (Ezra 4:2, 10–11).

A leading biblical historian concludes that the total impact of these depor-tations and wars was considerable, with "large population groups . . . trans-ferred to new homes throughout the empire" and significant "changes in the composition of the population of Palestine."[16] But again, even by the most maximalist of reckonings, these deportations did not leave the northern kingdom entirely depopulated. Another careful overview of an array of studies concludes, "most northerners were not deported."[17] It is likely that many groups throughout the territory were left in place. Many migrated south to Jerusalem. The story of Israelite deportation and exile is one subportion of a broader story of population movements into, out of, and around the region. Its biblical depiction exaggerates the totality of the deportations as part of a specifically Israelite narrative of loss and promised redemption, while the Assyrian sources seek to aggrandize their kings by emphasizing the sweeping devastation they were able to inflict through both the deportation and importation of multiple populations. Both sides of the narrative have clear ideological/theological motivation for inflating the scope of the deporta-tions.

Obviously, Palestine and the neighboring regions were not the only ones affected by Assyrian deportations. Mass deportations of conquered peoples were a frequent occurrence in the Assyrian world since the ninth century BCE and are a relatively well-researched topic. While certainly not a coherent imperial policy, deportation was an important tool of Assyrian imperial expan-sion and supremacy, and it was deployed over the centuries in order to serve the changing interests of an actively expanding empire. Tiglath-pileser is praised as the king "who exchanges the peoples of the upper land[s] with those of the lower land[s]";[18] it is clear that he used deportation as an effective tool both for punishing conquered peoples, explicitly engineering the demo-graphics of his territory, and for maintaining peace and stability in newly occupied territories which were designated as Assyrian. Postcampaign recon-struction rested in large part on repopulation. As Tiglath-pileser explains in another Assyrian inscription, "I rebuilt Nikur, together with its environs, [as Assyrian cities]. I settled therein people of foreign lands, conquered by me."[19] The Assyrian record of the period is largely one of multitudes of people deported and then resettled.

The paradigmatic biblical account illustrating the connection that the Assyrians saw between deportation and imperial stability involves the siege on Jerusalem in 701, the culminating point of which, as recounted in 2 Kings, is a dramatic speech delivered by Rabshakeh, Sennacherib's chief officer, to the besieged Jerusalemites. Standing on a ramp facing the walls of Jerusalem, the Assyrian official tries to persuade the besieged that resistance is futile and explains the advantages of surrender:

> [F]or thus saith the king of Assyria, [m]ake an agreement with me
> by a present, and come out to me, and then eat ye every man of his
> own vine, and every one of his fig tree, and drink ye every one the
> waters of his cistern. Until I come and take you away to a land
> like your own land, a land of corn and wine, a land of bread and
> vineyards, a land of olive oil and of honey, that ye may live, and
> not die. (2 Kings 18:31–32)

One should assume that this passage represents an idealized, heavily edited version of the speech, if it was ever made. Nevertheless, even this account makes clear that deportation was understood by the biblical authors as inevitably yoked to Assyrian conquest as its signature byproduct. Deportations and relocations were also seen, or at least presented, as a way to further the homogeneity of the empire by encouraging cultural change and interaction. As Sargon claimed, after deporting the Samarians to Assyria, he "counted them as Assyrians." Similarly, he "made one mouth" of the people of many languages whom he brought to Samaria. The success of these measures in achieving the goal of cultural homogeneity is doubtful. The biblical narrative discusses this precise point in the case of the people brought to Samaria by the Assyrians after the deportation of the Israelites; these are the people who later came to be known as the Samaritans, who feature so prominently in later literature and in the Christian Gospels. Upon their arrival, each group initially continued to practice its own religion "and did not pay homage to the Lord," the local deity. By the biblical account, this made the local god unhappy, "so the Lord sent lions to them to prey on them." Upon learning of this state of affairs, the Assyrian king ordered "that one of the priests taken captive from Samaria be sent back to live there and teach the people of the usage of the God of the country." The deportees to Samaria briefly learned how to pay homage to the local deity, but eventually "each of the nations went on making its own god" (2 Kings 24–33).

While the overall thrust is to affirm the Lord of Israel's divine supremacy over the region, the specifics are clues to the understanding in the period of the Assyrian policy of deportation. The Assyrian king is depicted as involved in the cultural life of the deportees, even to the extent of interfering in it in order to increase stability. The mention of the only partial success of his cultural engineering is significant. The (future) Samaritans learn the new ways, but stick to their old practices as well. The biblical knowledge of this hybridity was later a touchstone for thinking about deported Israelites. One central view holds that they, like the peoples brought to Samaria, had likely adopted the ways of their new cultural settings, but also might have retained a memory of their earlier, Israelite practices.

Even if we have every reason to question the on-the-ground success of the empire's cultural engineering projects, it is clear that, at the very least, Assyrian kings were eager that as many people as possible within their domain be "counted as Assyrians." At issue were the demographic, economic, and political needs of the empire. To be counted as Assyrian was not a matter of "becoming" Assyrian, but referred primarily to the duties that the original Assyrians incurred. One phrase that recurs in the inscriptions is "Corvée labor like that of the Assyrians."[20] To be counted as Assyrian also brought military service. Deportations were a useful way to populate the Assyrian army—a "truly multinational force!" as many scholars (glossingly) describe it.[21]

While the story tells us what happened to the imported peoples of the region, it leaves a gaping question as to the final disposition of the deported Israelites. Where did they go? Where were they taken? What was the fate of the deportees in their final location—did they, like the new Samaritans, continue their original worship? There is scattered evidence that provides only bits of an answer. The biblical source tells us that the king took the Israelites "away into Assyria, and placed them in Halah, and on the Habor, the river of Gozan, and in the cities of Medes" (2 Kings 17:6). All of these locations were within Assyria proper. The region of the "cities of Medes" was located to the east of the empire, beyond its original boundaries, and was fully incorporated into Assyria only after 716. It is also likely that many of the deportees were settled on farmlands owned by high-ranking Assyrian officials, priests, and aristocrats.[22] We know that many of them would have been equipped with skills beneficial to the Assyrian war effort and would have enjoyed "preferred or at least reasonable" or even "good [treatment]."[23]

Archaeological and documentary evidence from the region shows that many deportees were not completely dispersed but settled in groups in major cities. They were allowed to own property, marry, and conduct their own businesses—a semi-fulfillment of Rabshakeh's promise of a familiar "land of grain and new wine."[24] The deportation of many, though, was simply a form of punishment, and their experience was of "hardship and bare subsistence."[25] But it is possible to "trace the process of their assimilation into Assyrian culture."[26]

Overall, the story of the Israelite deportation is not at all exceptional for the period, which was characterized by a dizzying series of forced population movements. The Israelite deportation, in historical context, was just one among many such events and certainly not a standout story of the exile and eradication of an entire people. No one was truly lost, no one was sent to the ends of the earth. Like hosts of others, the Israelites—or rather, some subportion of them—were shunted from one zone to another as part of a broader imperial political plan.

Assyrian *Oikoumene* and the Edges of the Earth

The geographical context within which the deportation of the Israelites occurred, and was understood and recorded, shaped the story as one of irrevocable exile. The story would come to be embedded in Assyrian geography, ideology, and historiography as disseminated by Assyrian imperial propaganda.

Imperial communications and propaganda were important tools in the service of the Assyrian war machine. Assyrian rulers used these tools effectively to present a view of control and homogeneity within their dominions greater than what in fact prevailed. The Assyrian Empire was among the first to employ such tools. The world to which the biblical authors reacted, and which they largely reproduced, was the world of Assyrian propaganda, in which Assyrian dominion and primacy were complete and unquestioned, and it lasted long after the empire that created it was gone. Indeed, this propaganda has misled a number of Assyria's students. Earlier scholarly perceptions of the Assyrian Empire as having effective administrative control have undergone serious revision since the late twentieth century, and this scholarship notes that the empire was not, in fact, particularly efficient in its rule.[27] Yet all contemporary scholars agree on the effectiveness of its propaganda, which succeeded over millennia in conveying an overly rosy view of Assyrian dominance. The Assyrian claim to world dominance was "expressed openly and clearly in titles, epithets, phrases, statements, and hymns."[28] Most famously, Assyrian rulers made use of the visual arts, erecting huge monuments intended to convey the empire's messages.[29] Assyrian ideology was targeted at all and sundry in the empire's orbit and beyond, for all residents to hear, see, and heed. The world created by Assyrian propaganda and imperial communications was larger and wider than its actual political and military scope. Assyrian propaganda shaped the geographical imagination of the peoples within its (extended) boundaries, creating an impression of mastery over much of the known world.

Assyrian propaganda created a rich treasure trove of sources, including annals, summaries, and royal inscriptions. Some were produced around the time of the events they described; others were composed years later. Assyrian rulers erected steles marking the locations of battles, praising victories, and expounding the consequences of their wars.[30] The wealth of these sources, many of them discovered only in the nineteenth century, allows contemporary scholars of Assyria to provide us with a reasonable sketch of what might be called "Assyrian ideology."[31] Assyrian rulers invested great effort in providing justifications for their military expeditions and conquests. Assyrian wars were, of course, divinely sanctified, but there were plenty of more mundane, earthly justifications provided for them as well.[32] The twenty-first-century reader will probably be familiar with the claim that imperial rulers have the right to wage "preemptive wars." As today, the Assyrians' enemy in such cases was invariably cast as the aggressor, or at least the potential aggressor.[33] Similarly, Assyrian wars were often justified as the only means to "restore order" and "sustain peace" in places under the sovereign control of other powers.[34]

The eighth century BCE is a contender for the first "great century" in world history thanks to the Assyrians.[35] The Assyrian world was the first real *oikoumene*, created by the first world power truly far-flung in reach and diverse in culture. This world covered the entire Fertile Crescent from the Persian Gulf to eastern North Africa. It touched on the Zagros Mountains in the east and the eastern Mediterranean in the west, and in the north it reached the Taurus range. Its southern edges included "Egypt to the west and Elam to the east, even subduing the surrounding nomads—the Arabs of the desert and Medes of the highland." Indirectly, the Assyrian Empire reached even Arabia and Nubia along its southern borders (see figure 2.1).[36]

The incorporation of the Phoenician trade network, which was greatly affected by the rising imperial economy, brought an array of Mediterranean territories within the Assyrian periphery as well.[37] The limits of the Assyrian *oikoumene* were not the concrete limits of the empire itself. Rather, they were the outer limits of the world that the Assyrians knew and the world that knew them. The limits of the *oikoumene*, in short, were the limits of Assyrian propaganda. Indeed, Assyrian propaganda created this world, mapping it, as it were. Assyrian kings had a clear vision of this territory, conceptualizing the Assyrian realm both through the abstract term "universe" and by physical

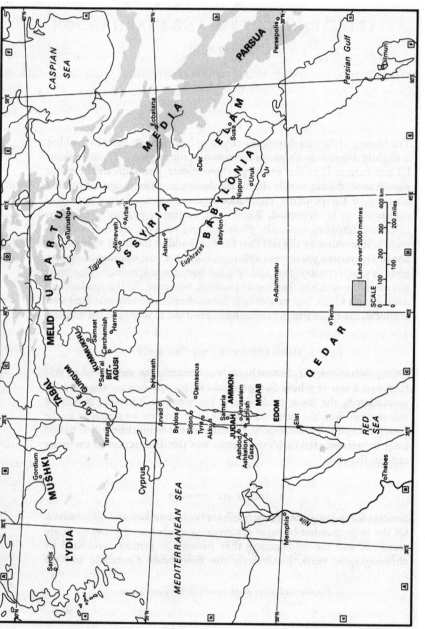

FIGURE 2.1. Assyrian and Babylonian empires. Source: Boardman, *The Cambridge Ancient History*, p. 104 (map 3).

markers ("the four corners") that set it off from other, lesser territories. The Assyrian king was "King of the Universe [everything]" (*sar kissati*), but also "king of the four regions/quarters of the world" (*sar kibrāt arba'i erbetti*). He was "Shepherd of the four quarters" (*rēū kibrāt erbetta*) and "king of all lands" (*sar matati*).[38] Assyria, we are reminded repeatedly, was ever expanding.[39] Honorifics invariably emphasize this. On one stele, Tiglath-pileser appears as "king of Assyria, king of Sumer and Akkad, king of the four quarters, shepherd of mankind . . . who enlarges the boundary of Assyria."[40]

The famous king Ashurbanipal was known as the ruler who "extends the borders of Assyria" and "enlarges the borders and territory."[41] Ashurbanipal, whose reign marks the culmination of the Assyrian Empire, was "the mighty king who has extended his conquests from the banks of the Tigris to Mount Lebanon and the great sea of the land of Amurru."[42] An inscription in Tiglath-pileser's palace calls him "Great king, the mighty king, king of the universe, king of Assyria, king of Babylon, king of Sumer and Akkad, king of the four quarters."

Recurrent themes in the inscriptions are the all-encompassing scope of the Assyrian kingdom and the territorially transformative effects of its rulers. Tilgath-pileser was memorialized as a "brave warrior" who "swept the [countries] like the flood." "I am Tiglath-pileser, king of Assyria, who from east to west personally conquered all the lands," declares an inscription found in Iran—the eastern territory of the empire.[43]

The tandem use of "universe" and "four corners/regions/quarters" was replicated in the Assyrian deployment of two distinct terms that referred to their power. One (*kissūtu*) denoted world hegemony, and the other (*bēlūtu*) world suzerainty.[44] This distinction was important because the Assyrians wielded power and control in varying degrees over vast territories that might fall under a number of categories: provinces, vassal states, buffer states, and enemies. In the words of archaeologist Bradley Parker, direct "annexation was not the only method of establishing Assyrian dominion."[45] The general term universe, the realm under the dominion of the "King of the Universe," was accompanied by the phrase "four regions of the world"—the vast, but finite and specific space that, while not within the physical limits of the Assyrian domain, was abstractly under Assyrian dominion.

The deportation of the Israelites was thus understood within a complicated framework that was already explicitly geographic. Indeed, the deported Israelites, in actual terms, were sent to places that would later become integral, core lands of the imperial domain. In subsequent memory, however, while they would retain their geographic groundedness—indeed, the promise that the ten tribes are actually here, in a real place on earth, was what gave such staying power to the myth—the borders beyond which the tribes were thought to have disappeared became ever receding, just like the borders that the Assyrian kings always recreated in their minds. With each expansion, first of the Assyrian Empire and, later, of human geographic knowledge as a whole, the lost tribes leaped back, forever remaining on the far side of the known horizon.

The Assyrian propaganda machine of the eighth and seventh centuries BCE, with its relentless emphasis on the vastness of empire; the horizon-expanding, unimaginable grasp of its rulers; and the constant reference to borders, markers, and boundaries were all part of the initial framing and reception of the story of Israelite deportation. As it first took shape, the biblical account of the lost tribes borrowed heavily, if unintentionally, from this same propagandistic repertoire. Even as Assyrian propaganda marketed the glory of its army and its kings, it also defined and popularized various notions of space. The Assyrians imposed upon their region a conceptualization of the world as a space divided into different polities, even as they proposed that all, ultimately, would become part of their empire. "King of totality of the [four] quarters including all their rulers" ran one particularly ambitious title.[46]

These differing notions of space had a great impact on biblical texts. Isaiah, Jeremiah, and Ezekiel, who all wrote under the shadow of empire, were keen observers of imperial activity, either Assyrian or Babylonian.[47] Most famous in this regard are Isaiah's "Oracles against the Nations" (Isaiah 13, 14:1–23), a reflection on the "international" context of the period.[48] The book of Jonah provides a superb expression of how the Assyrian *oikoumene* was lived by peoples on its margins and how empire was perceived and remembered. At the book's center is the city of Nineveh, the imperial capital, which, from the perspective of the book's Israelite author, is viewed from outside, as a destination to which Jonah is to travel. As the story has it, Jonah, son of Amittai, was a prophet who, according to the Bible, lived during the successful reign of Jeroboam II (r. 788–747; 2 Kings 14:25). One day, Jonah receives an order from God to go to the "great city of Nineveh" and tell its people that the city will be destroyed "for their wickedness" (Jonah 1:1–3). Jonah resists at first, fleeing God by hiding on a boat. When a storm threatens to throw its passengers into the sea, Jonah reveals himself as the target of God's wrath and tells them to throw him overboard to save the ship. No sooner do they do so than the waves calm. Famously, Jonah is swallowed by a great fish and, after three days in its belly, is spat up onto dry land. From there, he fulfills God's command, traveling to Nineveh to warn its wicked inhabitants of God's impending punishment: "in forty days Nineveh shall be overthrown!" Embedded in the prophecy is a dual meaning—while the focus of Jonah's story is the people of Nineveh, on a broader level it is a parable about Assyrian might as a whole. The Hebrew word for "overthrown," *nehepekhet,* literally means "turned upside down," and it has been taken as a word-play alluding to the ultimate repentance of the city's residents.

In Jonah's story, the prophet, a stranger, arrives at Nineveh and proclaims that it will be overthrown. The inhabitants do not argue. Improbably, they "take to heart this warning" (Jonah 3:5). Jonah's prophecy is one of pending repentance, implied physical destruction, and looming imperial collapse. But the story told in Jonah is also about imperial realities. We recall that, before actually delivering the prophecy as ordered, Jonah first fled. Jonah's journey away from, and then inexorably toward, the Assyrian capital reflects contemporary perceptions of the vastness and diversity of the Assyrian Empire, the geographical setting of the story.

At first, Jonah escapes the mission by running to the port in Joppa (Jaffa) and embarking on a "ship bound to Tarshish." Some scholars locate Tarshish in southern Spain; others consider it to be a legend. However, all agree that logically it was located in the opposite direction from Nineveh, somewhere in the Mediterranean. The scene on the ship reflects the multiculturalism of the empire; when God sends a storm, "everyone cried out to his own god for help," and Jonah is asked to do the same. When this does not work, the sailors ask Jonah, "What is your business? Where do you come from? Which is your country? What is your nationality?" To which the answer is "I am a Hebrew" (Jonah 1:7–9), one recognizable "nationality" among many.

The book of Jonah describes the diversity of Assyrian imperial society and teaches us about perceptions of distance to and from its capital. It also expresses, metaphorically, the sense of the empire's inescapable reach. Nineveh is described as "a vast city of three journey days' across" inhabited by a population of 120,000. Nineveh in both its proportions and distance is a known referent; it is, in its context, what "the City" means today. Jonah's prophetic travel is unwittingly a strong expression of the extent to which Israelite perceptions of geography and distance were drawn directly from Assyrian ones. This Nineveh maps the eastern Mediterranean world as a fundamentally Assyrian imperial one.

Nineveh also became intimately linked to the exile of the ten tribes. The apocryphal book of Tobit, produced around the second century BCE, tells the story of a righteous ten triber named Tobit who lives in Nineveh to which he was exiled by the Assyrians.[49] During the nineteenth century, when modern archaeologists began excavating the city, searching for evidence of the presence of the ten tribes in the vicinity was on scholars' minds.[50] In the city, the first modern Western observers found "the life-likeness of the very men who carried away the ten tribes."[51] Modern archaeological discoveries, which shed new light on ancient historical texts and provided a scientific basis for discussing the fate of the lost tribes, presented Nineveh as the place from which the captives were "distributed" to other locations following their initial deportation.[52]

While the geographical settings in Jonah reflect the scope of the empire, Isaiah echoes the power of its propaganda. Isaiah, an enthusiastic and at times uncritical consumer of Assyrian propaganda, refers to an idealized army drawn directly from the self-promoting image of the Assyrians. Of its soldiers, "none shall slumber nor sleep; neither shall the girdle of their loins be loosed, nor the latchet of their shoes be broken" (5:27).[53] Isaiah's words reflect the impact of the "terrifying mask [that Assyria] deliberately turned towards the outside world."[54] No wonder, then, that Isaiah has God declare: "O Assyria, the rod of mine anger...the staff in their hand is mine indignation" (Isaiah 10:5).

Isaiah describes the Assyrians as coming from the edges of the earth, with an army like a knife: "He [God] will hiss unto them from the end of the earth [mi-ketse ha-Aretz]: and, behold, they shall come with speed swiftly" (5:26). "In the same day shall the Lord shave with a razor that is hired, namely, by them beyond the river, by the king of Assyria, the head, and the hair of the feet: and it shall also consume the beard" (Isaiah 7:18–20). The image of the army as a razor echoes Bradley Parker's finding that "the Assyrian military traveled in [a] straight line from one destination [to] the next,"[55] and conjures up a vocabulary of demarcation and redistribution. In Isaiah's prophecy, the Assyrian army is in God's service, cutting out the contours of an oikoumene that stretched from the Persian Gulf ("Assyria") to Egypt. At these extreme points lay the edges of the earth. The phrase "edges of the earth" recurs throughout Isaiah's prophecies.[56] Parker has shown that the borders of Assyria proper were heavily garrisoned and guarded, and this was well known to Assyria's neighbors.[57] Words denoting boundary (missru) or territory/domain (tahūmu, of similar root as the Hebrew word tehum, means "pale," "domain," or "boundary") appear more than 300 times in Assyrian sources. Phrases referring to the "violation" of this territory occur at least 15 times.[58] These border garrisons may be the literal edges of the earth from which, in Isaiah's text, God will summon his avenging army.

Characteristic of a number of imperial boundaries, the border was not "a stark line, [but] instead a porous zone or continuum, often a hundred kilometers deep." It was strongly felt both in concrete and representational terms across a large swath of land, a further factor in the adoption of Assyrian notions of space and geography by a number of its neighbors and even its enemies. Isaiah's "ends of the earth" and "four corners of the earth" aren't a mere mimicking of Assyrian phraseology. They reflect what Mark Hamilton has called the "bidirectional and interactive" quality of Assyrian communication.[59]

Isaiah does not copy so much as *share* the geographical terminology and conceptual framework of the empire he so fears. To Isaiah, a would-be subject of the empire, viewing it from the marginal Judahite periphery, the Assyrian army was by definition always at the edges of the earth; its very mission was to expand them. In the biblical texts, the centrality of the Assyrian role in shaping and carving out geography is further underscored by a conflation of the emperor's role with that of God himself. Just as the Assyrian ruler "enlarges the boundary of Assyria," so too does God: "Lord, you have enlarged the nation . . . and won honour for yourself; you have extended all the boundaries of the land" (Isaiah 26:15).[60]

The geographic terms and symbolism of Isaiah were not theological metaphors nor hollow ornaments employed for the glorification of God. In the Assyrian context, they were concrete, meaningful terms that referred to geographic boundaries and imperial limits. Thus, imperial propaganda was closely linked to the geographic dimensions of Hebrew prophecy—a critical component of the environment in which the story of the lost tribes was cast and later elaborated.

From Deportation to Exile: Judahites and Israelites

The period between the mid-eighth and early sixth centuries BCE was one of rapid change and transition. Judah developed and flourished under the shadow of two empires, Assyria and Babylonia, the latter of which eventually destroyed it. Judah was continually affected by the power negotiations between the Egyptian kingdom to its south and the Mesopotamian empires to its north. The thinly populated, poor southern kingdom, born in the tenth century, saw the destruction of its sister and rival northern Israelite kingdom by the Assyrians.

Judah itself barely survived another Assyrian campaign and a siege on Jerusalem launched by Sargon's successor, Sennacherib, in 701. Emboldened by a perceived Assyrian weakness after the death of Sargon II and supported by Egypt, the Judahites tried to defy the world empire. Sennacherib's retaliatory campaign and siege left a strong imprint of Assyrian power in Judah; indeed, it was this Assyrian army that Isaiah saw coming "from the end of earth."[61] However, the Assyrians quite miraculously spared the kingdom after a mysterious military setback.[62] Later on, as Assyrian power waned and the empire retreated from the region, Judah was able to rise to a status of some regional significance. It became more populated, more centralized, and somewhat stronger in military terms. This uptick was mainly due to temporary changes in the regional power games between Egypt and the declining Assyria, and the disappearance of a powerful neighbor to its north, the kingdom of Israel.[63]

Judah went on to develop its own hopes and dreams of greatness and expansion. Most involved trying to capture territories that had once belonged to its northern neighbor and consolidating the rule of the house of David in the kingdom's old as well as new domains. Attempts to consolidate the rule of a national religion around the cult of the Yahweh divinity accompanied these political efforts. The culmination of this centuries-long transformation came under the reign of King Josiah (r. 639–609), during which Judah expanded northward, annexing territories that had belonged to the now-defunct kingdom of Israel, former home of the ten tribes. Josiah, a charismatic and active leader most probably moved by messianic motivations, presided over the "great reformation"—the triumph of the Deuteronomistic movement, which insisted on the cult of one god in the temple in Jerusalem and was violently opposed to other cults or locations of worship. The event that marks the beginning of this reformation, in 2 Kings, was the discovery in the temple in Jerusalem of a lost book, Deuteronomy, which would be the blueprint for the emerging faith.[64] These developments brought a further locative dimension to the Israelite world view; alongside the distant world boundaries marked out first by Assyrian propaganda came a very rigid sense of Jerusalem as the definitive center, the ultimate place to which one was to (re)turn.

In the end, however, Judah's ambitions were brutally crushed, twice. The Egyptian pharaoh Necho II (r. 610–595) killed King Josiah in Megiddo in 609.[65] Following Josiah's untimely and traumatic death, Judah was ruled by a series of mostly incompetent kings until its destruction by the Babylonians in 586 BCE; this destruction was followed by a deportation. But the decades before these calamities saw the Judahite production of the blueprint for an Israelite national history, one that included the story of two kingdoms and their fates. Significant portions of the story were written during this period.[66]

Here, we at last draw closer to the ten tribes themselves. The exile and salvation of the Judahites provided an important referent, alongside Assyrian propaganda, for the later reframing of the story in the biblical narrative. With the 589 arrival of a new imperial power, the Babylonians, the Judahite elite found itself, like the ten tribes in the north before them, sent into exile. In the Babylonian case, though, the destination was known: Babylon itself. The Babylonians, who succeeded the Assyrians as the major power in Mesopotamia, had crushed the Egyptians earlier and come to dominate the entire region. Once Judah was left with no major power behind it, it was doomed. In 597 BCE, Nebuchadnezzar II, king of Babylon, laid siege to Jerusalem, captured its king,

Jehoiachin (Jeconiah), and took him back to Babylon. The last blow came in 586. The Babylonian armies came to Jerusalem, sacked it, burned the temple, and exiled the Judahite elite to Babylon as captives. Miraculously, the exiled got to witness a speedy return to Judah: within a matter of decades, they were allowed to return, and the temple was restored. As the book of Ezra tells us, the Babylonian exile ended when a new imperial power, the Persians, defeated the Babylonians and allowed the exiles to return to their land and rebuild the temple, which they did in 518 BCE.[67]

Over this period, the Deuteronomistic history, the Bible's major historical narrative, was written. The history of one kingdom split in two (Judah and Israel) and next the disappearance of its northern half, Israel, became the larger context into which all biblically recorded events and subsequent interpretations are placed. The project of writing the history of Israel did not end with the destruction of Jerusalem, of course. It continued in the diaspora, intensifying when some of the Judahite deportees returned to Judah and rebuilt a new polity there. In these contexts of exile and repatriation, the story's basic contours were brought into further relief.

With the biblical transformation of historic events into theologically significant ones, "local histories" were transformed into expressions of "universal values," and "trivial events" underwent "significant re-elaboration," to borrow Mario Liverani's useful terminology.[68] The seeds of the story's main elements, namely, the exile of the tribes as a divine punishment, their loss, and their promised return, were written into the ur-text of the ten lost tribes in the period before Judah's destruction by the Babylonians. The final loss of the tribes occurred when the Judahite deportees returned to Judah and the Israelites did not.

The mainstream approach to the book of Kings holds that it began taking shape during the last decades of the first kingdom of Judah, most probably during the days of Josiah's reform. Among twentieth- and twenty-first-century scholars of the biblical period are many who suggest that this history was invented to serve the ideological and political programs of Judah under Josiah and to question the historicity of the Davidic united kingdom. By this view, the Judahites' plans to expand and take over the northern territories after the Assyrian retreat, and the consolidation and centralization of the one-god cult under their rule, were the real motives underlying the historiographic project.[69] This proposition (along with many others questioning the historicity of an array of biblical stories) is the subject of intense controversy.[70] But what is crucial is the fact that the biblical narrative of the ten tribes and their fate was taken as historical fact right up until the modern period. While elements of the story have been established as accurate—the Assyrian practice of deportation, for example—the question remains as to how these were transformed into a story of the exile of an entire people, indeed of ten entire tribes.

It is widely accepted that the biblical authors used existing chronicles that included data and information about the histories of Israel and Judah in assembling their accounts. Thus, the biblical narrative covering the Assyrian campaigns and the deportations that followed them begins with the campaign of Tiglath-pileser III. In 2 Kings 15:29, we read that Tiglath-pileser ultimately "came and seized Iyyon, Abel-beth-maacha, Janoah, Kedesh, Hazor, Gilead, Galilee, the entire region of Naphtali, and deported the people to Assyria."[71]

Thus, the Israelite kingdom became reduced both territorially and demographically. According to the biblical narrative, the Assyrian punishment did not impress Israel's subsequent rulers. Nor did the horrible fate of the Damascenes, who saw their king executed and their kingdom destroyed, and who were deported by the Assyrians during the days of King Hoshea (732–724 or 722), who apparently plotted with the Egyptians against them. Several decades after the first deportation, King Shalmaneser, who reinforced the arrangements his predecessor had made with the Israelites, "discovered that Hoshea was being disloyal to him, sending envoys to the king of Egypt at So, and withholding the annual tribute which he had been paying" (2 Kings 17:3). At this point, the biblical narrative skips one Assyrian king and, without mentioning Sargon by name, tells us that the king of Assyria seized King Hoshea and imprisoned him: "He overran the whole country and, reaching Samaria, besieged it three years. In the Ninth year of Hoshea he captured Samaria and deported its people to Assyria, and placed them in Halah, and on the Habor, the river of Gozan, and in the cities of Medes" (2 Kings 17:6).

Here recall Sargon's boastful, even chilling, summary of these same events; the biblical narrative seems to be echoing it quite accurately. The only substantive difference between the two accounts is that the biblical source provides the actual locations to which the Israelites were deported. These locations are not concocted; scholars have identified almost all of them as real places in the Assyrian Empire, either in Assyria proper or in the cities of Medes, that is, on Assyria's eastern borders.[72]

But while the named places were actual locations, it is not clear that these were the locations where the deported Israelites were actually settled. This is not a question with which the biblical authors, primarily interested in telling the story of Israel's exile and its promised return, were much concerned. While subsequent interpreters would make this their primary concern, at the time of biblical composition the location of the tribes seemed almost incidental.

At first glance, the story of deportation as told in 2 Kings 17 is very much as told in the Assyrian sources—a punishment that was limited to the people of the recently conquered region. But a closer reading betrays a tension between the proposition that only the people in Samaria and its immediate periphery were deported (as Sargon's inscription tells us), and the implication that the entirety of Israel was deported—exiled—as the final blow to its polity. The Hebrew original uses the account of the fall of Samaria as the platform for summarizing the fate of the entire Israelite people: the Assyrian king "captured Samaria and exiled Israel" (*lakhad et Shomron Va-Yigel et Yisra'el;* 2 Kings 17:6). All versions emphasize the totality of the "transfer," to use the Vulgate's rendering. The story of the third campaign speaks of one deportation—that of the people of Samaria—but is the platform for the story of the exile of the entire ten tribes.

The author of 2 Kings provides a capsule summary of the events that drives the point home. Sending a cautionary message to his Judahite readers, he concludes: "For so it was, that the children of Israel had sinned against the Lord their God, which had brought them up out of the land of Egypt . . . and wrought wicked things to provoke the Lord to anger. For they served idols, whereof the Lord had said unto them, Ye shall not do this thing" (2 Kings 17:7–13). The list of sins committed by the Israelites goes on and on, with constant reference back to their "original sin"—the building by Jeroboam of sites of worship, in competition with Jerusalem. The Israelites "persisted" in Jeroboam's sins "[u]ntil the Lord removed Israel out of his sight. . . . So was Israel carried away out of their own land to Assyria unto this day" (2 Kings 17:22).

The interpretation of the deportations as a single, divine act of punishment resulting in exile is reinforced in the following chapter, in which another Assyrian campaign, Sennacherib's, is the focus. Only two decades after the destruction of Samaria, the Judahites face the Assyrian army. As a preface to their account, the biblical authors briefly recap the story of Israel's fate: the Israelites were exiled to Assyria to "Halah and on the Habor, on the river Gozan and in the cities of Medes because they did not obey the Lord their God but violated his covenant" (18:9–12). Everything in the previous chapters is compressed into one simple story: the Israelites had sinned and were exiled. The complicated history of Israel as a vassal of the Assyrians and the history of the various campaigns and deportations are no longer relevant; nor is the fact of Assyrian might. Here, the Lord God is the agent of deportation, and the crime is sacrilege. Imperial expansion and forced migration are transformed into a narrative of sin, divine punishment, and exile.

That this backdrop stands as a lesson for the Judahites is underscored by the two tales' outcomes. While the Assyrian campaign resulted in deportation, this one was mysteriously aborted after the dramatic showdown outside Jerusalem (2 Kings 18:13–37, 19:1–37). The biblical authors describe the righteous Judahites as the direct opposite of their wicked Israelite counterparts. Despite his foolish and near-disastrous misreading of world political conditions, the Judahite king Hezekiah (r. 727–698) does everything right. He listens to Isaiah, God's prophet, and the people of Judah all repent and live to see, only two decades after the punishment of their northern brothers, the "angel of God" strike all Assyrian soldiers dead within one night. The Judahites are saved, for the time being at least, and will not go into exile.[73] The Israelites, on the other hand, failed to heed all warnings and are now gone.

The biblical depiction of the deportations as punishment and exile was further reinforced by the prophecies of the northern prophets Amos and Hosea and the southern prophet Isaiah, whose oracles postdate the fall of Israel and predate the fall of Judah.[74] These prophecies, which claim to have originated in times before the actual events took place (thus rendering them "prophetic"), commonly speak of exile as the ultimate and inevitable fate of the Israelites. Hosea (c. 760–720), who likened Israel to a whore, delivered his warnings to the Israelites during the reign of Jeroboam II, repeatedly urging them to repent and predicting, "They will not dwell in the Lord's land, Ephraim will go back to Egypt, or eat unclean food in Assyria" (Hosea 9:3, 11:5). Amos, a contemporary of Hosea from Judah who also prophesied in the northern kingdom, made several predictions relating to the Assyrian deportations: "Jeroboam will die by the sword, and the Israelites will assuredly be deported from their native land" (Amos 7:11, 17).

Isaiah, Hosea, and Amos illustrate how the lens of divine punishment transformed the deportations of the Israelites into the exile of an entire people. They were the first to put their oracles in writing; as such, they were hugely influential in turning the exile of Israel into a historical paradigm.[75] They elaborated the notion of exile as it appears in 2 Kings and transformed the kernel of actual history, the patchy narrative of deportations, into an invented Israelite history of sin and all-encompassing divine punishment. The mundane history of several small-scale Assyrian deportations was transformed into a large-scale forced migration enacted by Isaiah's "Rod of God." So it is that, while Assyrian kings deported some Israelites for military and political purposes, the Judahite authors of the biblical narrative "exiled" the entire Israelite kingdom for their own theological and ideological reasons.

Lost: Israel as a Diaspora's Diaspora

The reframing of the deportations as divine punishment is one central building block in the development of the story of the ten lost tribes. Another is the
reframing of the locus of exile. It too shifts in the lenses of the later biblical
material. The book of 2 Kings, as we have seen, makes reference to specific
locales and asserts confidently that the tribes are still "there, to this day." Again,
these were known places, touchstones in the quest for the tribes, with "Gozan"
read as "Ganges," for instance. Ultimately, though, it was precisely the fact that
they were lost that opened the door to infinite interpretation and speculation,
across oceans and continents.

How, with a few named, remote Assyrian provinces as a starting place, did
they become so very lost[76] that subsequent seekers could plausibly suspect
them to be found in the Americas or in East Asia, on the Hebridean islands or
in the South Pacific? The answer again lies in the ways in which the biblical
authors came to terms with, and transformed, the framework of the story. As
opposed to the ordinary locations specified in 2 Kings, the later prophetic texts
that processed the story worked to present the location of exile in more abstract
and value-laden terms. It was the prophets' job to lose the tribes, just as it had
been their job to render their exile so numerically complete. Just as the exile
itself was exceptional in the prophetic presentation, so too was the place of
exile. The extent of the exile (as presented by the prophets) was so complete,
and its means so otherworldly, that the site of exile itself had to take on a
greater mystery. At the same time, the increasing consolidation of Jerusalem as
the site par excellence around which all Israelite religious activity was to revolve
rendered all other locations blurry and insignificant. As the place(s) to which
the tribes had gone became blurred, the place to which they must someday
return stood out clearly: Jerusalem, the touchstone by which Israelite (and,
later, Jewish, Christian, and to a lesser extent Muslim) tradition was to emerge
as the definitively locative theological world view. As the centuries wore on,
with the tribes disappearing over each newly discovered horizon, Jerusalem
remained fixed as the pole star by which they took their bearings, the magnet
by which they would one day be drawn home. The lost tribes were turned into a
diaspora, and Jerusalem into a home.

Positioning is a crucial factor in the constitution of a diaspora.[77] The
locations to which the Israelites were exiled do not simply stand for themselves. They are reconfigured, in effect repositioned, in relation to home and to
the Judahites. Having first been cast as Judah's diaspora, the Israelites were

next redefined in terms of the Israelite *position* vis-à-vis Judah and the Juda-hites. An overlaying complication was the fact that the Judahites themselves contended with their own exile and their own diaspora, which was only partially resolved with their repatriation from Babylon.

What makes the Israelite diaspora amenable to endless repositioning is the way in which it is written into the biblical text as a silent diaspora, one that does not speak. This stands in sharp contrast with the Judahite diaspora. Even before their exile by the Babylonians in 589, the Judahites had a diaspora, *golah*, which had been formed during the seventh and sixth centuries BCE, composed of an array of small communities of Judahite refugees and soldiers, in various locations within Egyptian territories (the Nile's delta, Upper Egypt, and Nubia). More Judahites found refuge in Egypt after the destruction of Jerusalem as well.[78] Ultimately, the Babylonian Empire itself became the home of exiles from Jerusalem, first in 597 when King Jehoiachin was exiled with the elites of Jerusalem, and again after the final destruction in 589.

This Judahite diaspora differed from that of the Israelites in one basic condition: it was real. Contemporaneous with the Deuteronomistic history, its whereabouts and conditions were written into the biblical narrative itself. The circumstances, experiences, and setting of the exile make up a significant portion of the Bible itself. Large portions of Jeremiah, the entirety of Ezekiel, the later portions of Isaiah, and many of the later prophets were written in the diaspora and are part of its history.[79] The diaspora also kept in touch with those still in the land itself. Jeremiah, for instance, who prophesied before, during, and after the destruction of Jerusalem, corresponded with exiled communities both in Egypt and in Mesopotamia. Ezra and Nehemiah, as well as many of the smaller prophetic books, testify to intensive connections and movement be-tween the diaspora communities and the newly formed community in Judah after the return to Jerusalem and the building of the Second Temple. Even non-Israelites who were deported by the Assyrians to Palestine are recorded in the biblical narrative. Against this backdrop, the silence of the Israelite deportees resonates loudly. In this sense, their exile is not only from the "land of Israel" but from the Bible, where we read nothing about the Israelite diaspora after the actual moment of exile.

Edward Hine (1825–1891 CE), author of a series of books containing scriptural "proof" that the British are the lost tribes, begins his case with a discussion of this inaudibility, talking about "the lost tribes when last heard of."[80] In 1884, the Reverend Elieser Bassin, a Russian Jewish convert to Christianity, addressed the difference between the two diasporas: "The Lord, for his wise ends, separated and kept them apart for nearly three thousand years: and most of the time Israel was *unknown* . . . while the Jews were known" (italics mine).[81] Thus, two types of exiled diaspora emerge from the text. The first remains visible and audible; the second is invisible and inaudible—a lost diaspora.

The inaudibility of the Israelite diaspora first derives from its geographic framing. Between 2 Kings and the prophets, the Israelite diaspora is relocated to an undisclosed and hidden realm. The difference between the chronologies of the deportations in 2 Kings and in the prophets is striking. While the narrative in 2 Kings mentions specific locations, the prophets tend to be vague, general, and all-inclusive in their discussions of the location of the Israelite exile. It is as if the prophets themselves are wondering where their brethren have gone. Even before the Babylonian exile, the prophets Amos and Hosea express this same sense. Amos writes of "exile *beyond* Damascus" (Amos 5:5, 27). Hosea raises the possibility of assimilation and disappearance in the wake of exile: "Israel is *swallowed up* now among the nations" (Hosea 8:8), and "Israel will become *wanderers* among the nations" (Hosea 9:17). Isaiah, at the end of his most famous prophecy concerning the latter days, declares:

> And ... the Lord shall set his hand again the second time to recover the remnant of his people, which shall be left, from Assyria, and from Egypt, and from Pathros, and from Cush, and from Elam, and from Shinar, and from Hamath, and from the islands of the sea.
> And ... assemble the outcasts of Israel and gather together the dispersed of Judah from the four corners of the earth. (Isaiah 11:11–12)

The possibilities of location seem to be infinite. The tribes could be moving ever eastward "beyond Damascus." They could be assimilated and "swallowed up" within other nations, wandering endlessly among them. Or they could be scattered all over the world.

Isaiah's depiction of the two exiles—the first of Judah and the second of the Israelites—draws a clear distinction between them. Judah's was geographic— "mundane," calling for the gathering of Judah "from Egypt, Pathros, and Cush." The Israelite deportees, on the other hand, are cast into a far wider, ill-defined world.[82]

Isaiah's mimicking of Assyrian symbolism and rhetoric, such that the exile of the Israelites emerges in his text as a divinely mandated event rather than as the outcome of imperial politics, is crucial. The standard Assyrian formulation listed specific powers (Sumer, Akkad); included actual place names or geographic designators ("islands of the sea"); and generally concluded with the phrase "four quarters (or corners) of the world." Isaiah adopts this, whole cloth: he first lists the two powers dominant in Judah's world (Egypt, Assyria);

proceeds to a list of actual place names; and concludes with "the four quarters of the earth."

The tension between known, specific locations and general, abstract, unknown ones reflects the two diasporic geographies with which Isaiah was familiar: the known and unknown, close and distant. Judah marked the first, and Israel the second: "On that day a great trumpet will be sounded and those who are lost in Assyria [the Israelites] and those dispersed in Egypt [the Judahites] will come to worship the Lord on Jerusalem's holy mountain" (Isaiah 27:12–13).

The Judahites are "dispersed" in a familiar and close terrain, Egypt; the Israelites are "lost" in the outer reaches of an empire that stretched to the end of the earth. Isaiah's marking of two distinct diasporic conditions has been retained to the present day. The Judahites are the Jews scattered around the world, identifiable and diffuse. The Israelites—the lost tribes—are gone, hidden en masse. Isaiah's formulation underscores the emergence of Jerusalem as the geographic site par excellence around which messianic activity revolves: the definitive ingathering will bring Judah and Israel alike back to Jerusalem. If 2 Kings is the *ur*-text for the existence of the tribes, Isaiah is the *ur*-text for their single most defining attribute, their lostness.

The prophetic treatment of the historical event of the fall of the Israelite kingdom laid the theological infrastructure for all future speculation concerning the whereabouts and identity of the ten tribes. This theology was largely a tool for the education of the people of Judah: the deportations were synthesized into a single event, a divine punishment and exile that came with the messianic promise of ultimate return. Prophetic discussions took Assyrian imperial discourse as its point of departure, turning an Assyrian story of military conquest and territorial expansion into an Israelite story of messianic history unfolding in accordance with God's will. In the prophetic literature, theology and geography work in tandem.

From the prophets, the tribes made their way into the Torah itself. Deuteronomy, which depicts the history of the Jewish people as an exilic one framed by sin, punishment, and redemption, declares: "And the Lord rooted them out of their land in anger, and in wrath, and in great indignation, and cast them into *another land,* as it is this day" (Deuteronomy 29:28). As we shall see, though they are not mentioned in it, this verse became intimately linked with the ten tribes because of a clear hint to their fate in the words "as it is this day." The fate of the ten tribes thus was granted the highest possible authority as part of God's direct word, the Torah, which was handed to Moses on Sinai.

The tribes' transition from being political deportees to messianic exiles was complete.

But another key transition is embedded in Deuteronomy as well. Isaiah's phrase "lost in [the land of] Assyria" (*Eretz Ashur*) emerges here as "another land," *Eretz aheret*. Once lost in Assyria, by the time the tribes reach Deuteronomy they are, quite literally, in another place altogether. They now *are* a loss, an absence, residing in an *Eretz aheret*. Just what, and where, that other land was had become a matter wide open for ongoing speculation.

2

An Enclosed Nation in Arzareth and Sambatyon

I have heard indeed
Of those Black Jews, their Ancient Creed
And hoar tradition, Esdras saith
The Ten Tribes built in Arsareth—
Eastward, still eastward. That may be.
—Herman Melville, "Abdon," from *Clarel:*
    A Poem and Pilgrimage in the Holy Land (1876)

Loss after the Bible

Centuries after their disappearance, the ten lost tribes sent an indirect but powerful vital sign. It was encrypted in a prophetic vision. The ostensible recipient was Ezra the scribe, one of the last great figures of the biblical era, whose visions are recorded in the book of Esdras. In 2 Esdras, we read about the ten tribes and "their long journey through that region, which is called Arzareth." The book of the "Vision of Ezra," or Esdras, was written in Hebrew or Aramaic by a Palestinian Jew sometime before the end of the first century CE, shortly after the destruction of the temple by the Romans. The original is not extant, but Esdras was translated and preserved in Greek, Latin, Armenian, Coptic, Ethiopian, and Georgian.[1] It is one of a group of texts later designated the so-called Apocrypha—pseudoepigraphal books attached to but not included in the Hebrew biblical canon. Many were preserved and partially canonized by the various Christian churches and thus remained an important source of information about the ten tribes. Together with other "postbiblical" texts, such as the New Testament and rabbinic literature, Esdras contains critical further elaborations on the tribes' story as it appears in the Bible.

The legacy of these texts is the emergence of the term "ten tribes" and its Greek and Latin equivalents (*dekaphylon, decem tribubus*) as both a social entity and a theological category—a people and an exile. While, in the entire Hebrew biblical canon, the term "ten tribes" occurs only twice (and in one scene), in the postbiblical literature, it appears with striking frequency. The rudiments of a tale about the loss of an Israelite group were encoded in the biblical era. But the emergence of a distinct entity known as "the lost tribes" or the "ten tribes" is a legacy of the postbiblical period, and it is only then that the ten tribes come into being as a distinct collective category within "the people of Israel" and are assigned a distinct place within world geography and a role in world history. These transformations are intimately tied to the emergence during the Roman period of the Jews as a nation.

A crucial factor in the transformation of the ten tribes into a people is the emergence of the Jews as a community, certainly not homogeneous or unified, but defined by an acute sense of diasporic existence.[2] Had the Jews as a group not already been so clearly defined as in some sense diasporic, the inscription of the tribes as lost would not have been possible. The known lostness—the diasporicity—of the Jews rendered the unknown and complete lostness of the tribes potent and meaningful. The tribes became the ultimate missing diaspora. In the words of Flavius Josephus, the great Jewish historian of antiquity: "wherefore there are but two tribes in Asia and Europe subject to the Romans, while the ten tribes are beyond [the] Euphrates till now, and are an immense multitude, and not to be estimated by numbers."[3]

Josephus's geography of the people of Israel—Asia, Europe, and beyond Euphrates—is embedded in a larger world geography, that of the Greco-Roman world, first created by the Assyrian Empire and the crucible for the forging of the ten tribes as a known and motivating category. By Josephus's time, the world was a much larger one: the Greco-Roman *oikoumene*. The postbiblical period, broadly defined as from the late Second Temple period through Roman times and then well into the postexilic era, is the main time frame for the formation of the ten tribes as a category. It begins around the time of the Greek conquest of Palestine and ends shortly after the Arab conquest.[4] At its starting point, the story of the twelve Israelite tribes, and the disappearance of ten, was recorded in full with the completion and compilation of all the canonical biblical books. In the final phase of this period, in roughly the seventh and eighth centuries CE, came the fusing of the ten tribes to the coming of the Messiah.

The story's basics were laid out in 2 Kings and popularized largely through the creation of the Septuagint—the Greek version of the Hebrew Bible produced between the third and first centuries BCE.[5] Early on, the twelve (and ten) tribes had appeared in other Greek texts as well, notably in the writings of Flavius Josephus and other apocryphal texts.[6] The New Testament speaks of the "Twelve Tribes of Israel," which further popularized the notion that ten of the twelve tribes were missing—and laid the groundwork for them to later become a pivotal part of the Western Christian cultural and geographic imaginary.[7]

The popularization of the myth of the lost tribes made them a missing part of the whole of "Israel." "Knowledge" of the tribes was formed and generated within several contexts at once and recorded in a complicated set of dialogues among and between various postbiblical communities—what came to be "Jews" and "Christians."[8] Apocryphal texts, dressed in the guise of biblical books and even revelations, played an important role in the early stages of the creation of this new knowledge concerning the ten lost tribes. The story of Tobit (Tuviah), a righteous man living in Nineveh after the exile, was probably written during the second century BCE and is one of the earliest apocryphal books. Already, then, the ten tribes were an important *topos* in the imagination of those living in Judea. As revelations, such apocryphal books seem to attempt to tell us what the canonical biblical texts do not about the fate of the ten tribes: where they are and what happened to them. Above all, the books express a deepening sense of loss in relation to the ten tribes, marked by the tendency to use them as a mirror for the remaining two tribes: "Hast thou seen all that this people are doing to Me [the Lord], that the evils which these two tribes which remained have done are greater than [those of] the ten tribes which were carried away captive? For the former tribes were forced by their kings to commit sin, but these two of themselves have been forcing and compelling their kings to commit sin" (2 Baruch 1:1–3).

A number of recent tragedies lurked behind the author's words: the destruction of the Second Temple by the Romans, the loss of the second Jewish polity, and a new sense of exile that was bringing back memories of the Babylonian exile. The book of 2 Baruch is an early instance of the tendency, identified by Israel Yuval, to link the events of 70 CE with the Babylonian exile. The book of 2 Baruch also links the destruction of the temple with the exile of the ten tribes. Written close to the beginning of the second century CE, 2 Baruch pretends to have been composed during the early sixth century BCE, by Baruch, "son of Neriah the Scribe"—a biblical figure and a close associate of the prophet Jeremiah and his secretary.[9]

The book of 2 Baruch is replete with the warnings, admonitions, and promises of doom and destruction that are familiar from the period's literature. What concerns us, however, is an epistle to the lost tribes that begins in chapter 78 (1–2): "These are the words of that epistle which Baruch the son of Neriah sent to the nine and a half tribes, which were across the river Euphrates . . . : 'Mercy and peace.' I bear in mind, my brethren; the love of Him who created us. . . . And truly I know that behold all we the twelve tribes are bound by one bond, inasmuch as we are born from one father".

The letter in effect, updates the lost tribes on Israel's misfortunes since their disappearance. It is also an expression of missing them—speaking of the twelve tribes longingly as "bound by one bond." The author, Pseudo-Baruch, reassures the tribes, and himself, that the Lord "will never forget or forsake [them], but with much mercy will gather together again those who were dispersed." The lost brethren need to know all this, he writes, "[f]or what befell you we also suffer in a preeminent degree, for it befell us also" (2 Baruch 79:1–3). The narrative of lostness has become the narrative not just of the lost tribes, but also of Israel as a whole. Also significant is the link to the prophet Jeremiah and the framing of the text as an *epistle* to the tribes. As we have seen, already before the destruction of 586 BCE, Jeremiah was in contact with the diasporic communities in Egypt and in Babylon: he wrote them letters. He did not correspond, however, with the earlier third exile that supposedly existed— the ten tribes. They do not write letters, and no one writes to them.

Jeremiah, a prophet of the Lord endowed with supernatural powers, had corresponded with all diasporic communities but not with the exiles of Assyria. Baruch, his secretary, finishes the job: in 2 Baruch, we find at last the missing epistle written to the absent tribes by Jeremiah's faithful secretary. The "newly found" letter reestablishes the relationship between a far-flung community of exiles and a center in Jerusalem. The context of Jerusalem's destruction by the Romans fostered a sense of loss, prompting the yearning to speak with the tribes. Remembering the loss of the tribes provides a vocabulary for expressing the much more immediate loss of the temple and of political autonomy. A the promise of reestablished contact with the tribes bears the parallel prom of redemption from woes far more immediate. The *topos* of sending epistle the ten tribes would reoccur throughout their long mythic history.[10]

Arzareth: The Making of an "Other Land"

The book of 2 Esdras, Pseudo-Ezra, goes much further than 2 Baruch and solves a much bigger mystery. As Herman Melville attested in his poem, the word Arzareth, first coined in Esdras, became a ubiquitous code guiding the search for the tribes. Alastair Hamilton has shown that this was particularly true in Britain during the Renaissance and the Enlightenment, when "feelings about [the lost tribes] ran high."[11] Esdras was a decisive factor in the elaboration of both the theological and geographical dimensions of the ten tribes' story. Even though the visions it contained were ultimately rejected from the biblical canon, Esdras is crucial to the story, providing important clues as to how the story of the ten lost tribes was received during the postbiblical era, the questions it evoked, and the ways in which they were framed. In this regard, Esdras stands as a bookend opposite Isaiah—the first to declare the tribes lost and to frame the search for them. While Isaiah spoke generally of redemptive "latter days," including the gathering of the "lost in Assyria" as one of their features, Esdras speaks with specificity about how the tribes will return and explains where they are "now." The gathering of the ten tribes and their return is the culmination point of Esdras's marvelous apocalyptic vision.[12]

Esdras's visions stand at the intersection of postbiblical debates about the ten tribes. They draw on biblical history and geography and inform, directly or indirectly, future rabbinic and Christian discussions on the topic.[13] By Esdras's time, the essential parameters of the messianic idea and the redemption of the world had been popularized in the ancient Near East.[14] Here, too, begins the packaging of the ten lost tribes as a key narrative within a messianic world vision. The ten tribes thereafter would become attached both to peaceful messianic visions and to apocalyptic and eschatological ones. A well-known example is the image of the ten tribes as a mighty army of superhuman entities coming with the Antichrist. Such images were spread among various medieval Christian European communities, but had their roots in late antiquity.[15] Esdras's geography is not a matter of maps and accurate (or not) descriptions of the physical world. Historian James Romm emphasizes that "for the ancient Greeks and to a lesser degree for Romans as well," geography was "a literary genre more than a branch of physical science." This type of *geōgraphia*, Romm explains, "should be also seen as largely a narrative rather than a merely descriptive genre."[16] In approaching Esdras and anterior texts, we need to look for the geographical context, writ large, within which the tribes' lostness is embedded.

In the main frame of his vision, Esdras sees a man "coming from the sea," flying above the earth, wind coming out of his mouth, fighting a multitude of enemies.[17] Having defeated them, the man next "collect[s] a different company, a peaceful one":

They are the ten tribes that were taken off into exile in the days of King
Hoshea, whom King Shalmanesser of Assyria took prisoner. He
deported them beyond the River, and they were taken away into a
strange country [another land]. But then they resolved to leave the
country populated by the Gentiles and go to a distant land never yet
inhabited by man, and there at last be obedient to their laws, which in
their own country they had failed to keep. As they passed through
the narrow passages of the Euphrates, the Most High performed
miracles for them, stopping up the channels of the river until they
had crossed over. Their long journey through that region, which is
called Arzareth, was long, and took a year and a half. They have lived
there ever since until this final age. Now they are on their way
back and once more the Most High will stop the channels of the
river to let them cross. (2 Esdras 13:40–47)

Even a cursory reading uncovers that Esdras is referencing the core story in
2 Kings, the exile by Shalmaneser.[18] He also clearly alludes to the Deuteronomic
verse foretelling the exile of the tribes to "another land." The first usage merely
echoes the verse in Deuteronomy (29:28) and speaks of an unnamed land, an
"other" land—in Hebrew, *Erez Ahereth*. It is simply a land other than the land of
Israel. As opposed to known locations of exile ("the rivers of Babylon," "Egypt"),
it is unknown. Recall that Deuteronomy had addressed the lostness of the tribes
by emphasizing the total anonymity of their new place of dwelling. Esdras,
however, names the place by converting the Hebrew words *Eretz Ahereth* into
one designator: Arzareth (the replacing of the "e" with "a" is because when not
in construct state, the Hebrew word *Eretz* reads *Aretz*). That "other land" of
Deuteronomy, previously defined only by what it was not, becomes a real and
concrete entity with a proper name: "a region *which is called* Arzareth."

Here is an instance of the dialogical relationship between Jewish exile and
degeneracy: the Jews of the remaining two tribes have sinned (again) and lost
their temple (again); the ten tribes are faithful. The Jews are occupied, sub-
jugated, and dispersed across the known world; the ten tribes migrate beyond
imperial reach, beyond the known world, under the protection of God. The
exile of the Jews is the exile of sin and punishment; the exile of the ten tribes is
a voluntary exile that protects their purity and strength.

But while named, this Arzareth is beyond our reach. Explaining how the
tribes "became lost" in Assyria, Esdras reveals more about what happened in
the crucial days following their deportation from the land of Israel. After their
deportation, the tribes resolved to repent and rejected their wicked ways.

Instead of following the customs of the gentiles among whom they found themselves, they decided to go into isolation, living according to the divine laws given at Sinai. This called for another migration, this time voluntary, to a land located farther away from the gentile nations among which the tribes lived after their initial deportation. The gracious Lord led them to another land, never before inhabited by humanity, where they could live free of the danger of external influences. Millennia later, Joseph Armitage Robinson (1858–1933), a rather eccentric biblical scholar and cleric, would call this place "The Terrestrial Paradise."[19] As the tribes moved ever farther from the land of Israel and from the rest of humanity, the Lord "perform[ed] miracles," opening the "narrow passages of Euphrates," halting the flow of the river, and leading the lost tribes to their land of voluntary exile, Arzareth.

From a theological standpoint, Arzareth is of course a metaphor, an imaginary and pristine place juxtaposed with our mundane and tainted world. Yet, at the same time, it is presented as a real location, reached via familiar and known geographical markers. The word itself is simply a mistranslation of the Hebrew term for "another land."[20] Esdras's insistence on turning "another land" into an actual place (as the reconstructed Hebrew would have it, "it is a land which is called 'another land'") obscured the possibility of mistranslation for a strikingly long time. "Arzareth" wasn't taken as a simple error, a mistranslation or mistranscription or simple garbling of *Erez Ahereth*. Over the course of centuries, attempts to identify Arzareth, to pinpoint it on a map, and to understand the meaning of the name only underscored its presumed realness.

The possibility of mere mistranslation was raised only at the close of the nineteenth century, by William Aldis Wright (1831–1914), a leading British philologist and noted Bible and Shakespeare scholar. "Is not the *Arzareth* of our Apocrypha simply Eretz Ahereth ('another land') of that passage, corrupted by an ignorant translator into a proper name?" He concluded: "Arzareth of verse 47 is the '*terram aliam*' [other land] of verse 40."[21]

Meanwhile, the search for Arzareth had stretched over millennia. The story told by Esdras is a potent narrative about migration, exile, and the geographic imagination. In Arzareth, the real, historical circumstances of loss and exile found meaning as part of a cosmic narrative that culminated in repatriation and redemption. For many, Arzareth remained a real geographic entity, which appeared later in geographic narratives and maps. Arzareth is a stunning example of place making at work. (Witsius speculated, for example, that perhaps "Arzareth" really came from the Hebrew words '*Ir She'erit*, "City of Remnant," or *Har Sharet*, "Mountain of Ministry.")[22]

Unlike the more familiar Jewish exile in the known places of Babylon or Egypt, Arzareth is "another place" in the deeper sense of being *strange* or *different*. It is another place, but it is an Other place as well. Uninhabited and removed from humanity's reach, at the same time it is geographically close— we learn that it took the tribes only a year and a half of walking to get there, which was not so very far in the contemporary context. But to reach it would be a far-fetched hope. After all, it was the Lord himself who led the journey thither, performing miracles to get past the obstacles of geography and geology. Clearly, it will take an equally miraculous journey for the tribes to get back. Esdras tells us that God is "halting the river" (which has by now lost its name and is not necessarily the Euphrates any more) so the tribes can "cross again." The Jews were exiled to known locations, not removed from the land of Israel by impassable geographical barriers. The earthly mechanism that prevents their return is a set of unfavorable political—theological—conditions created by God as punishment. The lost tribes, on the other hand, are removed not so much as punishment but as reward, while access to them is blocked by geography alone. Their exilic state has become an emblem of their purity.

All told, Esdras seems to be crafting answers to the very questions that Isaiah left open when he spoke of the people "lost in Assyria." Why were the tribes lost? Where did they go? How did they get there? Why have we heard nothing from them since, and why can't we communicate with them as we can with our other diasporic exiles? Esdras also seems to be responding to Hosea's claim that Israel had been "swallowed by the nations," disappearing through assimilation. In Esdras, the tribes avoid such a fate, moving far away and resolving to keep to the laws of God.

In the face of the problems of assimilation and the loss of tradition and identity, Esdras imbues the lostness of the tribes with new meaning. Esdras's tribes are still lost, but not as a scattered group melting into the vast territories or human landscape of a distant empire. Here, they come into clearer focus, confined in one place outside the inhabited world: an enclosed nation.

However, in order to define a nation as enclosed within and yet shut off from the world, you need first to have a "world" in place. That is, to shut someone outside, an inside needs clearly to be defined. In his meticulous 1932 philological study, *Alexander's Gate*, Andrew Anderson referred to the ten lost tribes as one of the "Inclosed Nations" which the great conqueror had shut outside the world—outside the *oikoumene*. Anderson documented sources relating to "the exclu[sion] [of] Gog and Magog and other nations beyond the pale, such as the so-called Lost Tribes of Israel."[23] The study stood as an "authority for more than sixty years" on the subject of the lost tribes and still remains unique.[24]

Anderson defined the known world as the "oikoumene, the civilized world of common interests"; the gate marks its utmost limit. The quintessential Hellenistic creation, the *oikoumene* was "a new conception brought into being" by the "union established between Greece and the Near East by Alexander's conquests." Alexander was not only the "creator" of this "New World," but eventually became its "guardian genius to protect its civilization and to keep its frontiers inviolate against the barbarians dwelling outside." As such, Alexander gave "to the idea of world empire... a new, wider, deeper significance" and provided new meanings for the Babylonian, Egyptian, and Persian pasts. "The Roman Empire founded by Julius and Augustus Caesar was essentially the realization of his political ideal."[25] In world historical terms, Alexander's *oikoumene* was the huge river into which previous world empires—the Assyrian, Babylonian, Persian—flowed as tributaries.

This world's edges were strictly connected to human habitation and knowledge of it, not necessarily to the physical boundaries of the earth. Historian James Romm has shown that, beginning with Herodotus, the undefined Homeric boundaries of the earth vanish and an increasingly intense discussion concerning the boundaries of the world emerges among Greco-Roman authors. For Herodotus, the *oikoumene* was "an inner and outer space based not on the physical boundary between earth and sea... but on the presence of human inhabitants and resulting availability of eyewitness information."[26] Herodotus introduced the notion of *eschatiai* (literally, "most distant lands"). These lands "surround the rest of the world and enclose it within."[27] Though "attached to the known world, they are also distinct from it, much as the frame of a painting is distinct from the canvas."[28] Herodotus's distant lands were without inhabitants, like Arzareth, which had no residents to undermine the ten tribes' compliance with the law of Sinai.

Equally important was the enclosure of the ten tribes as specifically a "nation." In Esdras's presentation, they were migrants, wandering, homeless. The coming into being of the world as shared home—as *oikoumene*—enabled the positioning of the *a-oikos* (Diogenes' expression for "homeless") in a specific location. Seneca the Younger (c. 4 BCE–65 CE) observed that his world "was for the most part populated by people who were displaced," in which "whole tribes and nations [had] changed their abodes."[29]

The author of Esdras, a contemporary of Seneca's and a Jew in Palestine after the destruction of 70 CE, understood the ten tribes as removed from the *oikoumene*. If so many "tribes and nations [had] changed their abodes," as Seneca wrote, so too had the ten tribes. But while all humans were dispersed—and certainly, the Jews were—the ten tribes remained isolated and intact.

How Did Ezra Lose the Tribes?

In chronological terms, the canonical book of Ezra marks the last chapter in the biblical saga that tells the history of the children of Israel, beginning with the return of the Judahite exiles from Babylon to Jerusalem and the building of the Second Temple.[30] The book begins just as 2 Chronicles ends—with the dramatic declaration of Cyrus the Great (c. 559–530 BCE), ruler of the Persian Empire, which at its high point stretched from Central Asia in the east to Egypt and Asia Minor in the west. Having conquered the world and defeated the Babylonians, Cyrus proclaims the return of the Judahite exiles to Jerusalem. Ezra asserts at the outset that these developments are all the workings of the Lord and the fulfillment of prophecies that promised a return to Judah—now Yehud, a Persian province. This return would be marked by the building of a temple in Jerusalem:

> Now in the first year of Cyrus king of Persia, that the word of the Lord
> by the mouth of Jeremiah might be fulfilled, the Lord stirred up the
> spirit of Cyrus king of Persia, that he made a proclamation throughout
> all his kingdom, and put it also in writing, saying, Thus saith Cyrus
> king of Persia, The Lord God of heaven hath given me all the
> kingdoms of the earth; and he hath charged me to build him an house
> at Jerusalem, which is in Judah. (Ezra 1:1–2)[31]

The biblical authors were well aware of external sources, and they echoed them in writing Ezra's story.

Like his Assyrian and Babylonian predecessors, Cyrus left a monument. The Cyrus Cylinder proclaims that the Persian emperor was "king of the world, great king, legitimate king, king of Babylon, king of Sumer and Akkad, king of the four rims [of the earth]."[32] Restoring the Judahite exiles to Jerusalem did not contradict Persian imperial policies concerning conquered peoples. The Persians encouraged a great degree of cultural autonomy and deliberately cultivated local loyal elites. Furthermore, it is likely that, after Cambyses' invasion of Egypt in 525 BCE, a loyal and quiet province in Palestine ruled by a Jewish elite tied to the Persian court was desperately needed by the court.[33]

The book of Ezra tells us that the initial return of the exiles met with all sorts of trouble. By this account, the newly created province was socially and politically unstable. In response, Artaxerxes I (465–424 or 423 BCE) appointed Ezra the scribe, a Jew of dignified pedigree, to lead another, greater wave of returnees back to Jerusalem and to govern it.[34]

The imagery of a man leading people to the promised land is clear: Ezra is nothing less than a new Moses, and he is seen as such in Jewish tradition.[35] The book of Ezra depicts him as "a ready scribe in the law of Moses," who "had prepared his heart to seek the law of the Lord, and to do it, to teach in Israel statutes and judgments" (Ezra 7:6, 12). His journey, as head of a large select group of returnees from Babylon, is depicted as an "exodus." The voyage is completed, like the Exodus out of Egypt, with the direct help of God. At one point along the way home, we even find a dramatic river crossing fashioned on the fording of the Red Sea. But while Moses came out of Egypt with twelve tribes, Ezra comes out of Babylon with only two—Judah and Benjamin (Ezra 2:1). "All the men of Judah and Benjamin" gather in Jerusalem to hear his admonitions (10:9). Moses got to admonish all twelve tribes; Ezra painfully misses ten of them. Lurking behind the dramatic tale of return are unanswered questions: where are the other ten tribes, and why haven't *they* returned?

During the period following Ezra's return to Judah, such questions became pervasive. The deepened sense of the tribes' emphatic lostness is captured in the Greek translation of Isaiah. The original Hebrew, as we have seen, speaks of the ten tribes as being "lost." The Septuagint translates the same word very differently—here, the tribes are literally "those left behind" (Greek, *Apolómenoi*). This mistranslation makes sense only if read against the partial return described in Ezra, after which the remaining tribes appear even more deserted. The settling of Benjamin and Judah in Jerusalem sets up another apposition. While, before, the ten tribes were missing from the body of a collective—Israel—now they are also missing from a specific *place,* Jerusalem. The end of the Babylonian exile leaves the Assyrian one emphatically ongoing and renders its locative dimensions in sharper strokes.

The book of Ezra provides no answers as to why this second Moses left the other ten tribes behind, despite the strong specter of the Assyrian deportations that is present in the book. Rather then erasing any memory of the Assyrian deportations and the ten tribes with it, the book contains plenty of references and allusions to the more distant event. A locale frequently mentioned in Ezra is "beyond-the-river," once the core territory of Assyria and now a Persian province. While, for the Persians, "beyond-the-river" was likely a mere geographic/administrative unit, for the Jewish reader, it is a reminder of that first resettling of exiles, the ten tribes, in Assyrian times.

Moreover, the leaders of the returnee community in Yehud engage in constant battles with groups of local provincials, identified by the biblical author as the "adversaries of Judah and Benjamin." These people identify themselves as deportees brought earlier to Judah by "Esarhaddon king of

Assyria" (Ezra 4:3). They write a letter of complaint to the Persian emperor that is included in Ezra. It mentions several nationalities by name and classifies all "the rest of the nations whom the great and noble Asnapper [Ashurbanipal] brought over, and set in the cities of Samaria, and the rest that are on this side [of] the river." Elsewhere, these groups refer to themselves as people from "that side of the river brought to this side of the river" (Ezra 4:10). The backdrop is clear: the Assyrian deportations. The reader is reminded that, after the Assyrians sacked Samaria, they settled other peoples there. At the same time, the presence of the Samaritan deportees not only reminds us of the lost Israelites but also further presses the question of their whereabouts. If the deportees brought from the other side of the river are still here in Samaria, what happened to the deportees exiled from this side of the river to there?

Because the entire narrative is presented as "the works of God," the questions with which Ezra leaves us bear theological implications. The rise of the Persians to world dominance must have inspired shock and awe. Their empire was huge, much larger than any before. Its dramatic ascendancy came only seventy years—two or three generations—after the destruction of Jerusalem by the Babylonians. Memories of siege, destruction, and deportation were very much alive in the minds of the exiles from Judah and were recalled by their own captivity and punishment. Persian imperial policies, which in the Judahite case resulted in a reversal of Babylonian policies and the restoration of Jerusalem, must have been seen as an act of God. If God did all of this, just as the prophets promised, why didn't the ten tribes return? Can a divine promise be only partially fulfilled? The conundrum also had a geographic dimension. If Cyrus had indeed conquered the "entire earth," as he declares in Ezra, was in fact its ruler, then the ten tribes must by definition have been under his control. Therefore, his edict proclaiming the restoration of the exiles must have applied to them, too, and news of it reached their location.

The idea that the Persian king ruled over the entire world was well recorded in biblical and postbiblical sources. In the book of Esther, which is situated in the Persian capital, we read at several points that Ahasuerus, king of Persia (commonly identified as Artaxerxes II, c. 436–358 BCE), ruled an empire made of "127 kingdoms from India unto Ethiopia [*cush*]" (1:1, 8:9).[36] The phrase "from India unto Ethiopia" warrants some attention. It receives an illuminating treatment in the Talmud in a commentary dating back to Shmu'el of Neharde'a (c. 165–257 CE), a great rabbinic figure and astronomer from Babylonia, and his close associate Rav (Abba Aricha, c. 175–247 CE). The two agreed that the phrase meant that the Persian Empire stretched from one "end [edge] of the world" (*sof ha-'olam*) to "the other." Though they disputed the

geography, on one point there was clear agreement: India and Ethiopia represented the two edges of the world, "back to back next to each other."[37]

The notion of Ethiopia as the end of the world is as old as Homer, for
whom the Ethiopians were *eschatoi andrōn* ("the furthest of men").[38] This
image is fixed in Herodotus's narrative of the Persian conquest of Egypt by
Cambyses, who established Ethiopia as the outer limit of the Persian Empire.[39]
Centuries later, for the Roman Pliny the Elder (23–79 CE), the Ethiopians were
almost a miracle. "Who ever believed in the Ethiopians before he actually saw
them?" he exclaimed.[40] On the other hand, Alexander's conquests had stabilized India as the other end of the world. This idea was carried further by
the Greek geographer Strabo (65 BCE–24 CE) and the Roman Pliny.[41] For the
reader in late antiquity, the Persians in the book of Ezra did indeed rule
the entire world, and their empire touched its edges.

This perception was not entirely false. To rule over the entire world, the
Persians utilized a land communication system that covered much of the "four
rims" of the known world of the time, "from Sardis [in Asia Minor] to India." It
stretched from the Indus Valley in the southeast to southern Egypt and Yemen in
the southwestern corners of the empire and from Sogdiana to western Asia
Minor in the northern corners.[42] This system was uniquely effective. In the
book of Ezra, we find mentioned no fewer than six exchanges between the
Persian court and the province in Yehud. Famously, Esther details this communication process and describes how a decree allowing the slaughtering of the Jews
of the empire reached every locale in the "127 nations" of the empire "from India
unto Ethiopia [Cush] . . . every province according to its script and every nationality according to its tongue" (Esther 8:9). The decree authorizing Jewish resistance
and the slaughter of gentiles also reached every locale with even greater speed, or
so we read.[43] Is it possible, then, that Cyrus's edict did not reach the ten tribes?
Ostensibly, it should have, reaching as it did all the edges of the world.

Thus, postbiblical times—that is, the times that begin after Ezra's career
ends—inherited a series of nagging questions concerning the ten tribes.
Josephus, a near-contemporary of Esdras, the apocryphal Ezra, seems to be
struggling with them and to be doing so in direct relation to Ezra. When Ezra
received the Persian imperial order, says Josephus:

> He sent a copy of it to all those of his own nation that were in Media.
> And when these Jews had understood what piety the king had towards
> God, and what kindness he had for Ezra, they were all greatly pleased;
> nay, many of them took their effects with them, and came to Babylon,
> as very desirous of going down to Jerusalem; but then the entire body
> of the people of Israel remained in that country, wherefore there are

but two tribes in Asia and Europe subject to the Romans, while the ten tribes are beyond [the] Euphrates till now, and are an immense multitude, and not to be estimated by numbers.[44]

The phrases "beyond [the] Euphrates" and "till now" clearly show that, in putting together this particular passage, Josephus was working not only with Ezra but also with other related biblical material concerning the ten tribes. Josephus himself seems puzzled as to what became of the ten tribes, though he shies away from the problem. He instead consoles himself, like Esdras, by saying that the ten tribes are beyond the Euphrates and constitute a multitude immense in number.[45]

While neither the biblical Ezra nor Josephus answer the question of why the ten tribes had been left behind, the apocryphal Esdras, a visionary if not a prophet, does, through a quite significant reelaboration of the biblical story. To be sure, answering these questions was not the only thrust behind the visions of Esdras nor its attribution to Ezra the scribe. But it is not incidental that the first significant reelaboration of the ten tribes narrative is attributed to the person most associated with Israel's partial exodus/return from its *first* exile. Here, the tendency to reframe the Roman destruction of the Second Temple according to the template of the first Babylonian destruction and exile is crucial.[46] Reading the trauma of 70 CE through the lens of the Babylonian exile brings into the frame that earlier trauma, the ten tribes' exile. Writing after the Roman destruction of the Second Temple, Esdras emulates the "consolation prophecies" of Isaiah and Jeremiah, connecting the ten tribes to greater visions of redemption and restoration.[47]

The journey to Arzareth reads like another Exodus. Better yet, it is an Exodus in reverse: just as the Lord led the Israelites out of Egypt to the promised land of Israel, he now takes the ten tribes to a place of exile that is also a haven. The mention of God "stopping the channels" of the river is not only an allusion to the drama of crossing the Red Sea and the Jordan River during the original Exodus.[48] It is also a strong reference to what is described in Isaiah, which speaks directly of the "remnant rescued from Assyria" (11:15–16). In Isaiah's vision, the divine waves his hand "over the River" and "[splits it] into seven channels." Here, in Esdras, we see a new spin on another of Isaiah's prophecies:

And the Lord shall utterly destroy the tongue of the Egyptian sea; and with his mighty wind shall he shake his hand over the river, and shall smite it in the seven streams, and make men go over dry shod. And there shall be a highway for the remnant of his people, which shall be

left, from Assyria; like as it was to Israel in the day that he came up out
of the land of Egypt. (Esdras 11:15–16)

Esdras's vision encapsulates several important new features of the ten
tribes' condition. It affirms their existence "to this very day" and reinforces
the promise of their return. It then explains why they did not return with Ezra
the scribe during Persian times and reveals that they have migrated yet farther
off, into the strange land of Arzareth, a land "never inhabited by man." Finally,
we learn that a river runs between this uninhabited Arzareth and the inhabited
world. Implicit, but pretty clear, is the notion that this river cannot be forded by
humans—indeed, the Most High has to stop it so the ten tribes can pass
through on their way to Arzareth. When the time comes, he will stop it again
and allow their return. In the meantime, until that day, Arzareth is what
Herodotus would call an *eschatiai*—a most distant land. And the ten tribes
themselves become what the Greeks would call *eschatoi andrōn*—the furthest of
peoples, like the Ethiopians. Perhaps this is what God means when he cryptically says in Amos (9:7), "Are ye not as children of the Ethiopians [Cushites]
unto me, O children of Israel?"

The Place of an Invisible Exile

Esdras solves the problems created by the partial return to Zion under Ezra the
scribe by establishing the existence of the tribes and asserting their impending
return. These solutions mark one high point of the discussion concerning the
ten tribes that began at the time of the writing of Esdras and ensued in the
following centuries.

The basic idea here is that the ten tribes had moved away from their
original place of exile and away from the Assyrian world. The Vulgate's fifth-
century translation of Isaiah's "lost in Assyria" speaks of *qui perditi fuerant de
terra Assyriorum*—those lost *from* the land of Assyria. Similarly, the great
ecclesiastical writer Sulpitius Severus (c. 360–420) writes in his *Sacred History*
that "the ten which had previously been carried away being scattered among
the Parthians, Medes, Indians, and Ethiopians never returned to their native
country, and are to this day held under the sway of barbarous nations."[49] Note
how Severus adds the Indians and the Ethiopians—that is, the eastern and
southern boundaries of the Greco-Roman *oikoumene*—to the more biblical
Parthians and Medes.

A less veiled echoing of Esdras is found in the writings of the Christian
poet Commodianus (fl. 250 CE), who retells the story of how God "concealed"

the ten tribes, keeping them "enclosed [behind] a river across Persia" (*trans Persida flumine clausi*).[50] Commodianus is but one early instance of Christian apocalyptic writings relating to Esdras, which attached the ten tribes to visions of the end of the world. In the emergence of Jewish rabbinic tradition and its ongoing struggle with questions of exile and return in the wake of the temple's destruction, the question of the ten lost tribes was a complication.

Rabbinic sages, as cited in the Talmudic and Midrashic literature, obsessively reelaborated the questions and stories concerning the ten tribes. Like the author of Esdras, the sages contended with the questions posed by the partial return during Ezra's time. They belabored the question of return in the specific context of the reworking of the notion of Jewish exile and return after the Romans' destruction of the temple. This again raised the question as to why the ten tribes didn't return with Ezra the scribe, and it recast their original exile as well. These concerns were closely linked to the question of the full Jewish restoration promised in messianic times. If the exile under the Romans was to be framed by the parameters of the Babylonian exile, then surely it must ultimately end in the same way—with a triumphant, divinely led return.

If in later centuries, and in the Christian context, the obsessive quest would focus on the location of the tribes, for the rabbinic tradition the core question had to do with the notion of exile itself. Place was far less interesting, and its Talmudic treatment is quite literal. The literature nonchalantly identifies the place names of 2 Kings—"Halah is Halvan, Habor is Hadaib, the river of Gozan is Ginzak, and the 'cities of Media' is Hamadan and its surroundings, [though]...some say...it is Nahavand and its surroundings."[51] One might expect that the mention of these places, much less their clear identification with contemporary locales, would have led, as it did in the modern period, to deliberations about the ethnic groups living in these places and their possible relationship to the ten tribes. But in the Talmud, we see nothing of this sort. The places named in 2 Kings seem almost trivial to the sages. The rabbis seem to think that they know, with little pondering, the whereabouts of Gozan and the other places to which the Israelites had been deported. But, like the prophets before them, they are more interested in drawing lessons from the fact of the ten tribes' exile.

In one instance from the Talmud, the rabbis build on two dimensions of the story that are familiar from Esdras: the idea that the ten tribes migrated yet farther away after their initial deportation, and the implication that the place of their exile is beyond the rims of the *oikoumene*. In a *Gemara* (rabbinical commentary on and analysis of the older Mishnah) authored in Babylon, we come upon the rabbis in discussion of the names of various Assyrian kings, all of whom were connected to various deportations. The rabbis discuss the drama outside Jerusalem in 701 BCE when Rabshakeh had beseeched the people of the city to surrender, promising to take the surrendering Jerusalemites to a place of exile "just like their own" (2 Kings 28:32). "Rav and Shmu'el: According to one he [Rabshakeh] was a clever king, because if he had said that he would take them in a better land than theirs they would consider him a liar. And according to the other he was a fool, for what use could it be for them to go to a land which is not better than their own?" As is common in gemaratic discussions, a digression follows, here on the exile of the tribes:

> To where did he exile the ten tribes of Israel? According to Mar Sutra to Africa [*Afriki*] and according to R. Hanina to the mountains of S[a]lug. However, the ten tribes of Israel slander the land of Israel, for when they reached the city of Sus they said that it was like their own land. And when they came to the city of Elmin they said that it is like our Elmin [Jerusalem]. And when they reached the second Sus they said that it was much better than their own land.[52]

The thrust of the passage, obviously, is to insult the ten tribes by exposing yet another of their sins: slandering the Holy Land by suggesting that other places could be favorably compared to it. But it presents an itinerary of the migration of exile: along the route are Elmin and Sus (both in southern Iran), Africa, and the mountains of Salug (from the word *sheleg*, snow), ostensibly the final destinations of the tribes—and all real places.

"Afriki" and "Salug" require some thinking. In his *Geography of the Talmud*, Adolphe (Adolf) Neubauer identifies Afriki as either the Roman province whose capital was Carthage, or a stretch of countries from Ethiopia to today's North Africa. In either case, it marks the southern borders of the Roman world. It is not clear where the mountains of Salug are; many early modern and modern travelers would suggest that they could be the Elburz (Alborz) Mountains in northeastern Iran, southeast of the Caspian Sea, which marked the northeastern boundary of the Persian Empire. This almost Alpine snowy mountain range, 900 kilometers long and 300 kilometers wide, stretching from the borders of Armenia in the west to the borders of Turkmenistan and Afghanistan in the east, sounds like a good candidate for the Talmudic "Mountains of Snow." The Alborz range is not only a topographically ideal candidate for an impassable barrier beyond which the ten tribes reside; it is also the dwelling place of the Peshotan, a messiah-like figure in Zoroastrian Persian mythology.[53] Furthermore, according to several medieval Christian legends, Anderson's gates of Gog/Magog are located somewhere along this range.[54] In any case, we can assume that the name invoked a boundary of the world, paired as it is with Afriki, the location and identity of which are beyond doubt. Again, we see echoes of the Greco-Roman edges of the world, beyond which the ten tribes are located. Remarkably, while the sages discuss the actual geography, they do not discuss the question of what happened to the ten lost tribes—an ultimately far more important issue. And they debate it seperartly.

Theological deliberations over the meaning of exile end up creating a new place of exile, as did Esdras. This is evident in one of the earliest debates on the tribes found in the Mishnah (redacted and compiled in the early third century). The great sage Rabbi 'Aqiva (?50–135 CE) states the Talmudic problem of the ten tribes very clearly in his commentary on Leviticus 26:38: "and ye shall perish [be lost] among the gentiles." The passage, says 'Aqiva, "refers to the tribes exiled to Media [the ten tribes]."[55] The debate here is about the meaning of the Hebrew word *avad:* does it mean to "perish" (as 'Aqiva insists), or does it mean to be "exiled" and, therefore, as Neubauer puts it, to be "with the hope of returning"?[56]

The oldest Mishnah concerning the ten tribes discusses those "who have a share in the world to come." The chapter begins with the hopeful assertion that "[a]ll Israel has a share in the world to come," but proceeds to discuss individuals or categories of people who actually do not:

> The ten tribes who were exiled will not be returned, as it reads [Deuteronomy 29:27]: "And he cast them into another land, as to this day." As that day will not return, so will they not return. So R. 'Aqiva. [On the other hand,] R. Eli'ezer said: As this day means as usually a day becomes clouded and thereafter lights up again, so the ten tribes, who are now in darkness, the future will lighten upon them.[57]

The broader context is a discussion of the various types of people who have been "overturned," "covered," "swallowed," did not reach their destination, or simply disappeared from this world in all sorts of strange ways. It begins with the "generation of [the] flood," and follows with the "people of Sodom," the "generation of Israelites in the desert," and the "congregation of Korah," and ends with the ten tribes. Of the "congregation of Korah," who rebelled against Moses in the desert, we are reminded, tellingly, that "the earth covered them"— god's punishment. To complicate things, however, the biblical text cryptically says elsewhere (in Numbers 26:11) "the sons of Korah died not." This contradiction in the biblical text calls for rabbinic intervention: what is fate of the Korahites? The Korahites, insinuates the *Mishnah*, "are not going to ascend"— it is as if they are still stuck under the ground right now.

The inclusion of the ten tribes in such a fold of dubious cases suggests that, at least in the early stages of rabbinic deliberations, the question of return was a topic hotly contested by various rabbinic figures. It also suggests that the exilic status of the ten tribes was not quite the same as the familiar Jewish one, and their disappearance had somehow to be accounted for. At the same time, however, the Mishnah pools them with other "gone peoples," thereby reinforcing their peculiar status on earth. Only then does it establish their ultimate future return from exile as opposed to their complete disappearance with no return.

Later generations of rabbinic scholars were not willing to give up the ten tribes, and sided with Eli'ezer's claim that they were exiled, not lost forever. This position became the rule. But the idea that they might not return was nevertheless invoked later, as if the matter had not been definitively settled. Rabbi Yehudah Hanasi, compiler of the Mishnah during the early third century CE, had to give a ruling even long after 'Aqiva died: "They [the ten tribes] will have a share in the world to come, and they will return, as it reads [Isaiah 37:13]: "And then shall come those who are lost in the land of Asshur."[58] The jury, in short, was still out. But the view that dominated is the one that is softer on the tribes.

Why, despite the reaffirmation of Isaiah's prophecy concerning the return of the "lost in Assyria," do the sages repeat the debate as to whether or not the tribes will return? If there really is ultimately no uncertainty on this point, just what is it that the sages are uncertain about? The Talmudic sages, it seems, are actually contending with something else—not *whether* the tribes are in exile, but *what kind* of exile they are in.

Once they had established the exilic condition of the tribes (as opposed to their mere disappearance), the rabbinic sages had to confront the problem of a revealed exile, one that was not invisible but that could be seen. A later Midrash compares the two exiles thus: "Said Rabbi Yehouda Ben-Simon: the tribe of Judah and Benjamin was not exiled to the place to which the ten tribes were exiled, the ten tribes wandered into exile on the other side of the river Sambatyon, *but* the tribes of Judah and Benjamin are scattered throughout all the lands."[59] The two exiles have two distinct geographies. One exile is revealed and located all over the world ("throughout all the lands"). The other is concealed but apparently concentrated in one place "beyond the river" (perhaps an allusion to Esdras). The concealed, hidden nature of the ten tribes' exile is already suggested in Rabbi Eli'ezer's reference to the tribes as they "who are now in darkness." The notion of the covered or concealed exile appears frequently in a number of other Midrashic and Talmudic passages. An early passage in the Palestinian Talmud, for example, discusses the notion in detail:

> Rabbi Berechiah and Rabbi Helbo in the name of Rabbi Samuel ben Nahman, say, Israel [the ten tribes] wandered into exile in three divisions; the one to the other side of the Sanbatyon [Sambatyon],

another to Daphne in Antiochia, and the third was covered by cloud which descended upon them. Like them, tribes of Reuben, Gad, half Manasseh wandered into three lands of exile, as it is written [Ezekiel 23: 31] "Thou hast walked in the way of thy sister." And at the time of their return they will come back out of the three lands of exile, what is the meaning of this? as it is written [Isaiah 49:9] "That thou mayest say to the prisoners, Go Forth," which is said to those on the other side of the river Sanbatyon [Sambtayon]; "to them that are in darkness, Show yourselves," which is said to those who are covered in cloud; "They shall feed in the ways, and their pastures shall be in all high places," which is said to those exiled to Daphne in Antiochia.[60]

The notion of the three exiles, followed by the mention of the exile of specific tribes (Reuben, Gad, and half Manasseh), ties the passage directly to 2 Kings' detailing of the three deportations that followed each Assyrian invasion. The sages recover the trivial details of the deportations, which, as we have seen, had already been reworked into one single exile by the prophets Isaiah, Amos, and Hosea. The rabbis quoted in this passage, on the other hand, disaggregate the deportations into three types of exile, and the prophetic voice is used to support this move.

Each exile represents a different condition of concealment—imprisoned, in darkness, covered by a cloud. An early ninth-century Midrash explains: "In three Exiles the tribes were [divided] into three parts; one went to the Sambatyon, one was exiled beyond the Sambatyon, and the third [went] to the Daphne near Riblah and was swallowed there."[61] Here is yet another reelaboration of a prophetic reelaboration, in this case Hosea's (8:8) aside, "Israel is swallowed," which turned a story about forced migration into one of distance, place, and assimilation. Variants on this *topos* of the three exiles appear in Talmudic and Midrashic texts too numerous to count, developing well into the twelfth century CE. In most instances, the familiar locations repeat themselves, but in some cases new ones are added to the list.

Lamentations Rabbah, another old Midrash, discusses the three types of exile but adds, "all of them were ordered [by God] in one verse."[62] This seems to be an attempt to return to the prophetic tendency to lump all three deportations into one single event. *Numbers Rabbah*, a much later Midrash from the twelfth century, speaks of the three exiles but lists one of them as "those who are beyond the mountains of darkness."[63]

The thread running through these discussions is the notion of the concealed—invisible—nature of the ten tribes' exile, as opposed, again, to the exile of the remaining two tribes. The invisible tribes are under the ground, beyond mountains of darkness, or in darkness itself. They are beyond a river, or swallowed up, or covered by a cloud. The referencing of Isaiah's prophecy about the "prisoners" reminds us that the lost tribes are those that the king of Assyria "took captive." Yet theirs is not a simple captivity as commonly experienced by Jews in the postexilic period, but an invisible one. The Lord himself orders these captives to "show themselves."

Thus, much like the biblical inaudibility we've already noted, Talmudic invisibility becomes another feature of the ten tribes' exile. Indeed, it becomes its most dominant feature, because in the Talmudic literature, the exile of the ten tribes has been reworked against a specifically Jewish exile and not only against that of various diasporic communities. At the same time, Talmudic and Midrashic conversations and debates on the topic represent another, much more sophisticated reelaboration on the template of exile delineated in Esdras's vision, produced in the course of addressing new problems posed by the emerging notion of the Jewish exile under the Romans.

What, and Where, Is Sambatyon?

The term "Sambatyon"—a Hellenized distorted version of "Sabbath" that returned into Hebrew text—appears in conjunction with the ten lost tribes with striking frequency. In Jewish folklore and imagination, as Avigdor Shahan's testimony powerfully attests, Sambatyon plays the role of Arzareth, the place that must be reached, found, and crossed. At some point, the Euphrates ceased to be simply the Euphrates and became instead, as it sneaked into Esdras's vision, simply the "river."

Also clear is that Josephus's "beyond Euphrates" refers not so much to the actual River Euphrates itself but to a larger and ontologically deeper place than the actual terrain on the river's far banks. Just as the ten tribes' place of exile becomes ever more removed, the literal marker that initially separated it takes on a more elaborate significance. The Sambatyon becomes the river mentioned in Esdras, which God halted when the ten tribes crossed over and which he will break into seven channels when they come back. The Sambatyon marks the edge of the world. Neubauer aptly comments that the "river itself is as mysterious as the existence of the Ten Tribes. It would be lost time . . . to trouble ourselves about the identification of that stream."[64] But the Sambatyon, like Arzareth, has allowed for endless speculation: virtually every river on earth, from the Yangzi to the Amazon, has at some point been identified as the real Sambatyon.

Sambatyon appears at times as a river and at others simply as a place name. Similarly, there is an ambiguity about its function with regard to the ten tribes' exile. In some passages, we read that the tribes were exiled "beyond" Sambatyon. In others, we find them exiled "to" Sambatyon. A third instance posits that one exile went "beyond" Sambatyon while another went "to" it. A locative Sambatyon appears in many passages in the rabbinic literature, with Sambatyon not only the river separating the ten tribes from the rest of the world, but also the site to which they were exiled. The rabbinic literature, the later Midrash in particular, speaks explicitly of Sambatyon as a place of concealment and separation, concealment and protection. This is true not only for the ten lost tribes, the first group to be "admitted" to Sambatyon, but also for all sorts of people who are concealed and remain in a protected state.

The seventh-century CE Aramaic *Targum* (translation) of Pseudo-Jonathan for the Pentateuch refers to the Sambatyon as the river to which God dispatches another exclusive group of people, the sons of Moses (Benei Moshe). It refers to an episode in Exodus, when during a moment of extreme wrath against the Israelites, God promises to turn Moses's own offspring into a "great nation." Since Exodus fails to tell us if the Lord ever followed up on this promise, the *Targum* interferes in the text and tells us, in the voice of God, that after the initial Judahite exile to Babylon, the Benei Moshe were indeed whisked away and transferred elsewhere: "I will take them from the rivers of Babylon and place them beyond the Sambatyon and they will be different, no one as wonderful as them among the residents of the earth."[65] Crossing the Sambatyon means being in concealment, but crucially it also means becoming different from all the residents of the earth.

Similarly, a short Midrash entitled "Ten Exiles" ('*Eser Galuyot*) breaks down the exile of all Israel into ten different specific exiles and picks up on the same theme. It tells the story of some Levites who cut off their fingers since they did not want to play music in Babylon. The Levites express extreme sorrow for the loss of the temple and fear that they will be forced to sing in the new place of exile. The Levites are a special group within the children of Israel since they did not partake in the sin of the Golden Calf. Certainly Sambatyon material, these people are transferred to Sambatyon explicitly to be concealed: "and the Blessed be He saw that they did not want to sing and concealed them [*genazan*] beyond Sambatya [Sambatyon]."[66]

Sambatyon is also the place where another exclusive Jewish group, the Rachabites, sons of Yehonadav ben-Rechav, end up. Relatives of Moses, they are praised by Jeremiah for the extreme piety they exhibited in refusing to get drunk in the (first) temple. For this, they receive a promise from God that the horrors of the Babylonian exile will not affect them and that they will never be wiped from the face of the earth (Jeremiah 35). The Talmud and Midrash even claim that God's covenant with the Rechabites was superior to that of the house of David. (The Rechabites ultimately became the model for the Independent Order of Rechabites, an anti-alcohol organization founded in England in 1835.) They too ended up in Sambatyon.[67]

If early rabbinical treatment turned the river into a barrier enclosing the ten tribes, later rabbinical sources spoke of it explicitly as a "container," God's preferred location for all sorts of protected and concealed superior peoples. Thus, the River Euphrates undergoes a major transformation from a trivial and known geographical location to a river that defines the break in earthly space beyond which certain peoples exist in a concealed and protected state.

The origins of Sambatyon's name lie in its connection to the Sabbath. The Sambatyon is famous for its mysterious nature: it flows in different directions, changing in cycles, and legends about its wondrous qualities are very old and widespread. Pliny the Elder mentions in his *Naturalis Historia*, "In Judea is a stream that dries up every Sabbath" (*in Iudaea rivus sabbatis omnibus siccatur*).[68] Here Pliny unintentionally gave the river its name, "Rivus Sabbatis" because of the order of the words in the sentence—his phrase "rivus sabbatis omnibus siccatur" refers to the nature of the river and not to its actual name. But the notion of a river with mysterious powers and changing attributes, somehow attached to the Jews, was also probably before Pliny wrote his *Historia*. In his *Wars of the Jews*, Josephus reverses Pliny's order of things and describes a river that rests for six days and gushes on the seventh. He locates this "Sabbatic River" not in Judea but in Antiochia, saying that, as Titus Flavius was passing through Syria on his way to suppress the great Jewish rebellion:

> [He] saw a river as he went along, of such a nature as deserves to be recorded in history; it runs in the middle between Arcea, belonging to Agrippa's kingdom, and Raphanea. It hath somewhat very peculiar in it; for when it runs, its current is strong, and has plenty of water; after which its springs fail for six days together, and leave its channel dry, as any one may see; after which days it runs on the seventh day as it did before, and as though it had undergone no change at all; it hath also been observed to keep this order perpetually and exactly; whence it is that they call it the Sabbatic River [Rivus Sabbatis] that name being taken from the sacred seventh day among the Jews.[69]

Whether in Judea or Antiochia, this incarnation of the Sabbatic River was not attached to the ten lost tribes; neither Pliny nor Josephus mentions them in this context, and neither places the river at the edges of the earth. Just as the Euphrates in Esdras was transformed into the Sambatyon, Rivus Sabbatis underwent a transformation and became attached to the ten tribes.

How did this happen? An early Talmudic story recounts a dialogue about the Sabbath between the "wicked Turnus Rufus" and Rabbi 'Aqiva. Rufus asks: "Who tells you that this day is the Sabbath?" In response, 'Aqiva provides three signs: "Let the river Sabbation prove it; let the Ba'al ob [necromancer] prove it; let thy father's grave, whence no smoke ascends on the Sabbath [prove it]."[70] This dialogue is only one among several between the famous rabbi and Tinnieus Rufus (Roman governor of Judea under Hadrian, r. 117–138 CE) to be found in the Talmud. These dialogues, which supposedly took place when the tyrannical Rufus sentenced 'Aqiva to death in the wake of the Bar Kokhba revolt of 132–135 CE, revolve mostly around one central question—whose law is superior: God's or that of the empire?[71] In this instance, Rufus claims that the empire sets the time (and therefore determines the days of the week). Rabbi 'Aqiva claims that God sets the time, and provides proof of his claim.

As with Pliny and Josephus, 'Aqiva's reference to the River Sambatyon is not connected to the ten tribes. His position was that they were completely lost, perished. This is further evidence that the legendary river was probably not yet attached to the ten tribes at the time of the dialogue's recording. It is signifcant that the river is mentioned in the context of a fictional dialogue with a Roman governor, which suggests that, at this period, the Sambatyon was not uniquely Jewish but belonged in a cultural realm shared by Jews and Romans.

The evidence connecting Saturn, the Sabbath, and the Jews in the Roman period is vast and well known. Saturn, the seventh planet (if we include the sun and the moon) and a Greco-Roman god, was naturally perceived as governing the Sabbath, the seventh day or Satur(n)day.[72] Tacitus (56–117 CE), a great believer in a relationship between Saturn and the Jews, famously speculated that the "Jews rest every seventh day...in honor of Saturn...the seventh and highest of the heavenly bodies."[73] The logic is simple and hardly innovative—if Saturn governs or at least is linked to the Sabbath, it is most probably connected to the *rivus sabbatis*, the Sambatyon, as well. After all, from the Roman perspective, the river carries the very name of Saturn.

The similarities in the descriptions of the river's behavior in Pliny and Josephus, as in the dialogue between Rabbi 'Aqiva and Rufus, suggest a shared perspective; a Jewish-Roman cultural exchange existed on some level concerning the river. Could it be that Greco-Roman mythology dressed in Jewish lore helped to transform the Rivus Sabbatis into Sambatyon, the river enclosing the ten tribes? The myth of Saturn may explain the transformation of Rivus Sabbatis, a river ostensibly governed by Saturn, and in effect carrying its name, into the site of containment of the ten tribes and other groups.

Of course, not all of the features and facets of the Roman Saturn were duplicated in rabbinic literature. But some were woven into the basic framework of the ten tribes' story from early on. In Greco-Roman mythology, the insatiable Saturn/Cronus swallows his children one by one. Terrible for sure, but he does after all keep them alive inside him. This malevolent feature in the Greco-Roman myth is transformed in the Jewish version into the image of God placing the ten tribes—the children of Moses, the children of Levi, and the sons of Rechab—in Sambatyon. Again, we recall that Hosea's quip—"Israel was swallowed among the nations," which implies assimilation—was transformed into a story of being swallowed but remaining intact, as the Midrash suggest. As for the nature of these children, while we may still debate whether the ten tribes were a good nation or not, the Midrash is explicit about the superiority of those groups admitted later to Sambatyon. Consider Virgil's (70 BCE–19 CE) verse: "Justice now returns / And Saturn's realm, and from high heaven descends / worthier race of men."[74]

In the Roman version, in which Saturn plays a more positive role than in the Greek, Saturn represents a "golden age," a "glowing picture of blessed times where Saturn-Cronus ruled." Saturn, says Diodorus of Sicily (d. after 21 BCE), causes "all men who were his subjects to change from a rude way of living to civilized life."[75] While the Midrash does not speak explicitly about a change that the ten tribes undergo, Esdras's vision (which, again, provides the basic frame for the Midrash) explicitly speaks of the tribes' decision to change.

Finally, returning to the spatial from the temporal, the concrete physical position and behavior of Saturn as the planet in the sky show further links. In the ancient view of the solar system—that is, the five planets seen by the naked eye—Saturn appears as the most distant from the sun. In the ancient period, well before the heliocentric revolution, the planet's "vast distance from the earth" was key.[76] As Ptolemy (90–168 CE) observed: "Saturn is the farthest planet from the Earth and moves on the largest spheres around the centre of the zodiac."[77] To the ancient observer, then, Saturn's supposed orbit around the earth marked the outermost boundary and limit of our planet. In spatial terms, then, if one wanted to convey the message that the ten tribes were located outside the earth's outermost boundary, they would be placed beyond Saturn—beyond the Sambatyon.

Perhaps the best definition of Sambatyon is that of the German Orientalist and scholar of Ethiopia Hiob Ludolf (1624–1704). Discussing the rivers of Ethiopia in his history of the country, Hiob digresses suddenly and mentions "Sabbation of the Sabbath River," which as we shall see in the next chapter was held to be in Ethiopia. Having presented the "frivolous fiction" of the familiar description of the river's qualities, Ludolf mocks those who believe in it while being "ignorant where this River rises, or where it ends, whether in Asia, Africa, or in Utopia."[78] Ludolf probably uses the term "utopia" to mean "no place," but it seems to me that the more popular meaning of utopia as the ideal human *topos* is apt as well.

Wherever it is, the river, then, became attached to the ten tribes and underwent a transformation not dissimilar to the spinning of *Eretz Ahereth* from a vague other place into a real site of exile. When exactly the transformation of Sambatyon occurred is difficult to determine, but it emerged as an important element in the ten tribes package, not least, as we shall see, because it is the element of their story most strongly associated with redemption. And above all, Sambatyon represents the boundary between our world and a different world, between exile and redemption.

The Messiah and the Ten Tribes

Let's now recall the Talmudic use of Isaiah's verse (49:9) in relation to the ten tribes: to those who "are in darkness, Show yourselves," and "to the prisoners, Go Forth!" The messianic/redemptive overtones are clear. Indeed, a later Midrashic passage discussing the gathering of all exiles under the Messiah elaborates more explicitly on the subject. Asking, "what is meant by the Messiah's saying to the prisoners: 'Go forth'?" the Midrash answers:

> It means that the Messiah will say *Go forth*, and so on, to the Ten
> Tribes who were separated long ago into three companies of exiles,
> one which was banished to the [River] Sambatyon, one banished to the
> region beyond the Sambatyon, and one to Daphne near Riblah where
> it was said "Israel is swallowed up" [Hosea 8:8]. The Messiah will
> be *saying to the prisoners: "Go forth"*—speaking to those held in
> Sambatyon; and *to them that are in darkness* [he will say], *"Show
> yourselves"*—speaking to those held in the region beyond Sambatyon.
> As for those swallowed up in Riblah, the Holy One, blessed be He, will
> make passageway after passageway for them, and they will find their
> way underground [*mehilim mehilim mi-le-matan*] through them until
> they arrive under the Mount of Olives which is Jerusalem and come
> up. And [the] Holy One blessed be he, will stand upon the Mount, and
> after it is cleaved open for [the] exiles, they will come out of it.[79]

Mehilim—tunnels—is the plural of *mehila*, a tunnel or a burrow that an animal digs underground. The Midrash then uses the strangest and most rare of verbs in order to describe the motion of the tribes making their way under the ground—"being like a mole" (*mehaldin,* from the word *holed,* mole).[80] The image of the ten tribes returning to Jerusalem the way the blind small mammal burrows underground reinforces the invisibility of their exile. Here again is a stark juxtaposition between the visible Jewish exile and that of the ten tribes. The Jews will return on roads above the ground, or better, "on the wings of eagles" as the famous prophecy promises (Isaiah 40:31). The ten tribes, on the other hand, shall remain occluded until the Messiah gives the command and they make their way invisibly home through subterranean tunnels.

The rabbis follow this passage with several quotations from consolation prophecies foretelling the return of Israel to its land and end with a quote from Isaiah depicting God rejoicing at the sight of the return of the ten tribes: "Behold, I was left alone; these, where were they?" (Isaiah 49:21). Here, the return of the ten tribes is clearly and unequivocally tied to the coming of the Messiah:

> And these three companies of exiles [the ten tribes] will not come alone. Wherever there are Jews, they also will be gathered up and come. . . . Nay more! The Holy One, blessed be He, will lower the mountains for them and make them into highways for them; and so, too, He will raise up every deep place for them and make it level land for them, as it is written *I will make all My mountains a way, and My highways shall be raised on high.* (Isaiah 49:11)

Now it is the return of the "three companies of exile"—the ten tribes—that will stir the return of the Jews to the Holy Land. In spatial terms, the messianic return begins with them. The ten tribes, the most exiled of all, must lead the way for all the Jews. Talmudic discussions about the ten tribes deliberate as to whether or not they will return. Now, with the Midrash on Isaiah, all questions are over: the ten tribes are unequivocally tied to the Jewish return from exile—they even instigate it. The tribes are now an integral part of the messianic package— indeed, its very bedrock.

The potent messianic content of the ten tribes myth would fuse with its geographic dimensions to make the story a chief propeller of the Western geographic imagination—of its geographic theology: "These, *where* were they?" asks God, expressing his joy over the ten tribes' return. Location and topography emerge as key.

The notion of enclosure opened up the spatial dimensions of God's works in the process of return. In Esdras, we saw him breaking the river into seven channels. Now, we see him creating tunnels under the ground, lowering the mountains and turning them into highways, lifting the valleys. The return of the ten tribes entails the transformation of the physical geography of the earth.

This transformation is rendered in graphic detail, with reversals of every possible geologic or topographic obstacle: that which is low will be raised up; that which is high shall be leveled. Indeed, the world will be flat. The flattening of the world is the strongest expression of the idea that the return of the ten tribes will bring the repair of all the cleavages, ambiguities, barriers, and unknowns spread across the face of the earth. Until the messianic moment, we live in an age of spatial disconnection.

In Jewish thought and its later Christian inflections, the most basic definition of messianism as a category postulates "the certainty of the coming of a blessed world in some indefinable future moment."[81] At first blush, the concomitant question is a purely temporal one: when will the Messiah come? Indeed, most Jewish and Christian messianic calculations have focused on temporal considerations, signs, and signals. But it is God's question, "*where were they?*" that makes the spatial dimensions of messianism key: where does the messianic moment begin, and where—literally—can it be found?

3

Tricksters and Travels

And there are men of Israel in the land of Persia who say that in the mountains of Naisabur four of the tribes of Israel dwell...who were included in the first captivity of Shalmaneser, King of Assyria.

—Benjamin of Tudela

China, Spain, and Ethiopia: The World of the Ten Tribes

As the twelfth-century globetrotter Rabbi Benjamin of Tudela covered the enormous terrain stretching from the Iranian northeastern mountain ranges to the straits between southern Arabia and Ethiopia, he referred as he went to an array of people who had notices and news about the ten lost tribes. The famous Iberian traveler went as far as China and Persia, visiting 300 cities on the way. He did not, of course, come into direct contact with the tribes, but he seems to have been fairly knowledgeable about them and their great deeds. They are never seen, but the ten tribes are always heard, ubiquitously present as rumors about them roam the land. "Rumor" is perhaps the best way to characterize the space in which the lost tribes dwell, and Benjamin of Tudela was its quintessential consumer and conveyer. These rumors, in turn, became an important part of the accumulating "knowledge" about the tribes, bridging the textual traditions of the past and the contemporary talk of the people to bear on a growing body of scientific thought both about the tribes and their whereabouts and about emerging world geography.

The Jewish community of al-Qayrawan (in today's north-central Tunisia) was the first epicenter of major rumors about the ten tribes. In 883 CE, a mysterious man showed up one day and identified himself as a member of the tribe of Dan, one of the most enigmatic among the ten tribes, with a history of migration from its original place of dwelling recorded already in the Bible. After settling in the central coastal region of the land of Israel, the Danites ran into trouble with their neighbors the Philistines and had to migrate and conquer a new territory elsewhere. It was the first act of conquest after the initial and divinely guided conquests of Joshua, when the Israelites returned from Egypt. Dan was one of the first tribes to be exiled by the Assyrians; its territories were conquered by Tiglath-pileser, well before Sargon, during the invasion of 724 BCE. The judge Samson, a Herculean persona whose career was based on amazing physical strength and a mysterious relationship with the divine, was a Danite. He once wrestled and killed a lion with his bare hands and enjoyed the honey produced by bees that had settled in its carcass; he tormented the Philistines, his mortal enemies, with riddles about it. An unusually colorful judge, who always fought Israel's wars alone as an individual, Samson's wars with the Philistines combined the use of physical power, a great degree of intelligence, and a sense of humor. The book of Judges tells us that he once killed a thousand Philistines using a donkey's jawbone.[1]

The Danite who arrived in al-Qayrawan was certainly inspired by the stories of Samson's heroism and wit. The man, "Eldad son of Mahli, son of Atiel, son of Yekutiel . . . son of Hushim, son of Dan, son of Jacob the Patriarch," or, in short, Eldad Ha-Dani, said he was a merchant. He came to al-Qayrawan, a commercial center of major significance in North Africa, after a travel adventure in the depths of Africa, about which he told the town's inhabitants.

The encounter produced three important documents. The first is an epistle composed by Eldad telling of his adventures, *Sefer Eldad*. The second is a query about this man sent by the Jews of al-Qayrawan to the highest legal authority of the time; it includes his response. The third is a study of certain rituals described by Eldad and written by the Qayrawanis, which exists independently and was probably rewritten at a later point.[2]

A "modern" incarnation of Samson, Eldad provided a riveting account of his adventures: "Going forth from beyond the rivers of Ethiopia . . . I and a Jew of the tribe of Asher entered a small ship to trade." Suddenly, a great wind erupted and the ship was wrecked. The two clung to a box until they landed at last on a shore where they were caught by the "Romarnos, who are black Ethiopians, tall, without garment of clothing upon them, likened to beasts, and they eat human beings."[3] The Romarnos proved to be voracious but rational cannibals:

> They took hold of us and, seeing that my companion was fat and
> healthy and pleasing, slaughtered and ate him . . . but me they took, for
> I was sick on board ship and they put me in chains until I should get
> fat and well and they brought me all kinds of good but forbidden food
> but I ate nothing and I hid the food, and when they asked me if I had
> eaten I answered, yes I have eaten.

Eldad was imprisoned for quite some time until "[t]he Lord performed a miracle." His captors were defeated by a "great army [that] came upon them from another place." The mysterious army then took him captive themselves. Eldad told his Qayrawani hosts that his new captors were "wicked men and fire-worshippers." He lived with them for four years; they brought him to a country called Assin. This second captivity ended when:

> A Jew, a merchant of the tribe of Issachar, found me and bought me
> for thirty-two gold pieces and brought me back with him to his
> country. They live in the mountains of the sea-coast and belong to the
> land of the Medes and Persian[s]. They fulfill the command "the book
> of this law [the Torah] shall not depart from your mouth." The yoke of
> [foreign] sovereignty is not upon them only the yoke of [Jewish] law.[4]

Eldad proceeded to tell the whereabouts of each of the ten lost tribes, sketching a huge arc stretching from the borders of northwestern China through Arabia to Ethiopia in Africa.[5] Eldad's ten lost tribes are very much alive, engaging in business, traveling huge distances, waging war against various enemies. Most significantly, they are under the rule of no one. The tribe of Reuben, he mentions, engages in robbery and shares the loot with the neighboring Zebulonites. Eldad saves the best description for his own tribe: "But the descendants of Samson, of the tribe of Dan, are superior to all." While he implies that somehow all the tribes share territorial contiguity, Eldad locates four—Dan, Naphtali, Gad, and Asher—in the Ethiopian region of the ten tribes' domain:

> [T]hey see no man and no man sees them except these four tribes, who
> dwell on the other side of the rivers of Ethiopia. There is a place where
> these can see each other and speak if they cry out, but the River
> Sambation [sic] is between them. . . . When they want anything
> important, they have a kind of pigeon known among them and they
> write their letters and fasten them to the wings or to the feet of the

pigeon, and these cross the River Sambation and the pigeons come to their Kings and their Princes.

The now-familiar notion of the invisibility of the lost tribes is given a new meaning, perhaps so as to safeguard an otherwise not-so-coherent story. "They see no man and no men see them," explains Eldad, fearing perhaps that the Qayrawanis might attempt a trip south to visit the nearby tribes and fact-check his story. There is a designated place where they can meet and in times of need, they use special pigeons to cross the Sambatyon:

> The breadth of that river is 200 cubits bowshot, and the river is full of large and small stones and the sound of them rumbles like a great storm, like a tempest at sea and, in the night, the sound of it is heard for a day's journey and they have with them six wells and they all unite into one lake and therefrom they irrigate their land, and therein are clean edible fish. The river runs and the stones and sand rumble during the six working days, but on the seventh day it rests and is tranquil until the end of Sabbath. And on the other side of the river on the side where the four tribes dwell, is a fire which flames on Sabbath and no man can approach within a mile.[6]

Eldad is clearly familiar with the rabbinic information on Sambatyon up to his time. A careful reader would even note Eldad's echo of the Talmudic passage that speaks of one group of tribes "in" Sambatyon and another "be-yond" it. It is quite likely that Eldad is also mixing in Islamic traditions, which speak of a river of sand.[7] This description of the Sambatyon—with roaring water, stones, and sand—became the model for numerous folktales and stories. A Midrash from the eleventh century incorporates Eldad's version of the river verbatim into its discussion of the ten lost tribes, making it part of the recognized rabbinic literature as well.[8]

Before turning to the rest of the story, let us look first at its most basic geographic specifics. Eldad tells the Qayrawani Jews that he was originally from around the area of Ethiopia, where the tribe of Dan, and possibly Asher, resides. After his rescue from the cannibals, he ended up in a place called Assin. (This Assin [al-Sin] intrigued scholars until 1946, when Louis Rabino-witz, chief rabbi of Johannesburg, identified it as China.)[9] Eldad then relates that, after his rescue by the merchant from the tribe of Issachar, he spent his time visiting the rest of the tribes in Central Asia and Arabia. Finally, he arrived in al-Qayrawan on his way "to Spain." His purported travels cover the known world's corners, from China in the east to Spain in the west. Here, China appears in the context of the ten tribes' story for the first time, underscoring the link between the tribes and the edges of the world. The mysterious tribes that rescue Eldad from the cannibals come from "another place" (*makom aher*), which, eventually, turns out to be China.

Eldad's use of the Arabic word for China (Assin) is also telling. While China was certainly known during Roman times, it really became the world's new frontier only after the rise of Islam. While Alexander, who laid the foundations of the Roman *oikoumene*, reached as far east as India, the Arabs clashed with the Chinese in the battle of Talas in 751 CE. In 618 CE, after centuries of political disarray that rendered it globally marginal, China, under the Tang dynasty, had appeared as a major world power dominating the eastern parts of the Indian Ocean and Asian trade routes that connected it strongly to the Islamic world.[10] In the Arabic geographical imagination, China remained the final frontier, the most distant place one could go.[11] Eldad situates his story within this Arabic geographical imagination—a point under-scored by his claim that he was on his way to Spain.[12] While China represented the easternmost frontier in the Arabic geographical imagination, Spain (Anda-lusia) stood for its westernmost edge.

This view of a world with Chinese and Spanish boundaries is also implied in a ninth-century Midrash about the return of the ten tribes: "Behold, these shall come from far; and lo, these from the north and from the west (Isaiah 49:12), that is, those who were held in far places, such as Spain [Espamia]. And these from the land of Sinim." This is the first time in the rabbinic literature that the place names Spain and Sinim appear in the context of the ten tribes. Predictably, the passage begins with the familiar formula that all Israel "who were held in far places" (read, "the enclosed *eschatoi*") shall return "from the North and the West."

As for the specific places mentioned, there is no problem identifying Spain (Espamia), yet Sinim makes an interesting puzzle. Originally, Sinim was a biblical place just south of the Holy Land (Sini) and was used once by Isaiah to imply "south" (Isaiah 49:12). In this Midrash, however, Sinim is strangely juxtaposed with Spain. It only makes sense if we read it as the contemporary, post-seventh-century Hebrew word for China (Sin, or land of Sinim), and if we place it within the Arabic geographical imagination. Whether or not Eldad was familiar with this Midrash is less important than that, for him, Spain and China were the borders of the world; he shared its author's world view.

The impact of the much more informed and specific Islamo-Arabic geog-raphy, of which the first instance we see is Eldad, is also felt in later writings about the geography of the ten tribes. The notion of the "extreme Orient" was discussed and elaborated by several Jewish scholars in the period between Eldad and the appearance of the Prester John myth. Rabbi Sa'adya Gaon

(Sa'id al-Fayyumi, c. 882–942) commented that "there is not the slightest doubt that Halah, Habor, the river of Gozan, and the cities of the Medes (2 Kings 17:6), are to be found in Khorasan [in northeastern Iran]; Habor is most probably the river Khaboor. All this is well known here."[13]

"Here" for Sa'adya Gaon—the leading rabbinic authority of world Jewry at the time—was Iraq under the Abbasids. Khorasan—Persian for "where the sun arrives from"—was a much larger area than the contemporary Iranian province and included large parts of Central Asia and Afghanistan. Neubauer comments that the identification of Habor with the River Khaboor is indicative of Sa'adya's familiarity with Ptolemy's geography. Ptolemy, like many Greek authors, was translated into Arabic and was widely read by scholars under the Abbasids. Other contemporary readers of Arabic geography followed Sa'adya Gaon's initial identifications of eastern locations with increasing detail. A twelfth-century Arabic translation of Sa'adya's commentary on 2 Kings elaborates on his Khorasan identifications: "He placed them in Halwkn (a province of Nisabur), Herat, the rival of Azerbaijan (a Persian province, with the capital Tabriz), and the towns of Mahat (Nehawand)."[14]

Tricksters and Authentic Lies

Unlike these exegetes and the authors of the Midrash, however, Eldad was generating new knowledge about the ten tribes not by speculation, but by *pretending* to be one of them and to have traveled among them. His fantastic story—robed with cannibals and mysterious people coming from "another place," in addition to his pretension to be a member of the ten tribes—reminds us that Eldad, while no doubt a traveler of some sort, was also a trickster of the type so brilliantly profiled by Natalie Zemon Davis in her *Trickster Travels*.

Not many of his coreligionists, though, saw him as such. Abraham Ibn-Ezra (1092 or 1093–1167), a noted scholar of the sciences and an authoritative commentator on the Torah, mentions Eldad's as an example of a book "contradicting the truth," but he was almost alone in his suspicions.[15] Nineteenth-century depictions of Eldad alternated between two views. One of the first scholars of his story simply called him a "voyageur."[16] Another scholar called him "a rogue and a swindler," "devoid of any higher purpose," but at the same time also called him a "compatriot and counterpart of Ulysses." Heinrich Zvi Greatz (1817–1891), the great Jewish historian, called him "an adventurer and charlatan."[17] Neubauer dubbed him "a daring impostor, crowned with an unexpected success."[18]

Eldad was able to make the world of the ten lost tribes real for his listeners by blending it with tales and legends with which they were familiar. In fact, the complete inaccessibility of the world of the ten tribes is one of the main elements that serve him best in his tricksterism. His most basic trick is to change the identities of the speakers delivering parts of the story: instead of Talmudic sages speculating about the ten tribes, in his account the ten tribes speak for themselves.

Eldad the trickster was well aware of what his purported persona entailed. When he first introduced himself to the Jews of al-Qayrawan, he was careful to describe the ten tribes in apposition to the two that remained, just as traditional literature always set Judah and Benjamin against the missing ten:

> It is a tradition among us that ye are the sons of the captivity [of] the
> tribe of Judah and Benjamin under the dominion of the heathen in an
> unclean land, who were scattered under the Romans who destroyed
> the temple of our God, and under Greeks and Ishmaelites, may they
> pierce their heart and may their bones [be] broken.[19]

Echoed in this short passage are the ideas of Esdras about the ten tribes' exile to a pristine other land, as well as the observations of Josephus and Talmudic sages about the two different types of exile—the scattered Judah and Benjamin under a foreign political yoke, as opposed to the free but enclosed ten tribes. Here, however, we hear the story in reverse, from a pseudo-member of the ten tribes who presents his account as "a tradition *among us* [the ten tribes]," as if just as the Jews had developed their own traditions about their lost brethren, the latter had done the same. In his presentation of what we might term "the Jewish exile as seen by the ten tribes," Eldad is meticulous and creative. The Qayrawanis recounted: "their [the ten tribes'] only language is the sacred tongue, and this Eldad the Danite understands not a word of any other..., neither the language of Ethiopia nor the language of Ishmael, but Hebrew alone, and the Hebrew which he speaks contains words which we have never heard."[20]

As we shall see, these words that no one had heard are what would later betray Eldad's identity, but the trick worked for centuries, on the Qayrawanis and many others. Since Roman times, or even before, it is doubtful if there were Jews anywhere in the world who spoke only Hebrew—except of course the isolated ten tribes (or, more recently, some contemporary Jews born in modern-day Israel). The clever trickster also told the Qayrawanis that the ten tribes possessed the whole Bible—but did not read the scroll of the history of Esther, because they "had no part in that miracle."[21] After all, the ten tribes did not exist within the boundaries of the Persian Empire. Eldad was aware, no doubt, of the problems concerning the Bible's Persian context, and he made a point of telling his hosts that the tribes had no part in an episode that took place within it. Another nice trick was retelling the Midrash about the offspring of Moses and the Levites who refused to sing for Zion in Babylonian captivity and were taken to Sambatyon.[22] The quick reworking of traditions made Eldad look authentic in the eyes of the Qayrawani Jews. After all, they themselves held the same traditions; this man seemed to be confirming each one of them.

Trickster Eldad aside, who was the historical Eldad? This is a question that tormented historians critically engaged in his story, particularly during the later nineteenth century.[23] Linguist Shlomo Morag solved a major part of the mystery through careful scrutiny of Eldad's Hebrew (language, syntax, pronunciations) and specific words that he used during his exchanges with his audience. Morag was able to demonstrate that Eldad "certainly belonged to a community of Arabic speaking Jews from southern Arabia." That is to say, Eldad was a Yemeni Jew. Morag also found clear traces of Syriac in Eldad's speech, a point that prompted him to suggest that Eldad came from the "Jewish community of Najran, in northern historical Yemen [today's southwestern Saudi Arabia]." The Najrani Jewish community had been in close contact with Syrian Christian monks over several centuries, and the Hebrew spoken by its members had, in addition to Arabic, a strong Syriac influence and was a unique dialect. Morag also points out that the Najrani Jews enjoyed a special status under Islamic rule in Yemen, and "the Muslims generally treated them with great respect."[24] This might explain Eldad's arrogance and the fact that he dares to tell a story about Israelite military/political power in a Muslim city like al-Qayrawan.

Najran was the capital of the strong Himyar kingdom, ruled by a dynasty of Judaized kings, most famously Yūsuf Asar Dhū Nuwas (d. 525 CE), its last. From the early Roman period, Himyar was an active member of a vibrant trade network connecting Arabia, the Mediterranean, and the African kingdom of Axum in Ethiopia. It was certainly the most significant polity in Arabia before the rise of Islam, enough so to be at constant war with both the Ethiopians of Axum and the Persian Empire. The effective end of this turbulent kingdom came in 550 CE, when it was conquered by a Parthian army followed by an Ethiopian invasion in 570. Several decades later, the first Islamic messengers arrived.[25] Indian Ocean trade networks only grew larger during Islamic times, and southern Arabia continued to play a significant role in them thanks to its key location.[26] This would explain Eldad's great familiarity with Asian and Indian Ocean trade routes. Eldad himself, it should be recalled, told his hosts that his adventure began when "crossing the other side of the rivers of" Ethiopia, which contradicts his basic claim that the tribe of Dan resided there. Eldad therefore inadvertently revealed his secret, but it went unnoticed. However, his slip of the tongue suggests that he must have come from across the Red Sea in Arabia.

From a cultural standpoint, the Himyarite connection opens up an array of possibilities for understanding many aspects of his story. The long history of violence and confrontation with powerful Asian and African neighbors produced in Himyar a treasure trove of tales of warfare and glory that survived in Syriac, Byzantine, and later Islamic sources. Of particular interest are stories of Dhū Nuwas's war against the Christians of southern Arabia and against the Ethiopians. Even though he is defeated at the end, the Jewish king Dhū Nuwas is depicted as a ruthless killer and great military leader capable of mobilizing tens of thousands of men. Even in defeat, he dies with style—marching into the sea and drowning.[27]

The background of these wars as recorded by Christian authors was the Jewish king's policy of persecution of southern Arabian Christians, which prompted the Christian kings of Ethiopia to interfere on their behalf.[28] Early Islamic culture was a major consumer of such Himyarite tales, and Jews and some Himyarite characters made a nice career for themselves among early Islamic circles as transmitters of them. Most well known is Ka'b Ibn Mâti al-Himyarî, better known as Ka'b al-Ahbar (d. 652?), a Jew and early convert to Islam who became an authority on Islamic traditions concerning the Jews, which are known in Islam as the Isra'iliyyat.[29] Ka'b's title—al-Ahbar—is the Arabic translation of the Hebrew scholarly title haver (lit. "associate of the school"), and the wealth of knowledge about Jewish traditions that he displays indicates that the Jews of southern Arabia had a scholarly system connected to other centers of learning in the Jewish world.[30] This might account for Eldad's own wealth of knowledge of Jewish traditions a century and a half later.

A second important Himyarite figure is Wahb ibn Munabbih (c. 654–732), a man of mixed Persian and Himyarite descent who was also a source on Jewish traditions but, more important, on Himyari history. Wahb's main contribution to early Islamic literature is *The Book of Crowns, on the Kings of Himyar* [*Kitāb al-Tijān*], which reached its final form when compiled by Ibn Hisham (d. 833), himself of Himyarite origin and editor of an authoritative biography of the Prophet.[31] Full of lore, myth, and tales about great Himyari and Arab kings and heroes, it contains the genealogy of the "Children of Ham" and their offspring the Habbasha (Ethiopians) and recounts the wars between them and the Arabs.[32] For his part, Eldad dedicates several passages to the wars that the ten tribes conducted with the "Cushites" (Ethiopians). But in his account, it is not the Jewish Himyarite kings who fight the Ethiopians, but the ten tribes: "After the death of Sennacherib, three tribes of Israel, being

Naphtali, Gad, and Asher, journeyed on their own to the land of Ethiopia and encamped in the wilderness until they came to their border, a twenty days' Journey, and they slew the men of Ethiopia, and unto this very day, they fight with the children of the kingdoms of Ethiopia."[33]

Finally, *Kitāb al-Tijān* tells in detail the story of King al-Saʿb Dhuʾl Qarnain (Saʿb of the Two Horns), a legendary warrior king, a story that made its way also into the Qurʾan. In the Qurʾan, this enigmatic figure—who later became interpreted as an Islamic version of Alexander the Great, at war with Gog and Magog—appears briefly as the one defeating "Yajuj and Majuj" and shutting them somewhere in the far east: "until he came to the place where [the] sun rises" (Qurʾan 18:83–101). In *Kitāb al-Tijān*, however, a figure with a similar name is depicted as traveling from the far east to the far west, to "Andalus"— that is, Spain. He also goes "from the farthest north to the farthest south" and wages war in the "Land of Gog and Magog."[34] Eldad, who showed up a few decades after Ibn Hisham's version began circulating, might not have known that particular account, but he was certainly familiar with the local traditions as told by Wahb.

Placed within a milieu of storytellers such as Kaʿb and Wahb, Eldad's trickster character can be seen in a new light, which may partially explain his motivations. These stories' heritage was part of his *identity*. In other words, trickster Eldad was describing what historian Lev Gumilev calls "authentic lies."[35] Recall Morag's comment concerning the respect that Najrani Jews commanded among their non-Jewish neighbors even in modern times. Indeed, given its royal history, one can imagine why these Jews enjoyed such status, or at least thought they did, even centuries after these events. Among Jewish communities of the time, such a past was unique. Eldad was not completely lying, as many later historians have accused, when he sat surrounded by riveted Qayrawani Jews, telling them stories of huge Israelite armies fighting mighty enemies. He was not relying only on his imagination, but also on what he understood to be his own past, converting Dhū Nuwas and the Himyarite Jews of yore into an upgraded version of the ten tribes. At the same time, Eldad incorporated into the tale other bits and pieces of information about the wild Ethiopians; the world of trade that lay in the far east; and tales of a man between far east and the far west, a man just like himself.[36]

The Qayrawanis' Response: Law, Anthropology, and Scripture

"Be it known to your Lordship that a man has become our guest whose name is Eldad the Danite of the tribe of Dan, and he has told us that there are four tribes in one place, Dan, Naphtali, Gad, and Asher."[37] So wrote the Jews of al-Qayrawan to Rabbi Zemah Gaon (d. 895), head of the Yeshiva of Sura in Babylonia, then the highest rabbinic authority in the Jewish world and still widely regarded as such.[38] Turning to a legal authority for a ruling and clarification was, and remains, a common practice in Jewish (and Islamic) law.

The reaction of the Jews of al-Qayrawan to Eldad's fantastic tale had crucial implications for the later stages of the ten tribes' history since it tells us what kind of questions were to be asked in the first encounter with any potential ten tribers. The epistle that they prepared for the Gaon included a version of Eldad's story, a summary of its main elements, including the details of the Sambatyon as relayed by him. The epistle's authors noted that the tribes "use the four methods of death penalty and dwell in tents and journey and encamp from place to place." They explained that four of the tribes fight the "kings of Ethiopia" and that "the extent of their land is seven months' journey." Concerning scripture, the Qayrawanis reported that the tribes "posses the whole of the Bible [ve-yesh lahem ha-mikra kula]...and their Talmud is of a simple Hebrew and no [Talmudic] sage is mentioned therein, either Rabbi of the Mishnah or Rabbi of the Talmud, but in every Halacha [Jewish law] they say, 'Thus have we learnt from the mouth of Joshua, from the mouth of Moses, from the mouth of God.'"

There is only the faintest indication that the Qayrawanis had any doubt as to Eldad's identity as a ten triber: "We would show an object to him and he would tell us the name in the sacred language, and we wrote it down, and after a time we again asked him each word and we found it the same as the first word he had given." Evidently, Eldad knew how to present a solid case to a relentless interrogator and was not duped by the trap of repeatedly being asked the same questions. What bothered the Qayrawanis—and what prompted them to turn to the highest legal authority in the Jewish world at the time—was the discovery of some "slight" discrepancies between the laws practiced by the Jews and the laws practiced by the ten tribes according to Eldad: "We have seen that it is the same law but slightly different."[39] The Qayrawanis give as an example a lengthy description of Eldad's report on the ten tribes' rules of slaughtering;[40] slaughtering laws are one of the largest and most important bodies of Jewish law.

Delving into its minutiae is beyond our purpose here, but the nature of the exchanges between Eldad and the Qayrawanis and the questions that the latter ask are important. What is at stake is the anthropology of the ten tribes—a group of people that had supposedly existed in total isolation for over a millennium. The Qayrawanis were not only interested in the fantastic stories Eldad had to tell. They were more concerned about the life and conditions of a removed Israelite group. From a theological point of view, their findings raised a set of problems of major importance that they wished to clarify both with Eldad and with the Gaon.

The ten tribes were exiled many centuries before the Jews. They did not partake in major events of the biblical and postbiblical period, including the reign of Josiah and the finding of Deuteronomy, the great prophets, the Babylonian captivity, the return to Zion, the completion and canonization of the Bible, the Second Temple and its fate, the emergence of rabbinic Judaism, and the rabbinic monopoly on the interpretation and development of the law. But if the tribes were not part of biblical history, the covenant between God and Israel still bound them. Indeed, the Talmudic position implied that the ten tribes were enclosed in exile so they could continue to worship the Lord. From a rabbinic point of view, just as Mosaic law developed "here," in the Jewish exile, so too it must have developed "there," beyond the Sambatyon. Even if the ten tribes were removed from the rest of the children of Israel, they should have naturally or spontaneously developed the religious institutions and legal system of the Jews.

Some Christian theologies would develop the same expectation for "natural religious development," except that, in the Christian version, the ten tribes were to possess the New Testament as well as the Old. In its most radical version, this theology is also the basis for Mormonism. Recall, for instance, the story of the boy who found the ten tribes in the North Pole's Arctic Ocean, recounted by the explorer Lindelof. His encounter with the (good Christian) lost tribes reaffirmed his faith in the Bible.[41] That is, precisely *because* the ten tribes are outside human history, they hold the special power of affirming it, offering a link to an intact past. (Nineteenth-century Jewish historians read Eldad's story against this backdrop—and produced an array of bizarre explanations for his actions.)[42]

The question of the ten tribes' scripture, law, and religiosity was an important part of the Eldad episode. As we have seen, the Qayrawanis made a point of reporting that the ten tribes "possess [i.e., have access to] the whole of the Bible." This explains the seemingly bizarre note concerning the "four methods of death penalty." The Torah, the biblical basis for Talmudic law, specifies only three methods—stoning, burning, and decapitation by sword. Rabbinic sages introduced a fourth—strangulation.[43] The fact that the ten tribes had the fourth method was proof that Mosaic law in both exiles was similar, as was theologically expected. This had crucial implications relating to the authority of the rabbinic interpretation of Mosaic law—what is known as oral law, as opposed to the Torah, or written law. The fact that Mosaic law had naturally developed in the secluded land of the ten tribes validated its rabbinic interpretation, thereby affirming the monopoly on the interpretation of scrip-ture claimed by the rabbinic establishment. For all of these reasons, these "slight" discrepancies must be explained and accounted for. The Qayrawanis speak of their "bewilderment" (*temihah gedolah*) upon learning of them.

The Qayrawani report indicates that much of the encounter between Eldad and his hosts revolved around Eldad's language:

> [His is] neither the language of Ethiopia nor the language of Ishmael, but Hebrew alone, and the Hebrew that he speaks contains words that we have never heard. Thus, he calls a dove "tintar," a bird he calls "requt," for pepper he says "darmos." Of such as these, we have written down many from his mouth, because we pointed the matter out to him and he told us the name in the sacred language, and we wrote it down.

The Qayrawanis served as linguistic anthropologists, taking meticulous notes and examining the stranger's Hebrew. In another place in their report, they added, "Among [the ten tribes] there are no wild beasts and no impure, but only cattle. There are no insects and no creeping things. . . . They reap and sow themselves, for they have no slaves."[44] The Qayrawanis interrogated Eldad extensively about the rituals of the tribes.

All of this information was generated by a desire to know (Jewish) life in its primordial form. As an Israelite whose people had been in total isolation for over a millennium, Eldad represented a pure form of existence, a sort of control group for Jewish development, the ultimate survival, uncorrupted by years of encounters with foreign peoples, untainted by the yoke of non-Jewish rules. For the Qayrawanis, Eldad represented authenticity, an opportunity to get in touch with their own past as Israelites.

The Qayrawanis' questions present a research protocol that would guide future encounters with the ten tribes. In this early phase of ten-tribes-ism, it was basic. In its more elaborate form, this protocol would come to demand the extensive search for traces—for instance, of "Yahwehisms" among indigenous tribes all over the globe. Hebrew was from the start an important feature of this practice. The search for traces of Hebrew guided many such anthropologists as they encountered Native Americans.[45] The Irishman James Adair (1709–1783), for instance, based most of his well-known 1775 *History of the American Indians* on attempts to show affinities between Hebrew and Native American lan-guages: "The Indian dialects, like the Hebrew language, have a nervous and emphatical manner of expression. . . . Their style is adorned with images, com-parisons, and strong metaphors like the Hebrews."[46] Another example is the work of the Jesuit ethnologist Joseph J. Williams (1875–1940), *Hebrewisms of*

West Africa: From Nile to Niger with the Jews.[47] Both works suggest a link between modern ethnography and the Qayrawani interrogation of Eldad.

The Gaon's response to the Qayrawanis' query revealed from the outset his positive impression of Eldad, referring to him as "rabbi"; this rabbinization was a significant indication of authority. He also indicated that this Eldad had shown up elsewhere and caused a similar stir. The Gaon assured the Qayrawanis that there was no need to panic about the discrepancies they'd found in the course of their interrogations; others had dealt with them as well: "Wise men tell us that they heard from Rabban Isaac ben Mar and Rabban Simcha that they saw this Rabbi Eldad the Danite and were surprised at his words because some of them were according to the words of the Rabbis and some of them differed."

The crux of the matter, however, was halachic, and here, too, the Gaon gave Eldad the benefit of any doubt. He pointed out that, on the "big issues," such as methods of executions, the ten tribes' law was similar to Jewish law, in the sense that it also included strangling, which is not mentioned in scripture but is mandated by the rabbis. As for the slight discrepancies, the Gaon reassured the Qayrawanis that differences in ritual also prevail among different groups of Jews. "Do not be astonished at the variation and difference which you heard from Eldad," he urged them, "for it is a fact that the sages of Babylon and of Palestine study one and the same Mishnah and they do not add to or take away from it, but sometimes these give one reason and those another reason." In other words, since Jewish law allows a degree of pluralism and difference in interpretation, they must also allow for some differences between it and the ten tribes' law: "The law remains the same, whether in Mishnah or Talmud, and all drink from one well." Lest any doubt be left in his interlocutors' minds, the Gaon reminded them of the human dimension, as well:

> It must be said that it is not far fetched to think that Eldad has erred and confused things in consequence of the many troubles through which he passed and the stress of travel wearying the body, but the Mishna is one law... but the Talmud is studied by the men of Babylon in Aramaic and by the men of Palestine in *Targum* [translation into a different Aramaic dialect], and by the sages exiled to Ethiopia in Hebrew, which they understand.

Finally, the Gaon did not miss the opportunity to use the episode for didactic purposes, to confirm the supremacy of the Babylonian rabbinical establishment in the Jewish world:

> And as to what Eldad told, that they prayed for the wise men of Babylon first and afterwards for all Israel in exile, they do well, for the

chief sages and prophets were exiled to Babylon and they founded the law and they fixed the yeshiva [school] on the River Euphrates, from the days of Jehoyakin, King of Judah, until this very day and formed a chain of wisdom and prophecy and from them went forth the law to all the people and as we have already told you, all drink from one well, therefore, keep ye diligently what the sages preach unto you and the Talmud which they taught you, turn not to the right or left from any of their words.[48]

This is blatantly political. Perhaps fearing Karaite challenges, perhaps fearing challenges from elsewhere in the Jewish world, the Gaon could not avoid capitalizing on the notion that the ten tribes were "pray[ing] for the wise men in Babylon." Again, the primordiality of the ten tribes carried with it a special power of affirming certain histories. Indeed, this one nugget in the account may well be the reason that the Gaon was amenable to Eldad's story to begin with. Thus, we encounter, for the first time, a use of the ten tribes story for political purposes—in this case, the supremacy of the Babylonian rabbinical establishment. It was by no means the last.

Contrary to the Gaon's confidence in the supremacy and power of the Babylonian rabbinical establishment, it did ultimately give way to history, ultimately collapsing about one and a half centuries after his time and marking the end of the notion of a single or definitive Jewish legal authority. His ruling about the Danites in Ethiopia, however, was longer lasting and left a trail of rulings concerning the Danite origins of the Falasha, today called the "Ethiopian Jews."

Rabbi David ben Shlomo ibn Abi Zimra (Radbaz; 1479–1573), a Sephardic rabbi, ruled, based on the Gaon's response, that the Falasha are "without doubt" (beli safek) from the tribe of Dan. Four centuries later, in 1973, Rabbi Ovadia Yosef—then chief Sephardic rabbi of Israel and to this day the highest Sephardic legal authority—also ruled that the Falasha are the tribe of Dan. He reiterated this position in another, much longer response to a query in 1985.[49] These rulings were the basis for Israel's decision to bring the Falasha to Israel and naturalize them according to the Law of Return.[50]

Aside from legal issues, the entire Eldad episode marks a turning point in the development of the story told in this book. Eldad expanded the geographic horizons of the search for the lost tribes. Discussions up to his time revolved around real but removed places that no one was meant to recognize. Eldad himself maintained that the tribes were secluded, enclosed beyond Sambatyon: they see nobody, and nobody can see them. But he assigned the tribes to specific real locations in Asia, Arabia, and Africa. Working within an Islamic geography, he also introduced China—the frontier of the oikoumene after the

Islamic conquests—into the geographic frame. Many subsequent seekers went to look for the tribes in China. Similarly, Eldad reinforced Ethiopia's status as a possible candidate. Ethiopia already played a role in the Greek, Roman, and Jewish geographical imagination as one end of the world. Eldad introduced the Himyarite/Arab legacy with its stories about the wars with the kings of Cush and the wild Cushites. More important, Eldad the trickster introduced the possibility of a real encounter between the ten tribes and human beings on this side of the Sambatyon. If one of the tribes had made contact with "us," perhaps the reverse was also possible.

In Asia and in Africa, Eldad's tribes travel, trade, communicate with each other by pigeons, and fight with savage kingdoms and peoples. All of this opened up new horizons to search for, and talk about, the ten tribes. Perhaps the most important contribution of both Eldad the traveler and Eldad the trickster storyteller to the story of the ten lost tribes was the inspiration he gave to numerous travelers and seekers, Jewish and Christian. He had crossed over from them to us; so, perhaps, we could cross over to them.

Prester John and Benjamin of Tudela

The military character of the ten tribes as presented by Eldad brings to mind another of their occasional companions—Prester John, the legendary king and great Christian hope in the war against Muslims and other heathens. Along with Gog/Magog, he is one of their most common supporting actors. The story of this non-European Christian king is comparatively well researched.[51] It is worthwhile, however, to point to the connections forged among Eldad's story, the ten lost tribes, and Prester John.

The first recorded notice of Prester John appeared in 1145 when an emissary carrying a message of distress from the Crusader states in the Middle East arrived in Western Europe. The emissary, Bishop Hugo of Jabala (in today's Lebanon), recounted a story:

> Not many years ago a certain John, a king and priest, who lives in the extreme Orient, beyond Persia and Armenia, and who, like all his people, is a Christian although a Nestorian, made war on the brothers known as the Samiardi, who are the kings of the Persians and Medes, and stormed Ecbatana [Hamadan, in Iran], the capital of their kingdom. . . . The ensuing battle lasted for three days, since both sides were willing to die rather than flee. At last Presbyter John—for so they customarily call him—put the Persians to flight, emerging victorious

after the most bloodthirsty slaughter.... Victorious the said John moved forward in order to come to the aid of the holy Church.[52]

The king failed to reach the embattled Crusader states because he could not cross the Tigris River. As Gumilev points out, this story might be echoing an actual historical event, "the defeat of the forces of the Seljuk sultan of Sanjar by the levies of the Central Asian tribes...in 1141." Nestorian Christians, expelled by the Byzantines centuries earlier, did indeed migrate eastward. With this disconnection from European and Mediterranean Christendom, Nestorianism became a form of "lost Christianity." Some, such as the American physician and missionary Asahel Grant (1807–1844), identified the Nestorians with the ten lost tribes. Grant died in Ottoman Mosul, leaving a beautifully written memoir and a long book on his travels in northern Iraq and Iran, both widely published.[53] But mainly, the Prester John story "was more an aspiration than history."[54]

The legend of Prester John spread quickly across Europe, collecting a trail of "almost 100 manuscripts, written in several languages, including Hebrew," which purported to bring further notice about the Christian king.[55] It is clear that there is no connection between the legend of Prester John and Eldad's stories about the ten tribes, though "there are important elements common to the narratives."[56] A connection was created when the fictitious "Letters of Prester John"—in which the king describes his kingdom in detail—surfaced around 1165. These letters, which claimed to come from somewhere in the east, were of European origin and based in part on the "Romance of Alexander," a story of the wonder of the Mokdons which was popular in Europe at the time. The letters were addressed to the pope and several European rulers, most notably Emperor Frederick I Barbarossa (1122–1190). A tale about a river that throws up stones and about mighty kingdoms of "Jews" was included in all versions. In the letter to the emperor, Prester John specifically wrote about the ten lost tribes:

> On the one side of our country is a river, on the border of which all kinds of excellent spices are found. Near to it is another river, full of stones, which falls into the ocean, which flows between the sea and the Nine Tribes of Israel. This river runs all the week till the Sabbath day, when it rests.... it carries large and small stones to the sea, like a river of water does; consequently the Nine Tribes of Israel cannot pass the river. On the other side we have forty-four towns, built of very strong stones, and the distances between one town and another is not more than a bowshot. And in order to guard them we have 44,000 horsemen, 50,000 bowmen, and 30,000 men on horseback to guard

the cities from an attack by the children of Israel, for if they could pass the river they would destroy the world. The Israelites possess ten of the cities. We make known to you that for these ten cities, and for other expenses which we are obliged to make for the great King of Israel, he gives us yearly a hundred camels, loaded with gold, silver, precious stones and pearls; besides this he pays a tribute for our not ravaging the land which lies between us and themselves. Know also, that the great King of Israel has under his dominion 200 kings, who hold their lands only with his permission. Besides these kings, there are 2,300 governors and princes. In his countries flow two rivers coming from the Garden of Eden.[57]

As historian Andrew Gow has convincingly shown, this was the first instance of a potent medieval myth lumping together Prester John, the ten tribes, and, occasionally, Gog/Magog—a forgery that became chiefly responsible for the rise of the anti-Semitic eschatological myth of the Red Jews in fourteenth- and fifteenth-century Germany.[58] This is also the first clear instance of Christian interest in the ten tribes as depicted in a postbiblical Jewish source and of a dialogic process through which Jews and Christian fed each other ten tribes knowledge. Of course, each side reserved the right to cast itself in as positive a light as possible. Even if the "King of Israel" pays tribute to the Christian Prester John, he heads a strong polity with "200 kings" against which the Christians still need to gather a huge army.

Epstein comments that the purpose of the forgery was "to counter the story of Eldad of which the Jews were proud"[59]—one man's apocalyptic catastrophe being messianic hope for another. In the Hebrew version of the letters, the ten tribes are described as having still more power, and there is no mention at all of their subordinate status vis-à-vis the Christian king: "There are under the rule of King Daniel 300 kings, all Jews, and all of them possess countries under the power of King Daniel. And also under his governance are 3,000 dukes and counts and great men and we know that his country is unfathomable."[60] This is another instance of the invocation of the ten tribes' story for political purposes.

Whatever the reason for its composition, the story illustrates the extent to which Eldad's version of the militarized empire of the ten tribes, somewhere in the "extreme Orient" and/or Ethiopia, had become popular in Europe. In the wake of the letters, the ten tribes' importance in the European Christian imagination was certain. In many instances, a search for Prester John often implied, or triggered, a search for the ten lost tribes themselves.

The clearest proponent of this military image, and a sign of its dissemination, is Rabbi Benjamin of Tudela, the famous Iberian traveler with whom this chapter began. This prolific wanderer spent about thirteen years traveling mostly in the Mediterranean basin and in the Middle East, roughly between 1159 and 1173. Benjamin's travels came relatively soon after the first significant attack on the Crusader states by Zengi in 1144, which occurred after the defeat of the Seljuks of Sanjar by Central Asians in 1141—a moment of major global power shifts.

While most of the stories in his bestselling *Itinerario* are based on actual experiences, Benjamin incorporates numerous fictional anecdotes, traditions, and legends. In this regard, Benjamin's itinerary is at once concrete and mythical, and his travels can be read in real time and real space, as well as in a hypertext that reflects scripture, Talmudic and oral tales, and the history of the locations he visited. The result is a unified narrative made of actual geography, history, legend, and rumor. This hypertext is not only reserved to the ten tribes. Benjamin furnishes other *topoi*—Jerusalem, for instance—with similar lore. A learned scholar, Benjamin cites rabbinic literature and scripture. Unlike Eldad, he is not interested in concealing his movements or sources, and he takes care to record the details of his travels in space.[61] His meticulous accountings allow us to reconstruct Benjamin's course with a degree of accuracy. And since he does eventually discuss the ten tribes, Benjamin's itinerary allows us to view the world from which the ten tribes were imagined, to see them in the context of the real travel itself as a sort of ever-lurking point of geographic reference.

Benjamin's description of the ten tribes reflects in many ways the stories of Eldad in combination with Prester John's additions and adoptions. One can almost put one's finger on the page and mark the place where Benjamin enters the ten tribes' world, moving from the concrete map to the hypertext, as he moves from giving an account of places he has actually seen, to discussing places he has not physically visited.

Benjamin begins his hypertextual journey as he discusses Hamadan, formerly known as Ecbatana. Hamadan is a real place that recently had gained some new significance. Recall here that Hamadan is the city (according to Bishop Hugo of Jabala) that had been stormed by Prester John. Benjamin was undoubtedly aware that this ancient city was the capital of Medes. Located in the foothills of the Alvand mountain chain, it was close to the ancient city of Nahavand. The old biblical locations of the ten tribes were "the cities of Medes," and the Talmud mentions Nahavand and the mountains of Salug (Snow Mountains) in connection to them. No doubt, this came to Benjamin's mind as he approached Hamadan:

> [This] is the great city of Media, where there are 30,000 Israelites. In front of a certain synagogue, there are buried Mordecai and Esther.

From thence [Hamadan] it takes four days to Tabaristan, which is
situated on the river Gozan. Some 4,000 Jews live there.... Thence it
is seven days to Ghaznah the great city on the river Gozan, where there
are about 80,000 Israelites.... Thence it is five days to Samarkand,
which is the great city [in] the confines of Persia. In it live some
50,000.... Thence it is four days' journey to Tibet, the country in
whose forests the musk is found.[62]

The dramatic move from real to ambiguous geography is palpable and
leaps out with the utterly out-of-context reference to Tibet. Benjamin is not yet
talking about the ten tribes, but what is already striking is the number of
"Israelites" (as opposed to "Jews"). As Benjamin moves discursively east, the
numbers grow from communities of up to several thousand Jews in Iraq to
communities of tens of thousands of Israelites in eastern Iran. Josephus's "ten
tribes beyond the Euphrates, countless myriads whose numbers cannot be
ascertained" come to mind. One can sense that we are near ten tribes territory
with Benjamin's choice of the phrase "the confines of Persia."[63] Indeed, the
River Gozan, it seems, is the main axis of Benjamin's geography:

Thence it takes twenty-eight days to the mountains of Naisabur by the
river Gozan. And there are men of Israel in the land of Persia who say
that in the mountains of Naisabur four of the tribes of Israel dwell,
namely, the tribe of Dan, the tribe of Zebulun, the tribe of Asher, and
the tribe of Naphtali, who were included in the first captivity of
Shalmaneser, king of Assyria, as it is written (2 Kings 17:11): "And he
put them in Halah and in Habor by the river of Gozan and in the cities
of the Medes." The extent of their land is twenty days' journey, and
they have cities and large villages in the mountains; the river Gozan
forms the boundary on the one side. They are not under the rule of the
Gentiles, but they have a prince of their own, whose name is R. Joseph
Amarkala the Levite. There are scholars among them. And they sow
and reap and go forth to war as far as the land of Cush by way of the
desert.[64]

While the specific geographic identification comes from the biblical exegesis on the place name in 2 Kings, it is obvious that the most basic source for
information in this passage is Eldad. Benjamin's four tribes are the same as in
Eldad's story, as is the size of the tribes' land—"twenty days' journey."[65] So too
the insistence that they "are not under the rule of the Gentiles," the mention
that there are "scholars among them," and the description of how they "go
forth to war as far as the land of Cush by way of the desert." Suddenly, a real

geography has given way to a more mythical one, and the tribes are revealed as the pivot of the journey.

Indeed, a bit of Benjamin's tricksterism is exposed in this passage: he disguises Eldad as the source, pretending that his information is from "men of Israel in the land Persia." Part of this tricksterism is born out of geographic necessity: Eldad's four tribes live in Africa (Cush) and Benjamin is in Asia. Benjamin seems to be compensating for the disappearance of Eldad's African context when he says that the four tribes make war as far as the land of Cush. He also replicates Eldad's peculiar geography, which connected the various tribes located in Asia with their counterparts in Ethiopia.[66]

More significant is Benjamin's observation that the four tribes are "in league with the Kofar-al-Turak [heathen Turks], who worship the wind and live in the wilderness, and who do not eat bread, nor drink wine, but live on raw uncooked meat. They have no noses, and in lieu thereof they have two small holes, through which they breathe. They eat animals both clean and unclean, and they are very friendly towards the Israelites." He follows with several tales illustrating this friendly alliance. In his version, the four (out of ten) tribes were highly involved in the 1141 invasion of Persia. Benjamin's description of the Kofar-al-Turak makes clear that they are certainly not Muslims; they have no dietary laws whatsoever and are "friendly with the Israelites." Fifteen years prior, "they overran the country of Persia with a large army...took all the spoil thereof, and returned by way of the wilderness."[67]

The image of a huge army sacking Persia and then returning to the wilderness clearly references Prester John. Though Benjamin is inaccurate in his dating and location of the battles, he is evidently referring to the 1141 invasion of Iran that took Hamadan: "There can be little doubt that the Kofar-al-Turak, a people belonging to the Tartar stock, are identical with the so-called subjects of Prester John."[68] Unlike Hugo of Jabala, however, Benjamin erases not only the Prester's name but also any hint that his Prester John is Christian. He seems to be insisting that the people he describes have no faith at all. In the same manner, Benjamin reverses the tense relationship between Prester John and the ten tribes, perhaps echoing the Hebrew letters. This one passage references several sources: the historical events of 1141, real geography, the legends of Prester John and their inflections, the story of Eldad, and Talmudic and biblical exegeses.

Benjamin's treatment of the remaining six tribes elsewhere in his itinerary calls to mind Eldad's Yemeni/Najrani connection. Having completed his description of the city of Hilla (in today's southern Iraq), Benjamin proceeds with a discussion of Yemen and its Jews. His general description reminds us of the proud Jews of Najran who enjoy the respect of their gentile neighbors. "All the neighbours of these Jews go in fear of them," writes Benjamin, perhaps with a hint of vicarious arrogance. As in the case of the Central Asian ten tribes, the Yemeni ten tribes story begins with an exorbitant demography—"100,000 in Teima" and "300,000 in Tanai," the main city in the region.[69] But what concerns Benjamin most is the city of Kheibar (Khaybar), located not in Yemen, but "sixteen days' journey to the north" in the Hijaz:

> People say that the men of Kheibar belong to the tribes of Reuben, Gad, and Manasseh, whom Shalmaneser, king of Assyria led hither into captivity. They have built strongly fortified cities, and make war upon all other kingdoms. No man can readily reach their territory, because it is a march of eighteen days' journey through the desert, which is altogether uninhabited, so that no one can enter the land. Kheibar is a very large city with 50,000 Jews. In it are learned men, and great warriors, who wage war with the men of Shinar and of the land of the north, as well as with the bordering tribes of the land of El-Yemen near them, which latter country is [in] the confines of India.[70]

It is fascinating how persistent the story of the Hijazi ten tribes was. In 1665, at the height of the messianic fervor around the pseudo-messiah Sabbatai Zvi, rumors spread in Europe and particularly in England that the governor of Tunis had ordered the pilgrimage to Mecca be halted. According to the rumors, an army of the lost tribes had showed up at the gates of Mecca. *Annals of the Universe*, published in London in 1709, some forty years after the episode, summed it up thus: "the Jews reported at all places, that near 600,000 men were arriv'd at Mecha, professing themselves to be of [the] ten tribes and a half that had been lost for so many ages, but the story was false."[71] As Scholem has shown, though, many Christians in London in the 1660s had been more than ready to believe the rumors.[72]

Behind this *topos* of the Arabian ten tribes is the fact of Jewish tribes in Arabia up to the time of Muhammad; in this regard, Benjamin's "Kheibar" is not wholly fictional. Khaybar was "the great Jewish centre in the north of the Hajez" at the time of the Prophet Muhammad.[73] A rich oasis with a fortified Jewish village, Khaybar provided economic and political sustenance to the rest of the Jewish tribes in the Hijaz. A "hotbed of anti-Muslim intrigue," it was certainly a Jewish power with which Muhammad had to contend on his way to control of the region and of Arabia.[74] The siege on Khaybar and Muhammad's triumph there (629 CE) is one of the most decisive and glorious moments in the career of the Prophet and in Islamic history.[75] Classical Islamic historians tended to glorify the fortified village so as to aggrandize Muhammad's victory, which probably gave rise to an exaggerated image of a powerful and fortified Jewish Khaybar. As such, this image informs Benjamin's description, which reverses, in a manner similar to Eldad's, defeat into triumph and Jews into the ten tribes. Here again is an instance of fantastic geography, this time connecting Yemen with India—a testimony to the space-defying powers of the ten tribes' geography. Just as the "Asian" tribes reach Ethiopia, the land of the remaining tribes in Arabia borders on India. Benjamin's treatment of the familiar *topos* of the tribes' inaccessibility illustrates this surreal fluidity of space. The desert makes the eighteen days' journey to them impossible, he says. But how do we know that an impossible journey takes eighteen days?

Benjamin of Tudela's travelogue exposes the tensions between the biblical text and its derivatives and the real geography and history to which they supposedly correspond. Contrary to what one might expect, these tensions do not undermine the biblical text. Rather, the creative devices needed for reconciliation enrich the story. Yet while it is clear that Benjamin of Tudela borrows a great deal from Eldad Ha-Dani, there is a very basic difference between the two. Benjamin does not pretend to have made contact with the tribes and is careful to place them in distant, unreachable places. Rhetorically, too, they are distant, known of only through hearsay: in the Asian case, he comments, "there are men of Israel in Persia who say..." and in the Arabian, he prefaces the account with "people say..." This rhetorical device further strengthens the authority of Benjamin's text as travelogue; Benjamin uses this wording *only* concerning the ten tribes. All other things can be taken as authoritative fact.[76] His narrative carries the stamp of the travelogue, the story of a person who went there himself. Benjamin's *Itinerary* circulated widely and was known among learned Christians as well as Jews. In 1575, during a period when interest in the ten tribes reached a new height, it was translated into Latin.[77]

Benjamin's *Itinerary* makes significant contributions to the development of the articulation of the location of the tribes. He clearly places them in two different locations as opposed to one: the vast region in Central Asia between China and Persia in the north and the huge swath of land between Ethiopia, Arabia, and India in the south. The Talmudic idea of their unified exile, as opposed to the scattered Jews, remains. But the territorial coherence assigned to this exile is broken into two parts. Eldad had already suggested the same two locations, but insisted that somehow the tribes communicated with one another. Benjamin, more informed about the world and writing for a more informed audience, cannot allow for this and concedes that the tribes' locations of exile are indeed wholly different places.

In this regard, Benjamin sets the geographical record straight in terms of the possibility that the tribes are also in Africa. While Central Asia was from biblical times the most apparent candidate, Africa (i.e., Ethiopia) was not. The only two clues hitherto had been Talmudic comments that placed Ethiopia at one edge of the world that was ruled by the Persians and that some of the tribes were exiled "to Afriki." Three different figures are responsible for the African possibility as we see it emerge during this period: Eldad, the first to speak explicitly about the tribes in Africa; Rabbi Zemah Gaon, who turned this fantastic story into a legal reality; and finally Benjamin, whose itinerary organized this possibility into a coherent geography. This coherence of geography is possible thanks to what historian David Abulafia identifies as the "lack of sharp lines" of demarcation or boundaries, a lack that produced an array of political and cultural ambiguities in medieval European geographical thinking writ large.[78]

More than anyone before him, Benjamin was in dialogue with the geo-graphical traditions of an *oikoumene* dominated by Islam and Christianity. This did not, of course, transform the story of the ten lost tribes altogether, but allowed for an intensive, often implicit dialogue between Jews and non-Jews over the question of the ten tribes. Both regions were known as the limits of the old *oikoumene* during Roman times, and some of this status still lingered in medieval times. Ethiopia enjoys a unique status in traditional Islamic law. Before the *hijra* (migration) to Medina, Ethiopia was the first place to offer haven to the early Muslims, who were persecuted in Mecca. Muhammad never forgot this history. As a result, Ethiopia is neither of the house of Islam nor a "land of war," the only non-Muslim land in the world "immune from the *jihad*." "Leave the Abyssinians in peace, so long as they do not take the offensive," Muhammad is said to have declared in a *hadith* recorded in the eighth century.[79] Islam did not, however, leave the Abyssinians in peace so quickly, and the several invasions of Ethiopia during the early phase of con-quests failed miserably. Conversely, Islam expanded fast elsewhere in eastern Africa. As a result, Ethiopia, the first Christian kingdom, became the symbol of Christian resistance to Islam, and Europeans came to imagine it as a Christian enclave, an enclosed nation, surviving within an Islamic territory. Central Asia, as we have seen, is the original putative home of Prester John. The Central Asian origins of an ancient group, the Scythians, would in the early modern period give rise to the identification of them as the ten tribes. At the time of Benjamin, however, this region had long been perceived as the original dwell-ing place of many migrant groups and tribes that threatened the Islamic world, such as Tartars, or Turks, and, soon, the Mongols.

The Mongols and Sambatyon

A century after Benjamin's travels, the European perspective was quite differ-ent. Famously, in 1241, the Mongols appeared at the gates of Western Europe after defeating the Hungarians. This came on the heels of the fall of Kiev a few months earlier and within the context of smaller-scale forays into Moravia and toward Vienna. The Mongol threat to Europe seemed more real than ever.[80] In the face of the Mongols, eschatological and apocalyptic rumors and calculations sprang up everywhere.[81]

References to the ten tribes in conjunction with the Mongols show how potent was the Tartar ten tribes theory. The English chronicler Matthew of Paris (c. 1200–1259) gives an account of a Hungarian bishop who interrogated captured warriors from the Mongol army. He was very careful "to ask all the crucial questions," conducting what looked like an anthropological interview based on a specific agenda. He tried hard to find out if the strangers were "Jews," asking if the prisoners had any dietary laws. The answer was no; they ate "frogs, snakes, dogs, and all living beings indiscriminately." This evidence strengthened the suspicion that these were "Gog people." Yet, the possibility that these were the ten tribes persisted. The bishop's account produced mixed results: the prisoners knew nothing about the Jewish faith but apparently had started learning "Hebrew characters" from "some pale men who used to fast often and wore long vestments and did not attack anybody." The bishop believed that the anonymous teachers were "Pharisees and Sadducees."[82] Matthew of Paris, for his part, was adamant that they were the ten tribes. Attempting to reconcile these mixed impressions, he concluded:

> Indeed it appears doubtful whether these Tartars . . . are the people mentioned; for they do not speak in the Hebrew tongue, nor know the Mosaic law . . . nor are they governed by the legal institutes. But the reply to this is, that it nevertheless is probable that they are some of those who were inclosed in the mountains. . . . And as in the time of the government of Moses their rebellious hearts were perverted to an evil way of thinking so that they follow strange gods and unknown customs. . . . they are the Tartars, from a river called Tartar, which runs through their mountains, through which they made their way.[83]

But the Mongols' "roles and levels of eschatological meaning varied greatly as time went by."[84] Whereas the thirteenth-century account of Matthew of Paris unleashed the tribes from their enclosure, the fourteenth-century John of Mandeville enclosed them back inside, this time with the implied help of the Mongols. Perhaps no one better exemplifies the convergence of historical and geographical realities, political and theological aspirations and fears, imagination and myth than Mandeville. Published between 1357 and 1371, the *Travels* were studied and quoted extensively thereafter, with the result that commentary on the resultant "multitext," as one scholar has dubbed it, is well beyond the scope of this study.[85] Several virtually self-explanatory examples suffice to show how Sir John weaves all together in his travelogue. He writes of the "River Sabatory in Archas," somewhere in Syria, which "on the Saturday ranneth fast and all the week after this standeth still and ranneth not or else little."[86] Mandeville places another such marvelous river in his version of the land of "Emperor Prester John." Near the "land of the Great Khan, [this river] ranneth also three days in the week, bringeth with [it] great stones and the rocks also therewith and that great plenty. And anon as they be entered into the Gravelly Sea, they be seen no more but lost for evermore. And those days that [the] river ranneth no man dares enter into it, but in the other days, men dare enter well enough."[87]

Mandeville locates the ten tribes somewhere in Central or northern Asia, beyond the "Mountains of Caspia" where "the Jews of ten lineages be enclosed" together with Gog/Magog and "twenty-two kings with their people." While he does not specifically mention wars between Prester John and the ten tribes, the implication that they had taken place is clear.[88]

Mandeville's mention of the "Great Khan" betrays the triangle of power that connects the ten tribes, Prester John, and the Mongols. Benjamin of Tudela had written of the friendly relationship between the ten tribes and the Kufar al-Turk, the people with no religion who attacked the Muslim world. Mandeville, who writes two centuries after Benjamin and one century after the dramatic appearance of the Mongols on the world's stage, takes a different tack: he marries the two warring dynasties to one another. Writing after the initial scare of the Mongol invasion had abated, Mandeville again reframes the triangle of power and depicts friendly relationships between Prester John and the Mongol khan. "This emperor Prester John taketh always to his wife the daughter of the Great Khan, and Great Khan also in the same wise the daughter of Prester John."[89] While the great lords marry each other's daughters, the ten tribes are conveniently enclosed beyond the mountains.

The Mongol Messiah

In 1260, as Matthew of Paris was composing dreadful reports of the Mongols and arguing that they were the ten tribes, the young Rabbi Abraham Abulafia (1240–1290) left his hometown of Saragossa in Iberia in search of the Sambatyon. This youth set off for the land of Israel but discontinued his search shortly after landing at the city of Acre.[90] War was sweeping the country and on September 3, Mongol and Mamluk armies clashed in Palestine, and the Mongols were famously defeated in the battle of 'Ain Jalut.[91] Moshe Idel comments on the aborted journey that "it is quite possible that Abulafia thought, as did many others of his generation, that the Mongols were themselves the 'hidden ones,' *ha-genuzim*, the ten lost tribes of Israel reputed by legend to be dwelling beyond the Sambation River."[92] Idel also suggests that Abulafia's eventual rejection of "eschatological calculations" for the years 1270 and 1280 "might have been part of his disillusion when learning that the Mongols were not the ten lost tribes."[93]

Abulafia's interest was framed by the premise of "natural redemption," that is, a redemption of the Jews that was to occur in this world, involving this-worldly means such as, in this case, an army of the ten tribes interfering in global politics. As Idel puts it, "in an unstable situation such as this, it would be fitting to suppose that the Jews could also be integrated in an historical process that would allow them a foothold or even a victory by exploitation of a certain constellation of events." Abulafia, the messianic mystic, became "disillusioned" when he learned that the Mongols weren't, as he had hoped, the ten lost tribes.[94] The redemption they might have brought would have been natural and would not have necessitated any "disruption of nature."[95] The persistent search for the Sambatyon and the hope that the Mongols might turn out to be the ten tribes remind us that one man's dreadful apocalypse is another's messianic hope. They also remind us of the potentially vital role, particularly military, that the ten tribes could play in such a scenario—be it of natural redemption or apocalypse. The young Abulafia might well have hoped to enlist the Mongols—that is, the ten tribes—in this process of natural redemption. The Mongols turned out to be just Mongols, but Abulafia's logic was still valid. The sudden appearance of the ten tribes remained a possibility within the redemptive messianic scheme.

4

"A Mighty Multitude of Israelites"

Year 5354 [1594]: In that year, I had the same dream two or three consecutive nights. . . . I was walking along a great river, and I saw a large and mighty multitude of Israelites who were camping there in tents. I entered one tent and I saw their king reclining on his side. . . . When he saw me, he seated me at his side with great joy and said to me: Know that I am the king of Israel, of the tribe of Ephraim, and we have come now because the time has come for the ingathering of the exiles.

— Rabbi Hayyim Vital, rabbi and mystic, Safed, Palestine

An Arab Jew in Rome

In 1524, an unusual person arrived in Rome demanding to see Pope Clement VII (Giulio do Giuliano de' Medici, 1478–1534). He identified himself as "prince David son of King Solomon and brother of my older brother King Yosef, king of the tribes of Reuben and half of Manasseh," or, in short, David Reuveni. He bore a simple message from his brother. The king of the Israelites offered a military and political alliance between Christendom (Europe) and the kingdom of the ten tribes against the Muslim Arabs and Turks.[1] David presented himself also as "field marshal" of his kingdom's army of "300,000 combatants."[2] According to the Vatican's record of the interview, the pope identified David's homeland as a kingdom of "Arab-Jews"—

Hebraeis Arabibus. David testified that he had come from the "Desert of Habor in Arabia."[3]

David told the pope that his people were in the midst of a military struggle against the Muslims in Arabia and that the latter were winning because of their superior "artillery." David's people lacked knowledge in this type of warfare, and he asked that "armaments against the Muslim Arabs and Turks" and "a craftsman to make cannons and gun powder" be sent to help: "It could be done easily with a Portuguese boat that will come through the Red Sea." Valiantly, David offered to lead the expedition personally and promised that, when his people had the requested weapons, they would "overcome all Muslims in war and subjugate Mecca."[4] In his Hebrew journal, in which he detailed his journeys, David also claims to have offered his help in mediating between the pope and the various political powers in Western Europe.

David claimed to be many things, but the report of Giambattista Ramusio (1485–1557), an Orientalist who interviewed him several times in 1530 on behalf of the Venetian government, shows that the most frequent identification David used—and the one that was apparently universally received, at least initially—was his ten tribes affiliation.[5] David used important details from Benjamin of Tudela's *Itinerary* to help authenticate his identity as a member of the tribe of Reuben.[6] And Habor, as we read in the biblical narrative, was one of the locations to which the Assyrians had exiled the tribes. David, versed in the sources, said that was where he came from.

David's plan to redeem Israel by the might of the ten tribes represents what Abraham Abulafia would have called a natural redemption. The idea of a Christian alliance with a powerful non-European, non-Muslim force from the east that was to crush the Muslims was an oft-entertained idea over the centuries, and had been at least since Bishop Hugo of Jabala produced the story of Prester John.

If the Jews of Italy and Portugal saw David as a member of the ten tribes, the Christians were thinking of a possible link to the legendary Christian figure Prester John. It was widely known that missions on behalf of the pope had been made by merchants, monks, and all sorts of adventurers to the "Great Khans" in the east. These schemes were similar, in their basic parameters, to what David was now proposing to the pope—an alliance against the Muslims. Ramusio, who shortly after the David affair for the first time published Marco Polo's *Travels,* was certainly aware of Polo's mission to the Mongol great khan Qubilai (1215–1294).[7] Marco Polo (1254–c. 1324) also told a number of stories about Prester John, his family, and his territories in Asia.[8]

As we have seen, Ethiopia enjoyed a certain mystic glow among Europeans—either as the land of Prester John or, at the very least, as the imagined stalwart African Christian kingdom surrounded by Muslim lands.[9] All political parties involved—Venice, Portugal, and above all the pope—saw potential political gains if they properly exploited the story.[10] David's great conviction impressed Ramusio, who noted that David "was obsessed with returning the Hebrew people to the Promised Land....The Jews truly adore him like a messiah."[11] Later, when David appeared in Portugal, he caused an even stronger reaction among the local "converso" community—Jews who had been forcibly baptized just a little over two decades earlier.[12]

It is clear that the story of a man claiming to come from the ten tribes brought together a chain of connections. Yet, what counts in understanding the episode is not so much factual knowledge of specific events and history as a certain world historical imagination and the coming together of multiple regional threads. Talmudic and biblical prophecies and predictions concerning the ten tribes were at work both in David's self-presentation and in the reception to him. Contemporaneous elaborations on the messianic process and the possible role of the ten lost tribes within it played a key role as well. Finally, growing geographic knowledge about the east fused with mythic traditions such as that surrounding Prester John to create a context in which David was rendered intelligible—indeed, was rendered possible. These elaborations are significant, telling us the potent meaning of the ten tribes for Jews, for Christians, and for sixteenth-century Europe.

The Loss of a Nation

A rare document from the beginning of the fifteenth century sheds new light on the appearance of the ten tribes in European Jewish thought at the time. It involves a certain Solomon ha-Levi (c. 1352–1435), a noted Talmudist and the chief rabbi of Burgos, Spain, who converted to Christianity in 1391, in the wake of the notorious anti-Jewish pogroms. Shortly thereafter, ha-Levi—now Paul of Burgos or Pablo de Santa Maria—received an admonishing communication from his friend the physician Yehosu'a ha-Lorki (fl. 1400) of Alcañiz.[13] Ha-Lorki testified that, upon hearing news of his friend's conversion, he was greatly upset: "My thoughts were wandering and my heart won't rest and sleep." What had lured his friend to another faith? Was it material pleasures such as "money and majesty," or a desire "to see the pleasant face of gentile women"? Perhaps it was "philosophical inquiry" that "deceived you to turn things around"? Ha-Lorki's third guess touched upon the question of history: "Perhaps you have seen the loss of our nation [hefsed ha-ummah], and our recent troubles...and you began thinking maybe the name of Israel shall not be remembered any more?"[14] In case Israel's doom was indeed the reason for the conversion, ha-Lorki had a ready answer:

> I know that you are well aware of what is famous among us from the books of travels of those who pass through the itineraries of the earth . . . , from the epistle of Maimonides, and from what we hear from the merchants at the edges of [the] earth, that in this day the majority of our people is in the lands of Babylon and Yemen where the exile of Jerusalem first went, in addition to those who dwell in the lands of Persia and Media who are of the exile of Samaria, [the ten tribes] who are today a great nation [countless] as the sand of the sea . . . and according to the true faith, even if God decreed that the Jews of Christendom be annihilated and destroyed, still the nation shall exist and be whole, and this [calamity] shall not bring the weakening of the trust [in God].[15]

Pablo de Santa Maria answered the letter (in "bad" Hebrew, for which he apologized), but unfortunately restricted himself to general comments; we can only imagine what he made of ha-Lorki's argument. He went on to a career as a Christian theologian that culminated in his 1415 appointment as bishop of Burgos—a rare achievement, in that he managed over the course of his life to preside over two different religious communities in the same town.[16]

Ha-Lorki's letter is an excellent illustration of the potent and growing significance of the ten tribes within the context of an acute problem—the "perishing of the nation." The pogroms of 1391 had been the most destructive, in terms of the loss of Jewish lives, since the Crusades. The most significant outcome was a massive wave of conversion to Christianity that created a large converso community in Spain.[17] It is not clear how many lives were lost and how many Jews did convert, but the numbers were perceived, at the time and much later, to be very high.[18]

In such a context, the promise of the "countless" ten tribes, innumerable in person, was a source of hope. One can conjecture that the countlessness of the tribes was already a source of comfort for Benjamin of Tudela and perhaps even for Josephus—the first to discuss their large number. It is clear that Benjamin and Josephus were the source of ha-Lorki's confidence in his statements about the tribes. Ha-Lorki's argument provides us with the first clear sign, chronologically speaking, that in this period Jewish sources such as the Talmud were not the only ones considered authoritative. Books of travels and news from merchants at the edges of the earth were also referenced in support of the given truth of the tribes' existence.

It is not coincidental that ha-Lorki, a physician well versed in Greek philosophy, was the first to include travel accounts as evidence in support of scriptural statements on the ten tribes. Combining the two in relation to the ten tribes was a significant development and marks the beginning of what might be called the "scientific" approach to the topic. Implicitly, ha-Lorki also set the scientific parameters or methodology for a successful search: follow the itineraries of the travelers and merchants who have covered the length and breadth of the earth. With ha-Lorki's view, the ten tribes were now a provable fact, not only a note in scripture. It is not incidental that the first time that this idea appears is in the context of a debate—between a Jew and a (New) Christian. Over time, this would become the dominant mode of discussion of the tribes. The scriptural became the scriptural/scientific, which became the scientific alone.

Ha-Lorki closes with a confident statement about his "strength of faith in the physical continuity of the Jewish people." His inclusion of the ten tribes in this context was apt. After all, the loss of the tribes marked the greatest demographic defeat inscribed in Jewish memory since biblical times. To insist that they were not completely lost was one way to ensure faith and nourish hope—and bolster in number the total world population of Jews. The question of Jewish numerical insignificance became acutely connected to the question of the ten lost tribes.

A century later, as anxieties became even more acute, the role of the tribes as a source of hope became even more pronounced. The great Iberian Jewish statesman, philosopher, and scholar Don Isaac Abravanel (1437–1508) stressed that the three "unquestionable characteristics" of the messianic moment were its coming "only after long exile, [that] the Ten Tribes exiled in Assyria would return, [and that] God's terrible vengeance would be wrought upon the nation that persecuted Israel."[19] This leader of Iberian Jewry, whose political experience was unparalleled among world Jewry of the time, wrote in the wake of the 1492 expulsion of the Jews from Spain. Abravanel was mostly concerned with the Jewish sentiment "that everything was lost" and with the "growing despair" that was becoming prevalent among Jews. These feelings of despair were "largely inspired by the numerical insignificance of Jews."[20] Tragedy, conversion, and dwindling numbers—all called for the shoring up of the Jewish people with some massive influx. Who better to provide it than the long-lost tribes in their countless numbers and military strength?

The expulsion from Spain, the "last Jewish stronghold," worsened the despair. Not only were many lives lost, along with Jewish property, during and in the wake of the expulsions, but tens of thousands of Iberian Jews gave up their Jewish identity and chose to stay in Spain as Christians. Thousands more lost their Jewish identity in 1497, when the Portuguese Crown declared all Jews within Portugal's borders to be Christians.[21] To Abravanel, the numbers seemed massive. He estimated that the number of Jews expelled from Spain was 300,000.[22] The heavy sense of Jewish numerical insignificance cast a shadow on the "feasibility of Jewish redemption in a realistic manner." Restoring hope, forcefully, was of utmost importance for Abravanel, and "the very existence of the Ten Tribes refuted the contention that everything was lost."[23] To put it crassly, the game was not over; the Jews still had some cards up their sleeves.[24]

In addition to providing psychological comfort, the ten tribes played an important role in the theology Abravanel developed in the wake of Christian anti-Jewish polemics, which argued that the role of Jews in the divine plan had ended with the destruction of the temple. As Benzion Netanyahu explains, insisting that the return from Babylon to the Second Temple was not the complete and final redemption was crucial for Abravanel since he was determined to show that "not everything was lost." If the Second Temple was indeed the redemption promised by the prophets, then its destruction signaled what Christians had been arguing all along—that God had removed his grace from the Jews and initiated a new covenant with humanity. On the other hand, if the Second Temple was *not* the final redemptive moment, then the biblical promise was still valid. The central proof that the Second Temple period was not the final redemption was the fact that the ten tribes did not return with Ezra.

Ultimately, role of the ten tribes ends up embedded in the messianic process itself. Not only is their return one of the signs of imminent redemption, it also plays a "prominent part" in the "messianic wars" and the "destruction of Israel's enemies." In sum, "there had to be a realistic and positive answer to the feeling of national helplessness which was eating away the essential Jewish spirit. A this-worldly, concrete and understandable answer was provided by the Ten Tribes."[25] Abravanel upgraded the place of the ten tribes by making them an integral part of Jewish political thinking.

Abravanel, a Portuguese Jew who made a remarkable political career in Spain before the expulsion of 1492, finalized his ideas about the ten tribes' role in the messianic process in Venice, where he died in 1508. This was only sixteen years before David appeared in Italy, whose Jewry became toward the mid-sixteenth century what historian Yosef Yerushalmi aptly calls a "news-agency," copying and disseminating eschatological and messianic information and messages.[26] The this-worldliness of Abravanel's messianic scenario marks an important commonality between David's plan to start wars and regain Palestine and the role he assigns to himself as the spokesman for the ten tribes' plan. Perhaps more important than the plan to regain Palestine was the proof that David introduced that the ten tribes still existed in large numbers.

Abravanel expressed the anxieties and desires of his generation, into which the advent of David fit extraordinarily well. It is tempting to think that David had read or heard about Abravanel's messianic scenario and the role the ten tribes play in it. This is not possible, however; the latter's book was only printed and spread outside Italy from 1526.[27] David, it seems, was still working only with Benjamin of Tudela's accounts of the tribes. But whether or not he knew of Abravanel's ideas, David did indeed embody what the great statesman had articulated as the Jewish hope to see in the ten tribes an exhibit of Jewish power. That is to say, for people familiar with Abravanel's ideas, David must have seemed like the right man from the right place. Indeed, David did not leave anybody indifferent in Europe. As Rabbi Hayyim Vital's recurring dream shows, the military image of David was still evocative several decades after his death, even in Palestine.[28] It is time then, to turn our gaze to the Africa and Arabia of David's time and reincorporate them into the story.

News from Africa: Arabian, Ethiopian, Italian Connections

As we have seen, Ethiopia was tagged as a mysterious location, the home of different types of *eschatoi*, as early as antiquity. In the Jewish context, Ethiopia has been the putative location of the ten tribes, or some of them, at least from the eighth century on. Ethiopia also became the presumed home of Prester John. The process through which Prester John turned from a Central Asian khan into an African ruler is beyond the scope of this chapter. It is important to stress, however, that in this process Ethiopian and African rulers played a decisive role, more important than the European geographical and messianic imagination alone.[29]

African attempts to make contact with Europe steered the European imagination to look for Prester John in Africa and finally to fix on Ethiopia as the rumored home of the legendary Christian king. It was the Ethiopians who first initiated contact with Europe. In 1306, an embassy of thirty Ethiopians on their way to the king of "the Spains" was briefly detained in Genoa and questioned by the priest and cartographer Giovanni da Carignano (fl. 1291–1321). Carignano's report and map did not survive, but he is generally believed to be the first European to locate the Prester in Africa and not in Asia—Prester John's original home. In 1339, another mapmaker with ties to Genoa, Angelino Dulcert, specifically mentioned Ethiopia as Prester John's home in his nautical charts. By the late fifteenth century, Ethiopia was firmly established as such. The European tendency to confuse India—one of the original homes of Prester John—and Ethiopia plus the latter's fame for being the only Christian kingdom in Africa were at work as well.[30] That is to say, shortly before David's arrival in Europe, Ethiopia had already attained a special place in Christian as well as Jewish global geographies. For Jews, it was the alleged land of the ten tribes, and for Christians, it was the home of Prester John. Aspects of these two geographies converged in a way that strongly shaped David's career in Europe.

Several decades before his arrival in Italy, Italian Jewry, and perhaps some non-Jews as well, were troubled by news of bizarre happenings in Ethiopia and Arabia. The rumors depicted a decidedly new situation, one that involved both the ten tribes and Prester John. In 1488, the great Italian Talmudic commentator Obadiah di Bertinoro (c. 1450–1516) sent a letter from Jerusalem containing new information on the ten tribes and the River Sambatyon. Obadiah, a man of great reputation whose commentary on the Mishnah is considered an outstanding authority, reported on revealing conversations he had with pilgrims of all three religions, gathered near the Temple Mount in Jerusalem:

> I made enquiries concerning the Sambatyon. . . . I have no clear information, just hearsay, but one thing I know without doubt: in one of the borders of the kingdom of Prester John there are high mountains and valleys that can be traversed in ten days' Journey, and which are certainly inhabited by descendants of Israel. They have five princes or kings, and people say that they carried on great wars against the Prester John for more than a century.[31]

Obadiah was in the right place to hear such rumors. The area around the Temple Mount, or Haram al-Sharif, in Jerusalem was, and still is, one of the busiest locations in the world, bringing in pilgrims, travelers, merchants, and adventurers of all religions. In 1489, he sent another letter relating conversations with Yemeni Jews whom he had met in Jerusalem, who told him, "It is now well-known through reliable Ishmaelite merchants that the river Sambation is fifty days' journey from them in the wilderness, and like a thread, surrounds the whole land where the descendants of Israel dwell." Obadiah also met an "old Ashkenazi Rabbi" who told him:

> The Jews of Aden also say that the Israelites dwelling on the borders of their territory, of whom I wrote in my first letter, are now at war with the people of Prester John (the Abyssinian), and that some of them have been taken prisoner and brought to Cairo. I have seen some of these with my own eyes; these Jews are a month's journey in the wilderness from the others who live on the Sambation. The Christians who come from the territory of the Prester John relate that the Jews there, who are at war with the people of Prester John, have suffered great defeats, and we are very anxious to know if these accounts are true.[32]

It seems, then, that some Christian Ethiopian monks along with Muslim merchants coming from Africa supported the stories told by the Yemeni Jews. Evidently, the Yemenis had been telling these stories in Jerusalem over a long period; no one refuted them. Yemeni Jews feature as the main informants in similar letters sent to Italy by other rabbis.

It seems that Jerusalem and, consequently, Italy had been inundated with news relayed by Yemeni Jews on this particular issue for about a century prior to David's arrival in Italy.[33] Yemeni Jews served as an important source of information about the goings-on in Ethiopia. They were not only the community closest to the African kingdom, but the only one in the vicinity. They enjoyed a great deal of authority because no one else could corroborate or refute the stories they told. As for the content of the news, one senses that the developments in Ethiopia were quite new to the Yemenis themselves, as they began relating the stories only around the mid-fifteenth century, when the "old Ashkenazi Rabbi" was young. Finally, they themselves—not only their listeners—seemed to be fascinated with what they had to narrate. Was there a Yemeni conspiracy to spread lies about Ethiopia, and why did it all start in the mid-fifteenth century?

The recent historiography of the Falasha Jews and of Ethiopia in general suggests that these Yemeni informants were telling a version of real events. Steven Kaplan, a historian of Ethiopian Jewry, has convincingly shown that, around the beginning of the fifteenth century, amid efforts of the Solomonic Christian dynasty (which began c. 1270) to strengthen the Christian grip on Ethiopia, certain peripheral groups resisted state policies and assumed a "Jewish" identity. These groups, recognized in various Ethiopian chronicles as *ayhud* (Jews), became over time a more cohesive group mostly because of the economic sanctions that a resistance to Christianization entailed: the "previous inchoate group identity began to take on new social and economic overtones." The religious articulation of this new identity as "Jewish" took place under the leadership of monks (*falasyan*), who introduced "biblical-Hebraic elements found in Ethiopian Christianity," which "were adopted and adapted to develop a distinctive Jewish identity." This became eventually the "far more centralized and distinctive group known as the *Falasha* [Beta Israel]."[34]

The group's appearance was noticed to some extent by Jewish communities in the Middle East when "Jews from the land of Prester John" began appearing in slave markets at the beginning of the sixteenth century.[35] Its rise did not please the state's ruling fanatical Christian dynasty; there was a series of violent conflicts between the new Judaized group and the emperors. Of particular importance was the period of Zra'a Ya'ecop (1434–1468), a zealot whose reign was characterized by "religious nationalism" and punctuated by repeated attempts to forcibly reincorporate the Beta Israel into Christian society.[36] After Ya'ecop's death, state pressure eased, and the balance tipped slightly in favor of Beta Israel: "During the period from 1468 to 1632 the Beta Israel displayed their most sophisticated political-military organization." These new Jews "were involved in some of the most dramatic conflicts with the Ethiopian Emperors."[37]

This generally corresponds with the basic description of the happenings in Ethiopia as told in Jerusalem by the Jews of Yemen. To Jews outside Ethiopia, the Falasha must have seemed to appear out of nowhere—as indeed they did, since they did not exist previously. The stories of Eldad and of Benjamin of Tudela about the tribes' military prowess must also have played a decisive role in the Yemeni interpretation of the news of intrareligious violence involving a military order of "Jews" and mighty Christian kings. With the newly added dimension of Prester John's residence in Ethiopia, news of the events in that country led the Jews of Yemen to interpret the violence as the struggle between Prester John and the ten tribes.

Already in the early 1400s, the Iberian ha-Lorki had written with great conviction about the ten tribes' cycles of war and truce with Prester John in the land of the Cushites. But while ha-Lorki was simply reelaborating the story of the ten tribes in order to accommodate the legend of Prester John, the Yemenis and their European interlocutors worked with real events, giving rise to news about the ten tribes that was grounded in historical reality rather than elaborate speculation. By the mid-fifteenth century, stories of Prester John and the ten tribes provided an indispensable, ready-made tool with which Jews could interpret the real events in Ethiopia. It may well be that Yemeni Jews were reporting on wars between the ten tribes and Christian kings and that their Italian, European, and Jewish interlocutors were adding another layer to this interpretation by identifying the Christian kings with Prester John.

David Reuveni himself spent time in the Middle East just before coming to Italy. Letters sent to Italy from Palestine and Syria during the 1520s show that David indeed visited various Middle Eastern communities—Alexandria, Gaza, Safed, Jerusalem, Beirut, and Damascus—in the early 1520s, leaving in each a trail of stories and impressions. All tell more or less the same tale: a story about a "dark man" who said that he was from the "tribe of Re'uven" and who told stories about the ten tribes and their wonders somewhere in the area of Ethiopia and Arabia. In one, he mentions an army of the tribes of Dan and Re'uven composed of "600,000" (*shishim ribo*) men. Another recounts the wonders of the River Sambatyon.[38] While Bertinoro's Yemenis simply related their stories of the ten tribes, David went further and invented a ten tribes identity.

In the later part of the fifteenth century, Yemeni Jewry was swept with yet another messianic fervor, one that resulted in a major violent conflict with the southern Arab tribes that rushed to quell it. We cannot tell to what degree this Yemeni Jewish messianic fervor was at work in David's mind and helped to shape his own aspirations, but it is clear that he was intimately familiar with Arabian military might.[39] It is also probable that David witnessed another violent development in Arabian history: the Ottoman advent to the Hijaz and Arabia. By 1517, the Ottomans had taken over Mecca and had control over the caravan routes leading back and forth to Arabia.[40]

So it is that two momentous political and military events took place in David's lifetime before he left Arabia: the suppression of a Jewish movement by southern Arabian tribes and the Ottoman takeover of the peninsula and Mecca. (The Ottoman control of the peninsula in 1517 may explain why David traveled to Palestine through Africa and not via the Arabian side of the Red Sea trade route.) David's plans to "fight Islam" and specifically "to subjugate Mecca" in the context of war with the Ottomans shed further light on David's state of mind and motives. David's focus on Mecca also betrays the Arabian context as the one with which he was familiar. The Arabian context is not complete, however, without the Portuguese one.

The Red Sea Trade Route and the Portuguese

David outlined his plan to take over Mecca, stating that it would be easily accomplished by a "Portuguese boat coming through the Red Sea." He was familiar, then, with Portugal's naval power and was aware of the Portuguese presence in his native region; he had probably seen Portuguese ships and was able to assess their military applications. There is some novelty in the plan that he suggests, using gunpowder-based warfare on boats to decide the battlefield on land. It had already been experimented with in the Venetian-Ottoman wars of 1499–1503, but this was twenty-five years prior to David's appearance in Europe and in the Mediterranean, far from his own home region. David could not have known much about naval warfare without first-hand experience. He must have seen Portuguese boats elsewhere, that is, in the Red Sea.[41]

The Red Sea provides access to the Indian Ocean and connects Ethiopia with Arabia. Even after the discovery of the Cape of Good Hope, it remained important as a major stronghold en route to India. The trade route is one of the most ancient in world history, connecting, eventually, the Mediterranean world with the Indian Ocean. On land, the route stretched from Alexandria and Cairo, up the Nile and along the East African coast, all the way south to the

Aden straits. On the eastern African side of these narrow straits was Ethiopia, endpoint on a trail of several important city ports.

Admittedly, David's "reputation for veracity does not stand very high," but "there is no doubt...that he had first-hand knowledge of Eastern Sudan, for the details set out in [his] note are remarkably accurate, and could not in his time be derived from any literary source."[42] We know that he began in Jiddah, Arabia, and then crossed the Red Sea to Africa and proceeded from Suaqin to the Nile Valley, and from there to Egypt. David's descriptions of the "Blue Nile region in the Sudan is not only considered accurate, it is also the earliest we [have] available."[43]

David's suggestion to involve the Portuguese also made sense to Pope Clement VII. Indeed, he eventually did send David to them with a letter requesting that they assist him. In this regard, the pope acted in a manner similar to that of al-Qayrawan's Jews after their encounter with Eldad: the pope turned to the highest relevant authority on the matter in question. Portugal was the recognized authority on the region featured in David's stories and the only European power active in that district of the world. Portugal had knowledge and interests in that region that no one else in Europe shared.[44] In his letter of September 17, 1524, to the king of Portugal, Clement VII specifically stated that he was interested in information that only the Portuguese could have had at that point: "We, who are very distant from these places, could not recognize [as truth] and thoroughly assess the nature of said David's story. On the other hand, we did not want to dismiss [him] completely. Therefore we decided to send him to your highness that has numerous people traveling frequently to these places and tour[ing] them."[45]

Portuguese involvement in Africa began as early as 1415, when they conquered Ceuta in North Africa. They are, of course, famous for their series of navigations along the African coasts, the discovery of the route to India and the Indian Ocean, and the voyages that produced such heroes as Magellan, da Gama,[46] and Dias. Portuguese maritime activity in Africa was accompanied by voyages on land that were not insignificant.

On February 4, 1525, a few months after he wrote to the Portuguese k Clement VII also wrote a letter to the king of Ethiopia, David Alnaza. (Emperor Lebna Dengel David II). He introduced David Reuveni and h story and asked for Ethiopia's general support for David's plans to fight the Muslims. Justifying the bizarre letter of recommendation on behalf of a Jew, the pope explained: "God sometimes uses enemies in order to punish ei mies."[47] Clement VII did not have anything specific to ask from the Ethiopian emperor with respect to David, and David himself did not even mention Ethiopia in his plans. Yet, Clement VII clearly saw the African Christian kingdom as an integral part of any future Portuguese move following David's appearance in Europe—and so should we.

Portuguese activities in Africa and the Indian Ocean were related to the objectives and plans David had lauded in various places in Italy. As historian John Thornton has summarized, "the search for Prester John and a route to his lands was a way to find support behind the Muslim power of Northern Africa." This objective was interconnected with such other Portuguese goals as war against the Muslims of North Africa, exploration of the Atlantic, and "developing trade in more prosaic commodities such as gold and slaves."[48] Finally, within the broader context, the Portuguese kings had only a few decades earlier been commissioned by the Vatican to carry out the mission of finding the eastern Christians.[49] For Western Christendom, eastern Christians were a bit of an anomaly and represented the lost sons of the church. The quest was an enduring mission that fed on rumors and encouraged travel.

Here, we have an intersection of the imperial and religious desires in the region where the Red Sea runs into the Indian Ocean and the history of communication between Portugal and Ethiopia and particularly the role of diverse individuals in it. The Yemeni connection of the late fifteenth century helps us to situate David within the context of Yemeni pilgrims reporting rumors of Ethiopia as the land of Prester John and the ten lost tribes, but it is in the early sixteenth-century Portuguese/Ethiopian context that David's plans finally fall into place.

The convergence of these various contexts in Ethiopia, the presumed location of Prester John, was highly charged at the time of David's arrival in Rome. This was so not only for political reasons, but also for geographic ones, which became meaningful for the first time in history with the coming of the first European Christian imperial power to the region. Ethiopia was located across the straits from Aden and was a gate to the Indian Ocean. It was also located behind North African and Mediterranean Muslim powers. The Portuguese, therefore, were highly interested in finding access to the land of Prester John and to East Africa, and they tried to obtain them by using both seafaring and espionage. These Europeans were maritime pioneers off the African shores, and the Portuguese did not waste any time as they completed their Atlantic explorations along the West African coast—which would have yielded a sea route to Ethiopia. They sent emissaries and spies to the Christian kingdom through the Mediterranean and Egypt. On May 7, 1487, a year before the return of Bartolomeu Dias (1450–1500) from his famous tour to the Cape of Good Hope, the enigmatic Pedro da Covilhan (c. 1450–1530) left for Ethiopia and India in search of Prester John.[50] Covilhan was not the first nor the last to be sent to gather information, but his trip was the most remarkable. While he might not be directly connected to David's story, his career and character are a wonderful illustration of the culture of rumors that revolved around Portuguese activity in the region.

Covilhan's story is full of inconsistencies and complications,[51] but we can be sure that he visited India, the Middle East, and various regions in Africa. He knew North Africa well; he carried out delicate missions there for the Portuguese Crown. Most of what we know about him comes from the contradictory accounts of persons who met him in Ethiopia and from the few letters he sent to Europe. The most important account is from Friar Francisco Alvares (1465–1541), who met him in Ethiopia in 1520, many years after Covilhan had first arrived.[52] "This man Pedro de Covilhan knows all the languages that can be spoken, both of Christians, Moors, and Gentiles, and who knows all the things for which he was sent; moreover he gives accounts of them if they were present before him."[53] What was needed on the Red Sea trade route was the ability to engage with a diverse mix of languages, religions, and cultures. Covilhan, a master storyteller in Alvares's portrayal, clearly had a truly remarkable career as a loyal soldier, spy, and diplomat.[54]

This experience made Covilhan the perfect man for forging Portuguese alliances in East Africa and finding a way to the land of Prester John. Originally, Covilhan set out for Egypt without a clear assignment except to find an overland spice route. Covilhan then headed to India, then back to Cairo, where two Jewish spies sent by King Joaõ II intercepted him to deliver special instructions from the king. Covilhan was to concentrate on finding the Prester, for whom the spies were carrying a letter. Addressed to the "Precious King," it inquired whether Prester John could provide "entrance" to India, the final Portuguese destination.[55] Beckingham observes, "the difficult decision which the King of Portugal and his advisers naturally hesitated to make in the years from 1488 to 1497 was whether to send a fleet to India without first discovering what help if any might be obtainable from the Prester John."[56] The question of Prester John was not merely a romantic pursuit but a concrete military question.

Upon receiving his new directions, Covilhan sent an update to Lisbon, narrating his travels so far. He then set out on a long series of journeys, ultimately crossing the Gulf of Aden to Zeila (in today's Somalia), then made his way to Ethiopia, having become convinced that this country indeed was the land of Prester John. His career in Ethiopia was astonishing.[57] He was well received by Negus Eskander (1471–1494), a member of the Solomonic dynasty who was happy to receive foreign Christian attention. There were a few Italians there already, but Covilhan was certainly seen as the first official European representative in Ethiopia. When Eskander passed away in 1494, however,

Covilhan found himself detained, or so he claimed, by Eskander's successors. The Ethiopian rulers apparently loved him so much that they simply wanted to keep him at the court forever. Covilhan married an Ethiopian woman and had in the following decades a Rasputinesque life in the Ethiopian court. He lost virtually all contact with Portugal until 1520, when Father Alvares discovered him. By that time, he spent thirty-three years in Ethiopia.

To Alvares, "this honorable man of merit and credit" seemed to be well established. He was living near the court, and the only thing he seemed to complain of was the fact that in "the thirty-three years that had passed he had not confessed . . . because in this country they do not keep the secret of confession." Covilhan instead had been accustomed to go "to church and there confessed his sins to God."[58] Deeply affected, the monk immediately adopted Covilhan as his "spiritual son." Covilhan told Alvares about Prester John's wars with the Moors in the region and how, he, Covilhan, had taken active part.[59]

Though one gets the impression that Covilhan was the only foreigner in the region, we know that Italians were there as well. Alvares describes the seaport city of Manadeley (in northeastern Ethiopia) as swarming with "merchants of all nations."[60] Covilhan was able to furnish his Portuguese guests with a wealth of information on the geography of the land and the East African region, mentioning to Alvares that "the Nile rises [in] or issues from" the "kingdom of Gojama" (Gojam, in northwestern Ethiopia).

The report turns vague, however, with regard to what lies beyond the borders of the kingdom of Gojam. Alvares says that all that he was able to learn is that "there are deserts and mountains and beyond them Jews." Alvares adds a strange disclaimer: "I do not credit it or affirm it; I speak as I heard general report[s] and not from persons whom I can quote."[61] Clearly, a discussion of Jews in Ethiopia was problematic. Was he referencing the *ayhud,* who still opposed and resisted the ruling dynasty?

Covilhan's career illustrates the extent to which European powers seeking paths to the Indian Ocean relied on information supplied by individuals and their investment in maintaining a network of information gatherers. In the absence of widely accessible geographic knowledge, such individuals were of immense importance. Europeans also had to rely heavily on Others to guarantee safe travel in non-Christian lands: "On many occasions . . . a messenger, often a Jew, an Armenian, or a convert from Islam, traveled overland through the Moslem countries, in disguise if necessary."[62] Such conditions produced the marvelous careers of, among others, Leo Africanus—a Christian convert from Islam—and the Moroccan Jewish spy Samuel Pallache (b. 1550), who was able to inhabit no less than "three worlds."[63] In this regard, the early success of David Reuveni in Rome and Lisbon was not unusual at all and belongs to what historian Miriam Eliav-Feldon aptly describes and analyzes as European "credulity."[64] Outside Europe, on the Red Sea, there was also a reasonably active trail of spies, merchants, and messengers of all sorts. Like other projects related to the quest for Prester John, it was a scene that constantly bred rumors.[65]

The Portuguese were by now able to monitor significant sectors of traffic in the Indian Ocean, but could not gain control of Aden. And "control over [Aden] was crucial to the maintenance of Portuguese presence in the Indian Ocean and beyond."[66] This rendered Ethiopia central to Portuguese plans. With Ethiopian supplies and armies, they could lay a much more effective siege on Aden. In 1510, the Ethiopian queen Eleni, wife of Zra'a Ya'ecop, sent a letter to the king of Portugal, Manuel I (1469–1521). On behalf of her son, she wrote: "I wish that finally and totally, the vermin of infidel Moors be wiped off the face of the earth.... If we combine our... military powers, we shall have... sufficient forces to destroy and eradicate [them]." She offered precisely what the Portuguese most needed: large numbers of ground troops and logistical support for a fleet operating far from home.

An envoy working for the Ethiopian court and carrying Queen Eleni's letter slowly made his way to meet the Portuguese. An Armenian merchant based in Cairo, as an Ottoman subject he was able to move freely in Muslim lands. This Matheus headed east to Zeila en route to India. Disguised as a Muslim, he was hoping to meet the Portuguese in their newly acquired post in the Arabian Sea and sail to India. In 1513, after many troubles, Matheus arrived in India, where he finally met Afonso de Albuquerque in Goa. Afonso promptly sent the man to Lisbon, where he arrived in February 1514.

Matheus was well received in both Goa and Lisbon: "Catholic Europe and the Portuguese Court were excited by this appearance." Soon after, the Portuguese king, Dom Manuel, was publicly endorsed by Pope Leo X to spearhead Christendom's war against Islam and was promised all future spoils from infidel lands—this just after Manuel dutifully informed the pope that an "ambassador" from Prester John had arrived in his court. King Manuel ended up sending two delegations to Ethiopia following Matheus's appearance in Lisbon;[67] one of them finally arrived in Ethiopia in 1520 (without Matheus, who died en route) and spent six years there before its members were dispatched back to Lisbon. Thus, shortly before David's "embassy," a Prester John "equivalent" was really in motion.

References to Matheus as a "liar" who took advantage of both the Ethiopians and the Portuguese occur several times in Alvares's narrative. The Ethiopian emperor first disavowed Matheus, then changed his mind and, in a letter to Dom Manuel, acknowledged that it was Queen Eleni who had sent

Matheus "because at the time I was eleven."[68] (This letter arrived in Portugal in 1527 and was partly responsible for the demise of David and his fall from grace in the Portuguese court. If Matheus was a liar, maybe David was one too.)

It is tempting to look for a direct connection between Matheus and David Reuveni: both arrived in Europe and proposed military alliances and cooperation against Islam. Aaron Aescoly, who dedicated years of work to David, considered the possibility that Matheus was an imposter and even wondered whether he and David had met at some point and exchanged views. But rather than search for evidence of such links, I would like to focus on the African/Middle Eastern realities that produced certain crucial aspects of David's story. As we have seen, the Yemeni Jews who reported on the wars between Prester John and the ten tribes were in fact interpreting contemporary reports about the events in Ethiopia between the 1460s and 1480s. News about clashes between a zealous Christian dynasty and a Jewish opposition were read as ten tribes wars. Just as Christian Europeans tended to translate the core features of the legend of Prester John into Ethiopia, Jews from across the Aden straits translated them along the lines of the ten lost tribes.

Ultimately, David's story allows us to see how the ten tribes were present in a complicated web of converging forces: European expansion in the Indian Ocean, perceived global conflict between Christianity and Islam, hard-to-decipher events in a still-mysterious African land. Clearly, David's own creative personality had a lot to do with bringing the ten tribes to Europe's attention. But what enabled his story was the long legacy of debates about the tribes that placed them in the distant, old, southern edge of the world—somewhere between Ethiopia, Arabia, and India—and furnished them with military prowess. This legacy was created long before David and was part of the context that received him. We return now to Italy and to the relationship between the ten lost tribes and global geographical thinking.

Itinera Mundi: Lost Tribes in an Exposed World

In 1525, two years after David showed up in Italy, Rabbi Abraham Farissol, a resident of Ferrara originally from Avignon, composed the first Hebrew geography of the world. *Igeret Orhot ʿOlam*[69] (Itineraries of the World) is a typical Renaissance tome, similar to many other works produced at the time. It is, as its author called it, a *cosmografia*, based on the most recent news of the geographic discoveries of, mostly, the Spaniards and the Portuguese. It is a unique document, a Jewish global geography written in Hebrew as an "entertainment." Farissol says that he wrote it for the consumption of "those who distract themselves from the troubles and the sorrows with poetry of lust and books of ancient wars that never took place."[70] The comment underscores Farissol's scientific approach to geographic facts. Historian David Ruderman has shown that Farissol was well educated in the recent scientific and geographic discoveries of his time and shared the values of other scholars of the Renaissance—among them a curiosity and fascination about the natural world and world geography.

Reading the *Igeret* against contemporary geographic works reveals its author to be highly conversant with them. Ruderman convincingly shows that the *Igeret* was part of the humanist project as envisioned by Farissol. Above all, he wanted to bring to print, in Hebrew, all the "innovations" (*hidushim*) in world cartography of the time.[71] The *Igeret* is a superb example of the intense sixteenth-century dialogue between Jews and Christians in Italy. Historian Amnon Raz-Krakotzkin has shown it to have encompassed many forms of knowledge, mostly religious but also scientific.[72] Farissol exemplifies this dialogue, deploying "gentile" knowledge in the preface to his work, with information from "their" books. Apologizing for the limited scope of the *Igeret*, he writes: "even the Christians, leading authorities of this craft [of geography] could not say everything." Christian geographers determined facts and named places by "way of agreeing on them"—by using evidence, testimony, and proof and drawing on a shared and growing body of knowledge deemed to be accurate and authoritative. His text "follow[ed] them" in this regard.[73]

Despite the disclaimer about its limited scope, the *Igeret* is conceived as comprehensive, promising to "teach [the] Seven climates, and three inhabited parts [of the world]: Asia, Europe and Africa," including "the distant islands recently discovered by the Portuguese boats next to the South Pole." His reader would also "find [information] about the river Sambatyon, and locations of the enclosed Jews, where they are."[74] Comprehensive world geographies, according to Farissol, should include both the *oikoumene* and "distant islands," but also the enclosed Jews and the River Sambatyon. The geography of the world was made up of three categories of habitation: the classical inhabited and known world; its newly discovered parts, not yet fully known; and the enclosed realms.

The notion that humans inhabited the entire planet was hotly debated during the later parts of the sixteenth century, bearing serious theological implications for Christianity, a supposedly universal religion. Triggered by the dramatic discoveries of the preceding few decades, which exposed the world as something radically different than what the Europeans had imagined, the center of the debate was Italy, particularly Venice—Europe's foremost center for world cartography, where new geographic data were processed and mapped.[75]

Though Farissol was writing a few decades before the idea of total habit-ability took final shape, he was aware of the problems arising from the assumption that the world was totally inhabited. The crucial issue for him was the ten tribes. Talmudic and medieval sources had no problem distancing them ever farther. For Farissol, writing in the context of an exposed and mapped world where all territories seemed to be accounted for, the idea of a lost and unknown people was a problem that required care. His inclusion of the ten tribes as a third category, after the inhabited and the newly discovered, is an indication of this dilemma and an attempt to resolve it.

Farissol uses the term *Yehudim Segurim* (enclosed Jews) when referring to the ten tribes. As we have seen from Esdras on, the enclosure of the ten tribes was implied in different and elaborate ways: they were in another land, con-cealed, under the ground, beyond rivers and mountains or great walls; they were invisible. Only the third-century Commodianus had explicitly used the term "enclosed": *iudaei clusi*. Abulafia had used the term "concealed Jews" (*Yehudim Genuzim*). Writing in the sixteenth century, Farissol had difficulty representing the tribes' special condition in a world that seemed to be fully exposed, or at least exposable; no river or mountain now seemed beyond reach. So, for the first time, "enclosed" in its most simple sense seemed the only possible descriptor. The hidden Jews were human islands, a real entity on the world's map—among us, but set apart.

Like most Italian Jews of his time, Farissol had followed David Reuveni closely since his arrival in Italy. While it is clear that David's appearance in Italy in 1523 did not lead to the writing of the *Igeret*—Farissol probably was already working on it well before—the work is closely related to him. Historian David Ruderman points out that Farissol was greatly encouraged by the attention given to the ten tribes by non-Jews.[76] David appears in the book despite Farissol's skepticism about David's messianic aspirations, and he also sus-pected David's ten tribes identity. At moments, he identifies David as a man from the ten tribes, but adds that "he might be from Yehuda"—that is, a simple, garden-variety Jew. Farissol, even as early as 1525, likely did not fully believe in David.

Ultimately, though, the identity of David was far less important than the challenge of inserting the ten tribes into world geography. To a certain extent, Farissol wanted not only to incorporate them into the dramatic discoveries of his age, but to do so in a manner that would conform to the contemporary method of writing world geography as a form of agreement between experts. This bore a burden of scientific proof from which Talmudic authors or Benja-min of Tudela, for example, had been immune. To write about the tribes and the world in Farissol's day, scientific approval was required. It was in this regard that David was of use. "I, Abraham Farissol, wrote in order to expose to the uninformed the itineraries of the world; I chose to write this chapter that concerns the itineraries of the Jew from the tribes, or maybe from Yehuda, whose name is David son of Shlomo, Commander of Israel's Armies."[77] David's story serves to introduce the reader to world geography. The power of Farissol's faith in the existence of the ten tribes clearly overrode any doubts he might have had in David himself: "I have seen all this in truthful writings, and my ears heard [this] from important people, men of truth, and the Lord God. . . . the complete truth . . . does not lie . . . and all those who seek his shelter shall not be ashamed, and the truth shall naturally grow forth and will make its way." The power of his faith in the final redemption of Israel and in its God is more important than the question of David's honesty.

Farissol here calls to mind Zemah Gaon, who centuries earlier was faced with the mystery of Eldad Ha-Dani. The Gaon could not afford, and did not wish, to deal with the identity of the person himself. Faith was more important. The restoration of the people of Israel and their return to the Holy Land was the "complete truth." It seems that Farissol understood that to doubt David was to undermine his messianic project. Farissol saw signs of the truth "making its way" in the fact that David's episode won the recognition of the gentile authorities of the existence and the power of the ten lost tribes. It is not clear how he came to this conclusion, but Farissol wrote that the Portuguese king's response to the pope's inquiries corroborated David's claims about the ten tribes. This of course was not true, but for Farissol the mere fact that David was received by the leaders of Christendom was enough to suggest that they had information corroborating his story. He also maintained that Portuguese explorers brought news that proved David's story to be true.

For Farissol, this would have signaled a triumph that cannot be underestimated. Writing in 1525, only two years after David's arrival in Italy, Farissol was quick to identify the one substantial benefit of the whole episode: "Now it became truth to all the kings and the rulers and among the masses and in the streets of Rome that there is still existence to the numerous tribes of Israel and they have many kings. . . . And the Jew who came let him be whatever he is."[78]

Whereas the Talmudic authors or medieval writers hardly considered concrete or external geographic knowledge in their discussions of the ten tribes, a sixteenth-century Renaissance man was required to consider them in writing a *cosmografia,* as Farissol subtitled his *Igeret.* Farissol's joy that now it "became truth" to the gentiles that the ten tribes exist reveals how important it was to him to provide substantiated information in his work—that is, information acknowledged by the gentiles' geography. In this regard, Farissol was the first modern researcher of the ten tribes who was burdened with the challenge of proving their existence.

Farissol's actual treatment of the ten tribes is rather disappointing, despite the fact that they appear as a distinct item in the title page of the *Igeret* and although he dedicates a whole chapter to David. Farissol does not have much new to report and, by his own admission, resorts to the familiar Talmudic "India." The big change is that he includes the tribes for the first time within a real charted geography.

Commenting several decades later, Rabbi David Gans (1541–1613) dismissed Farissol's treatment of the ten tribes, calling it *gimgum*, which implies stuttering or diffidence.[79] He also expressed dissatisfaction with another Italian writer, Azariah dei Rossi (1513 or 1514–1578), who had commented on the location of the tribes in his huge *Sefer Me'or 'Enayim* (Light of the Eyes, 1575). Albeit not writing a *cosmografia*, dei Rossi, like Farissol, simply repeated scripture and Talmud when he commented on the tribes' location.[80] Gans was dissatisfied that Dei Rossi and Farissol did not really provide any new geographic news about them. Gans said he was preparing to write his own, presumably superior, geographical treatise with a better account of the geographic location of the ten tribes. If he ever completed the task, the fate of this book is not clear.[81]

Historian André Neher explains that David Gans was already more informed than both dei Rossi and Farissol.[82] But one could also say that David Gans was too harsh in his judgments, missing the ultimate point: not to provide new information about the ten tribes, but to better locate them within newly charted territories. Which is what Farissol did. Whereas previously, the ten tribes were located in an unknown location within the unknown world, they were now located in an unknown location within known locations. As a Renaissance humanist, Farissol realized that his real challenge was to engage his wider intellectual audience, and it was in this spirit that he engaged the challenge to inscribe the ten tribes into the new world geography of his day. His effort underscores the predicament that the Age of Discovery presented to the story of the ten lost tribes. How to remain lost in an exposed world is the puzzle that would dominate its remaining chapters.

5

Concordia Mundi

Inasmuch as the body became torn asunder [when Jeroboam led away the ten tribes], the Prophet says, Together shall be gathered the children of Judah and the children of Israel.

—John Calvin, *Commentary* on Hosea 1:1

And when the ten tribes of the Israelites set out, the clouds of glory and majesty of God will surround them, and God himself will set off before them.

—Johannes Buxtorf, *Synagoga Judaica* (1603)

In the Cordilleras, Peru

One boiling day in the summer of 1647,[1] a deathbed was brought into the synagogue of Recife. Upon it lay a man in his mid-forties, Aharon ha-Levi, better known as Antonio Montezinos, taking an oath that all that he had told over the past two years was true. The people around his bed, all former "New Christians," had taken refuge from the horrors of the Iberian Inquisition in this new colony, where they were able to return to Judaism. They were taking notes, which they planned to send back to Amsterdam, Montezinos's last residence before coming to Recife, then briefly under Dutch rule.[2] The scene at the synagogue was meant to resolve any remaining doubts about Montezinos's story; the Talmud says that a man on his deathbed does not lie. Montezinos had a fabulous story to tell. In Amsterdam, where he had stayed for six months, there were several important people who were particularly interested in its veracity and were waiting to hear from Recife.

Born around 1604 in Villaflor, Portugal, to a Marranic/New Christian family, Montezinos's Jewish ancestors had been forced to convert to Catholicism by the 1497 decree of Manuel I. As a young man, Montezinos left Portugal for the West Indies where, like many other Portuguese New Christians, he secretly returned to Judaism. He lived in the Americas for about twenty years and then returned to Europe, to Amsterdam, where a community of former New Christian Jews now thrived. Protestant Amsterdam, getting free of the yoke of Spanish rule, was tolerant enough to attract numerous Portuguese New Christians who wanted to return to their Judaism freely. For a long while, Portuguese returnees to Judaism dominated parts of the Atlantic trade networks. Upon arriving in Amsterdam in September 1644, Montezinos began spreading the story of his adventures in the Americas.[3] It was incredible.

In the Americas, Montezinos had made a living trading with Indians and normally traveled accompanied by natives. Trekking through the Andean mountain range from Honda (in modern-day Colombia) to Quito (in Ecuador), he met an unusual mestizo Indian. Named Francisco, he was called *casique* by the other Indians, which in their language meant "leader." Several incidents that took place as they were crossing the Cordillera Mountains gave Montezinos the impression that the other Indians treated Francisco with a strange deference. Francisco also had open contempt for the Spanish Empire and did not hesitate to voice it, telling Montezinos that Spaniards were cruel people who would soon be "punished by a hidden people."

Shortly thereafter, Montezinos arrived in Cartagena de Indias and was thrown in prison by the local Inquisition. In his cell, he had an epiphany—the Indians were Hebrews! Francisco and the other Indians must have known the truth, which Montezinos vowed to confirm as soon as he got out of prison. When he finally arrived back in Honda, he sought out Francisco and asked to travel with him alone. On the track, Montezinos turned to him: "I am a Hebrew from the tribe of Levi and my God is the Lord God, and all the rest is just a disguise."[4] The Indian Francisco, "shaken," inquired about Montezinos's ancestors and, after much negotiation, became convinced that Montezinos was indeed an "Israelite." He told Montezinos that he was going to take him on a journey. They marched for a week, "crossing rivers and swamps" and eating only some "toasted corn." On the Sabbath, they rested. On a Tuesday morning, they reached a huge river. Francisco said to Montezinos: "here you shall see your brothers." It seems that these mysterious brothers already knew that the two visitors were coming: in a few minutes, a small canoe came across the river paddled by "three men and one woman." Francisco spoke with them; then all four jumped up and hugged Montezinos. Two of the men started reciting the Shema, from Deuteronomy (6:4), which calls upon all Israel to affirm that the Lord God is their one God and is recited by Jews worldwide

The men and the woman were ten tribers, "Children of Abraham, Isaac, and Jacob." They gave several signs showing that they were Israelites, but did not volunteer much information about how they got to their location, telling Montezinos that Francisco would tell him the rest of their story later. They also averred, cryptically, that "soon enough" they would make contact with the outside world, but before that, they asked him to send them "twelve men, all bearded and literate." They refused to let Montezinos cross the river. When he tried to cross on his own, they became very angry.[5] After some time, Montezinos and Francisco headed back to Honda. After some pleading, Montezinos convinced Francisco to tell the rest of the story. "Know that your brothers the Children of Israel, God brought them to this land, he did miracles and wonders for them. . . . When we Indians came to this land we fought with them and we treated them poorly, more than the Spaniards treated us." After a series of massacres and bloody exchanges between the Israelites and the Indians, eventually the Israelites disappeared, losing contact with the outside world. Only a limited number of *casiques* was allowed to see them once every seventy months. Outside this rule, a *casique* was allowed to come see the Israelites only under unusual circumstances—such as the coming of Montezinos. Francisco finished with a prophecy to which they held: "One day the Israelites will take over this country as before and will rule the world."[6]

It was after this episode that Montezinos set out to spread the word about the future return of the ten tribes, ending up in Amsterdam where Manasseh Ben-Israel (1604–1657) would eventually put it into writing, producing the famous 1650 *Miqveh Israel* or *Hope of Israel*.

At first blush, Montezinos reminds us of David Reuveni, but his story is more complex. Whereas the Yemeni Jew was working with an older narrative that placed an intact collective of the ten tribes at the southern boundaries of the world, Montezinos's story was embedded within the significant changes and transformations of a dramatically short period. The tribes were relocated from the world's eastern and southern edges to its northern and western ones; theologically, there was a new emphasis on the meaning of the restoration of the tribes to humanity. The book of Esdras's presence in Montezinos's story is much felt. It tells of the tribes' further wandering into another land, led by a God who performs miracles and quarrels with gentiles; it tells of the huge river that none can cross. Most important of all is the prophecy of their triumphant return and reuniting with the rest of Israel, also prominent in Montezinos's story.

Esdras had begun its rise to prominence in Europe almost two centuries earlier, during the 1480s, when humanist scholarly circles in Italy, most notably that of Pico Della Mirandola (1463–1494), took new interest in Near Eastern languages, Jewish texts and Kabbalah, ancient Greek thought, and Islam. In this context, the Apocrypha, particularly the prophetic/apocalyptic Esdras, a book that speaks of the climactic return of a lost people, were very attractive. The encounters with peoples in the Americas also made this book acutely important. In Spanish America in particular, the book of Esdras was much on many people's minds.[7]

In 1572, several decades before Montezinos, the Franciscan Fray Francisco de la Cruz was interrogated and tried by the Inquisition in Lima, Peru. Among many other crimes, de la Cruz confessed to an interesting heresy. He declared that the Turks—since the fifteenth century a rising Muslim power—would eventually destroy Catholicism in the Old World. The only hope for survival was a Catholic alliance with the ten tribes—the Indians—in the New World. De la Cruz, who wished to be the head of this New World–reinforced Catholicism, based his argument on his belief that the Indians were the ten tribes of Esdras. Less fortunate than Montezinos, he was burned to death after the trial.[8]

Beyond Esdras, the adaptations that Montezinos adds are fascinating. His setting is the Andean mountains, a huge range in South America, and the gentiles from whom the ten tribes are hiding are the Indians. The story also develops from revelation to revelation: Montezinos's realization (in the Inquisition's prison) that some of the Indians are Hebrews, and his own self-exposure as a Jew, lead to the exposure of the ten tribes. An evil empire—the Spanish—provides the basic setting for the drama. In its most basic elements, Montezinos's story, however unique and bizarre, belongs in a much wider realm of speculation, hopes, and fears concerning the ten tribes. Montezinos's version adds an interesting dimension to the prospect of finding them, one stemming from his own identity. As a returnee to Judaism, Montezinos was very familiar with the actual meanings of return and restoration. And as a Jew hiding his identity, he understood the invisibility of the ten tribes as a problem not only of reaching them, but also of identifying them. Being hidden does not only mean living behind impassable geographical barriers, but also hiding one's identity. It is thus not surprising that he finds the tribes in the same place where he himself returned to Judaism. Yet, just as he has still at times to hide his identity even in America, so too the ten tribes: the moment of full return, the moment of revealing their true identity, has not yet come—though the encounter in America signals the possibility of its future arrival. Montezinos's encounter with the ten tribes stems from this broader context, a horizon of possibilities which began to be seen around 1492.

Horizons and Possibilities

On April 21, 1519, a small Spanish army led by Hernán Cortés (1485–1547) landed in Ulua, the gate to the Aztec Empire. Thirty bloody months later, Cortés was the ruler of a vast Mesoamerican empire—Nueva España. In October 1522, he was officially appointed its governor and began building the city of Mexico, in Tenochtitlan, the site of the ruined Aztec capital, and started importing people and goods from Spain. Cortés was followed by Francisco Pizarro (1471–1541), who sailed southward from Panama in 1524 toward the Incan Empire in the southern part of the continent. By around 1550, Spanish America—Peru and Mexico—was a vast territory stretching from present-day Mexico in the north to Argentina and southern Chile in the south (though Spain, of course, did not control every single square mile within these territories, which bordered and included major natural barriers—the Amazon jungle, the Andean mountains, vast deserts, and tropical forests). In 1572, the last independent Native American ruler, Túpac Amaru, was beheaded in Cuzco. Spain remained the only power on the continent.[9]

This history had started with the sailing of Christopher Columbus, under the Spanish flag, toward the west in 1492, ushering in an active century of sail, exploration, conquest, and colonization. Not only military efforts were involved in this project. Intellectual endeavors accompanied it from the very beginning. The existence of the American continent, its wonders, and, more important, its people needed to be explained and thus "possessed" or "assimilated."[10] Religion, clergy, and scripture played a pivotal role in the creation of this vast empire.[11]

The advent of empire was accompanied, sometimes preceded, by intense searches for all sorts of things. One of the more interesting places that travelers sought in the Americas was Ophir. In 1 Kings, we read that King Solomon's messengers "went to Ophir and brought back four hundred and twenty talents of gold" (1 Kings 9:28). Ophir had already been sought elsewhere as well. (Vasco da Gama had suggested in the late fifteenth century that Ophir was East Africa.) In the context of the Americas, interest began with Columbus, and later explorers dedicated much time to finding this legendary biblical location,[12] along with El Dorado.[13] Other quests included those for the fountain of eternal youth for which Juan Ponce de León (1460–1521) went to Florida and the Amazon; and for the legendary women in honor of whom Francisco de Orellana (1500–1549) insisted on naming the Amazon.[14]

Searches for the ten tribes in the Americas certainly belong on what historian Anthony Pagden calls the "horizon of possibilities," for which America emerged as a "greenhouse."[15] But whereas the fountain of eternal youth would make one forever young and El Dorado would make one forever rich (not to mention the implications of an encounter with the Amazon women), there was a greater value still in finding the ten lost tribes. In addition to prophecies that promised their return at the end of days, the possibility of an encounter with the ten tribes had a deeper theological dimension. Their horizon of possibilities was a place where time, geography, and prophecy met.

It is now well known that not only the Christianization of conquered peoples but deeper theological considerations and aspirations accompanied (perhaps better, "enveloped") European expansion and colonization virtually from the start. Literary scholar Djelal Kadir has shown, for instance, that Columbus saw himself as a "divine instrument in the eschatological plot of providential history." The great Spanish Dominican theologian Bartolomé de las Casas (1484–1566) commented on Columbus's invocation of Isaiah (in his letter on the third voyage): "since Isaiah was a prophet, he could have well been prophesying the discovery of the New World."[16] Isaiah's prophecies, particularly those foretelling the end of days, the unification of humanity, and the restoration of world peace, occupy a major place in Columbus's *Libro de Profecías*, a text that reveals Columbus to be intimately familiar with biblical prophecies and to have understood his biography as the fulfillment of them.[17] In the selections Columbus made for this book, he meant to show that his discovery was "no mere accident, but an integral part of providential history."[18] Columbus came to view his accomplishment as "not so much a 'discovery' but a revelation—an important step in uncovering God's plan."[19] As Columbus pondered his voyages, his "eschatological awareness" became more acute, and he sought a "historic and theological context in which he could locate his geographical discoveries."[20]

Historian Pauline Watts has shown that Columbus was particularly interested in the prophecies of the medieval mystic Joachim di Fiore (1135–1202) concerning the restoration of Jerusalem to Christian hands: "He who will restore the ark of Zion will come from Spain."[21] "In Columbus's mind," concludes Watts, "the New World was identified with the end of the world."[22] That end of the world was closely associated with the ten tribes. Columbus was likely familiar with Joachim's view that the fall of Jerusalem into "Saracen" captivity was nothing less than a repetition of the fall of the ten tribes into Assyrian captivity.[23]

The "islands of the sea," identified by Isaiah as a place from which the ten tribes would return, were particularly significant for Columbus, who quoted Isaiah 11: "It will happen on that day the Lord will extend his hand a second time to gather up the remainder of his people from Assyria, Egypt, Patros, Ethiopia, Elam, Shinar, Hamath, and from the islands of [the] sea; etc."[24] But not only Isaiah and other biblical prophets were on Columbus's mind. Most significantly, there was Esdras,[25] an important element in Columbus's thought and world, used even in making his case before Isabella and Ferdinand "to prove how small was the ocean."[26] In the letter he wrote about his third voyage (1498), Columbus spoke of it as a "godly pilgrimage to the prophetic tradition's ends of earth."[27]

Columbus had an "unmistakable...sense of his own apostolic and providential election."[28] As Kadir has shown, this sense of being a tool in the fulfillment of prophecies was closely connected to later speculation concerning the ten tribes in the Americas.[29] Columbus twice refers to the world he found as "another world" (*otro mundo*).[30] Could it be that Columbus's "another world"—as opposed to Vespucci's *Mundus Novus*, or New World, coined in 1504[31]—is in fact Esdras's "another land," in turn the *Aretz aheret* of Deuteronomy? In Hebrew, *Aretz* could also mean "world/earth." And after all, Columbus found this other world by "arriving at the end of the Orient [*fin de Oriente*] where East and West meet."[32]

The geographical fact that the world is round (and therefore east and west must meet) went hand in hand with the prophecy that another world—another land—existed somewhere. A combination of geographic determinism and interpretations of prophecy were at work. The newly acquired ability to reach the "end of the east" and the "end of the earth" allowed one, if one looked hard enough, to find the ten lost tribes. In addition to geographic search, an active measure of consultation with and interpretation of prophetic texts was necessary as well. The prospect of finding the ten tribes was very real. Both prophecy and the exposed and revealed geography of the real world enabled (but certainly did not mandate) it.

As Tudor Parfitt thoroughly documents, the Americas were the center of what later came to be known as the "Jewish Indians theory,"[33] according to which the Native Americans or some of them were the ten lost tribes. Other versions had one or two tribes of the ten migrating to the Americas among other groups—Egyptians, Phoenicians, or others. The Jewish Indians theory generated heated debates that lasted for centuries, first in the Spanish world, but particularly (later) in England and the American colonies. The notion that the Indians were related to the ten tribes was a useful political tool, helping Europeans to "possess" them, to borrow Stephen Greenblatt's terminology,[34] and was often employed to justify conquest, colonization, and the deprivation of property. At other times, it was employed to condemn these very same acts.

Among the many peculiar twists of this theory, one can count the conversion to Christianity of Gallegina Watie (1802–1839), a Cherokee noble who was adopted by Elias Boudinot (1740–1821), among other things a famous ten tribes scholar, and the development of an Incan ten tribes identity. In the United States, President Thomas Jefferson found it necessary to issue a ruling that the Indians were not the ten lost tribes, though some of his closest associates, such as Elias Boudinot, passionately believed that they were. The theory was potent and seductive. Boudinot was not the only American prominent leader to believe in the Jewish Indian Theory. Already in 1682 William Penn (1644–1718), wrote about the Indians: "As to the original of this extraordinary people, I cannot but believe they are of the Jewish race, I mean of the stock of the ten tribes so long lost; . . . The ten tribes were to go to a land 'not planted nor known,' which certainly Asia, Africa, and Europe were."[35]

The Jewish Indian theory was attached to two critical questions. The first is the familiar "where are the ten tribes?" The second was far more important at the time: "how had humans arrived in America to begin with?" "There was a problem accounting for who [the Indians] were and where they came from. If everyone on the surface of earth [were] the descendants of Adam and Eve and the seven survivors of the flood, then the Indians had to be connected to the Biblical world."[36] This charge became particularly acute after the May 1537 encyclical "Sublimus Deus" by Pope Paul III (1468–1549). Addressing the question of the enslavement of the Native Americans, the pope stated that they "and all other people who may later be discovered by Christians" were "truly men."[37] But what men were they? To be sure, the early modern period was imbued with theories about the origins of different recently discovered races. Yet the ten tribes theory was certainly the most persistent among them.[38]

The Jewish Indian theory raised other questions that are still much overlooked, which revolve around the theological and geographical aspects of the horizon of possibility that the ten tribes posed in the Americas. Why was it so important during the early modern period to find the tribes? And if they were to be found in the Americas, how did they get there in the first place?

The Nordification of the Ten Tribes

In 1544, Arzareth, the land of the ten lost tribes, made its first appearance on a map, a small woodblock entitled "Asia wie es Jetziger Zeit" (Asia in Current Time; see figure 5.1) prepared by the German cartographer Sebastian Münster (1488–1552). Listing it as "Arsare[t]," Münster located it in the northeasternmost corner of Asia, south of the Scythian Sea (*Mare Scythivm*). The broader region within which it appeared is part of a peninsula surrounded by seas to the north and the east, and separated from the rest of Asia by a wide river to its west. China is positioned to the south of this peninsula.[39] Münster—a theologian, cartographer,

FIGURE 5.1. Münster, "Asia in Current Time." Courtesy Rolf Stein.

cosmographer, mathematician, and professor of Hebrew at the universities of Heidelberg and, later, Basel—is best known for his *Biblia Hebraica,* the first Protestant translation of the Hebrew Bible. He is also known for his *Cosmographia Universalis,* a compendium of maps and scientific treatises describing the world, published in 1544, and for his edition of Ptolemy's maps.[40] The connections among Hebraism, biblical studies, theology, and the geography of the ten tribes are strongly attached to a new Christian sensitivity concerning the tribes that emerged in the sixteenth century. Christian Hebraism, a form of Renaissance scholarship rooted in earlier periods and the contemporary quintessence of Jewish-Christian dialogue, was chiefly responsible. Hebraism, which was not confined to only one Christian denomination, involved the translation and study of "kabbalistic books, Jewish biblical exegeses and Talmudic texts."[41] Münster himself was well known, and often criticized, "for his close engagement with rabbinic literature."[42] (Münster also published the book of Tobit, so one could say he was familiar with the life of at least one ten triber already.)

Hebraist practices produced a wealth of new material on the ten tribes, marking the beginning of a direct, if not quite transparent, dialogue between Jews and Christians over the subject. As we have seen, Jewish and Christian discussions about the ten tribes had long been carried out on separate tracks. From this moment on, they would proceed through a more intense and direct dialogue concerning not just their location but the meaning of their story as well. If up until now only Jews discussed the tribes in terms of loss, from now on the implications of their disappearance would be a Christian question as well.

Only two decades prior, in the midst of David Reuveni's escapade in Italy, Abraham Farissol had gleefully noted that "now" the Christians "knew" about the ten tribes. Farissol's contentment underestimated the long history of Christian sentiments about the ten tribes, yet suggests that the inclusion of the tribes in his *cosmographia*—a narrated cartography of the world—was part of an ongoing Jewish-Christian dialogue over, among other things, the issue of the ten tribes. The appearance of Arzareth in a cosmography prepared by a Christian Hebraist signals the shift of geographical speculation about the ten tribes from being an almost exclusively Jewish exercise to a Christian one as well. This was one of many major shifts in the debate that came in the early modern period.

Just as the Jewish and Christian texts and ideas engaged one another, so did geography and biblical studies. Moreover, European geography during the period was in many respects a religious, sacred project. Cosmographies were "the discourse that brought together celestial and geographic exploration, represented space and scale, and theorized the place of humans within nature."[43] One's religious beliefs shaped one's geography. During the sixteenth century, there was also no "clear-cut distinction between cosmography and geography"; the two terms "coincided in the writing of world geographies." Geographer John Short aptly refers to Münster and others as "cosmo-geographers" writing "geographies of the world," and defines their work as "adapting the cosmographical project to write universal geographies at a time when the known world was rapidly increasing in size and complexity."[44] Münster's cosmography, a popular book published numerous times well into the seventeenth century, was "an eclectic collection of material, some old, some new, part old myth, part new fact."[45] The 1628 edition of his cosmography, for instance, identified the newly explored Southeast Asian kingdom of Siam with the legendary Ophir.[46] This description is quite apt when we come to evaluate the way in which Münster, "a prisoner of classical errors and medieval prejudice," as Short mercilessly defines him, inscribed Arzareth on his map.[47] "Arsare[t]" is seemingly no different than most of its other place names, a mere notation with no boundaries or any other special markings or explanations.

Its inclusion seems connected more to the cosmographer's commitment to biblical legacies than to geographical fact. Münster's choice of location for Arzareth—in northeast Asia—is more interesting.

The "idea of north," to borrow a phrase from another context, is crucial here.[48] Against the backdrop of a known world that "was rapidly increasing in size and complexity," one could no longer place Arzareth in its traditional Central Asian location. Southeast Asia and the Indian coast, other putative locations of the ten tribes, are represented rather accurately on Münster's map. European knowledge of the geography of Central Asia, centuries after the Mongols and in the wake of numerous Turkic migrations westward, was sufficient to determine that no ten tribes lived in that region of the world. European knowledge of the geography of China and far eastern Asia had also increased significantly. Thus, northeast Asia, still a century before the beginning of the Russian advent to that region and before the rise of the Manchu Empire, was the only location where the tribes could still "travel." The unexplored and unknown north was simply the only remaining option. Indeed, as late as 1596, the Fleming cartographer Jodocus Hondius (1563–1612) declared: "The northern area of Asia is indeed uncertain."[49] Northern Asia had become, in its turn, the new edge of the world. Other mysteries, among them Gog and Magog, underwent a similar relocation. The great Flemish cartographer Gerardus Mercator (1512–1594) placed them in northeastern Asia in his famous 1569 *weltkart,* an endpoint in a gradual north-ward migration produced by the northward expansion of European knowledge of "Tartary" and the Tartars.[50]

Another important clue hinting that the nordification of Arzareth on Münster's map was not a mere capricious notation is the movement northward also of the Scythian Sea. Originally, the Scythian Sea was one of the names of the Black Sea, which is situated far south of the Arctic Circle. The Black Sea was in ancient times understood to be on the northern "edge of the world."[51] It was, in a way, the world's "first north." It was known in Roman times as an "inhospitable place of exile," an image adopted by Byzantine authors.[52] In its earlier incarnations, the Black/Scythian Sea was imbued "with the same fantastic qualities that defined all the outer limits of [the] world."[53] The nordification of Arzareth is also its mystification—relocated to the north, in a region of the world conceived as home to the fantastic. Just as the Black Sea, a former northern edge of the world, traveled north to a new edge, so did the ten tribes. Their nordification was the result of a cartographic necessity, but also came about because of the invention of the north as the new site where "treasures and marvels" were located, the seat of "all virtues" and "all evil."[54] The linkage between the Scythians and the ten tribes—most probably made here for the first time—is significant. The Scythians were the root for numerous legends like "the unicorn, Prester John, and Atlantis."[55] Black Sea historian Charles King notes that, for "ancient writers, the label 'Scythian' was primarily geographic. To be Scythian was to reside in a cold climate and probably live [a] nomadic life." This image of the Scythians, for which Herodotus is responsible, "became the one that most ancient geographers accepted as a true depiction of all the barbarian[s] of the north."[56] Their image as people "roaming the seemingly endless spaces on the peripheries of the civilised world" is key. The Scythian domain, large and vaguely defined, was also seen as "a region which no foreigner was allowed to enter and no one was allowed to leave."[57] The Scythians themselves would later be identified with the ten tribes, an identification that perhaps had its inception in Münster's cosmography. Racist theories seeking to establish the supremacy of the Anglo-Saxons by identifying them with the Scythians and the ten tribes also began here.

Restitutions

During the sixteenth century, millennial anxieties and apocalyptic expectations in which the ten tribes, or "verities" of them, played a significant role and swept the German-speaking world, particularly at the time of Martin Luther's activities and the various religious movements that they stirred. One can hardly follow the many inflections and variations that the rather simple biblical story of disappearance and loss produced in such a short time. Following the fall of Constantinople in 1453 into Turkish hands, the discovery of America, and the widening schisms among Christians, there were plenty of reasons to be deeply fearful of an approaching end of the world. Although he rejected some of the popular legends about the ten tribes, Luther fanned the fire with his writings on the Jews and his comparisons between the Turks and Gog/Magog.[58]

But far more important in Münster's world were the Swiss context and the connection to John Calvin (1509–1564). Münster, who came to be one of the most famous Calvinist scientists, published his cosmography in 1544 in Basel, his home since 1527. The city had separated from the Holy Roman Empire in 1501 to join the Swiss confederation and was an important center for Protestant activity and home to many French Huguenots fleeing persecution in France. It was there that Calvin published his seminal *Institutes of the Christian Religion* in 1536. Calvin and Münster knew each other well; the latter served as the former's Hebrew teacher for a while.[59] While one cannot catch Calvin and Münster red-handedly exchanging views about the ten tribes, Calvin's ideas about them reflect the changing approach to the issue of the big split in the

Davidic kingdom that had first created the ten tribes and their disappearance thereafter.

In earlier periods, the search for the ten tribes was mostly fueled by the desire to solve a biblical mystery or was an expression of Jewish messianic hopes. The desire for restoration and restitution certainly existed in Jewish thinking about the ten tribes, but by the later parts of the sixteenth century, the ten tribes had become much more pronounced as a Christian code for restitution. Calvin played an important role in this shift. Recall that the first book dedicated solely to a theological treatment of the ten tribes was the seventeenth-century Calvinist Hebraist theologian Witsius's *Dekaphylon: Sive De Decem Tribubus*. Restitution, however, was not unique to Calvin or Calvinism. Calvin should be viewed as an expression of a much more general European mood. He, of course, did not represent all of Christendom at the time, but his *Commentaries* on the ten tribes shed light on a much larger frame of mind for which he serves as an example. And, as one of the most influential early modern Christian thinkers, Calvin's overall impact is not to be underestimated.

Calvin's *Commentary* on Hosea ("Inasmuch as the body became torn asunder... Together shall be gathered the children of Judah and the children of Israel") graphically expresses the anxieties produced by the ancient story of David's kingdom split into two parts, one eventually punished for its sins and banished. For Calvin, the ten tribes were the perfect example of a people who had sinned and been punished. The schism was a body torn asunder, an idea repeated in his *Commentary* on Jeremiah 33:23–24, which speaks of the "body of the people that had been torn asunder." No one had written about the schism between the two and the ten tribes with such imagery, likening schism to the dismemberment of the human body.

Calvin, a French Protestant who had left France and witnessed the migration of many French Protestants out of the realm of the "elder daughter of the Church," was very sensitive to divisions. Indeed, he tended to notice them everywhere in the Bible:

> Not only were the twelve tribes divided, but the tribe of Benjamin was split in two also. Again not only was this tribe divided, but of the sons of Joseph, Ephraim dominated his brother Manasseh. And although members of the ten tribes wanted to worship in Jerusalem, Jeroboam saw to it that they received their own religious sites. The tree of Israel, grown from one root with various branches, was cut into pieces.[60]

Yet, just as Calvin emphasized schisms and splits, he stressed restorations and restitutions. While the body may be torn apart, there is the hope that unity will be restored and that what was lost shall be returned. He can be read here as an example of the contemporary sentiments about the ten tribes. While these sentiments represent the non-Catholic side, they arguably also reflect Catholic sentiments concerning the ten tribes as well.

The circumstances of the next appearance of Arzareth on a map reveal the idea of restitution forcefully.

Theater of the World

While Münster's *Cosmographia Universalis* certainly represents "classical error [and] medieval prejudice," it still "was creating the basis for a more accurate universal geography."[61] In the case of Arzareth, Münster's contribution was putting this place on a map and designating northeast Asia as its location. He turned an old myth into a new fact. Until Münster's map, Arzareth was just a place name appearing in texts such as 2 Esdras and medieval travelogues. Now, it became a fact on a map, a further step in the inclusion of the ten tribes in early modern world cosmo-geographies.

The modern geographical facticity of Arzareth became more evident still in an atlas of the world published two decades later by the great Flemish geographer and cartographer Abraham Ortelius (1527–1598). His map of Asia indicated the location of Arzareth in the same place as on Münster's map. Ortelius's map of Tartaria, or the kingdom of the Great Khan, was later included in his famous *Theatrum Orbis Terrarum* (Theater of the World), "the first true modern Atlas."[62] Thereafter, Arzareth appeared on all of Ortelius's maps of Asia and Tartary. One of the most authoritative atlases, and certainly the most popular, the *Theatrum* was an ambitious and comprehensive collection committed to the idea of "global territoriality."[63]

After its inclusion in the *Theatrum*, Arzareth became known to a wide readership of world geography. The *Theatrum* was widely popular in Europe, quickly translated into six languages. As on Münster's map, Arzareth appears in what would be the Arctic Circle, to the east and therefore farther north of "Tartaria" (see figure 5.2 for details). It marks the northeasternmost point of Asia, north of China and Japan, very close to today's Alaska. In short, it is very close to the North Pole. The viewer can learn from the map that Arzareth is the peninsula that sticks into the Scythian Ocean, or Oceanus Scythicus, which "according to Pliny" "has sweet water." So far, Ortelius had followed Münster's formulation in terms of the nordification of the ten tribes. But he added more.

Münster's location of Arzareth in North Asia returns us to the question of the relationship between the ten tribes and the Tartars, the region's traditional inhabitants. In Matthew of Paris and John of Mandeville, the ten tribes and the "tartars," broadly defined, were considered one and the same thing. Thus, the inclusion of Arzareth in a map of "Tartary" required Ortelius to rework the geographical and historical relationships between the ten tribes and the Tartars. Ortelius cannot leave the two entities entangled, so he divides Tartary between them. What he accomplishes is a marvelous patchwork of new facts and old myth,[64] meant to disentangle the two entities and situate them in relation to each other in a manner that makes sense.

The northern part of Asia on Ortelius's map is indeed a region imbued with fantastic qualities. A close look at the northeastern corner reveals a concentration of legends, myths, and facts denser than anywhere else in the entire *Theatrum*. In this little corner, we find Prester John, St. Thomas, a horde named after the tribe Dan "residing in the dark north." North of Tartaria, touching the North Pole itself, is another territory, much less defined geographically, which is designated as home to the horde of Naphtali (*Nepthalitarū horda*), "named after one of the ten tribes" (*ab una 10 Tribuum Israelis nomine*): "others call [these hordes] incorrectly Euthalites [Hephthalites]." That is to say, the horde of Naphtali is named after one of the ten tribes, but it is not that tribe. Ortelius does not tell us why the Hephthalites took the name of the tribe of Naphtali. Why does he bother with such a bizarre story?

The Hephthalites, or White Huns, were a real entity, Central Asian no-mads whose original homeland was northwest of the Chinese Great Wall (whence they had been displaced by the Huns). Their moment of glory came during the fifth and sixth centuries when they defeated the Scythians and invaded northern India and parts of Persia, making themselves known not only to Chinese but also to Persian and Byzantine historians. Best known for defeating the Sassanid king Peroz I (r. 458–484) in 476 and the Indian Guptas in 480, the Hephthalites were driven away in 561 by a coalition of Persians and other nomads led by Peroz's grandson, the illustrious Khosro I (or Anushir-avan, r. 531–579). The Hephthalites were then quite forgotten, their memory kept alive mostly in histories that relied on the Byzantine chronicles that mentioned them.[65]

A wandering people in Central Asia with a name similar to that of one of the ten tribes was enough to demand an explanation. It seems that Ortelius was unsure if the Hephthalites were indeed an Israelite tribe, but could not ignore the similarity in name. Perhaps he was also aware of the traditions, expressed by Benjamin of Tudela, according to which the tribe of Naphtali at one point settled in the region where the Hephthalite kingdom existed. He thus came up with the story that the Naphtalite horde was given the name of

FIGURE 5.2. Detail from Abraham Ortelius, "Tartary; or, Kingdom of the Great Khan." Courtesy *Cartographica Neerlandica*.

S SCYTHICVS
Plinio auctore, qui multas in eo
dicit, vt etiam M·Paul: Vene:
auter neq, situm neq, numeru tradit.

typus

Tabin Prom·Plin.

ARSARETH.

ANIA.

Quinsai id est
ciuitas cœli

QVINCI

MANGI

XAN
TON.
NANQVI.

CHEQVAN

STRETTO DI ANIAN

MARE
CIN.

Rio T

Sierra

Minas BAN
de plata. DVMIA.
Occote

BVNGO
Bungo

Amanguro

IAPAN

Meaco
inunde sixi:
tas prima to
ra

Osaqua

S·Thontas   TONSA.

Cogoruma   Osecti
mia

S·Maria   Taxuma

Isola di
fogo   7·Islas

Lequino grande

Japan insula, à M·Paulo
Veneto Zipangri dicta,
olim Chryse, a Magno
Cham olim bello petita
sed frustra.

the tribe of Naphtali.[66] There is much in support of the idea that Ortelius had Benjamin in mind as he wrote about the Hephthalites and the tribe of Naphtali. Among Ortelius's close associates in Antwerp was Benito Arias Montano, the translator of Benjamin of Tudela into Latin. His "sacred history" maps, depicting the itineraries of such holy men as Abraham, Moses, and Paul, were inspired by Montano's work.[67] Montano, who spent several years in Antwerp, published a translation of Benjamin in 1575.[68]

Whether he consulted Benjamin or not, Ortelius's explanation seems to be a compromise among various conflicting issues: the facticity and the wealth of information about the Hephthalites, the power of the traditions that placed the ten tribes in Central Asia, combined with the nagging similarity he detected between the names "Hephthalites" and "Naphtali." The result is an apparent attempt to organize the stories into a coherent narrative: the one-time rulers of an empire stretching between eastern Iran and northern India are linked to the ten tribes, but are not themselves the ten tribes. Ortelius next discusses the real ten tribes, providing two locations. The first, supposedly their original, is in a place called "Turcestan," east of the Caspian Sea. Dutifully placed beyond a mountain range, Ortelius mentions that the tribes had been living there when they were "allies" in the war against the "Ishmaelites" some "900 years ago." Their "current" location, however, is way up in a northeasterly direction. Underneath the word "Arsareth," and on other maps next to it, Ortelius adds the following notation: "4 Esdras v. 13: Arsareth. Here the ten tribes retreated, and changed from the Tatar or Tartar area to Scythia. Since then they are called Gauths or Gauthens, confirming God's highest glory."[69]

The map provides a full narrative and visual account of the ten tribes' wanderings. The map's viewer can even measure the way and examine their route from their original location beyond the Caspian Sea to the northeastern corner of Asia, just as "a merchant could certainly use the maps of the *Theatrum* to trace the route of his goods, and a scholar could study the movements of mankind over the physical earth."[70] Arzareth's location, at the edge of the Asian land mass, surrounded by seas on three sides and by hordes and a river on the fourth, suggests a commitment to scripture.[71] Ortelius was committed; at the foot of his map, he quotes Cicero, "What of human affairs can seem great to him who knows all eternity and the entire universe?"[72]

We can read Ortelius's inclusion of Arzareth in more than one way. On one hand, the map is a quintessential instance of early scientific approval of Arzareth as a real geographical location. There can be no doubt that Ortelius copied the location of Arzareth from Münster, whose *Cosmographia* was one of the inspirations for the *Theatrum*.[73] Here is the transformation of Arzareth from a mere word on a 1544 map in Basel into an elaborate story on another map produced just two decades later. This transformation still begs the question, however. While we can be sure that Ortelius borrowed the location from Münster's map, we still have to explain the source of Ortelius's explanation of what Arzareth itself is and why it is in northern Asia.

While we cannot explain Ortelius's motivations in full, his relations with the Frenchman Guillaume Postel (1510–1581) may explain a second and more signicant insipiration for his thoughts and ideas about the ten tribes. The correspondence between Ortelius and Postel has only recently been uncovered, and knowledge of the extent of it is far from complete,[74] but it is clear that the link between the French mystic and the Flemish cartographer was unique. It helps us to understand the connections among the ten tribes, geography, and restitution.

A Hebraist, Arabist, astronomer, mathematician, and Kabbalist (among many other things), Postel's character was popularized in Umberto Eco's *Foucault's Pendulum*.[75] However, already in 1678, a century after his time, he was described in *The Wonders of the Little World* as a sort of holy man: "William Postel a Frenchman [who] lived to an hundred and well high twenty years, and yet the top of his beard on the upper lip was black, and not gray at all."[76] Eco's Postel, not far from the historical figure, was described as in a "fit for mystical fervor and spiritual regeneration."[77] He maintained close relationships, if often tense, with thinkers from all Christian denominations, as well as with Jews and Muslims. Postel was very excited about Ortelius's inclusion of the ten tribes in his *Theatrum* and expressed his feelings about it in a letter to Ortelius in 1579. In this letter, Postel celebrates the common opinion that both he and Ortelius held about the ten tribes. Ortelius's "cosmographic depiction" would now show that "the ten tribes are in Scythia."[78] Evidently, Postel had very good reasons to rejoice about the *Theatrum*'s Arzareth. The question is: why was it so important to him?

Postel is mostly known for being an advocate of universalisms, who sought to "harmonize Christian, Jewish and Mohammedan [Islamic] thought" and who prophesied about a "universal religion, universal monarchy and world peace."[79] Against the backdrop of schisms, Postel deeply believed in *Concordia Mundi* or *Orbis Concordia*—the universal "triune ideal of unity, order, and peace."[80] The ideal of universal peace prompted Postel to explore and write extensively about the common origins of humanity and about the origins of, among others, "mysterious" peoples such as the Turks, Samaritans, and Scythians.[81] One could say that he was one of the first to conceive of world history as "human history" or as the history of humanity.[82] However, in addition to his scholarship, he reserved a special role for himself in bringing on this age of peace. Postel was not only the prophet proclaiming the coming of restitution, but he also believed that he was chosen to serve as "congregator."

His restless engagement with all sorts of religious strands was part of his self-understanding as a mystical peacemaker—the *congregator mundi* of the "Ecclesia Universalis, God's respublica on the earth."[83] One can suppose that, for the *congregator mundi* seeking the restitution and unification of all humanity, a lost collectivity such as the ten tribes would be highly interesting.

A variety of passages surveyed by historian François Secret suggest that Arzareth as a distinct site occupied a special place in Postel's world. An array of other clues indicates that this enigmatic man placed special importance on the ten tribes in his messianic *Concordia Mundi* schema. As Secret points out, the starting point of Postel's interest in the tribes was a 1516 Venetian exposition of the prophecies of Joachim di Fiore. This document, the *Expositio magni prophetae Joachim,* provides a hint at the tribes' location, prophesying: "[the ten tribes] will leave the Caspian Mountains through a certain valley, and will miraculously cross a river with the blessing of Christ that will calm down the incredible velocity [of that river] like it is said in Esdras 4, 13."[84] Intimated in this prophecy are traces of the Jewish legend of the Sambatyon, a river impassable because it is too fast for human crossing, and of Benjamin of Tudela's geographical speculations. However, the real innovation is the clear idea that Jesus performed the miracle of the crossing—obviously absent in Esdras.

The tribes were no longer beyond the Caspian Mountains, and Postel set out to identify and locate them. His eyes were on Central Asia and its various peoples, notably the Turks, whom he suspected were somehow related to the lost tribes.[85] In 1560, he cited "secret Jewish doctrines" that made it necessary to "infer that the Tartars are the successors of the Ten Tribes."[86] A year later, he wrote in his own *Cosmographicae Disciplinae Compendium* that Arzareth was in northern Asia close to the North Pole.[87] Postel most probably borrowed this idea from Sebastian Münster, whom he considered "so erudite and so well versed in all kinds of subjects."[88] Finally, Postel fully exposed his ideas about the location of the ten tribes in a letter of 1579 to Theodor Zwinger (1533–1588), in which Postel traced their entire journey. They were first "led by Shalmanesser to the Western borders of Persia and then until the river Gozan or Ganges." They then proceeded "to the extreme angle of Asia, that is to say, to Arzareth, which is the best part of the land of the Scythian people, or their ancestors. They arrive in there spontaneously while singing Gaou or Gaoth, or Oaoth, that is a word employed by Moses in the song of crossing the sea, [a word] that by secret mystery sings the victory of God."

The "Song on the Sea," sung by Moses after the crossing of the Red Sea (Exodus 15:1–18), describes the great victory of the Lord after he drowns the Egyptians in the sea. Central in both Jewish and Christian (Catholic) liturgy, it is one of the most powerful expressions of praising the Lord in the wake of his most crushing victory.[89] One can see the parallel between the breaking of the Red Sea and the ten tribes crossing the river on their way to Arzareth as a basis for a possible link between the two. There is also an interesting parallel between the Father breaking the sea and leading the redeemed Israelites to the promised land and the Son, Jesus, breaking the river and leading the ten tribes to Arzareth.

But Postel the mystic offers a more recondite connection, using the Zohar, the book of Splendor—the famous Jewish mystical interpretation of the Torah.[90] The song's second sentence, "I will sing unto the Lord, for he hath triumphed gloriously," contains the repetitive phrase "Ga'oh Ga'ah," which cannot be fully translated. In his 1573 preface to the Zohar, Postel noted the shape of the Hebrew letter aleph, which occurs in the word Ga'ah (*in voce Gaah notandum est literam Aleph*), explaining enigmatically that this shape points to the ten tribes. Yet there is nothing in the verse from the Zohar about the meaning of the biblical repetition "Ga'oh Ga'ah" that is connected to the ten tribes. Esdras said that the tribes moved to Arzareth to be away from sin.[91] For Postel, this is not enough. In his Arzareth, the tribes not only avoid sin, they also confirm God's glory. Postel's Arzareth also brings us back to Ortelius's map of Asia, the only other text where it is said that the ten tribes confirm the Lord's glory in this place. And Ortelius's notation next to Arzareth ended with a cryptic remark about the ten tribes' being renamed "Gauths or Gauthens, confirming God's highest glory," after their arrival in Arzareth. Another important allusion to Postel's theories about the ten tribes is the indication on Ortelius's map that the ten tribes' original location was a place called Turcestan from which they set out to Arzareth.

We can now understand Ortelius's map better: the tribes originally lived in the area from which the Turks also originated. They then moved to Arzareth where they assumed the name "Gaoths," and it is there that they confirmed God's glory. Clearly, Ortelius misunderstood Postel's quasi-Kabbalistic take on the word Gaoth and took it to be the tribes' new name. However bizarre and wild Postel's ideas were, the inclusion of his Arzareth in Ortelius's *Theatrum* was crucial. Nothing else gave it stronger purchase than the combination of a visual representation accompanied by an (enigmatic) text drawing on scripture, included in one of the most popular and authoritative atlases of the time.

From North Asia to the Americas

The placement of the ten tribes in North Asia and Ortelius's depiction of a retreating Arzareth solved the question of how the tribes had arrived in the

Americas. In 1580, thirty-six years after the first map with Arzareth appeared, the French Orientalist and Hebraist archbishop Gilbert Génebrard (1537–1597) provided the track of the ten tribes from North Asia to the Americas. He did so not in a *cosmographia* but in a *chronographia*, a chronology of Israelite/Jewish history largely based on Jewish sources. In the first edition of his chronography, published in 1567, Génebrard simply notes that the Assyrians deported ten tribes. In the 1585 edition, he adds a lot more. Génebrard's notation is "3434 to the Creation," the year the deportations of the tribes took place. Génebrard goes into a lengthy explanation about their history after the destruction of their state, quoting 2 Kings. Following the well-known passage from Esdras, Génebrard states that they went "to a region called 'Asereth'" (*region voactur Asereth*) by crossing the Euphrates and the "desert of Tartary." Alluding to Ortelius, Génebrard locates Asereth/Arzareth first in the "Northern Regions" (*partibus Septemtrionis*) in Asia or in the "Grand Tartaries" (*Tartariae Magnae*). His goal, however, is America. The tribes then continued to walk through an "unknown land towards Greenland" (*terram ignotam versus Grotlandiam*) until they reached the outer boundaries of America. Thus, the tribes first went northeast toward Tartary but then headed west. Now that we know that humans did cross the Bering Straits to the Americas, Génebrard was not really far from the truth.

However, Génebrard's concern was the ten tribes, and it is for this reason that he needed to invent that unknown land, somewhere in the most distant north, that connected North Asia and Greenland. It solved a geographical problem stemming from his acceptance of two facts—Arzareth was in North Asia and the ten tribes moved from it to the Americas—and covered for any geographical inconsistency that a route from North Asia to America near Greenland suggests. A look at Ortelius's world map shows Greenland as a very small island stuck between northwestern Europe and northeastern America and very close to both; it is also very close to an unknown and uncharted large island lying to its north. This unnamed island, which Ortelius counts as part of several large bodies of land collectively named Septentrio, touches Tartary. The route Génebrard limns seems a bit bizarre but makes sense—from Tartary to Septentrio toward Greenland and then to America. Génebrard was not the only one contending with the problem of passage to America to solve it in this way. As for "why America?" Génebrard says that it has been "long held by tradition and Kabbalah that the [ten tribes] are called enclosed, also the Americans are enclosed by seas from every side, and also America indeed is a large island, or peninsula." While, for the most part, America is separated by sea, the northern part of the continent is "covered" and is not.[92] America is enclosed enough to be similar to the ten tribes' home but connected enough to allow for their passage to it.

Thus, the ten tribes' road to America that culminated with Génebrard was long and involved a mixture of geographical logic, early modern cartography, theology, and mysticism. In Génebrard's speculations, we see how all converged, forcing searchers to ponder the physical shape of the world itself. Like Génebrard, others suggested specific paths based on actual maps. In the American context as well, this feature of the ten tribes' geography would become more pronounced in the debates about their route to America.

First Contact: The Canary Islands

The first encounter with the ten tribes begins not with America, but with an earlier sighting of the Canary Islands, some 200 miles west of Africa, well before Columbus's journeys. The Spanish pondered if they had found the ten tribes. The Canary Islands were not exactly a discovery (Europeans knew of them at least since 1339), but they were certainly the first colonies of the Spaniards. The Spanish conquest of the Canaries, which began in 1402, took a long time. Hugely significant in the development of Spanish maritime activity, they provided a deep-water harbor in the Atlantic from which Spanish ships sailed west. Their position within the Atlantic wind system was vital for sailing. All of Columbus's voyages began there.[93] In many respects, the people of the Canaries were the Spaniards' "first encounter" and Europe's first "New World," or first "other world."

A rare early history of the conquest of the Canaries, written before the end of the sixteenth century by Friar Juan de Abreu de Galindo (b. 1535?), reports on debates concerning the people of the Canaries and the ten lost tribes that took place after the islands' discovery. Opinions holding that the ten tribes came to the Canaries have not survived, but are expressed in de Galindo's history, where they are refuted. According to one opinion, the ten tribes had been exiled to the islands. The basis for this theory lies in Esdras's prophecies, says de Galindo, who reasons that, after their initial deportation, the captives received God's permission to go "much farther to a land never inhabited by people." The islands were chosen because they were not populated at the time. The tribes came in order to populate them and to remain "concealed."[94] In this regard, the island fit the prophecy that, it is clear, de Galindo accepts as truth, though for other reasons (the absence of traces of Hebrew language and customs), he rejects them as home to the tribes.[95]

Another history of the conquest of the Canaries, published much later (in 1772), suggests that the question of the ten tribes in the Canaries kept tormenting scholars. José de Viera y Clavijo (1731–1813), a botanist who settled in Gran

Canaria, wrote that "there was not even a single trace of Hebrew, or custom, or rite, or idiom" that would support the theory that the tribes ever landed in the islands.[96] In the case of the earlier instance, not only sophisticated ethnography, but also plain geography helps de Galindo's refutation:

> Although Esdras says that [the] ten tribes went to distant regions after being deported, one must consider what he also says namely, that the journey took a year and a half. If we compute the leagues from the city of Nineveh, which was the principal and metropolitan [center] of the Assyrians, to these islands of the Canaries, there are 1435 leagues, or a bit more or less. Now, counting seven league[s] of journey for each day, there are 250 days of journey that one has to do in this respect from the city of Nineveh to the Canary Islands. However, Esdras says that the journey took a year and a half which means that they went much farther [than the Canaries]. . . . in this we have for sure a proof that Israelites who were deported are Indians that were discovered in New Spain and all over that land and not those [natives] of these Canaries.[97]

Here, in the strict demand that geography fit prophetic text, we have perhaps the clearest example of theology and geographical imagination at work. The Canary Islands were not the land of the ten lost tribes. They are simply too close to Nineveh.

Speculations about a possible relationship between the Canaries and the missing tribes surfaced as soon as the Spanish began colonizing them, before Columbus's voyages farther into the Atlantic and before the discovery of the Americas. From early in the Age of Discovery, the possibility of finding the tribes loomed large. De Galindo's commentary on the length of the journey from Nineveh to the Canary Islands related to the big questions: was this they, and were the Americas their home? An affirmative answer in turn raised another: what had led the ten tribes to leave their traditional locations in Asia and eastern Africa and migrate to the Americas?

The theory of Canary Islanders as ten tribers was ultimately abandoned not only for the absence of supporting evidence, but also because a better candidate was discovered—American Indians. Unlike the natives of the Canaries, the "Mexican Indians" were said to have many traces of Hebrew and Israelite ritual, and the Mexican language had many Hebrew words. Many Indians practiced circumcision, and like the Jews, they often bathed in rivers. The Indians also held to "many other Jewish rites and ceremonies." Even the existence of sorcerers among them was marshaled as evidence: "we know from sacred scripture that the Israelites had many sorcerers who worshipped the idol of the Baal." De Galindo even offered an explanation as to why America,

which appeared too far from Nineveh geographically, met the biblical specifi-
cations: "In the sea one covers 50 leagues per day."[98] Travel over water was
quicker than over land.

The Canaries appear to mark the first instance of speculation as to whether
an existing group had any connection to the ten tribes. And it is certainly the
first case in which a combination of geographical calculation, ethnography, and
prophecy was employed in the effort. Up until this moment, all news of the ten
lost tribes had been the product of rumor, outright lies, and speculations. We
have seen in the case of Eldad's interrogation by the Jews of al-Qayrawan how a
sort of ten tribes protocol of investigation and examination was in place. But in
Eldad's case, it was Jews who interrogated a claimant. In the Canary Islands
case, we find Christian clergy examining an indigenous people.

It is perhaps not surprising that the Spanish were the first Christians to
entertain the possibility of actively finding the ten lost tribes. Spain had one of
the largest and most well integrated communities of Jews in the world,
certainly in Europe. From 1391 on, a large converso (converts to Christianity)
community existed in Spain, giving Jewish ideas about the ten tribes more
exposure to Christians than in any other country in Europe. (Here we recall the
discourses of ha-Lorki and Abravanel; and the first publication of Benjamin of
Tudela's travelogue in a language other than Hebrew was in Spain.)

There is more, however, deriving from the specific Spanish context of that
period. De Galindo's knowledge of "Jewish ceremonies" indicates that he is
familiar not only with Jewish rites and rituals, but also with a protocol of
recognizing and identifying Jews. The fact that he is able to compare freely
among Jewish rites, Indian rites and customs, and Canary Islanders' culture
and language suggest that he is very familiar with the methods entailed in
gathering such information. One does not need to look far to find out why. As
is well known, a highly elaborate and sophisticated protocol for recognizing
Jews and Jewish practices—the Inquisition—had existed in Spain since
the creation of the first large converso community after the pogroms of 1391.
Later waves of conversion, culminating in the mass conversions of 1492,
intensified the needs (and abilities) of this institution.[99] There were simply a
lot more New Christians (conversos) to spy on, and far more interrogations
were conducted in order to identify and root out Jewish rites. Manuals that
instructed the good Catholic, and of course the inquisitor, in identifying
"tricky and deceiving" conversos were popular. One such, the *Alboraique*,
published in the 1480s, displays "an astounding range of erudition, combining Christian, Muslim and Jewish sources."[100] De Galindo's sixteenth-century
discussion concerning the existence or absence of Jewish rites or "traces"
among indigenous peoples came out of this environment.

His comparisons between Jewish and Indian rites can also be seen as a precursor to practices that in time would become increasingly common. Historian Irene Silverblatt has exposed the many affinities and connections that existed between inquisitorial discourses about conversos and discourses about Native Americans: "Jews and Indians, according to seventeenth-century lore had their own special ties," thanks to their "common Semitic heritage"—an assumption in part derived from the theory that the Indians were the lost tribes. Silverblatt shows how the inquisitorial registers, particularly in New Spain, became intertwined with regard to Jews and Indians.[101] Inspecting Indians alongside or in contrast to Jews was a common practice.

The connections among inquisitorial practices, Marranic Jews, Jewish rites, and the ten tribes are reflected conspicuously in Montezinos's story. It is in prison, after being interrogated by the Inquisition, that Montezinos concludes that the Indians are the ten tribes and that the *casique* is hiding something. Later on, his encounter with the ten tribes involves identification of their rites. The idea that the ten tribes are hiding within another people or hiding their identity is represented quite literally in the story. Now the question was no longer "where are the ten tribes?" but also "who are the ten tribes?" Finding the ten tribes had now become a matter of identifying them within another group of people or as another group of people. Ethnology would become another way, indeed, the most common way, of seeking them out and finding them.[102]

The Tribes' Paths to America: Atlantis, Greenland, and the Anian Straits

Diego Durán's (c. 1537–1588) *Historia de las Indias de Nueva-España y islas de Tierra Firme* was an early central proponent of the ten tribes in America theory, a study of the newly found continent, and a history of its natives. Virtually all studies of America in this period dealt with the ten tribes question as a derivative of a larger issue: how did the continent first become populated, and by whom? The question of the Indians' origins didn't matter only for science's sake. Determining who they were was a serious concern of the Spanish Empire since its answer would prescribe the way in which they should be treated.[103]

Discussions about the ten tribes in America to which de Galindo's study of the Canaries pointed had been in place for decades. Already in the 1540s, one Dr. Roldán, from Spain, used Esdras to argue that Native Americans were the ten tribes.[104] Roldán calculated that the tribes walked eastward from Nineveh at a pace of twenty miles (seven leagues) per day. He also used Hosea to justify their treatment by the Spaniards, the first instance in which the biblical text, promising punishment for the ten tribes, was used to justify the dispossession of Native Americans. Bartolomé de las Casas, a major proponent of the Indians' human rights, refuted the theory but to no avail; it gained more purchase with Durán.

A Dominican friar probably of Jewish descent, Durán was one of the most vocal early proponents of the idea that the American Indians were the ten tribes.[105] Born in Spain and raised in Mexico, Durán acquired a great deal of knowledge about America's natives and their languages. Durán's key goal was to establish that the Spanish colonization of the Americas was part of a divine plan,[106] and he declared that understanding the origins of the American Indians was a work of "divine revelation." Proving that the Native Americans were members of the "Hebrew people" was supported by the sacred scripture.[107] A key feature in his account is the natives' "inclination to idolatry," held up as proof of their connection to the ten tribes, which are condemned in the Bible for their idolatry. God, Durán reminded his readers, promised the tribes the "most rigorous punishment" for their "great evil deeds and abominations."[108] However, as Kadir rightly points out, Durán's interest in identifying the American Indians with the ten tribes was not just a scriptural exercise. He was "explicit in remarks that not only proclaim the Indians to be Jewish, but serve the unmistakable purpose of justifying the Conquest."[109] Linking the Native Americans with the ten tribes helped to justify the Spanish conquest of the Americas and its horrors. The conquerors were merely serving as the hand of God. Durán's theories about the ten tribes in America were based on scriptural interpretations and driven by political and theological considerations. This was not the first time that political and theological considerations used the story of the ten tribes, nor was it the last. But Durán's justification of the advent of empire and its horrible consequences is probably the most blatant example.

Durán was familiar with the criticisms of Spanish attitudes toward American Indians. The first to voice them, in a spectacular speech in 1511, was another Dominican friar, Antonio de Montesinos (not to be confused with Aharon ha-Levi). Standing at the podium in Santo Domingo Church, Hispaniola, the friar promised the Spaniards "hell" for what they were doing in America. The sermon was recorded and relayed back to Spain by las Casas, who was greatly influenced by Montesinos.[110] The idea of punishment for the Spaniards resonates strongly in the story of Antonio Montezinos/ha-Levi over a century later, which tells of an encounter with the hidden and embattled ten tribes, who suffered terribly in the wake of the Spanish invasion. Their return, as Montezinos envisions it, is not only a restoration with the rest of the Israelite people, but a promise of punishment and even revenge for Spanish crimes in the New World. Recall that in the account, just before he leaves the secret location of the ten tribes, one of the mysterious men gives Montezinos a promise with a threatening message to the Spanish. It seems to be a reversed echo of Durán's logic: instead of the Spanish punishing the ten tribes, the ten tribes will punish the Iberian colonizers.[111]

But if the Indians were the ten tribes, how did they get to the Americas? Let us first look at Atlantis.

Atlantis is mentioned in Plato's *Timaeus and Critias* as "an island that disappeared in the depths of the sea." "The island was larger than Libya and Asia put together, and was the way to other islands, and from these you might pass to the whole of the opposite continent which surrounded the true ocean."[112] Plato comments that, in "those days," before Atlantis sank, "the Atlantic was navigable." The newly acquired European navigability of the Atlantic brought to the fore the issue of the sunken continent as a cosmographical problem.[113] Where (if at all) was Atlantis, and what was its relationship to the New World? The new interest in Atlantis was a derivative of the big question concerning the populating of the Americas. Already in 1535, Gonzalo Fernandez de Oviedo y Valdes (1478–1557), one of the earliest historians of the New World, suggested that the people and culture of the New World originated in Atlantis.[114] Shortly thereafter, Atlantis attached itself to the lost tribes. Atlantis is similar to the unknown land that Génebrard invented in the north in order to bridge North Asia and Greenland. We do not know who was the first to make this move. As in the cases of the Canaries and the torture of the American Indians, it is an opponent who first brings the theory to light in a coherent manner.

The great Jesuit scholar José de Acosta (1540–1600), the "Pliny of the New World," was hugely resistant to the Indians/ten tribes theory: "The opinion of many, who believe that the Amerindians come from the lineage of the Jews, is false."[115] A "heavy man, of uncertain, melancholic temper, a Jew by descent,"[116] Acosta had spent almost two decades in Peru, during which time he wrote the *Historia Natural y Moral de las Indias* (1590), an impressive work on the natural history of South America that won him the comparison to Pliny, whom he referenced frequently. For Acosta, the story of Atlantis was just plain nonsense, but it had to be refuted since proponents of the ten tribes theory claimed that the tribes got to the Americas through that continent. "I have no reverence for Plato [the source for the Atlantis myth] no matter how divine they may call him." In fact, Acosta had no reverence for several legends, among them, Ophir and Prester John, which he also rejected.[117] Atlantis simply was far too big to sink in the ocean without a trace: "What sea could be great enough to swallow such a vast extent of land . . . so completely that not a trace has remained?"[118] Acosta's blunt, authoritative manner did not put the debate to an end, however. Perhaps it even further promulgated the notion that the ten tribes had passed through Atlantis, since it is only after and in response to his angry dismissal of Atlantis that the first study of the subject saw light.

A Dominican friar, Gregorio García (c. 1540–1627), took on Acosta in his 1607 *Origen de los Indios del Nuevo Mundo*. García's main concern was the question of how America had been populated, but he also dedicated time to the derivative questions of the ten tribes and Atlantis. García insinuated that Acosta's Greek was poor and that his erroneous conclusions stemmed from having read Plato in Latin. He offered a systematic set of refutations of Acosta's statements against Atlantis. The result is a learned assembly and discussion of all sources relating to Atlantis from Greek and Roman times onward. Its most interesting feature is a form of ethnolinguistics. "In the Mexican language the word for 'water' has the letters 'Atl' . . . which are at the very least the first three letters of the word 'Atlantis.'" Atlantis is closely associated with water since it gave the Atlantic Ocean its name. Having established this connection (ignoring the fact that "Atlantic" is a European word), García points out that the combination "atl" occurs frequently in the Mexican language, particularly in important words denoting gods (as in Quetzalcoatl), place names, etc. "It is certain that the combination of the letters T.L. does not occur in all the nations of Asia, Africa, and Europe, and in [other languages] in the New World . . . more than in the Mexican language."[119] The Mexicans thus were shown as uniquely and intimately connected to Atlantis. (Two centuries later, when the great German scientist Alexander von Humboldt [1769–1859] traveled to Latin America, he commented in his diary, "I am rather disposed to think that the grammatical system of the American idioms has confirmed the missionaries of the sixteenth century in their ideas respecting the Asiatic origins of the nations of the New World. The tedious compilation of Father García, *Tratado del origen de los Indios,* is a proof of this.")[120]

However, García's main question was who had populated the Americas, and how. He was convinced that the earliest ancestors of the American Indians were in fact Hebrews. To be sure, García mentioned other ancient peoples who also came to the Americas, such as the Egyptians and the Phoenicians who, he said, had first populated Atlantis and then the Americas. Each, by their own right, could be considered the original Americans.[121] Yet, García insisted, the Hebrews had arrived there first. García, it seems, was more interested in establishing the ten tribes theory than in proving the validity of the Atlantis theory itself, and therefore was careful to also cite the theory that the tribes actually migrated to the Americas through North Asia—as science would one day actually prove to be possible.[122] The Asian theory was not only much stronger in that it involved no need to revive Atlantis, but it was closer to older and more familiar speculations about the North Asian location of Arzareth and the possible Arctic track to America. Here, García employed another tedious method of finding Hebrewisms in Native American rites and languages—a systematic presentation of an array of clues and evidence drawn primarily from biblical sources, but also from classical texts and contemporary studies, most notably those of Juan de Torquemada (1562–1624).[123] Among other things, he claims that the root "Mexi" came from the Hebrew word "Messiah." "The word 'Mesi,' which is actually Hebrew," in the Mexican language indicates "the commander, the head, the captain."[124]

Asking "How could those tribes go to the Western Indies crossing such an immensity of water and infinity of land?" García's answer sticks to the concrete: "From Grand Tartary they could go via land until Mongolia and from there, pass the Straits of Anian, which are very narrow and go to the kingdom of Anian that is already the Tierra Firme of New Spain."[125] The "Straits of Enian," separating Asia and America, appear on Ortelius's map as a sea above the China Sea (*Mare Cin*), just north of Japan. They are apparently named after a locale named Ania, found just south of Arzareth. The kingdom of Anian, or *Anian Regnum*, appeared first in a 1559 map of Asia made by Giacomo (Jacobo) Gastaldi (c. 1500–1566). This Italian cartographer, whose map was the basis upon which Ortelius created his own map of Tartary, decided that the locale "Aniu," mentioned by Marco Polo, was a kingdom north of China important enough to have the straits between Asia and America named after it.[126] They appear on maps by several major cartographers, such as Hondius, Mercator, and Ortelius. The straits inspired several expeditions attempting to find a path between Asia and the Americas. Henry Hudson (1570–1611), for instance, was among those who tried to reach the straits from the American side.[127] The Streto de Anian also appeared on an "accurate" map by Bolognino Zalteri (fl. c. 1555–1576) as very narrow straits parting northeast Asia from Mesoamerica, somewhere in the area of Panama. Zalteri's (distorted) map was probably the inspiration behind the expedition of Lorenzo Ferrer de Maldonado, who "discovered" the straits in 1588. Maldonado was greatly concerned with the "security hazard" that such an easy path to Panama could pose to Spain's assets in the Americas. "The Strait of Anian is fifteen leagues, and can easily be freed in a tide of six hours, and those tides are very rapid," he commented in a 1588 letter to Philip II of Spain (1527–1588).[128] Several decades later, Ben-Israel commented that "among the miracles the Blessed be He did with the ten tribes, he also created this Strait known as the Strait of Anian, so they can remain separated and hidden from the nations."[129]

García was very familiar with both Zaltieri's map and Maldonado's description of the straits; he referenced both in his narrative. Perhaps he also was attracted by the comment on the "rapid" tides that governed them, which may have struck him as a possible allusion to the River Sambatyon's mythic behavior. Using Ortelius's map, which places Arzareth on the Asian side of the straits, he was able to come up with a plausible trajectory leading the ten tribes all the way to New Spain. The path he proposed also explains some of the American Indians' rites and customs. On their way from Arzareth to the kingdom of Anian, the ten tribes, he asserts, "picked up some customs and rites observed in that kingdom and province." Careful to provide a complete picture of the possible paths to America, García also discusses the Greenland routes, providing a review of several suggestions put forth by other scholars, among them Génebrard, who "[m]aintains that Arzareth is [in] Grand Tartary... that as it is said in Esdras it is across the river Euphrates. [The ten tribes] went to the deserts of Tartary and from there to that land towards the Island of Greenland, because in that part it is said that America is not surrounded by sea and in other parts it is enclosed by the sea and is almost an island."[130]

Thus, we have at least three paths the ten tribes could have taken to America: Atlantis, the Straits of Anian, and Greenland. In toto, García's argumentation is an illustration of the various exercises in global geography that the ten tribes triggered. They involved early modern geography as well as scripture. Once one sought to establish the existence of the ten tribes in America, one had to deal with the question of their route there. Simply saying that God, or an angel, or Jesus performed some miracles en route was not enough. With the existence of "accurate" maps and a growing scientific/ geographic culture, one had to sketch the trajectory as clearly as possible. As geographical knowledge of the world expanded and was recorded on increasingly accurate maps, the exercise had to make geographical sense.

This mode of argumentation peaked in 1681 with Diego André's Rocha, a physician from Lima who had served in different capacities in Spanish America. Rocha's lengthy *Tratado Único y Singular del Origen de los Indios* is indeed unique and singular—covering all peoples from "Santa Fe" in the north through "Mexico and Peru to Chile." Rocha, "an ardent Spanish patriot," as his nineteenth-century editor dubbed him, makes the argument that the Americans' ancestors were descendants of "ancient inhabitants of Spain in the first place, and of the Israelites and Tartars in the second."[131]

Rocha's problem was how to explain differences among the Native Americans, particularly differences that made some "very valiant" while others were not. His solution was simple: the "valiant" Native Americans were descendants of the ancient Iberians; the others were either Tartars or Israelites.[132] Following

García, Rocha identified the Toltecs as the descendants of the ten tribes; his treatment involved careful readings of all the relevant prophets and numerous scholars, ethnographers, geographers, and cartographers from the ancients Josephus, Pliny, and Strabo to Ortelius and other early modern figures.

"How did the ten tribes arrive from the East to the West?" This, in Rocha's view, was the main "difficulty that the Prophet Esdras left open" when he described the route to Arzareth.[133] Rocha tracked the tribes' route from Samaria all the way to Mexico, leaving no theory untouched and no map unexamined (except Postel, who is conspicuously missing). The result is a marvelous treatise on world geography, including a meticulous analysis of several of Ortelius's Asian maps in conjunction with biblical prophecies tracing the tribes' routes through northern Assyria to Armenia and the Caspian Sea and from there to Turkestan and Arzareth. Rocha paid heed to the Greenland and Atlantis theories, reviewing every piece of evidence. He also discussed the possibility that the ten tribes might be on other continents, such as Africa.[134] In the end, he came up with an all-encompassing hypothesis that combined all of the previous ones: some tribes had come through Atlantis, some through Greenland, and the majority from Arzareth through the Straits of Anian. Some even remained in their original Old World locations, with others staying on in different locations through which they had passed en route. This allowed Rocha to encompass all of the locations ever discussed as putative homes of the ten tribes and to bring many of their residents along to the Americas:

> The lost or exiled tribes . . . and their descendants and the other
> nations came from Asia and from Grand Tartary, populating all
> of Northern America [la America Septentrional] and all parts of
> Mexico. . . . The first that entered Mexico were the Toltecs, who were
> the main bunch of the ten tribes and many of them came from
> Arzareth penetrating through the Kingdom of Anian and passing
> the Straits of the same name.[135]

Rocha adds to the list other members of the ten tribes, who had remained in Arzareth and then arrived in the Americas in a later wave (which sequencing explains the ethnic differences among the various peoples of Mexico). The most important innovation in his treatment is the idea that the ten tribes are not located in one place; their remnants could be found anywhere along their way from Samaria to Mexico. In short, Rocha tells a well-documented story of a global migration and wandering centered in part on the ten tribes. This set the stage for the global search for the tribes that began in the later part of the eighteenth century.

Between Gregorio García's 1607 *Origen de los Indios* and Rocha's 1681 unique and singular *Origen de los Indios* stood Menasseh Ben-Israel's 1650 *Orígen de los Americanos,* in which the story of Antonio Montezinos/Aharon ha-Levi appeared. Ben-Israel's erudite tome shared with the other two the premise that the ten tribes, or part of them, had arrived in the Americas, and in this respect it sits squarely in the Spanish context of the debates about the peopling of the Americas. But Ben-Israel's book, better known as the *Hope of Israel,* truly belongs in a different context—that of the English romance with the ten lost tribes.

6

Hopes of Israel

My brethren, as thou call'st them, those ten tribes I must deliver,
if I mean to reign.
—John Milton, *Paradise Regained* (1671)

Biblical Culture and Political Perceptions of the Ten Tribes

During the late seventeenth century, England emerged as the site
of the hottest debate over the ten lost tribes. By Milton's time and
beyond, even when ideas about the tribes were generated elsewhere
in Europe, they were echoed most strongly in the English-speaking
world, notably the United States and the empire.[1] The English phase
of the story, while not the last, was certainly the high point of the world
history of the ten tribes, intimately connected to the strong desire, as
Milton put it, to "deliver" them. While the ten tribes appear in *Paradise
Regained,* they—or, more precisely, their lostness—are part of the
condition that characterizes *Paradise Lost.*

In 1652, the historian, geographer, and theologian Peter Heylyn
(1600–1662) published *Cosmographie in Four Bookes,* a "chronography
and history of the whole world." The book, based on *his* 1625
Microcosmus of the *Great World,* taught the reader that the "apostacy
[*sic*] of the ten tribes at once from the Law of their God and the
extermination of the other two in short time, abundantly declare[s] the
frail condition and estate of the Jewish Church." Reading on, one

learns all about the ten tribes—a featured, lengthy chapter on Palestine gives a detailed account.[2] Two centuries later, Palestine would be a topic of central interest in England,[3] one connected to the ten tribes.

These were the times when the Bible, the King James edition in particular, was hugely influential in English thought.[4] Milton's England was a "biblical culture" where "[m]en knew their bible very well . . . and could convey messages through allusion to it."[5] Politics was a favorite realm for such. In a political climate that saw many dramatic shifts, the story of the ten tribes—one of secession, with divine blessing, from the kingdom of a legitimate, but tyranni- cal, king—was continually invoked. Daniel Defoe (c. 1659–1731), for one, wrote a 1706 satire that included the lines "when Israel's tribes from Judah's scepter stray'd and laws of nature, not of kings obey'd . . . God justified the revolt of Ten Tribes for the Tyranny of Rehoboam."[6] Note the tension between "aposta- sy" and "revolt." The latter would become part of the political rhetoric popular in England at the time.

One of the legacies of the Glorious Revolution and the political upheavals that followed it was the sensitivity to royal tyranny. In 1681, for instance, the Parliament heard a speech: "For Parliaments and against Favourites." The speaker invoked the example of King Rehoboam "who forsook the counsel of old men and inclined to that of young men." "Why were the ten tribes taken from him?" the speaker sternly asked the king. The answer: the ancient king had not heeded counsel. The hint was clear: the English king must listen to his Parliament.[7] The warning reflected the recent and contemporary political goings on in England. Charles II (1630–1685) had been installed by the English Parliament twenty days before the fall of Cromwell in 1658. Charles II's father, Charles I (1600–1649), had been beheaded after a trial at Parliament.[8] Justify- ing this later, Sir Edward Peyton (1587–1657) invoked Rehoboam, "who justly lost the ten tribes," as his first justification for the Parliament's acts. "If the Parliament had not opposed King Charles, God would have been revenged on them."[9]

In the background were strong tensions between the kingdom's Protestant subjects and its Catholic rulers. In 1688, during the Glorious Revolution, James II (1633–1701), the last Roman Catholic king of England, was deposed by a group of parliamentarians. The king, whom Defoe would later depict as a modern-day Rehoboam, was distrusted for his religious policies and authori- tarian manner of rule. A Collection of State Tracts, Publish'd on the Occasion of the Late Revolution of 1688 cited the ten tribes at least twelve times to the effect that "if the King did change the form of government to Tyranny, the people had a right to reject him." The "history of the ten tribes" was invoked as "a proof" that the people had the right to change the government.[10]

An even more bluntly political use of the ten tribes story came after the ascension of the house of Hanover to the English Crown amid political upheavals. In 1714, the year George I (1660–1727) was installed as the first Hanover monarch, George Ridpath (d. 1726), a prolific journalist and pamphleteer, published a lengthy treatise "in Defence of the late Revolution and the Hanover succession" that he sent to all members of the English Parliament. "The late King James...came with a French power to wreath the yoke of popery and slavery on our necks," wrote Ridpath, "an overt act more express than that of Rehoboam." And, as he pointed out, Jeroboam had been given the divine order to secede in direct response to Rehoboam. Ridpath traced the history of the ten tribes down to their exile, reminding his readers that "the Israelites were forever dispers'd among Foreign Nations for their concurrence with their kings in Idolatry, Tyranny, and the Breach of Leagues."[11] Never mind that the ur-text in 2 Kings mentions no crimes other than idolatry. The addition of the political crimes of tyranny and deceitful diplomacy to the ten tribes' story nicely shows the politicization of the story characteristic of eighteenth-century England. After all, what could be more authoritative than the Bible? Ridpath's justification of the Hanovers' coming to power did not make them immune to the criticism that had befallen their predecessors: the ten tribes could be used to undermine any regime and justify any revolt.[12]

Just as the pains of schism were not lost on Calvin during the sixteenth century, political thinkers in the seventeenth and eighteenth focused on the legitimacy of the tribes' secession from and revolt against a rightful king. On December 12, 1776, the Scottish priest William Thom (1710–1790) delivered a lengthy sermon on "The Revolt of the Ten Tribes": "Is there not cause to look on this war...which threatens a division of the British Empire, as a judgment of heaven, for our impiety and wickedness?"[13] Thom was not the only one to tie the impending schism to the split in ancient Israel. The great Scottish jurist and theologian John Erskine (1721–1803) discussed the case of the ten tribes as an example of the sort of bad administrative "measures that have unhappily occasioned the American revolt."[14] One magazine of 1777 opined that the ten tribes' revolt was "a defensive war exactly upon the same ground as that of the Americans, a refusal to submit to the arbitrary imposition of taxes."[15] Across the Atlantic, the famous revolutionary preacher and New York politician Abraham Keteltas (1732–1798) reminded his listeners that "when Rehoboam and Judah went out to fight against [the ten tribes] to bring them back to subjection, God sent his prophet...saying 'ye shall not go up and fight against your brethren.'"[16] Perhaps within the political rhetoric surrounding the revolutions of 1688 and 1776 lurk the roots of both the United States' and England's nineteenth-century identification with the ten tribes. As a theological and political question, the history of the ten tribes was evidently very much on people's minds throughout the seventeenth and eighteenth centuries.

The ten tribes also surfaced in the context of the American debate over slavery. The *Quarterly Anti-Slavery Magazine* from New York told its readers in 1836 that "with all the wickedness of these apostate ten tribes they were stricken with remorse" when the abolitionists were "convinced by a prophet of the lord" that owning slaves "was a flagrant violation of the law."[17] Supporters of slavery, on the other hand, enslaved the tribes themselves as proof of divine approval. The 1852 *Pro-Slavery Argument* explained that "slavery existed in Assyria and in Babylon" and that "the ten tribes were carried off in bondage to the former by Shalmanezar."[18]

Finally, the Civil War, the second major political schism to devastate the English-speaking world in less than a century, reintroduced the ten tribes yet again. George Junkin (1790–1868), an educator and Presbyterian minister, discussed the ten tribes' rebellion in a treatise on the Civil War and urged the "southern people," whom he likened to the ten tribes, to prove that "the sovereign powers vested in the United States have been forfeited by cruel and tyrannical abuse."[19] The Reverend John H. Aughey (1828–1911), a "refugee from Mississippi," warned the "supporters of secession who [were] advocating the way of the ten tribes" that "if we, as the ten tribes, resist the ordinance of God, we will perish."[20] Less than a hundred years since it had been invoked in support of the secession of the colonies from the British Empire, the secession of the ten tribes was now used to condemn the Confederates who wished to do the same to the Union. Such was the power of the ten tribes story to attach itself to different political events in a culture in which the Bible played a central role.

From at least Milton's time, the combination of a specific biblical culture and a unique political trajectory introduced the ten tribes into the realm of political thinking and kept them there as long as scripture enjoyed a dominant cultural status. Their messianic promise, however, was much more powerful.

Millenarianism and Irenic Scholarship

In 1701, Daniel Defoe invoked the ten tribes in yet another context: the gloomy fate of the "Protestants of France." Once "a powerful bunch," he lamented, the French Protestants were now "quite lost, sunk and gone." Complaining about the poor treatment of the Huguenots by France's Catholic government, Defoe depicted them as "either suppressed or driven to paupery at home, or like the Ten Tribes of Israel, scatter'd abroad into so many unknown countries that they have lost themselves."[21]

The ten tribes, it seems, had a monopoly on lostness and on the condition of being lost in an unknown country. Defoe was perhaps not surprised to see that the first modern comprehensive history of the Jews had been authored by a Huguenot refugee, Jacques Basnage (1653–1723), who settled in the Netherlands.[22] Basnage, who was undoubtedly inspired by Calvin's emphasis on schisms, wrote of the "body of ten tribes [that] remained in the schism."[23] His favorite term for the tribes was "Schismaticks."[24] The schism of the tribes was not merely a singular event in history, but a *condition of existence*—and mending the schism would come to be a hugely important goal.

Jews and the ten tribes featured still more prominently in early modern scenarios of a millenarian or messianic nature, as is well researched.[25] Jews and their conversion were central in almost every one. "The conversion of the Jews in the 16th and 17th centuries was part of a package of ideas about the approaching end of the world and the millennium," the most popular target years for which fell between 1650 and 1666.[26] The conversion of the ten tribes was depicted as a harbinger of the conversion of their brethren from the remaining two.

In Jewish millenarian thinking, too, the tribes featured prominently. Waves of messianic expectation had erupted periodically since the expulsion from Spain in 1492. As we have seen, the appearance of David Reuveni in Italy and Portugal in the 1520s and 1530s entailed and fed a particularly acute messianic aspiration among Portuguese conversos. The seventeenth century was even more turbulent. The 1648 pogroms in the Ukraine brought a wave of messianic expectations that culminated in the appearance of Sabbatai Zvi (1626–c. 1676) in various parts of the Ottoman Empire just before the crucial year 1666. As Gershom Scholem has shown, the ten tribes surfaced repeatedly in the two decades before Zvi's rise.

Various European Christian theologians and millenarians listened attentively to the Jewish rumors about the coming of the ten tribes. While Jewish sources were not fully explicit about the arrival of the ten tribes, Christian rumors were unambiguous.[27] While the ten tribes issue was not particularly salient in the messianic message of Sabbatai Zvi, certain Christian observers of the movement were more than ready to insert it. The man most associated with rumors about the appearance of the ten tribes during the days of the Sabbataian movement was Peter Serrarius (1600–1669), who, only a decade before, was engaged with others in a dialogue with Manasseh Ben-Israel,[28] who stood at the center of this cultural climate of intense interest in the ten tribes.

Ben-Israel's *Hope of Israel* and the circumstances of its writing and publication in 1650 first belong to the Spanish phase of the ten tribes' history. Both Ben-Israel and his hero, Antonio Montezinos/Aharon ha-Levi, came out of the

milieu of Iberian New Christians returning to Judaism in the sixteenth century. The broader setting for the story was the Spanish Atlantic world. Yet at the
same time, the author and his book were connected to the Protestant and
English milieux. Indeed, one could say that the English version of *Orígen de los
Americanos* was a different book altogether, so different was its reception in
England, where it caused a major stir.[29] English theological interest in Montezinos's story was huge.[30]

Shortly after Montezinos testified in 1644 in Amsterdam about his encounter with the hidden tribes in the mountains of South America, Ben-Israel
was "bombarded" by Christian scholars "from all parts of Europe" with inquiries about his story. English scholars, with whom Ben-Israel—a rabbi of great
fame among both Jews and Christians—had been in contact for some time,
were particularly interested in Montezinos's report.[31] A small circle of English
and Dutch philo-Judaists, who were highly interested in signs of the impending mass conversion of the Jews, engaged Ben-Israel in dialogue over many
theological and scholarly matters; they considered him, quite rightly, the father
of Judeo-Christian friendship.

Born in 1604 to a converso family who escaped Portugal and settled in
Amsterdam, where he became a rabbi, Ben-Israel made a name for himself
among Christian Hebraists and scholars as the "chief Doctor of the Jews."[32]
Hope of Israel came as a result of Ben-Israel's correspondence with John Dury
(Durie) (1597–1680), a "chaplain at The Hague," and Nathaniel Holmes (or
Homes; 1599–1678), a "notorious millenarian" who had a career at Oxford and
served as a minister in London. Both independently wrote to Ben-Israel and
asked about the ten tribes in Jewish theology and thought. They were interested to know what the "Jewish Divine" had to say about Montezinos's story—that
is, about the ten tribes in America.[33]

There was an immediate reason for that correspondence. In 1648, Thomas
Thorowgood (1595–1669), a Puritan minister from Norfolk, had circulated a
manuscript that argued that the ten tribes were in America. His was probably
the first comprehensive treatise on the subject in English.[34] Thorowgood was
not interested in the geographic problems that concerned the Spanish scholars
but rather in the possibility of converting the Native Americans to Christianity.[35] Thorowgood had read about the successes of another Puritan, John Eliot
(1604–1690), in converting the Native Americans. For Thorowgood, this was
proof that a distant Jewish past was still present in America.[36] If the Indians
were the descendants of the ten tribes, he reasoned, that would explain why it
was easy to carry out missionary work among them. Note the Puritan emphasis
on "cultural grooming" and "civilizing" as an integral part of conversion to
Christianity. Having an Israelite past, as the ten tribes did, would help to

facilitate the missionary project, since the Indians' path to civilization would consequently be "shorter."[37] As descendants of the ten tribes, the Indians were at once an "other kinde of being, and condition, and may yet happily, by divine appointment, be restored and recovered."[38] The project of restoring the Jews should begin with the first exile—that of the ten tribes. Without finding the tribes, the restoration of the Jews could never be complete.

The language of "recovery" and "restoration" provided a different, powerful framework for the missionary work among the Indians. The cultural grooming of Indians was not simply a "civilizing project" of the "natives," but a work of recovering lost and forgotten practices. Thorowgood's treatise is important as the first to articulate the project of the Christianization of the Native Americans as a fulfillment of the restoration of the ten tribes. Once the Indians became Christians, they would not only be restored as God-fearing people, but also restored to the body of "Israel"—that is, the church—as the old biblical prophecies promised. Furthermore, Jesus's dictum to his disciples to go to "the lost sheep of Israel" was hereby reinvigorated as well. The prophecies of Isaiah, Ezekiel, Jeremiah, and others promising the return of the lost tribes in the latter days had gained a new, Christian meaning at the same time. Thorowgood's articulation of the conversion of the Indians charged the project of Christianizing the newly discovered peoples with a compelling new rationale, one that was to last long after this particular millenarian moment had passed.

The idea that evangelizing the Indians was in fact a work of restitution according to biblical messianic visions did not remain confined only to Puritan circles.[39] Several decades after Thorowgood first articulated this idea, Herman Witsius elaborated on it in his *Dekaphylon*.[40] Hundreds of years later, one can still find numerous books and sermons expressing the same logic. Nearly two centuries after Thorowgood, one author, the aforementioned Barbara Simon, spoke of the conversion of the Indians/ten tribes as an act of "saving" them from the state of being "ready to perish," as the King James Bible translated Isaiah's "lost in Assyria." As proof that the prophecy was right, the Native Americans were described (with tragic accuracy) as "a nearly extinguished race."[41]

Thorowgood's manuscript was important enough to prompt Durie and Holmes to turn to Ben-Israel and ask him for his opinion. By then, they were used to writing to discuss different questions relating to Jewish theology. The rabbi responded with *Hope of Israel*. He was hoping that his relationships with English scholars would help his efforts to obtain English permission to settle in the kingdom that had expelled its Jews in 1290, the efforts for which he won lasting fame. He was able to go to England in 1655 to plead with Cromwell for the readmission of the Jews. Partly thanks to his efforts, Jews were allowed to settle in England starting in 1664. (Ben-Israel had passed away seven years earlier, under the impression that his two-year mission in England had failed.)

There were also *Jewish* messianic overtones behind Ben-Israel's wish. Resettlement of the Jews in England would be the fulfillment of a prophecy in the book of Daniel (12:7): "When he shall have accomplished to scatter the power of the holy people, all these things shall be finished." Taking into account that the ten tribes were considered to be in America, England was the only location on earth with no Jews. A Jewish presence in the British isles would fulfill a "necessary condition" for redemption. Ben-Israel was also attentive to Jesuit reports in Europe about the discovery of Jews in China—at one edge of the earth—which he combined with rumors about the ten tribes in America, at a new edge of the earth. All this, together with prospects of Jewish settlement in England, might indeed bring the redemption.[42]

While Ben-Israel did not share the theological perspectives of his Christian colleagues, he certainly believed that he was living in an age that might see the beginning of the redemption of the Jews. His book's title, *Esperança de Israel,* points to the *Esperança de Portugal, Quinto Imperio do Mundo* by Antonio Vieira (1608–1697). Vieira, a Portuguese-born Jesuit who moved to Brazil, met with Ben-Israel twice, in 1646 and 1648, in Amsterdam. A prophetic figure in his own right, he developed a messianic vision centered on the mystical figure of the Portuguese king Sebastian (1557–1578), killed in a battle against Morocco. After his death, Sebastian became the core of a messianic cult to restore Portuguese power and unity. The slain young king was supposed to return and unite all of humanity under Portugal's rule. In Vieira's upgraded formulation, Portuguese Jews were to play a crucial first role in this process by rejoining the Portuguese nation and embracing Jesus.[43] This was the background for his contacts with Ben-Israel, a leading Jewish figure of Portuguese decent. While the two obviously disagreed on the role that the Jews were to play in the coming messianic era, the similarity of the titles of their books suggests a degree of mutual influence and dialogue. Vieira's bizarre ideas were somewhat substantiated by his incarceration by the Inquisition as a "Judaiser," but his call to restore the Portuguese Jews to Portugal should be seen as yet another variation on an idea that was on the minds of many at the time. Restoring the Jews—to the body of the church, to the Portuguese people, or to their land—was considered an important step in many millenarian or messianic scenarios. Isaac La Peyrère (1596–1676), a French millenarian of Marranic descent who was famous for his pre-Adamite thesis (which claimed that there was a human stage before the biblical Adam), called in 1643 for both Jews and Christians to return to an old form of Christianity to be shared by both.[44] Ben-Israel was certainly part of this restorative frame of mind. The

Hebrew title of the book, *Miqveh Israel,* while alluding to the Hebrew root *qvh* ("to hope"), alludes also to the restorative messianic vision; *miqveh* also means a "concentration of water." Historian Ernestine Wall puts it well: "The Jewish Rabbi and his millenarian friends were all living in the 'miqweh Israel,' the hope of the assembling restoration of the Jews. There was a kind of brotherhood between them."[45]

In addition to consolidating this brotherhood, the discussion regarding the ten tribes provided the rabbi with an opportunity to perform a sort of irenic scholarship intended to alleviate conflicts rather than deepen them—as Erasmus (1469–1538) conceived of its role. While the great Dutch theologian thought of irenism in the context of removing conflicts among Christians in the wake of the Reformation, Ben-Israel expanded it to Jewish-Christian relations. His *Conciliador,* which reconciled thousands of conflicting passages in the Bible, was intended for a Christian readership.[46] Even though it was not a work of scriptural exegesis, *Hope of Israel* is full of irenic statements.[47]

Hope of Israel, then, was born amid millenarian and messianic moods, in the context of a friendly, brotherly, Jewish-Christian dialogue over questions of the restoration of the Jews. The ten tribes were considered an important part of Israel and mattered in the context of its restoration, within either the Christian or Jewish realm. In this regard, Ben-Israel's *Hope of Israel* represents the culmination of centuries of Christian-Jewish exchanges and dialogues, direct and indirect, over the significance of the lost part of Israel, and the concord of the two religions. As Ben-Israel wrote, "All which things of necessity must be fulfilled, that so *Israel* at last being brought back to [its] own place; peace which is promised under the Messiah, may be restored to the world; & concord, which is the only Mother of all good things."[48]

A Historical Portrait of World Wanderers

The more practical issue at stake, however, was the *location* of the people of Israel. In this regard as well, *Hope of Israel* is the climax of a tacit Jewish-Christian dialogue. Truthful to his ideal of irenic scholarship, Ben-Israel produced the most inclusive treatise on the ten lost tribes ever undertaken up to his time: "I have collected many acts of the Jewes, and many histories out of the Hebrewes, the Arabians, the Grecians, the Latines, and other Authors of other nations."[49] Ben-Israel covered almost every Jewish source available to him at the time, up to Isaac Abravanel. He also included every well-known Roman and Greek geographer and historian. The list of Christian sources was equally comprehensive, including several church fathers, such thinkers as Postel and Génebrard, and Spanish writers such as José de Acosta and Gregorio García. With respect to geography, the list included contemporary geographers and cosmographers from the Jewish Abraham Farissol to Abraham Ortelius and many others. Ben-Israel also included Jewish chroniclers such as Joseph ha-Kohen (1496–1575) and Azariah Dei Rossi, whose works are considered the earliest examples of modern Jewish historiography, and also Josephus, the last Jewish historian before the early modern period.[50]

The inclusion of these historians was significant and bespoke a highly inclusive approach: "And because I intend a continuation of Josephus' *History of the Jews,* our famous historian; I entreat, and beseech all Learned men, in what of the World soever they live (to whom I hope that shortly this Discourse will come) that if they have any thing worthy of posterity, that they would give me notice of it in time," asks Ben-Israel.[51] The request that every learned man in the world send materials on Jews to Ben-Israel is very revealing. *Hope of Israel* was only one chapter in a "world history" of the Jews that meant to pick up where Josephus left off. Quite significantly, the circumstances within which this Jewish world history was conceived and produced involved an intense dialogue about the ten tribes. In fact, the history of the ten tribes, as recorded in *Hope of Israel,* was the very first chapter of the comprehensive Jewish history that Ben-Israel planned to write, but never completed.

Ben-Israel's request that all learned men from all parts of the world, not necessarily only Jews, send him materials relevant to this Jewish history he envisions further accentuates the inclusive drive of his project and his desire to have as knowledgeable a common ground for it as possible. The theological common ground upon which *Hope of Israel* rested was sufficiently vague so that Christian readers could interpret it according to their own theological considerations. On the other hand, the geographical common ground was simply presented as one whole. Following the story of Montezinos, with which the book itself opened, the geographical trajectory tracing the ten tribes that Ben-Israel presented to his readers followed all sources of Jewish and other nations alike, resulting in a rich jigsaw puzzle of world geography in relation to prophecy. Ben-Israel seems to have left no writer, prophet, or traveler unmentioned, nor any place unspecified. In this regard, he gave new and concrete meaning to Isaiah's prophecy of the return and, more important, presented a potent tool, perhaps even a method, for further accommodation of prophecy and geography. The global aspects of Isaiah's prophecies, discussed at length in the second chapter of this book, came to life forcefully in *Hope of Israel,* which quoted this particular prophet more than anyone else. But whereas Isaiah's world was the world created by Assyrian imagery, Ben-Israel's Isaiah now referenced a much larger one. In discussing the various possible paths the tribes took to the America, he wrote:

[A]nd why not some of them sail from *China*, and Anian . . . which do
border upon New Spaine; and from thence they went to Panama,
Peru, and those thereabout. These in my judgment are those Chinese
of whom *Isaiah* speaks, chap. 49 ver. 12 . . . *Behold these shall come from
afar, and these from the North, and from the West and from the land of
Sinim.*

The little issue of the term *Sinim* is a wonderful illustration of the change in
the relationship between scripture and geography that characterized this context. I showed earlier in chapter 2 that Isaiah's original *sinim*, which meant
"south," turned, implicitly, to "China" in a Midrash that was embedded in early
Arabic world geography. Here, we see a third twist of the prophecy; whereas the
aforementioned Midrash on Isaiah in the eighth century CE juxtaposed Sinim
with Spain, now Ben-Israel uses the same verse in order to tie together China
and New Spain. Furthermore, whereas China in the Midrash was just a reflection of the Arabic geographical imagination, which placed it at the far eastern
edge of the earth, Ben-Israel's China is far more real. He mentions several times
in his book the recent Jesuit reports "that there is a great number of Jews" in
China who might be descendants of the ten tribes. Ben-Israel is fully aware of
his accommodative move in this particular case. Invoking the Jesuit reports,
and even Ptolemaic geography, he thinks to refute a great medieval exegete,
Abraham Ibn-Ezra, who located Sinim to the south of the land of Israel, judging
Ibn-Ezra to be "mistaken."[52] Ibn-Ezra was, in fact, correct in his literalist close
interpretation of scripture in locating Sinim somewhere between ancient Israel
and Egypt. However, in the context of new times, new geographies, and new
theological demands, Ben-Israel did not hesitate to dismiss him in a way that
exposes his own accommodative interpretation and the huge extent to which his
views on the tribes were shaped by the culture and geography of his time.

However, the book's major contribution is the image it created of the tribes as
global wanderers. Ben-Israel's method of conciliating the anterior conflicting
geographical accounts was simple: parts of the ten tribes lived in different parts
of the world because they had arrived in these locations during the different stages
of their wanderings. Their wanderings were crucial for Ben-Israel, as they are for
the final stages of this book. It was at this moment in history, albeit after a long
period of incubation, that the image of the ten tribes as nearly nomadic wanderers
emerged clearly and in a world context. Ben-Israel draws a direct line to Esdras,
the first to suggest that the biblical locations of exile were not the final ones:

The first ground of that opinion is taken from 2 *Esdras* 13, v.
40 . . . [who says that the ten tribes] had passed over to . . . *Arsareth*
from whence we may gather that the 10 tribes went to New Spaine. . . .

Genebrardus, quoting *Esdras* concerning the wandering of the 10 tribes, saith, the *Arsareth* is *Tartaria the Greater* and from thence they went to Greenland.[53]

Ben-Israel also turns to more accepted scripture: "You must know that the ten tribes were not carried away at the same time . . . as I shew in the 2nd part of my Reconciler [*Conciliador*]."[54] At the same time, Ben-Israel resorts to contemporary geography in order to explain what happened next:

I could easily believe the 10 tribes as they increased in number, so they spread into more Provinces before mentioned, and into *Tartary*. For Abraham Ortelius in his Geography of the world, and Map of *Tartary*, he notes the place of [the] Danites, which he calls the Horde, which is the same [as] the Hebrew *Jerida*, signifying *A descent*. And lower, he mentions the Horde of Naphtali.[55]

Ben-Israel is able to place the ten tribes in every place ever suggested. As *Conciliador* harmonized conflicting biblical verses, *Hope of Israel* reconciled the geographical conflicts of the ten tribes story: some remnants of the tribes are behind the Sambatyon, some in China, some in Tartary, some in Ethiopia, and some in America. Rather than decide which of the conflicting sources is correct, Ben-Israel establishes that they *all* are. Accordingly, one could say that *Hope of Israel* is a sort of an irenicon, an instrument of peace, expanding the common ground between Jews and Christians and reconciling conflicting opinions.[56] Ben-Israel is happy to use the apocryphal Esdras as a hermeneutical device; if the ten moved once, they must have moved again—and again.

Esdras's logic served Ben-Israel well. If different parts of the tribes were wandering, there was no contradiction between the accounts placing them in different locations. The image that emerges is of nothing short of a global migration. Ben-Israel never got to write his intended world history of the Jews, but *Hope of Israel* is a seventeenth-century world geography, narrated through the search for the lost tribes—a cosmo-geography of loss. In Farissol's *Igeret* (which he cites), the ten tribes are in the old southern location somewhere between Arabia and India. The meticulous Farissol had little to contend with. In Ben-Israel's account, they are everywhere. His account reflects the various opinions that had proliferated in the century since Farissol. In sum, "[t]he Tribes are not in one place, but in many; because the prophets have foretold their return shall be into their Country, out of divers places."[57]

Thus, it was in terms of the geography of the ten tribes that Ben-Israel deviated from the Talmudic formula of a single location behind the Sambatyon—a position that was, for instance, still maintained by Farissol only a century before. In deserting the single-location theory and embracing this new geography, Ben-Israel brought the globalization of the ten tribes to a new height. They could potentially be everywhere, firmly fixed as the ultimate world wanderers.

Ben-Israel articulated new, flexible ways of accommodating prophecy and geography, while his history of wandering opened the opportunity of finding the ten tribes virtually anywhere. The appearance of the apprehension that the ten tribes had been "heathenized," any indigenous population in the world could now be a possible candidate for ten tribes ancestry. Many of these elements had appeared in earlier sources. But only with Ben-Israel's irenic approach was the wealth of the Jewish and Christian writings on the ten tribes organized and presented systematically as a coherent, unified body of knowledge. Not only could the tribes now be anyone, they could also be anywhere—and everywhere.

Thomas Thorowgood replicated the spirit of Ben-Israel's global approach, though he was first and foremost invested in the American theory. In 1652, two years after the publication of Ben-Israel's book, Thorowgood produced *Digitus Dei: New Discoveryes with Sure Arguments to Prove that the Jews (a Nation) or People Lost in the World for the Space of Near 200 Years, Inhabite Now in America*. While Thorowgood maintained the centrality of his American thesis, Ben-Israel's conclusions had clearly affected him. He now spoke of "bringing back ...the ten tribes from all the ends and corners of the earth."[58] In fact, *Digitus Dei*, the finger of God, was simply a new edition of the earlier *Iewes in America*. However, this new version included the correspondence between Durie and Ben-Israel. By then, *Hope of Israel* itself was circulating widely, and Thorowgood was clearly interested in linking his work to the authoritative book of the famous "Chief Jewish Divine." The Jewish identity of the author seemed to lend further authority to Christian motivations and goals.

The Jewish Indian theory persisted, developed into many variations, and resonated strongly on both sides of the Atlantic for centuries to come.[59] As Colin Kidd puts it, "Amerindian ethnography was strongly inflected by theological anxieties about the real identity of the native Americans." These theological anxieties were created chiefly by "scriptural parameters," which originally permitted only a monogenist explanation for the origins of humanity.[60] This reasoning brought the ten tribes, through the use of scripture, into the realm of racial thought on both sides of the Protestant Atlantic.

In the particular context of the ten tribes, these anxieties were fueled and driven not only by scriptural parameters that mandated all humans to be of Adamite and Noahid descent, but more acutely by the restorative promise embodied in *Hope of Israel*. "There is a strong argument in favor of the Indians being converted to Christianity, their being descended from the Jews," wrote Charles Crawford (b. 1752), a typical observer, in 1801.[61] Viewing the Native Americans as lost brethren added more power to missionary zeal. The ten tribes were terribly missed, and reuniting with them was the great hope of many. A "Song Millennial," sung in 1832 by preacher Harriet Livermore of Massachusetts, expressed this sentiment well: "How happy is Judah to meet his lost brethren / Tribes of the red man from forests afar; / 'These were they have been' the long outcast Ephraim / We've missed them e'er since the Assyrian war."[62]

The combination of the scholarly accommodation of prophecy and geography supplied by Ben-Israel and Thorowgood's theology of restoration furthered knowledge produced on the ten tribes in the American context. The sermons, news, reports, and attempts to prove the theory are too numerous to count.

Of course, not everyone in America agreed with the notion that the ten tribes were the ancestors of the Native Americans. Thomas Jefferson, a biblical scholar in his own right, entered into a debate with his colleague Elias Boudinot over the issue. He was but the most prominent. More and more evidence based on increasingly sophisticated and less passionate ethnography pointed to the simple reality—the Indians were not Israelites. This was, as Popkin stated, one of the most important reasons that the Jewish Indian theory eventually died.[63] There was simply no plausible evidence for the claim. The only real evidence found in America was a strange earthwork (a mound) discovered in Philadelphia in 1772, which, for a while, was taken to be the work of the ten lost tribes. The debate gradually dissipated as increasingly sophisticated archaeological and ethnographic research tied it to known Native American practices.[64]

On the whole, only those who initially set out to identify the Native Americans as the lost tribes were able to do so, for example, Boudinot in his *A Star in the West; or, A Humble Attempt to Discover the Long Lost Ten Tribes of Israel*. Its very title bespoke a strong messianic ambition: Jesus's birth, of course, had been foretold by the star in the east. Discovering the tribes was "preparatory to their return to their beloved city, Jerusalem"—as Christians, of course. Boudinot later would serve as the president of the American Society for Meliorating the Condition of the Jews, which sought to improve the circumstances of the Jews before their conversion to Christianity. Ultimately, he would engage the discovery of the tribes at all levels: accommodating prophecy, providing an ethnographic survey of Native American tribes, and discussing global geography and migration, with special attention to recent discoveries and voyages.[65] Writing at the beginning of the nineteenth century, Boudinot was quite convinced that the discoveries made since Ben-Israel's time only further corroborated the case for the tribes:

> It is now asked, can any one carefully and with deep reflection, consider and compare these traditions with the history of the ten tribes of Israel, and the late discoveries of the Russians, Capt. Cook and others, in and about the peninsula of Kamschatka and the northeast coast of Asia and the opposite shore of America, of which little was before known by any civilized nation, without at least drawing strong presumptive inferences, in favour of these wandering nations being descended from some oriental nation of the old world, and most probably, all things considered, being the lost tribes of Israel.[66]

In London in 1829, Barbara Anne Simon directly considered Ben-Israel in her own *Hope of Israel*. "Presumptive evidence" was put forward that "the aborigines of the Western hemisphere" were descended from the "Ten Missing Tribes of Israel." Simon was much more informed in the nineteenth century about world geography than Ben-Israel had been, and her narrative was far richer in detail than his. Still, he was crucial as an authority on accommodating scripture and geography. Nearly 200 years after him, Simon was certain that the hope of Israel—"the general restoration of the ten tribes"—was within reach. The appropriation of Ben-Israel's title reflects an underlying theme persistent for centuries, indeed since the birth of Christianity: "Israel" is the Christian church, not necessarily the Jews. When Harriet Livermore sang of "Judah missing his brethren," Judah signified not the Jews, but her Christian listeners.

Simon's project began as a purely theological speculation about the possibilities of restoring the Native Americans to Christianity. However, as she already had notified her readers in a special advertisement, a fresh 1836 volume with "new evidence about the Western tribes" was forthcoming. The ten tribes were now "historically identified" with the "Aborigines of the Western Hemisphere."[67]

The "new evidence" turned out not to be so new, given the research on Mexican antiquities undertaken by the relentless Lord Edward Kingsborough. Kingsborough is mostly associated with his marvelous collection of codices of Mesoamerican art and culture, the preparation of which cost him his fortune. An "amiable and talented nobleman" of Irish decent, Kingsborough devoted his life to studying the Spanish histories of North American indigenous peoples, particularly those of Mexico, hoping to prove that they were descendants of the ten tribes. Impoverished, Kingsborough died of typhus at forty-two in "the sheriff's prison in Dublin."[68] To the *Antiquities*, mostly facsimiles of art works, Kingsborough added an extensive text that was a summary of the many Spanish accounts he spent his lifetime reading. Ben-Israel and Montezinos were both cited as sources of inspiration.[69]

This book was what Barbara Simon used as her historical evidence. She simply republished Kingsborough's text, with some of her own commentary added at the front. In an appendix, she placed Ben-Israel's interpretation of prophecies foretelling the ten tribes' return.[70] Sandwiched between Simon's introduction and Ben-Israel's prophecies, Kingsborough's book reads rather differently from the original version. The original *Antiquities* had relied heavily on Spanish authors and on ethnographic and linguistic studies. It was thus not theological enough—that is, not embedded in the interpretive view that placed the ten tribes within the restorative messianic project.

By the beginning of the nineteenth century, the idea that Indians were Israelites had exhausted itself in the face of the overwhelming evidence to the contrary. Only a renewed theological thrust could keep it alive. In 1832, the polymath and natural scientist Constantine Samuel Rafinesque (1783–1840) attacked in his *Atlantic Journal* the "singular but absurd opinion that American tribes are descended from the Hebrews or the ten lost tribes."[71] He was outraged by the news that "Lord Kingsborough, having adopted [this] delusive idea . . . ha[d] vainly spent 80,000 pounds Sterling, or \$135,000!!!" on his *Antiquities of Mexico*. But the thing that most angered Rafinesque was the appearance in the United States of "a new religion or sect [that] has been founded on this belief!" Rafinesque identified the new sect of fanatics as "[t]he Mormonites thus called after a new Alcoran, or book of Mormons." The comparison to the Qur'an was intended as the ultimate insult."[72]

The Ten Lost Tribes and the Birth of Mormonism

The Book of Mormon, a collection of unknown Mesoamerican prophecies thought by Mormons to have been compiled by the prophet/historian Mormon, was first published in 1830 in Palmyra, New York. The publisher, Joseph Smith (1805–1844), claimed to have found the book in 1827 in the form of gold plates, the location of which was given to him in revelation by the last of the prophets, Moroni, who had buried the entire collection. The basic theological premise of the movement identified America with "Zion," and the Church of the Latter-day Saints as "Israel." Rafinesque's outrage reveals much about the cultural moment when Mormonism first appeared. What mattered was rational thought; indeed, Rafinesque seems as annoyed with Kingsborough's idiocy as with Mormonism itself. Kingsborough's sad fate—to have lost all in pursuit of the tribes—marked one of the last attempts to prove the Israelite identity of the Native Americans by way of ethnographic research, a tradition that had begun with the early Spanish writers whom he translated. The Jewish Indian theory as a scientific project died more or less with him. However, the elaboration of theology based on the idea that the ten tribes had arrived in America had only just begun to prevail. Mormonism is its most significant product.

The well-researched history and tenets of Mormonism are beyond the scope of this book.[73] Yet it is worth stressing here one important Mormon principle: the transposition from theology to revelation of the principle of loss. Whereas Simon had tried to resuscitate the Jewish Indian theory by evoking its theological value, the Book of Mormon breathes life into it with revelation. Colin Kidd points out that "the book of Mormon is particularly rich with ethnological and genealogical lore" describing the roots of all sorts of biblical "ethnicities" found in America, thereby making its terrain and history part of the Bible.[74] America was thus imbued with a biblical past that predated European colonization. What the Book of Mormon takes from the debates about the ten lost tribes is the singular possibility acknowledged since the early sixteenth century: that a biblical people had arrived in America. This new biblical past was implied in the sacred Mormon texts. Crucial in this regard is the idea that knowledge—or, more aptly, revelation—accompanied the Israelites who came to America. If the exile of the tribes were the miraculous work of God, he surely knows where they now are: "But now I go unto the Father, and also to show myself unto the lost tribes of Israel, for they are not lost unto the Father, for he knoweth whither he hath taken them," declared the Mormon prophet Nephi (3 Nephi 17:4). If God carried the tribes away, he also revealed himself to them; and this revelation is to be united with the Old World revelation. This unification is carried out in the Book of Mormon: "And it shall come to pass that the Jews shall have the words of the Nephites, and the Nephites shall have the words of the Jews; and the Nephites and the Jews shall have the words of the lost tribes of Israel; and the lost tribes of Israel shall have the words of the Nephites and the Jews" (2 Nephi 29:13).

Loss is central in Mormon prophecies. Isaiah speaks only once about the "lost in Assyria"; Jesus commands his disciples only once to "go unto the lost sheep of Israel." The Book of Mormon, however, deals with loss profusely, echoing the language of the older prophecies: "And behold, there are many who are already lost from the knowledge of those who are at Jerusalem. Yea, the more part of all the tribes have been bled away; and they are scattered to and fro upon the isles of the sea; and whither they are none of us knoweth, save that we know that they have been led away" (1 Nephi 22:4).

Even with the revelation of the Book of Mormon, loss does not end. In fact, it becomes more acute, as it is revealed that there are more lost peoples, lost even to our knowledge. We find the ten tribes "bleeding away" from the body of Israel, scattered all over the earth in the "isles of the sea," not only in the Americas. Herein lies the moment of turning loss itself into revelation. The finder of the Book of Mormon, Joseph Smith, turns at the precise moment of finding into a prophet himself. In 1831, Smith was given his own revelation: "After this vision closed, the heavens were again opened unto us; and Moses appeared before us, and committed unto us the keys of the gathering of Israel from the four parts of the earth, and the leading of the ten tribes from the land of the north" (Doctrine and Covenants 110:11). The "land of the north" appeared again in another vision promising "they who are in the north countries shall come in remembrance before the Lord" (Doctrine and Covenants 133:26). The North Pole and the idea of north play an important role in the Mormon geographical imagination. Orson Pratt (1811–1881), one of the original twelve apostles of Joseph Smith and a leading Mormon scholar, wrote:

> When the Ten Tribes left Assyria they crossed the Euphrates River from west to east, miraculously. They must have repented of their sins or God would not have miraculously divided the river for them to pass over. They likely passed between the Black and Caspian Seas and continued on through Russia to the extreme north shores of Europe, i.e., 2500 miles north. But this could not be a year and a half's journey: indeed, it would not be an average of five miles a day. From many intimations of ancient prophecy they evidently had a highway made for them in the midst of the Arctic Ocean and were led to a land in the neighborhood of the North Pole. This region would be about 4000 miles north of their Assyrian residence and could be traveled in eighteen months time at an average of a little less than eight miles a day.[75]

Isaiah's "highway for the remnant of his people, which shall be left, from Assyria" (11:16) resonates here. Smith too claimed that a "highway shall be cast up in the midst of the great deep" (Doctrine and Covenants 133:34). Pratt's calculations resemble those made by de Galindo who, in the 1580s, contemplated the tribes' path to the Canaries. The early Mormons, too, debated the geography of the ten tribes and the status of the knowledge they introduced. Pratt—in a fascinating passage that reveals that even geographical science could never rest on its laurels—also wrote, "The Prophet Joseph [Smith] once in my hearing advanced his opinion that the Ten Tribes were separated from the Earth; or a portion of the Earth was by a miracle broken off, and that the

Ten Tribes were taken away with it, and that in the latter days it would be restored to the Earth or be let down in the Polar regions."[76]

As revelations, Mormon claims are immune to any scientific challenge—not the case with the Jewish Indian theory, which relied on ethnographic findings. Nevertheless, scientific challenges to Mormonism have been an integral part of its history since its inception.[77] And for its part, Mormon science is interested in proving the correlation between the various nations mentioned in the Book of Mormon and, for instance, the mound builders.[78]

The power of the Mormon Church of Latter-day Saints lies, however, not in such proofs so much as in the conversion or restoration of the lost into the center of its revelation and in the commissioning of its prophets to the task of "gathering Israel from the four parts of the earth," as Joseph Smith commanded. The Book of Mormon and the subsequent revelations represent one of the most radical reactions to the idea of the hope of Israel. The church, "Israel," is engaged in an unrelenting effort to reunite with the lost—the rest of humanity—a true fulfillment of the hope of Israel and a true *Concordia Mundi*.

Ephraim's Empire: England and Anglo-Israelism

Mormonism had a lesser-known British precursor some two decades earlier. In 1794, Richard Brothers (1757–1823), a retired naval officer who was a radical Calvinist, revealed himself in London as a prophet. Brothers called himself "Prince of the Hebrews" and promised that the end of the world was very near. The basic premise Brothers propagated in *A Revealed Knowledge, of the Prophecies & Times* was a return of the Hebrews to Jerusalem. The moment would come in 1798, when he would lead the Jews and his followers back to Jerusalem and build it anew. He devised a complete project of colonizing the Holy Land.[79] Brothers was quickly arrested on the grounds of insanity and remained in an asylum until 1806. Nevertheless, he managed right from the start to attract followers, and his numerous missives from prison were published in multiple editions. As is often the case in other unfulfilled millenarian or messianic movements, the fact that nothing transpired in the predicted year did not matter much,[80] and the small movement gained more followers (although some left him for another prophet).

Thus originated Anglo-, or British, Israelism—the belief that the Anglo-Saxons (and related Europeans) are the descendants of the ten lost tribes, a superior chosen race, destined to rule the world. The movement's proponents and opponents—in the United States and in England—focus on Anglo racial supremacy.[81] The pamphlets, sermons, and books that this movement generates to this day are numerous and in most cases repetitive. The best summary of Anglo-Israelism's main tenets is provided by David Baron (1857–1926), a Jewish convert who became a fierce opponent—not for rational reasons but because he served as the messianic leader of the Hebrew Christianity movement, a competing sect that did not focus on the ten tribes: "The theory is that the English, or the British, are descendants of the 'lost' Israelites, who were carried away captives by the Assyrians, under Sargon, who, it is presumed, are identical with Saxae or Scythians, who appear as a conquering host there about the same time."[82]

Richard Brothers espoused "the fantasy of belonging, literally, to God's elected race." At the time, he was unique in making genealogical arguments for that case in England.[83] Historian Eitan Bar-Yosef has argued that the origins of Brothers' visions were rooted in "English dreams about the Holy Land." This specific strand was most concerned with Palestine's geography and symbolic religious status under British rule. This interest in the Holy Land was itself embedded in earlier forms of radical piety and the desire to "build Jerusalem in England." During the eighteenth century, "as a metaphor the 'Holy Land' was much more accessible, and endlessly more useful, than the geographical place itself." Only later, with the rise of the eastern question at the beginning of the nineteenth century, did English attention turn compellingly to the idea of the actual colonization of the Holy Land.

Brothers stands at the moment of transition from interest in a "British Jerusalem" to interest in the actual Middle Eastern one.[84] British interest in Palestine and the possibility of restoring the Hebrews to it grew throughout the nineteenth century, famously culminating in the Balfour Declaration of 1917.[85] Although Richard Brothers did not mention the ten tribes at all in his initial prophecies, they entered his later visions. Basing himself on clues from the book of Daniel, chapter 12, Brothers claimed that he was "a descendant of David, King of Israel, who will be revealed to the Hebrew[s] as their Prince"—a basic messiah who met all the requirements for the title. As for the origins of at least some of the English, Brothers had more exciting news: "Though very long residents in this far northern part of the globe," at least some of the English "were members of the twelve tribes of Israel."[86] Writing from the confinement of "Fisher Mad-House, Islington," Brothers preempted ridicule with an invincible argument:

> I am certainly liable to be contradicted, not only on account of my own immediate confinement . . . but also by their having lost all remembrance, either by tradition or genealogical manuscript, of such distinctive origin; and again because they are different in dress—manners—and religious ceremonies from the visible Jews.[87]

Brothers spoke of "Hebrews" who "undoubtedly are concealed among the Gentiles, and are apparently as such; some of whom are *now*, multitudes will be soon, recognized to be of Hebrew extraction."[88] He told a story of migrations and wanderings that spread Hebrews throughout different parts of the world and "others who went into Assyria, Egypt and the northwestern parts of Africa," imitating *Hope of Israel*'s portrayal of global migration. More noteworthy was his *en passant* phrase "the visible Jews," contrasted with those "concealed among the Gentiles."

As we have seen, invisibility has been one of the markers of the ten tribes' exile, and it was often contrasted with the visibility of the Jews. In different contexts, this idea was expressed or implied in varying ways. Brothers took the idea to a new height: the invisibility of the ten tribes was caused by their "loss of Israelite memory" and by the fact that other traditions or "genealogical manuscripts"—false pedigrees—covered their real identity. Of himself, Brothers wrote, "it is fifteen hundred years since my family was separated from the Jews, and lost all knowledge of its origin." (Indeed, the last Jew "on record" in Brothers' family was James, which made Brothers Jesus's distant nephew.)[89] Finding the ten tribes now meant revealing the true identity of the Britons/Anglo-Saxons. This notion supplemented that of a British "return" to Jerusalem.

The roots of Anglo-Israelism lay also in geography and ethnography. While America reigned as the center of ten tribes debates throughout most of the sixteenth through the nineteenth centuries, eastern and northeastern Asia were not entirely forgotten. Jacques Basnage had boasted already in the 1680s that he had "reviv'd the Ten Tribes, which seem'd to be buried in the *East*."[90] As historian Richard Cogely has shown, English interest in the Tartars and the possibility that they were the ten tribes was reinforced by Giles Fletcher the Elder (c. 1548–1611), a poet, diplomat, and parliamentarian, who became involved in Tartary when he visited Russia, the history and geography of which interested him greatly.[91] Tartary and the Tartars had long been associated with the ten tribes, since the appearance of various Central Asians on the world's stage. Although the notion of the Tartars as the ten tribes declined with the Mongols, it never disappeared. The rise of the Ottoman Turks to global prominence drew more attention to Tartary, the vast territory of Central and northeastern Asia east of the Caspian Sea. Tartary gained currency in Postel and Ortelius. Fletcher infused this subject with new content.

In 1610, he wrote a short treatise: "The Tartars; or, Ten Tribes." The treatise was published only in 1677, but reveals changing ideas about the ten tribes at the time:[92] "That [the tribes] have lost their name, and the distinction of their Tribes, is more than probable, for that no Nation of the World are called *Israel*."

The tribes are obscured in that they no longer exist as "Israel" and have lost the "distinction of their tribe."[93] Fletcher was deeply invested in the idea of the reversal of fortune for the Jews and the Israelites—now in a state of punishment. As they were once a "holy Nation elected by God, out of all Nations in the World," they would one day unite and "Palestine shall be famous in all the world." Employing the principle of the reversal of fortune, Fletcher argued the best of futures for the Tartars, since they had been punished even more than the Jews. Fletcher maintained that, since they had been degraded to be "the most vile and barbarous nation of all the World," because of their grave sins and idolatry, they would be the most elevated. As Cogley explains, "the greater the Israelites' degradation, the more dramatic their eschatological deliverance, and there was no greater degradation than being Tartars."[94]

We can already identify some of the elements—the great expectations of a return to Palestine, the unique chosenness—that would surface later in Brothers' visions. However, another leap was needed to connect the Tartars to the Britons. It is to be found in Uppsala, Sweden, where Olof Rudbeck Jr. (Olaus Rudbeckius; 1660–1740) was inquiring into the origins of various Scandinavian and Baltic peoples. Scandinavian philology had a considerable influence on English romanticism and imagination, particularly in the context of northern antiquities.[95] A polymath trained at Utrecht, Rudbeck held a position as professor of medicine at Uppsala University and was a well-known botanist and ornithologist. In 1695, he went on a mission to study nature in Lapland.[96] He was greatly interested in the possible connections between Asian and Scandinavian languages and Hebrew.

Rudbeck inherited this interest, together with the position at Uppsala, from his father, Olof Rudbeck Sr. (1630–1702), "the greatest Gothic patriot," who had also devoted attention to Norse mythologies and the Scandinavian past. A proud Swede, Rudbeck Sr. was convinced that all European cultures originated in the north and espoused ideas about a Northern European super-race. The Scythians, long thought to be the putative ancestors of the Goths and many European peoples, occupied a special role in his early quest for roots; among the Scythian languages, Swedish is the oldest.[97] Rudbeck's thought and ideas about the origins of the European races came at precisely the time when linguistics was intimately associated with the rise of the racial theory in Europe. Linguistics in the eighteenth century opened a wide door for all sorts of theories[98] that matured later into European forms of racial thought and helped to shape the tragic racial pair—Aryans (Indo-Europeans) and Semites. The pair was fully formed only during the nineteenth century, but as historian Maurice Olender has shown, Rudbeck Sr. is one of its early fathers. The main thrust of linguistics at the time was the search for the *ursprache*—"the lost language of paradise," the language once used by all humans. Later, the search was rerouted to the origins of the European peoples.[99] Among the plethora of related hypotheses produced at the time, Rudbeck's theories stood out when he began arguing that Sweden was in fact Plato's Atlantis. The legendary land itself was now portrayed as the original homeland of most Northern European races, where Japheth, the third son of Noah, took refuge after the flood. The "Oracle of the North," as Rudbeck Sr. came to be known, spent a lifetime trying to prove his theories.[100]

We have some reason to believe that Rudbeck Sr. became familiar with Ben-Israel's work on the ten tribes more or less around the time it was written. He was a member for a while of the large international circle of scholars around the eccentric Queen Christina of Sweden (1626–1689). Ben-Israel was trying, unsuccessfully, to gain access to the queen's entourage in the early 1650s. Isaac Vossios, whose son was a student of Ben-Israel and the translator of his *Conciliador,* had a long and complicated relationship with the queen.[101] Thus Ben-Israel and Rudbeck Sr. may have met or been familiar with each other. In any event, Rudbeck Sr. was more concerned with his *Atlantica* project. But Rudbeck Jr. took up the ten tribes, which he thought were ancestors or relatives of the Scythians and, therefore, the progenitors of the various European peoples. The idea of the Scythian origins of the Europeans had been in circulation at least since Gottfried Wilhelm Leibniz (1646–1716), a German philosopher and linguist.[102] Rudbeck Sr. had already noticed that there were connections among several Asian and European languages, a fact that he took as proof of Gothic migrations to and domination of parts of Asia.[103] Rudbeck Jr. transformed his father's quest for Atlantis into the more promising (and less disputed) subject of the ten lost tribes. In 1717, he published a lengthy study of several European languages (including Finnish, Laponic, and Hungarian) in which he identified a relationship between the Laponic and other Gothic languages and Hebrew. There could only be one explanation for this finding: the speakers of these tongues were "those ten Israelite tribes led by Shalmaneser to captivity."

Rudbeck traced the tribes to Arzareth using a language basically similar to that of Postel and Ortelius, but for the most part upheld Ben-Israel's theory of wandering tribes that had separated en route. A number of tribes went to Persia, India, and China, until they finally penetrated "our north" (*Septentrionem nostrum*).[104] In locating Arzareth, he cited Esdras and Hosea, Ptolemy and Pliny. The "many Hebrews" living among the Russians and Slavs he saw as further proof supporting the theory about the trail from Asia to northeastern and Northern Europe. Rudbeck suggested that the Scythian city "Arsaratha" (north of Armenia), mentioned in the writings of Berossus, a third-century

BCE Hellenist/Babylonian historian, was in fact Arzareth. And he indicated the resemblance among the words *kong, könig,* and *king*—all Gothic words signifying royalty—and the Hebrew word *cohen* (priest),[105] a compelling case, in his view, for the ten tribes ancestry of the Scythians, the fathers of Europe. This new approach to the ten tribes was a result of the quest for the ethnic and racial genesis of Europeans, which was gaining momentum at that time. Just as the ten tribes had been attached to debates about the origins of peoples in America, they now became attached to debates about the origins of Europeans.

The long history of European imaginings about the Scythians, and the fact that Postel and Ortelius had already located the ten tribes in Scythian territory, encouraged the reception of these theories. We can assume that Rudbeck was not alone in assigning a Scythian relationship to the ten tribes, though his training as a scientist and his Swedish background must have given his ideas special purchase. In 1727, Rudbeck Jr. further developed his ideas in the essay "Of the Origin of the Estonians, Finns, and Laplanders," published in the *Acta Literaria Suecia,* Sweden's first scientific magazine. These three peoples were "referable to the remains of the tribes of Israel." Claiming that "no historian since Esdras" had written on the matter, he continued: "I know not whither the *Israelites* betook themselves unless to that part of the north, where mankind never inhabited; and that journey from the *Euxine* sea [Black Sea] to Lapland requir'd, on account of their children, flocks, effects, &c, the time, he [Esdras] mentions, of one year and a half."

Despite the claim that "no historian" had written about the ten tribes since Esdras, it is evident that Rudbeck Jr. had been reading what Génebrard, at least, had to say about them. Calculations about the time it took the ten tribes to get from the Black Sea (the original Scythian Sea) to Arzareth were considered key to accurately locating them. He listed a number of names of locales in Finland, Estonia, and Lapland that corresponded with the names of locales in Asia, "traces left by [the ten tribes] between *Persia* and Finland." He provided (laughable) examples of Hebrewisms to be found in Scandinavian dialects and cultural practices that could be traced back to the Israelites:

> The customs of the ancient Hebrews in entering upon an inheritance,
> in saluting, in embracing, in crossing their legs sitting, and in other
> respects, swell the number of my arguments. . . . the *Laplanders*
> worship the deity by sacrifices, falling down on their faces, by
> anointing, by building temples and by calling their Gods *Jumala,*
> *Thor,* &c. in all of which, they imitate the *Hebrews.*[106]

Rudbeck Jr. did not comment as to whether the famous red-bearded Thor, god of thunder in Norse mythology, and the Finnish god Jumala were also circumcised. But other than this little detail, in his account everything Norse seems to be of Hebrew origin. Ironically, the Laplanders and the Finns were later famously the subject of intense research carried out by Himmler's SS in Germany. Just as Rudbeck Jr. had found them to be remnants of the Israelites, the Nazis considered them remnants of the great primordial European races; the Finns and the Laplanders had been assigned to very different ancestors.[107]

Similar arguments were central in later Anglo-Israelist thought, which looked to such northern precursors. There were several advantages to focusing on the ten tribes: as part of Israel, they were chosen, blessed by God, and—most important—they were not Jews. Exiled seven centuries before Jesus, they could not be guilty for the Crucifixion. "The Ten Tribes, being the main mass of the Hebrew Nation, were not in the land to share in this crowning crime," ran the argument.[108] This idea, despite its philo-Jewish beginnings, would later pave the way for some radical forms of anti-Semitism within the various Anglo-Israelist offshoots.

By the second half of the nineteenth century, Anglo-Israelism was a popular "madness," an "Anglomania." Numerous people were tediously working to prove that the ancestors of the English were the ten lost tribes and to solve the "Anglo-Saxon riddle" of origin.[109] One of the favorite slogans of proponents was that the word "British" was in fact made of the two Hebrew words *brit* and *ish* and thus meant "man of the covenant." (Instances of such "primitive philology," as one angry observer called this, were quite frequent.)[110] Thus, Britain alone, or the Anglo-Saxon race, was the sole inheritor of God's blessings to Israel.

A few examples are representative. Edward Hine, in 1880 the founder of the British-Israel Identity Corporation, was particularly diligent, proving that "Anglo-Celto-Saxons" were the ten lost tribes. By 1870, he had found "seventeen positive identifications" that the "English nation" was "the Lost House of Israel." By 1874, the number had stabilized at forty-seven identifications, resting on no less than "five hundred" scriptural proofs. When his book was republished in New York years later, Hine was careful to trade the phrase "British Nation" for the more inclusive term "Anglo-Saxons."[111] The Reverend William H. Poole (fl. 1870–1890s), a Canadian proponent of the theory, used the same tactics in his influential *Anglo-Israel; or, The British Nation the Lost Tribes of Israel*, published in Toronto in 1879. When republished in Detroit a decade later, it turned into *Anglo-Israel; or, The Saxon Race*.[112] The theory's proponents were fanatical in their commitment. One gets the impression that Hine, a bank teller, spent every single minute away from his bank combing the Bible, matching verses with British historical and geographical facts, and generating more and more "identifications." Hine confessed his obsession:

"I found myself in possession of light that I had received in boyhood . . . [and] the matter grew upon me until . . . I clearly saw that Identity of the Lost Tribes of Israel was one grand essential of the age."[113]

In 1891, an essayist writing on "The Art of Conversation" compared the "believer in Anglo-Israel identity" to the "vegetarian, or the anti-tobbacoist," categories of people fixated on one topic which, endlessly, they discussed.[114] In the Anglo-Israel theory, a long and complex history of geographical theology was brought together.

Isaiah's prophecies concerning the Israelites on the isles of the sea became the most basic geographical tenet of the Anglo-Israelist creed. Mormonism offered new revelations in order to override science. Anglo-Israelism, on the other hand, used science, or scientific modes of argumentation, in order to support its arguments. The grounds for this were already formulated in 1836 by William Carpenter (1797–1874), who, like many biblical scholars, was also a natural scientist. His *Biblical Companion* instructed the reader on how to read the Bible in conjunction with, among other things, "biblical criticism, history and natural sciences."[115] Carpenter announced in 1874 that "the Israelites found in the Anglo-Saxons were of the isles of the sea." In a manner that may seem paradoxical today, modern science and modern disciplines such as biblical criticism together helped Carpenter to ground his argument. Carpenter was the first, for instance, to incorporate Sargon's inscriptions about the deportations, which were discovered in 1845 by archaeologists in northern Mesopotamia. That Sargon's number of deportees—27,280 or slightly more—dwarfed the grandiosity of the theory did not discourage Carpenter. After all, the prophet Isaiah had said, "The little one shall become a thousand; / And the small one a strong nation."[116] That strong nation was the Anglo-Saxon race.

Like Rudbeck Jr. before him, Carpenter also focused first on Gothic history and ethnography, albeit in a more informed and detailed way, in order to show the relationship between the Goths and Israelites. Yet he eventually focused on the fact that the Britons, as opposed to other European nations, dwelled on isles—which must be the isles of the sea mentioned by Isaiah. Several years later, the relentless Edward Hine collected all the biblical verses in which isles were mentioned in his discussion of "identification the fifth," which concerned the British isles. "Listen O Isles, unto me," he quoted Isaiah (49:1) and explained, "Israel must be found in the Isles." The following identification relied on Isaiah 24:15 to show that these isles must be northwest of Palestine since "the name of the lord God is in the Isles of the Western seas." The absence of the north from the verse should not discourage the believer. Isaiah, as we have seen, also prophesied that the ten tribes shall come from the north.

Furthermore, generations of scholars had already established the northern affinity of the ten tribes. "The identity is obvious. The British Isles are to the North west of Palestine—they are 'afar off' from there—they are in the 'Western Seas' and they constitute most emphatically a 'North Country.'"[117]

Carpenter and Hine did a sufficiently good job of establishing the identity of the ten tribes as the Anglo-Saxons who resided in the British isles, but not of explaining how they got there. The story of Israel's path to the isles still needed to be detailed. In 1881, a fascinating study of Israel's wanderings from Palestine to isles in the northwest was published under the pseudonym "Oxonian." Its purpose was "to work out a connected account of the Wanderings of the Lost Tribes between Palestine and Britain, which will at least show the possibility, historical and ethnological, of our Identity with Israel." And indeed, *Israel's Wanderings* told a story of migrations to Europe in different stages: first from Palestine to Arzareth, somewhere in Asia north of the Black Sea; then from Arzareth—led by Odin through Scandinavia—to the British isles. The author made brilliant use of the contemporary modern historiography of European migrations, which had traced back to Asia the roots of most European languages and, therefore, ethnic groups. However, he was careful to suggest that philology's authority should be questioned: "The theory on which philology has been resting hitherto—namely, that language is a certain test of race—has been entirely cut away by the recent declarations of eminent philologists, that *language is only a sure test of social contact.*" Languages do not constitute races; at best, linguistic similarities can convey contacts between peoples and cultures. Therefore, he concluded, "there is no *known* fact in the sciences of race and language which is violated by the supposition that the British belong to the Hebrew race."[118] Oxonian was well versed in nineteenth-century European debates on the relationships among race, religion, language, and philology.[119]

The desire to identify the inhabitants of the British isles with Israel was so strong that Oxonian developed an elaborate story. It told how the tribe of Dan, which we first met in Ethiopia, arrived in the isles well before the rest of the other tribes and spawned the ancient Celtic culture. This contravened the biblical story that mentions a mysterious migration of the tribe of Dan at some point in early Israelite history. Eldad had used this story to establish his Danite identity somewhere in Ethiopia. A millennium later, the same point was used to establish a Celto-Israelite identity. Dan is the "remnant that escaped" the Assyrian calamity.[120] The rest of the tribes follow the more familiar story and arrive in Britain, now as Scythians, between the eighth and the eleventh centuries. In the previous period, these Scytho-Israelites inhabited the original biblical locations of northern Persia and then northern Asia. Oxonian diligently showed that the description of migration in Esdras, although hardly rich in geographical detail, corresponds with the accounts of Scythian migrations in Herodotus, a point he even illustrated in maps (see figure 6.1). Oxonian dramatized the migration as a story of escape from Asia to a safe dwelling in Northern Europe. This wonderful saga only occurs by virtue of the divine blessing on Ephraim, the lead tribe in the ten tribes' nation. This was all "God's merciful assurance, delivered through the mouth of Hosea, at the very time when He was allowing His ungrateful children to be removed into captivity. How then could their future be to continue in captivity and eventually become absorbed in alien races?"[121] Esdras's story about the need to protect the ten tribes from idolatry is reworked here into a story of protecting the purity of the British races, and the history of the Britons emerges as a story about an exodus from Asia to Europe.

This was all about the British past, but their present and future were equally important. Here, the equation of the destiny of Britain with the destiny of Ephraim and his brother Manasseh was essential. In fact, it was nothing short of the destiny of the world, and therefore the history of the lost tribes *was* the history of the world. All Anglo-Israelist thinkers since Brothers strongly embraced this idea, for without it Anglo-Israelism was nothing but another version of the many variants on the story of the ten lost tribes:

> How can the unique position of the British Nation and Empire be
> accounted for, except on the supposition that it is the Nation and
> Empire of the seed of Abraham? Certain it is that this Nation fulfils at
> the present day the destined *role* of Israel. This can only be due to the
> fact that Israel is in Britain: no other nation can have stepped into the
> promises entailed by God on Israel, for God cannot lie.[122]

The unprecedented global success of the British in the nineteenth century could only be explained as the fulfillment of God's blessings, given through Jacob to the leader of the tribes. The British Empire, its colonies, and its offspring polities were "His throne on earth."[123]

The emphasis on empire derived in part from the enigmatic book of Daniel—an eschatological vision involving rising and falling empires. So too the idea that Ephraim was blessed with colonies as one of the most important identifications or marks of the tribe's glory. All Anglo-Israelists insisted on this point. Jacob had promised in Egypt that Ephraim was to "become [a] nation and company of nations" (Genesis 49:22–26). And what was an empire if not "a company of nations," and what was the British Empire if not the greatest of all empires? A similar, lesser role was assigned to the United States, "whose growing greatness, its increasing population are due to elements in it of Manasseh."[124] In Egypt, recall, Manasseh had received the lesser blessing;

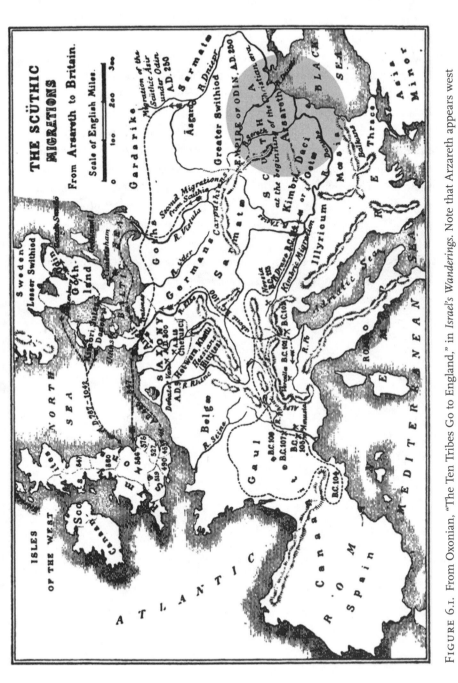

FIGURE 6.1. From Oxonian, "The Ten Tribes Go to England," in *Israel's Wanderings*. Note that Arzareth appears west of the Black Sea.

this, too, became an element in the emerging political theology of the empire. When the British Empire declined and lost its colonies during the twentieth century, thereby putting the whole theory in jeopardy, the rising United States would become Ephraim, and England would be demoted, albeit implicitly, to being Manasseh, as the two traded places in the schema.[125]

Like Mormonism, Anglo-Israelism can be described as another Christian derivation of the hope of Israel. Both rework the story of loss, wanderings, and restoration into a new theology that through revelation identifies Israel in an existing human group. Anglo-Israelism, like Mormonism, overcomes loss, replacing it with an aggressive restorative theology. Whereas Mormonism restores the loss through conversion, Anglo-Israelism does so by reminding the Anglo-Saxons of their lost identity. In both cases, the original fervent search for the lost tribes dissipates. The romanticism and the passion of searching fades, since, as one later Anglo-Israelist proclaimed, the "lost tribes: found!"[126]

But, of course, they were not. Despite the revelatory power of Mormonism and Anglo-Israelism, the ten tribes persist as one of the geographical mysteries of an exposed world.

Conclusion

To Find the Ten Lost Tribes

Question: Whither went the Ten Tribes?

Answer: This Question is not so difficult, if we compare their Laws and Customs with those of other Nations; and where we find the greatest Agreement in practice, we may with the greatest probability fix the Affirmative of the Question. But before I discuss that, I shall give you the received Opinion which the two Tribes entertain about their lost Brethren. There is, say they, a great Lake in Asia, which is always toss'd with Tempests and Storms, so that it is un-navigable, except on the Sabbath day, upon which day the ten Tribes being still Jews, are unwilling to travel, or contradict so great a part of the Old Law, as a Prophanation of their Sabbath, and therefore must tarry there; but this seems very unlikely, for the Question recurs, How they could get over at first, unless upon the Sabbath, when, according to their Saying, the Lake is then only free from Tempests. But to satisfie the Querist, we have the Testimony of Josephus, That they were in great Numbers in the Land of Media under the Parthian Princes; also Sulpitius Severus says, that they were dispersed amongst the Parthians, Medes, Indians, and Æthiopians, all which exactly agrees to my Notion in the first part of my Answer, that in these Places above the rest of the World, are retained Washings, Sprinklings, and other Jewish Ceremonies; but by a long Tract and Series of time, the Ten Tribes are now really Heatheniz'd.

—*Post-angel; or, Universal Entertainment* (April 1701)

Global Empire, the Ten Tribes, and Knowledge

The author of this anonymous query was not alone in his interest. Such queries and commentaries appeared regularly in English publications of all sorts, for both "the Gentleman" and "the Lady" reader. Asking about the ten tribes was in part a matter of "universal entertainment," as the *Post-angel*'s subtitle suggests, and is a symptom of the emergence in the seventeenth century of a lay or secular interest in the lost tribes. This is not to imply that the concerned individuals were not religious or faithful; most probably, the overwhelming majority were. Rather, the interest stemmed from titillated curiosity and was not part of a broader theological quest. Learning about issues such as the tribes was considered part of the English's universal, that is, global education.[1]

We have noted the popularity and authority of Abraham Ortelius's *Theater of the World*. The first (among many) English editions was published in London in 1601.[2] "Whither went the ten tribes?" was a question in the purview of world geography and also an "entertainment," in the eighteenth-century sense. Common among queries to such publications as the *Post-angel* were "where was the soul of Lazarus while he lay in the grave?" and "[do] fleas have stings?" For Britons of the less sophisticated sort, the ten tribes belonged in this same realm of entertainment.

The answer to the ten tribes question, however, was not of interest only to "rural Saxons."[3] There was an avid higher-brow audience as well. Contemporaneous with the *Post-angel*, the brothers John (fl. 1690–1714) and Awnsham Churchill (c. 1681–1728) published *A Collection of Voyages*, a widely subscribed geographic journal with frequent notations about the tribes. Its circulation list included "commissioners from the admiralty," attorneys, attorneys general, ministers, booksellers, merchants, and nobles.[4] John Churchill was at some point in his career a politician, and he was well and widely connected. Geographical literature was wildly popular at the time, and most of its consumers read religious literature as well.

The question "where are the ten tribes?"—with us since biblical times— has undergone many transformations of context. The editorial observation that the question was "not so difficult" did not, paradoxically, imply that its answer was known; John Dunton (1659–1733), the journal's editor, doesn't actually say where the tribes are. Rather, the answer was not so difficult in that, by the early eighteenth century, there was an abundance of knowledge available to anyone who wished to ponder it. Jewish and Christian views about the ten tribes had meshed to a considerable degree (though they did not assign the same meaning to the question), providing by way of answer a dense body of knowledge.

The *Post-angel*'s answer also shows the method of searching to have changed: to find the tribes, look for the "greatest agreement in practice" and compare the laws and customs of many nations so as to sleuth out the tribes among them. By the eighteenth century, no group was really lost any more in the simple sense of that word. All human groups were either already found or, at least in theory, findable, discovered or discoverable. Paradoxically, this in a sense rendered the ten tribes more lost than ever.

Finding the ten tribes now also meant *identifying* them. In the early sixteenth century, a cosmographer like Abraham Farissol could engage the simple question of the tribes' location. It was assumed that, if they could physically be found, they'd be instantly recognizable. By the early 1700s, after more than a century of debate over the Native Americans and other newly discovered groups, the ten tribes had moved from world history as the history of the globe to world history as human history, and the tribes' own history had been normalized: they had been exiled, had migrated ever farther, and in the course of movement through time and space had undergone various social and cultural transformations. Consequently, discussions about them had come to involve not only earlier questions about world geography, but also questions about global human migration, cultural practices, and languages. Spanish discussions had revolved largely around questions relating to the shape of the world—as the discussions of Atlantis, Greenland, the Straits of Anian, and the Canaries exemplify. Next, ethnography of a sort was increasingly the pivot. Now, the moral and cultural status of the tribes emerged as the new concern.

Before the Americas theory, the expectation had been to find an intact Israelite entity. In the Americas in the sixteenth century, however, empirical experience led to the notion that the ten tribes had lost their old customs, and it was the question of their Israelite-ness that drove the ethnographic and linguistic investigations. Now, in the 1700s, a new frame emerged: the ten tribes had been "heatheniz'd"; the tribes had somehow fallen from grace but had not physically disappeared. No matter that the whole world had been discovered and held no further unknown peoples. The tribes were here among us, hidden, waiting to be redeemed. Rather than geographic knowledge extinguishing the possibility that the tribes were actually out there, it paradoxically increased it. The idea that the ten tribes had evolved culturally opened the door to an exciting new possibility: if they had changed over time and were the descendants of earlier peoples, it was possible that recognized world nations—anyone, perhaps even the Britons themselves!—could be the descendants of the ten lost tribes. The ten tribes had become truly global: anyone could be a candidate. The idea of cultural change preserved the lostness of the ten tribes, transforming it into a new question, more complicated than its predecessor.

All earlier speculation about the ten tribes had understood their lostness as a geographic matter—they were beyond impassable barriers (a wide river, a range of mountains), or in another land, or in Sambatyon, enchanted domains that represented the edges of the earth. But by the mid-seventeenth century, with the realization that the world has no real edges—humans could inhabit its every corner—the ten tribes became lost not *beyond* the world, but *in* the world. The ten tribes ceased to be "spatially transcendent" and became lost instead in an "immanent" world with no geographical "beyond."[5]

Biblical and, later, Talmudic and medieval discussions placed the ten tribes outside the world in which these discussions took place—some by enclosing them, others by placing them literally beyond the world's limits or on its edges. Before the early modern period, the ten tribes were simply lost, invisible, hidden, beyond, or enclosed. In this regard, late sixteenth-century debates about the ten tribes—which placed them in America or in northern Asia—can be viewed as transitional. The beyondness of America, even the mini-beyondness of the Canaries, was an important factor in the debate about these places as possible residences of the ten tribes. As we have seen in the cases of Ortelius and Postel, northern Asia was imbued with many old and familiar markers, and the north to which the ten tribes were assigned was in large part a mystical and almost unreachable one. More than a real place, it was where the tribes "sing to God." Yet the Canaries and America were, at the same time, real places which had been "discovered." They, by definition, were no longer beyond the world.

Of course, the old beyondness of the ten tribes did not disappear completely. It still worked well as a poetic metaphor, as exemplified in Milton's famous *Paradise Regained:*

> Deliverance of thy brethren, those Ten Tribes
> Whose offspring in his territory yet serve
> In Habor, and among the Medes dispersed:
> The sons of Jacob, two of Joseph, lost
> Thus long from Israel, serving, as of old
> Their fathers in the land of Egypt served,
> This offer sets before thee to deliver.
> These if from servitude thou shalt restore
> To their inheritance, then, nor till then,
> Thou on the throne of David in full glory,
> From Egypt to Euphrates and beyond.[6]

This is poetry. But in reality, the beyond that began as a mere geographic notation, and that was later transformed into an "iron curtain" of sorts, had dissipated by the seventeenth century.

Comparing the various phases of the debates about the ten tribes reveals another aspect of this transformation. Portuguese and Spanish debates were limited in temporal and spatial terms—and they were not unconnected to immediate political motives. They were confined to those regions of the world where the empire was active at any given moment. In the Portuguese case, the region in question was at the southern boundaries of the ancient world—from Ethiopia through Arabia to India, where the ten tribes continued to play their traditional role as a supernatural and unreachable group of people. In the Spanish case, interest was confined to the colonies in the Americas.[7]

In the case of the British Empire, the frame was radically different, and discussions about the ten tribes eventually encompassed the whole world. As we have seen, debates within the English context were informed by and fed the rise of an increasingly acute sense of loss. Here, empire played a crucial role. The sheer size of the British Empire and, most important, the perception that it truly was a *world* empire, "where the sun does not set," as the famous cliché had it, made England at once the clearinghouse and crucible for ideas about the ten tribes, which were spread through its vast information networks. This corresponds with an observation from the second part of the eighteenth century: "Britons increasingly thought of their empire in global terms and . . . increasingly imagined the world generally, and their empire more specifically, within a global framework." British officials were encouraged to "consider the whole globe."[8] A sensitive ear can detect the distant echo of Assyrian claims to the "whole world" that lay beyond the boundaries of their empire. Assyrian rulers, too, and their admiring listeners—such as the prophet Isaiah—had thought in terms both of empire and of the whole globe beyond it. The more the British Empire became global, so too did the possibilities of finding the ten tribes.

Historian Edward Beasley's survey of the founders of the Colonial Society— "the first major pro imperial pressure group," founded in 1868—characterizes its members as the people who invented a "world-historical mission for the British Empire." Its founders were all gentlemen from different social strands across the empire who shared "globe-spanning ideas of the place of the British Empire in geography and history."[9] One of the active founders was Sir Henry Drummond Wolff (1830–1908), son of Joseph Wolff, among the most active tribes seekers in history. Many of the tribes' seekers saw a connection between their individual activities in searching for the tribes and the empire as a whole. The empire broadened the field for the search, just as searching helped the expansion of empire.

When, in 1823, Reginald Heber (1783–1826) was appointed bishop of Calcutta, he went to visit a friend of his mother, whom he told he was leaving for India. The lady said, "yours is the Quixotism of religion, and I almost believe you are going in search of the ten lost tribes of Israel."[10] Her comment revealed the irony of the romantic period concerning the lost tribes, but Heber himself was a true believer. "Your joke may have truth in it," he replied, open to the possibility that he would find the ten tribes there. The tribes existed at the margins of fact and fancy, with just enough possibility of the former remaining to make them of ongoing interest. And in missionary activity, particularly, the frame of a global empire widened the scope of possibilities.

Only ten years earlier, the Reverend Claudius Buchanan (1766–1815), a Scottish missionary appointed to a chaplaincy in Calcutta, declared that he had found evidence of the tribes' residence in India or in neighboring Afghanistan: "we have reason to believe that the Ten Tribes so long lost if they exist in a body at all have at length been found."[11] Just as earlier seekers preceded or followed the imperial expansions in the Americas, in the British imperial context they accompanied expansion in Afghanistan, India, and Africa. Indeed, it is often forgotten that David Livingstone (1813–1873), the great Scottish explorer of Africa and a national hero, was a missionary who did not distinguish among "Christianity, Commerce, and Civilization."[12] Though he despised ten tribes seekers, he was wedded to them by his context, a fusion of Christianity, commerce, and civilization: in short, empire.

Heber and Buchanan epitomize the genre of imperial travelers most concerned with the ten tribes—the missionary on a mission of conversion. In this context, even if the expedition was not specifically designated as a search for the ten lost tribes, they always lurked in the background as a possibility. One could hope, in Ezekiel's words, to "take the children of Israel from among the heathen." As Thorowgood had put it centuries earlier, the conversion of indigenous peoples might actually be the restoration of the ten lost tribes. The nineteenth century provided plenty of opportunity for such missionaries/travelers to discover, convert, and restore, and the empire—specifically, imperial expansion—enabled it. Even though India, writ large, had been considered the place of the ten tribes since Roman times, it only became a major site for searches during the times of British colonization.[13] The British Empire and its fringes—indeed, potentially, the entire globe—had become the zone and the economic force that sustained interest in the ten tribes and presented the possibility of finding them. The search for the tribes had come, to an extent, full circle. Alongside British imperial expansion, its epicenter had returned to Africa and Asia.

The Lost Tribes as a Modern Geographic Mystery

From the seventeenth century, it became clear that a major trouble with the ten tribes was the sheer abundance of views and opinions on the subject of their whereabouts. The very multiplicity of opinions on the matter and the debates as to whether the tribes were in America, Africa, northern Asia, or India—all of this added another dimension to the simple question, "Where are the ten tribes?" The question now meant, rather: "Where are the ten lost tribes *really*, as opposed to other putative locations?" And the question, "Who are the ten tribes?" now actually meant something more like, "Are the Native Americans the ten tribes or not, or is it the Tartars who are the descendants of the ten tribes as opposed to, say, the Chinese?"

As early as the first two decades of the seventeenth century, the educated person could read about the ten tribes in, among other places, Samuel Purchas's (c. 1575–1626) huge and popular *Pilgrimages and Relations of the World* series, a collection of world geography, voyages, and navigations. The kingdom of the ten tribes first appeared as part of biblical history, on its maps of the Holy Land (prepared by Hondius) with Samaria, the capital, in a large font.[14] Similar maps, portraying the territories of the tribes before their exile, had been popular since the mid-sixteenth century. (For instance, Walter Raleigh's [1552–1618] influential "history of the world," published for the first time in 1614, provided detailed information about the territories of each tribe during the period of the settlement of the Holy Land after the Exodus.)[15]

About the ancient geography of the ten tribes in Palestine, there was little dispute. Purchas, however, placed great importance on the religions attached to each region of the world. The ten tribes after exile, a group whose location and religious status were highly unclear, were a matter of particular concern. Purchas was an attentive collector of materials on the subject. In 1613, Purchas discussed—and did not rule out—the possibility that the ten tribes were in Tartary, relying, apparently, on Ortelius.[16] In 1625, a year before his death, he declared, "The Tartars are not Israelite," and spent time on Esdras's allegations that this was the case, reviewing in the course of doing so all other possible locations in Asia, America, Arabia, and Ethiopia. Even after years of study, he could not be sure.[17]

Despite his skepticism, Purchas liked to tell tales about the "closed Jews." In a section dedicated to the Persian Gulf, Purchas "intreate[d]" his readers' "patience," digressing to discuss at length "the Jewish fables" about the "Sabbatical streams"—the River Sambatyon. This comes just after mention of European travelers who had lost their lives or fortunes looking for the legendary river—something he called a "Jewish tragedy." The learned geographer ridiculed the lack of geographic knowledge displayed by Jewish writers and could not resist a witticism concerning "the Sabbatical river: now you shall understand how the Jews generally drowned their wits therein." He had as his two examples "Rambam [Maimonides; 1135–1204] who called it [the River] Gozan," and Eldad Ha-Dani, whose story should serve as "favorable entertainment." Purchas tells a version of Eldad's story, which he claims to have read in a "translation of Génebrard."[18] Fable or not, Purchas did not deny the existence of the "closed Jews" and encouraged his reader to become acquainted with the fascinating story of the "traveler Eldad."

From still earlier times, readers had available to them the Latin translations of Benjamin of Tudela, published in Antwerp in 1575. These placed the tribes in Central Asia, Ethiopia, and Arabia. In 1691, the great Arabist and scholar of Islam Thomas Hyde (1636–1703) published the *Itinera Mundi*, a bilingual Hebrew and Latin edition of Abraham Farissol's *Igeret Orhot 'Olam*.[19] The *Igeret*, it should be recalled, had placed the tribes in India and in Taprobanne (Sri Lanka), the old Far East of the Roman *oikoumene*. But it was not only Jewish thinkers who were "drowning their wits" when it came to the matter. So were Christian ones.

Churchill's *Collection of Voyages and Travels*, which reached final shape in 1732, dedicated pages to the possibility that the ten tribes were in China, only to negate it by publicizing the views of Domingo Fernández Navarrete (c. 1610–1689), a leading Dominican missionary who debated the issue. The Chinese could not be Israelites, insisted Navarrete, since "China was ancienter than the captivity of the ten tribes."[20] Navarrete also refuted similar suggestions of the Jesuit João Rodriguez (1558–1633). Rodriguez, who spent his lifetime in Japan, had ended his great dissertation on the Japanese language with the suggestion that the great Chinese thinker Confucius and some other Chinese originated in the ten lost tribes. *Travels of the Jesuits, into Various Parts of the World,* published in London in 1762, also discussed Jesuit reports that people in India, China, or Japan could be the tribes' offspring. The book's English editor, John Lockman (1698–1771), cited a long list of sources—Eldad, Benjamin of Tudela, and Farissol, among others—in an attempt to evaluate the Jesuit accounts. The deliberations over the subject thus included medieval sources, sixteenth- and seventeenth-century Jesuit accounts, and eighteenth-century editorial opinions, all massed together in a few brief pages. After much deliberation, it seems that all that Lockman could say was "some remains of [the] ten tribes existed in Upper Asia."[21]

Perhaps the final stamp on the ten tribes as a modern geographic mystery—indeed, a modern geographic problem—came with James Rennell's most learned "Concerning the Disposal of the Ten Tribes of the Jews, which were Carried into Captivity to Nineveh: Commonly Called the First Captivity." Rennell (1742–1830), one of the most important modern English geographers and known for his works on India, was one of the first world oceanographers. He considered the ten tribes to be one of the key "subjects of history and geography," and he included them in a massive study that sought to compare and reconcile ancient and modern geographies.[22]

Readers were thus exposed to a wealth of contradictory information concerning the geographic location of the ten lost tribes. But the numerous contradictory accounts did not result in the conclusion that there was no such thing as the ten tribes. Rather than making the mystery evaporate, the contradictions made it more acute. And all along, of course, to many, their location remained a matter of great theological concern.

In 1750, the Italian Isaac Lampronti (1679–1756), a rabbi and physician from Ferrara, wrote an entry on "Sambatyon," or *Fiume Sabbatico*, for his *Pahad Yitzhak*, a huge encyclopedia.[23] This source sheds light on the volume of tribes-related geographical knowledge that had accumulated over the years since Ben-Israel's treatise and shows the degree to which the tribes were understood as an elusive and problematic geographical item. A wide-ranging, well-educated man, Lampronti did not hesitate to confront rabbinic authorities on questions of Jewish law if science contradicted them. For the entry on Sambatyon, Lampronti surveyed sources from antiquity to his time, covering virtually all regions of the world. However, he appears to be selective in what cites. The entry cites close to thirty sources, all by now quite familiar to us. Strikingly, none of the sources quoted by Lampronti came from ancient or medieval Jewish text. Also strikingly, some of his citations come from other encyclopedic works, such as the *Universal Geography* by La Croix (c. 1640–1715) or the *Geographical and Historical Dictionary* by Thomas Corneille (1625–1709).[24] In all of these texts, as Lampronti was careful to quote, the ten tribes were presented as a geographic problem, a matter of debate and of differing opinions. But their existence was factual enough to be included in encyclopedias.

This shows to what degree the issue of the tribes' location had become common in global geographical writing. And the absence of Jewish sources in Lampronti's list exposes the momentous transformation that geographical knowledge concerning the ten tribes had undergone. From late antiquity to the late fifteenth century, geographical information about the ten tribes could be found almost exclusively in Jewish sources: Josephus, the Talmud and Midrash, medieval biblical exegeses, the travelers Eldad and Benjamin. The few non-Jewish sources, such as John of Mandeville and Marco Polo, derived their information, if indirectly, from Jewish lore. Beginning in the early modern period, the sources of knowledge changed dramatically, to almost exclusively Christian. These sources are newer—much newer—and are based on observations of the world, not on divine revelation or inspiration.

In Abraham Farissol's *cosmographia* from the 1520s, notations on the ten tribes drew on Talmudic sources, though his information on other issues was based on new gentile geographies; indeed, his brilliance lay in placing Talmudic geography in the context of the global geography of his time. (Recall his rejoicing that gentile geography seemed to be accepting Jewish notions of the tribes' existence and location.) Just over a century later, Ben-Israel's 1650 *Hope of Israel*—while referencing Talmudic sources and biblical exegeses—placed the weight of geographic authority on the contemporary gentile geography to which Farissol had alluded. Another century later, though, in Lampronti's *Fiume Sabbatico*, the Talmudic sources have disappeared altogether. By the 1750s, Lampronti's entry on the ten tribes pretty much ignored them.[25] Over two centuries, the transformation was complete: by the late eighteenth century, the overwhelming majority of opinions on the tribes were generated by non-Jewish sources. This gradual shift does not mean that the original biblical and Talmudic sources had lost their authority, nor that the ten tribes had lost their special place in Jewish thinking. Rather, what these changes reflect is the decline in their relevance for this particular debate. After nearly three centuries of dramatic transformations in geographical writing and thinking, the new world geography increasingly ruled the day.

This posed one problem: while earlier Jewish sources enjoyed the authority of scripture and divine inspiration, these much later geographies did not. Perhaps this accounts for the fact that the final section of Lampronti's treatise resorts to reaffirming the most basic Jewish belief that the ten tribes were to remain hidden until the end of days, when they would reunite with the rest of the Jews. It is as if he was troubled by the emergence of the ten tribes as a geographic and secular (or at least gentile) mystery and wanted to remind both himself and his readers that whatever others might be debating about the tribes and their location, what the Jews really ought to do is to stick to the prophecy promising their return. This reunion, he assures his readers, is going to be the work of God, not of modern geography, and will happen "according principally to the prophecy of Ezekiel in chapter 37" (*principalmente di quella d'Ezechiel cap. 37*).[26] Ezekiel 37 consists of the so-called dry bones vision, in which God orders the prophet to take two sticks and write upon them the names of Judah and Ephraim: "Join them one to another into one stick; and they shall become one in thine hand." And indeed, the two sticks become one. "Behold, I will take the children of Israel from among the heathen, whither they be gone, and will gather them on every side, and bring them into their own land.... I will save them out of all their dwelling places, wherein they have sinned, and will cleanse them: so shall they be my people, and I will be their God" (Ezekiel 37:16–23).

Lampronti's strange phrase "according *principally* to ... Ezekiel 37"—as opposed to other prophecies of return—begs some consideration. Why not Isaiah? Why only Ezekiel, and why "principally"? The answer perhaps becomes clearer if we think in light of the problem of locating the tribes in the context of modern geography. Recall that Isaiah—the master of latter-day visions—speaks of a highway bringing the ten tribes from specific geographic locations (Assyria, beyond Euphrates, from the isles of the sea, from the north). Ezekiel, on the other hand, typically talks about a reunion in dramatic visual—and abstract—terms. Whereas Isaiah builds a highway to facilitate the tribes' return from named locations, Ezekiel's reunion is effected as simply and inexplicably as the two sticks merging in his hand. Lampronti, acutely aware of the problems of locating the ten tribes in the discovered and cartographized world, prefers this presentation. He, too, feels the need to escape geography: "If someone, after all, still wonders how come these ten tribes can remain hidden from the eyes of the geographers, particularly after the last navigations, please consider how could the region of Las Batueças, in the kingdom of Leon, between Salamaca and Placentia, remain hidden in the middle of Spain until the time of Philip the Second."[27]

In other words, the familiar old hiddenness of the tribes did not derive from some sort of mystical invisibility or enclosedness as Esdras, Eldad, Postel, and many others had implied, but was simply a failure of modern geography. Indeed, the modern navigations Lampronti mentions had made the tribes *more* hidden, because they had failed to produce them. This failure of geography might in turn produce a failure of faith—one that Lampronti hastens to remedy (in his readers and perhaps also in himself) with a return to scripture. But whereas Isaiah might lead us back to geographical conundrums because of his mention of specific locations, the more general and mystical Ezekiel does not bother us with specific geography.

The failure of modern navigations to find the tribes brought with it the final dimension of their lostness: over time, with progress, the tribes became more lost in that even the most self-confident, scientific, geographical methods and the close of the Age of Discovery had failed to point decisively to where they were. The mystery had grown more mysterious than ever. Was there still out there on the globe one place which had, against all odds, yet to be discovered, traveled, and mapped? The sixteenth-century rabbi Maharal had implied that an infinite number of new worlds might lie out there as yet undiscovered; Lampronti already knows that this proposition is impossible.

So he takes a different tack, reminding his readers that even within the finite and fully exposed world, there could yet be places not out in the open.

As we reached the end of the eighteenth century and entered the age of romanticism and romantic adventure, here was a final reason to go on searching. If, earlier, the whole point was to *find* the tribes, in the romantic era the point of attraction was perhaps their very *lostness*. The lostness of the ten tribes, first encoded by Isaiah in the context of ancient Judah in the Assyrian world, had now taken on its final dimensions.

Adventurers, Romantics, and Romantic Travel

In the romantic era, and particularly in the era of romantic travel, even if one were not particularly invested in bringing the ten tribes back because of some grandiose theological purpose, one looked for them simply because they were an item to be found, something to report in the travel diary. They were mysterious and the search for them exciting. At the very least, there was an expectation that a traveler would make ironic mention of whether or not he had run into them. Fictional romantic travel accounts routinely included an encounter with the ten lost tribes. Karl Friedrich Hieronymus von Münchhausen (1720–1797), famous for his unbelievable feats (and the syndrome named after them), recounts in *Münchhausen at the Pole:*

> I am not so strict a Christian but I can fraternally embrace a Jew. Here
> I had stumbled upon the ten tribes of Israel unaccounted for in
> Scripture, who had existed here under the good old law unknown to all
> the world: in truth, they believed no nation existed but themselves.
> Their temple was [a] fac-simile of that built by Solomon the apostate. I
> intended to have sketched it, but as Saint Martin's church is an exact
> resemblance, I spared myself the trouble. These good people direct[ed]
> my course to the north.[28]

Other fictional travelers followed protocol and came across the tribes as well. Don Manuel Alvarez Epriella, the fictional Spanish traveler created by the romantic poet Robert Southey (1774–1843), is described as touring England in 1814. Epriella/Southey writes of a visit to the Jewish quarter of an undisclosed English town. There, he says, "I saw so many Hebrew inscriptions in the shop windows, and so many long beards in the streets, I began to fancy that I had discovered the ten tribes."[29] Southey, of course, did not really think one could find the tribes. For him, they represented the ultimate example of something that is gone, a fantasy never to return.[30] An 1835 novel about the notorious pirate Blackbeard (Edward

Teach; c. 1680–1718) included a character "whose thoughts were wholly devoted to that abstruse and perplexing search after the lost tribes of Israel."[31] The ten tribes also continued to feature in nonfictional travel literature.[32]

Finally, the same period also saw the translation and republication of a raft of older narratives touching on the ten tribes theme. Benjamin of Tudela, for instance, was popular in London during the 1780s, when a new, detailed, critical, and annotated translation (from the Hebrew) of his travelogue came out in several editions.[33] The geographer John Pinkerton's (1758–1826) *General Collection of the Best and Most Interesting Voyages and Travels in All Parts of the World* featured Benjamin of Tudela's narrative, translated from Montano's Latin version.[34]

By the nineteenth century, as opportunities for travel increased dramatically, the ten tribes became an integral part of it. One could run into the tribes pretty much anywhere in the world, or at least hear rumors about their residence, which was always "nearby." One could also always run into other people who were looking for the ten tribes, as happened to David Livingstone during his famous Zambezi expedition. The celebrated traveler apparently ran into numerous ten tribes seekers; at least, this is the impression one gets from his diaries and letters. At one point, he tells about annoying encounters with a type of traveler who complains "that his proper position was unjustly withheld because special search was not directed toward 'the ten lost tribes.'" Mentioning the ten tribes in such a context presented an occupational hazard; Livingstone wryly notes, "It is dangerous to rally such a one, for the irate companion may quote Scripture, and point to their habitat 'beyond the rivers of Ethiopia.'"[35] Livingstone bitterly complained about all those who "had come to discover the 'Ten lost tribes,'" as if, of all things in the world, we had not plenty of Jews already."[36] One gets the impression that Africa was swarming with travelers looking for the tribes; evidently, Livingstone had come to loathe both them and the ten tribes they were seeking.

Livingstone himself ultimately went missing. Henry Morton Stanley (1841–1904), whose own obsession and mission was finding the Scottish explorer in Africa, later became the subject of a parody in New York in which the ten tribes played the key role. The spoof depicted a conversation between Stanley and James Gordon Bennett (1795–1872), the *Herald* owner who had paid him to find Livingstone and generate a good adventure story:

MR. BENNETT (in bed, 4 A.M.)   Mr. Stanley, have the Ten Tribes ever been found?

MR. STANLEY (in room adjoining, also in bed)   No, sir; not to my knowledge.

MR. BENNETT   Can they be found?

MR. STANLEY   I should judge so.

MR. BENNETT   Will you find them?

MR. STANLEY   I will, sir.

MR. BENNETT   Start immediately; draw on me as large a sum as you like, and don't come back until you have found all the Ten Tribes, whom you must send to America as speedily as possible. And Mr. Stanley takes the first boat—anywhere; and depend on it, the news will soon be flashing along the line: "Glory! I have just found Tribe Number One. The Reubenites are well, and send congratulations!"[37]

By the nineteenth century, a quasi-ironic culture had developed around the search for the ten tribes, a precursor of the adventure stories that would center on them decades later. This culture was so prevalent as to generate countless parodies, sarcastic asides, and other popular cultural references.

Increasingly, the tribes existed in the realm of cavaliers and "Quixotism," and the search for them was considered a titillating adventure. A good example is Ben Aronin's fictional hero Raphael Drale, who searches for the lost tribes in one of the earliest Jewish science fiction books.[38] But still, at least a small part of the titillation lay in the possibility of their really existing. The 1903 *A Trip to the North Pole; or, The Discovery of the Ten Tribes, as Found in the Arctic Ocean* by O. J. S. Lindelof was an adventure story, to be sure. But its Mormon author was quite serious about the theory that the tribes were at the North Pole. He was religious, but his decision to dress up his argument as an adventure book was connected to the romantic aspect that the search for the lost tribes had taken on.

Increasingly, though, as adventure and romantic discovery became their context, the tribes were relegated to the realms of fantasy and fiction. An 1837 history of global circumnavigation criticized the fantastic depictions of Tahiti by the French Louis Antoine de Bougainville (1729–1811). Obviously hostile to and critical of the idea of French circumnavigation, its English author compared Bougainville's reports to "tale[s] better fitted for the dark times and heated imaginations of the earliest adventurers; when Juan Ponce de Leon sailed in search of the Fountain of Youth; when golden regions were sought for every day; and when the lost tribes of Israel were so often found in the Islands of the Caribbean Sea, or on the shores of Tierra Firme."[39] The ten tribes, increasingly, were for cranks.

The Search Returns to the Jews

The search for the tribes had begun in Africa and Asia and, with the British Empire, had returned there. So, too, in the wake of empire, active searching became again the domain of Jews. Seven centuries after Benjamin of Tudela undertook to find the tribes in Asia, a Jew who converted to Christianity, resumed the search. Joseph Wolff (1795–1862) is perhaps the nineteenth-century figure most associated with romantic missionary travel and the quest for the restoration of the ten lost tribes.[40] Born in a small town in Bavaria, the son of a rabbi, David Wolff, Joseph called himself a "restored Israelite," after baptized into Roman Catholicism in 1812. Perhaps he was echoing the afore-mentioned idea of conversion to Christianity as "restoration" articulated by earlier theologians in the seventeenth-century.

Originally planning to be a Jesuit missionary, Wolff spent several years learning Hebrew, Arabic, Chaldean, and Syriac. In England, he joined the Anglican Church and was naturalized as a British subject. The declared purpose of his Oriental studies was to "preach to the Jews" in the "east." And indeed, he spent most of the 1820s in the Middle East, preaching to everyone: "Jews, Mohammedans, and other Sects." But what gained him fame in Eng-land and the United States, and among missionary circles worldwide, was a lifetime of searching for the ten tribes all over Central Asia, Afghanistan, and India.[41] There is perhaps no one more responsible than Wolff for making eastern Persia, India, the cities of Bukhara and Samarkand, and above all Afghanistan hunting grounds for the ten tribes.[42] Wolff explained the impetus for his travels:

> In the first place, it was my earnest desire to make known to my
> brethren of the Jewish nation, Jesus Christ. . . . Besides this, I often
> asked myself, how my brethren fare, whose ancestors were scattered,
> after the captivity of Babylon: those tribes of Israel, who, according to
> the sacred oracles, shall be united to the house of Judah; and whose
> present abode is a matter of speculation among many Christian
> Divines, and Jewish Rabbies. The latter assign to them a fabulous
> country, which they call "The land of darkness, beyond the Sabbathical
> river." Benjamin Tudela, and the Jews of Jerusalem boldly asserted,
> that they were residing at Halah and Habor, which they state to be the
> present Balkh and Bokhara. In the year 1829, being then at Jerusalem,
> I said to my wife, "Bokhara and Balkh are very much in my mind, for
> I think I shall there find the Ten Tribes." "Well," she replied, "I have no
> objection to your going there."[43]

Armed with Christian zeal, a training in both Jewish and Christian scrip-tural traditions, and a love of what today would be called "exotic" travel (not to mention an amenable spouse), Wolff was fueled perhaps most of all by his own Jewish roots. He wrote his first memoir (of four) at the age of twenty-nine; he was evidently a self-absorbed man, a proud "religious fanatic," and a romantic. His *Travels and Adventures of the Rev. Joseph Wolff*, published two years before his death, is riddled with self-aggrandizing stories of disease, suffering, courage, and near-death. There was a good market for his stories, as they were read both as missionary material and as travel and adventure literature. Wolff had "Adventures in Abyssinia" and was "beaten by Wahabitics" in Mecca. In between adventures, Wolff told his readers about the ten tribes:

> Some of the [Yemeni] Jews [in Bukhara] say, that the Ten Tribes are beyond China, and one must cross the Sambatyon, in order to reach them; but the river is stormy through the whole week, except on a Sabbath day: on the Sabbath, Gentiles are allowed to cross it, but not the Jews. . . . Though this [is] mixed with fiction, there is no doubt that some of the tribes are in China; as I hope to prove when I come to the narrative of my journey to Cashmere.

Wolff was also convinced that the "Benee Israel of Bombay" were descendants of the tribes.[44] Wolff concentrated his searches in Central Asia and India after having first spent time in West Africa, Ethiopia, and Arabia. (This geographical focus was clearly related to the decline of the Jewish Indian theory.)[45]

Wolff's love for adventure, his zeal for finding the ten tribes, and his intimate familiarity with the Central Asian regions eventually made him useful to the British government—at least, he thought so. When two British diplomats (and spies), Arthur Connolly (1807–1842) and Charles Stoddard (1806–1842), were captured by Emir Nasrullah Khan of Bukhara (r. 1826–1860), Wolff undertook to rescue them. At the time, Russian-British rivalry over control of part of Central Asia was growing: the so-called Great Game was becoming increasingly heated, attracting all sorts of adventurers and self-appointed spies.[46] Wolff failed, the men were executed in 1842, and he barely escaped. The story he wrote about the mission became a bestseller in England. Everybody read how Wolff, dressed in his "clergyman's gown, doctor's hood, and shovel hat; with a Bible in Hebrew and English . . . in his hand" introduced himself to the emir as "Joseph Wolff, the grand dervish of England, Scotland, and Ireland, and of the whole of Europe and America."[47] After him, Wolff's son Sir Henry Drummond Wolff made a great career as a diplomat in regions where his father was active, and the younger Wolff raised funds for yet another ten tribes expedition to Central Asia. Both Wolffs functioned in the broader frames of empire, romantic adventure, and missionary zeal. But they also marked the beginning of a transition back to a specifically Jewish interest in finding the ten lost tribes, one that was soon to shift the interest in their restoration to a desire to bring them "home."

In 1837, the Reverend Jacob Samuel set out from Tehran to the Caucasus, looking to see if the ten tribes were still in their oldest "place of hiding" since biblical times. In his *Remnant Found*, in which he recounts having found the ten tribes in the contemporary Jewish community of Dagestan, Samuel presents a long and coherent case in support of the claim, drawing on a wide range of sources.[48] Samuel, like Wolff a Jew who converted to Christianity, was determined:

> This discovery of the Ten Tribes at the present important crisis [the rivalry between Russia and Britain] must appear a wonderful event. The preservation of them through so many ages, in the very heart of their enemies, must be acknowledged as a most signal act of Divine Providence; and we need no stronger or more convincing proof of the time of their restoration being at hand, when they shall be taken from the place of their interment for near two thousand five hundred years, and be restored to their own land.[49]

Once again, the question of exile had returned. And for nineteenth- and early twentieth-century Jews, a way to solve it seemed increasingly close to hand.

Wolff and Samuel escaped death, but Uziel Haga, who went to find the tribes in China, was not as fortunate.[50] In 1900, U.S. president William McKinley (1843–1901) gave Haga, an Orthodox Jew who was an Eastern European immigrant to Boston, permission to join the U.S. military and relief forces being sent to China. Haga claimed that he had proof that the ten lost tribes of Israel were hiding there; he wanted the chance to find them. The time and the place of the mission were highly significant. Over a year earlier, the militarized religious sect known as the Society of Right and Harmonious Fists (Chinese, *Yihe tuan*) had erupted in China, triggering a wave of anti-foreign and anti-Christian violence that sent shock waves throughout the world. The mysterious Boxers, poorly armed but fully motivated with "fanatic zeal," killed about 230 foreigners, mostly missionaries, and tens of thousands of Chinese Christians. At the peak of the rebellion, they invaded Beijing and besieged the foreign embassies quarter. The Boxers believed themselves immune to Western weaponry and employed traditional martial arts.[51]

To the outside world, it seemed that the Boxers had appeared out of nowhere. Thus, Haga, an American Jew, decided that the mysterious, violent, anti-Christian, militarized movement was connected with the ten tribes. Various sources had placed the ten tribes in China since as early as the eighth-century Midrash. Many exegetes had insisted that Sinim in Isaiah's vision of redemption, from whence the ten tribes were to return, was China. Other

Jewish sources had depicted a violent appearance of the ten tribes as the first step in the redemptive process that would usher in the coming of the Messiah. Could it be that the Boxer Rebellion was the beginning of the messianic process?

The violence was put down by international forces led by Britain, among them a rather small U.S. contingent. Haga went with this latter group. He tells us that he begged McKinley—"sobb[ing] in front of the president"—that he be allowed to go with the American ships. McKinley "willingly" agreed, equipping Haga with a special letter explaining his mission and even paying all of his expenses. This was the immediate context of Haga's mission. However, it had a much longer history. Haga was not just going to search for the ten tribes. He was going to bring them back. His "soul was yearning" to make a "new covenant" (*Berit Hadash*) with the children of the "Ten Tribes who were torn away from us, a huge tear that does not heal" (*qeri'ah gedolah she'eina mita'aha*).[52] One cannot miss the messianic overtones. The phrase "new covenant" in this context speaks volumes. The Bible tells the story of the children of Israel as a series of progressing covenants with God—first with Abraham, then with the whole people at Mount Sinai. After the flood, God made a covenant with humanity and vowed not to destroy it again. Haga's mission, then, was to pave the way for a new covenant, by bringing back the ten tribes and overcoming the Sambatyon. The only report Haga managed to send to his relatives from China was entitled "The Book of the New Covenant with the River Sambatyon in the Land of China." The odd phrase, a "covenant with . . . Sambatyon," calls to mind the notion of Sambatyon as not only a place but also a condition—a utopian, but exiled, state of existence.

Here, then, was the old messianic yearning for restitution through reuniting with the ten tribes and an end to exile. We have considered here just some of the many stories from Jewish tradition that had this as their theme. Such quests had intensified in the nineteenth century in the wake of new messianic expectations based on the calculations of the Vilna Gaon (Eliyahu ben Shlomo Zalman; 1720–1797). The Gaon, one of the greatest and most powerful rabbinic authorities in Eastern Europe and a central figure in the rise of Jewish Orthodoxy, placed great importance on the return of the ten tribes as part of the messianic process whose beginning, he predicted, was imminent. Arie Morgenstern has shown that, in the Gaon's view—and this was a true innovation—the ten tribes were supposed to take an active part in the renewal of Jewish *political* institutions as part of the redemptive process. This new interpretation triggered a new, more intense interest in the tribes, involving mostly writing and speculation but also some real attempts to find them.[53]

China occupied a special place in these quests. The Alsatian rabbi Abraham Stempel had also been there and claimed to have found the ten tribes. Stempel's trip, too, came in the context of upheaval—in his case, in the midst of the Taiping Rebellion, a devastating wave of violence that shook China when forces led by a man who claimed to be Jesus's brother swept the country.[54] Stempel was allowed to join the British forces going to China, arriving in Shanghai in 1860. His tale is not unlike that of Montezinos: the Alsatian rabbi saw a "great river" that reminded him of the Sambatyon. But interestingly, he places the ten tribes in the province of Sichuan, known for its cloudy mountains—and allusion, perhaps, to the cloud that covered the ten tribes in one of the Talmudic passages. And, as in Montezinos's story, the ten tribes were initially unwilling to engage. After some hesitant overtures, a mysterious man admitted to Stempel that he was the local rabbi in a ten tribes community. In conversation with this "Chinese rabbi," Stempel learned that the community was "of the ten tribes that were exiled by King Shalmaneser to Assyria, and then moved eastward to China," where they had lived for "2450 years."

Stempel's account of China during the rebellion seems fairly accurate, but he was also a trickster with an agenda about the vexing problem of Jewish assimilation into European gentile culture. The Chinese ten triber, so reported Stempel, was very proud of the fact that, even after 2,450 years the ten tribes had kept their traditions. "We heard," he told Stempel, of "the [European Jewish] desire to become like the [gentile] natives of the lands in Europe." As long as this was the situation, concluded the Chinese rabbi, no reunion with the ten tribes was possible.[55] Stempel—who was from the German world, where assimilative tendencies were strongest and conversion to Christianity at a peak—was really after a powerful argument against Jewish assimilation.

Stempel's report was published in 1864 in the Jewish journal ha-Magid. It was this report that prompted Haga, who never doubted it, to try to reach the ten tribes in China, seeing it as a sign from God that he should go to China.[56] Haga suffered greatly on his trip, evading death by a hair on numerous occasions. In one sense, Haga's mission was successful: he managed to tour huge swaths of territory and produced a detailed and largely accurate account of turn-of-the-century China, which he sent to relatives in Europe. In broader terms, though, the trip was less of a triumph. While Haga apparently did—to his mind—find the offspring of the ten tribes, he had little chance to write about his discovery. He sent only one report while still in China, and then he disappeared. His relatives eventually surmised, but there is no evidence for this, that he was ultimately captured by the "Wrestling Chinese" (the Boxers), imprisoned, and tortured to death. Perhaps the Boxers mistook him for a Christian missionary. The only trace left of his journey was that first report he had sent to his relations, which was published in 1906 with Stempel's original account. The jacket copy read:

> In this book one tourist will tell how he traveled with the forces of the armies of America with the permission of President McKinley to trace the sealed and the hidden of the Kingdom of the Chinese during the war of the European kings in the year 1900 in China. He will describe reliably the history of this pagan and savage people; their customs, processions, laws, war stratagems, etc. etc. etc., and will shed bright light on the Jews that are to be found there, and will prove with clear cut signs and paragons that they are the true descendants of the Ten Tribes exiled by the King of Assyria to Lahlah and Habor. He will also resolve all questions about the River Sambatyon, and will provide an honest call to unite with the Jews and remove the curtain separating them and us, and many advantages will spring forth from this for the sake of lifting Israel.[57]

Ramaswamy observes that "loss [is] an irresistible and inevitable condition of modernity."[58] The urge to "heal the tear," as Haga put it, could not be resisted by latter-day Jewish travelers. To be sure, Haga was not the first Jewish traveler who went to look for the tribes. But Haga's journey was different in the fusion of its contextual factors: modern global imperial expansion and the globalization of transportation and communication routes combined with a millennia-old aspiration for restitution and reunification with that which had been so painfully lost. Unlike the Christian searchers of his time, Haga was not looking for a "heathenized" or transformed ten tribes. He sought the very same entity that had been lost 2,700 years before—ten intact, isolated tribes, which had been carried away so many years before by the long-gone Assyrian king. His was an atemporal search, framed and contextualized—enabled—by historical context. His loss was atemporal, but it was also a distinctly modern one, a loss that was felt and expressed most strongly precisely when the chances of overcoming it seemed most present.

But Haga's ultimately tragic attempt to reach the tribes in China was most striking in that he was determined not only to find the tribes but also to bring them back and to renew and restore the covenant. The possibility of bringing the tribes home was very real and could be accomplished through mundane means, via the institutions of his day, including permission and financial sponsorship from a major world leader and a knowledge of geography. Haga's journey signaled a vital departure from the traditional trajectory and shape of Jewish trips seeking the ten tribes, which long had been, for the most part, marked by a fictional expression of longing and yearning for their restitution and for the end of exile. Haga's endeavor foreshadowed the coming of a new Jewish quest for the ten tribes, one that would confidently find them— and bring them back.

Over the centuries, geographical knowledge had grown; anthropological accounts had accrued; and traveler after traveler had contributed his or her latest knowledge about who and where the tribes were. Paradoxically, far from limiting the field of possibilities—far from leading to the conclusion that perhaps the ten tribes were no more, or never were—this body of knowledge only served to make finding them ever more possible, and their loss ever more acute. Haga's "Book of the New Covenant"—and the very idea of a new covenant—brings this study to a close. The publication of Haga's book coincided with the appearance of the first major movement that sought above all to establish a covenant with all the world's Jews. The story of Zionism, writ large; its relationship with the various groups identified as the ten tribes; and other Judaizing movements is well researched and represents a different type of history than the one told here.[59] What matters most here is what Zionism shares with Mormonism and British Israelism: the power to actually discover the ten tribes.

To Search and Bring Back

In 1904, Yaacov Jacques Faitlovitch (1881–1955) arrived in Massawa, Sudan. David Reuveni had passed through this city/port centuries earlier on his way to Europe. Faitlovitch, however, was going in the opposite direction, toward Ethiopia—where rumors of the ten tribes' existence had a long history. A scholar trained in Europe who was active in lost tribes committees in Tel Aviv, Faitlovitch marks the shift of ten tribes attention from Europe back to Palestine, which at the time was the Zionist Yishuv under the British Mandate.

Faitlovitch had studied Ethiopian languages at the Sorbonne's School of Oriental Languages and would later, in 1907, complete a doctorate on the subject. Born in the Polish city of Lodz, then under Russian control, he had a self-assigned mission: to "discover the Falasha" in Ethiopia. As his biographer Emanuela Trevisan Semi notes, Faitlovitch was motivated by a verse in Isaiah (49:6): "I will also give thee for a light to the Gentiles, that thou mayest be my salvation unto the end of the earth." And, indeed, Faitlovitch covered the various (historical) edges of the world, traveling to Afghanistan, India, China, and Japan to try to "create links between Jewish communities."[60] But his central and earliest focus was Ethiopia.

The arrival in Ethiopia of this "Jewish missionary," as some disturbed rival Protestant missionaries called him, started a long relationship between him and the Falasha community there. The Protestants had good reason to feel threatened. Faitlovitch, "a tough man," fought hard to "protect" the Falasha from Christian missionary drives. At the same time, Faitlovitch introduced Jewish customs and liturgy and helped to build Jewish schools in Ethiopia. Between 1904 and 1950, Faitlovitch made several long visits, looking for traces of the ten tribes—and bolstering the Falashas' Judaism. In between trips, he published reports on the Falasha in Europe and raised money for his Ethiopian activities, skillfully maneuvering among various world powers, the Italian colonial administration in Ethiopia, and worldwide Jewish and Zionist organizations.[61] These were the beginnings of a long and complicated relationship between the Zionist movement and, later, the state of Israel and the Falasha of Ethiopia.

The modern Jewish gaze turned elsewhere as well. In 1928, Zvi Kasdoi (1862–1937) published *Tribes of Jacob and the Preserved of Israel*, arguing that the ten tribes were located—no surprise here—somewhere in the Caucasus. He particularly pointed to the "Dagestanis, and Georgians," but also suggested that many of the Armenians were also related to the ten tribes. Indeed, a great deal of the book was a rewriting of Armenian history—combined with numerous clues from Talmudic and biblical sources—in an attempt to expose Armenia's Israelite past.[62] What was really at stake was what had troubled ha-Lorki five centuries before him: acute anxiety about the size and fate of the Jewish people in modern times. He was trying to combat this fear with the reassuring claim: the ten tribes are not lost, they are still here, they are part of "us."[63] Kasdoi was the brother-in-law of none other than Yitzhak Ben-Zvi (1884–1963), the future second president of Israel, who was busy at the time in a vast effort to collect information on the ten tribes and other "distant Jews" from all corners of the earth.[64]

These efforts are characteristic of the growing links between study of the ten tribes and Zionist thought. In the same period, Aaron Zeev Aescoly, the David Reuveni scholar, produced the monumental study *Israel*, covering "the essence of the Jewish people" and the "history of the Jewish race." Including the fields of anthropology, geography, linguistics, and demography, Aescoly's study—published only after he died—was meant to assess the scope of the Jewish people.[65] Special appendixes discussed converts to Judaism and, predictably, the ten tribes. Aescoly was also a scholar of messianic movements in Jewish history,[66] and he saw a clear connection between the scope of the Jewish people and Zionism.

The logic of this new breed of seeker was simple: if the Zionist movement was engaged in bringing the redemption of the Jews, why not bring the ten tribes into the picture as well? Faitlovitch, Kasdoi, and Ben-Zvi might be seen simply as just another phase in the ongoing search for the ten tribes and the creation and accumulation of knowledge about them. But this conclusion would miss the fact that they were operating in a radically different and utterly unprecedented context: that of the very real possibility of Jewish political sovereignty.[67] The ten tribes had been used in the past for political ends. But now, for the first time, they were politicized in aid of a *Jewish* political movement. The inclusion of the ten tribes in the scope of the Jewish people meant, in Zionist terms, the politicization of their return.

In 1928, Menahem Mendel Emanuel of Jerusalem, a rabbi, historian, and traveler, published *The Lost Tribes of Israel: A Call in Time and the Redemption of Israel*. Published in Hebrew and English, the book on the surface looked like many that had come before it, advertising itself as using "the latest critical analysis, scientific, historical and biblical investigation" in the effort to answer the question of where the lost tribes were to be found. Emanuel was yet another member of this new Jewish genre of scholar/seeker, though not one with the European university credentials of many of his confreres. David Wishenewitz, the author's old high school teacher from New York, testified that "Rabbi Menahem was always interested in Geography...and passed with honors... Geography and Ancient history."[68] Like many of its predecessors, the book relied on the "Talmud, Midrash...mystic Kabbala, and the famous Travelers of the world, ancient and modern" up to the year of its publication. But *The Lost Tribes of Israel* was, above all, "an appeal to all the Nations, and to all the world" for a concentrated global effort—of Jewish organizations supported by world powers—to bring back the lost tribes: "The aim of this book, is, to wake up the Jews and all the liberal Nations of the world, and to make them interested, to send out an expedition, to look for them...and re-unite all the Jews in the world."[69] It recorded the many notices sent to world leaders and dignitaries calling on them to help and outlined a clear plan to bring the ten tribes home with the help of world powers. In this, it was the first text of its kind.

And, indeed, leaders of the world responded, politely if not resoundingly, to prepublication copies of the book presented to them by Emanuel. "Wishing you...success...I remain Respectfully yours," wrote Theodore Roosevelt from Oyster Bay, New York. "Worthy Rabbi: I have the honor to acknowledge receipt of your letter and a copy of your book, which contains patriotic articles by a loyal citizen of honour," wrote Woodrow Wilson. Oscar Heizer, the American consul in Jerusalem, acknowledged receipt on behalf of President Calvin Coolidge. So, too, the assistant district commissioner in Jaffa on behalf of King George V. Among the many rabbis endorsing the book was Simon Hurwitz, the author of *Kol Mevaser* (Voice of Annunciation), a book on the ten lost tribes that provided notices on them from traditional sources as well as "wonderful news on the Jews of China."[70] Another endorsement was from Abraham Isaac Kook (1865–1935), chief rabbi of the Yishuv Palestine and a great theologian of modern political Judaism.[71] A number of other dignitaries and rabbis also endorsed the book. What mattered to Emanuel and the rabbis was the place of the quest for the ten lost tribes within their own contemporary context. In 1923, Kook had written about the "thirst" and the "desire" to see the "disappeared brothers" whose absence he likened to the "most basic deficiencies inflicted on Israel by the bitter exile." The ten lost tribes, in his view, had played a vital role in putting Jewry on the world stage:

> Our eyes have seen the great wonders of how the idea of finding the ten tribes became rooted so deeply.... [We saw] the return of our brethren children of Israel to Britain ... and from this development we [see] the signs of some emergence of salvation in our days, after the horrible pogroms, the war, and the British declaration concerning our national home. Surely, this is all the act of God.[72]

There was a clear progression as Kook saw it: ten tribes mania had led to Britain allowing Jews to return to its shores and, later, to the Balfour Declaration. Now, interest in the ten tribes might help bring them back to the Holy Land—not to the biblical one, but rather to a national Jewish homeland. British interest in the tribes was, in Kook's view, hastening a Jewish *political* redemption.

Kook's direct referent of course, the "British declaration," was the Balfour Declaration, which recognized the right of Jews to a national home. Kook recognized the various strands feeding Britain's interest in the ten tribes and the global implications. Chief architect of the potent theological interpretation that considers the modern Jewish state to mark the beginning of redemption, Kook forged a direct link between the ten tribes and Zionism. Just as redemption involved ending Jewish exile, it also meant ending the exile of the ten tribes.

Zionism presented itself as messianism without a messiah, a movement (and salvation) with its sole focus to bring all Jews into a modern Jewish polity. The two other long-standing elements in the messianic package—the rebuilding of the temple and the return of the ten tribes—were initially understood as exceeding (or irrelevant to) the earthly charter of the Zionist movement. The Zionists would leave them up to God. Kook's intervention changed this view and brought the ten tribes squarely into the Zionist frame. Faitlovitch, Kasdoi, and Ben-Zvi took much the same view. Kook's insertion of the ten tribes into the Zionist context of a pending Jewish national home, promised by the British government in 1917, raised the possibility of a return of the tribes not simply to the Jewish people, but specifically to a Jewish polity.

It is here that the long history told in this book reaches its culminating point. Kook returns us to the prophet Isaiah's first call, from millennia before, for the ten tribes' return—a call issued, like Kook's, in Jerusalem. Kook's call for the restoration of the ten tribes to Palestine is directly linked to Isaiah's original prophecy of their ultimate return to the Holy Land and rests also on the millennia-long history of theological and geographical searchings for the ten tribes. All previous strands of pursuit—theological, geographical, scholarly, and imperial—converge in Kook's simple analysis of the history of his time. Isaiah spoke of a highway that would bring the ten tribes from Assyria back to the Holy Land. That highway initially stood outside history and outside geography. But on its way to Kook's vision, that highway was, as it were, paved— brought into real history and geography—by the numerous seekers and searches recounted here.

And indeed, most of this has come to pass. With the creation of the state of Israel in 1948, the world saw the establishment of the first and sole institution in history vested with the political power to declare certain groups to be of the ten lost tribes. Through formal, state-dictated processes, Israel, whenever it wants to, can now overcome loss.

New Study Shows: Conversion of Jews to Christianity in Western Europe in Late Antiquity Was More Dramatic than the Loss of the Ten Tribes
                                    —Headline in *Haaretz* (February 11, 2007)

On January 11, 2000, the Israeli Parliament (the Knesset) convened for the gathering of the Committee for Immigration, Absorption, and the Diaspora (*'Aliyah, Klitah,* and *Tefutsot*). On the agenda was "the bringing [to Israel] of the groups of the Benei Menasseh who are living as Jews in India."[73] The people in question, the Mizu, are a group from southeastern India. In addition to the chair, Naomi Blumenthal, and three other parliamentarians, there was a large group present, among them several officials from various relevant ministries. Also in attendance were several officials from the Jewish agency which oversees Jewish immigration to Israel. So too was Hillel Halkin, a prominent Israeli-American writer and translator, author of *Across the Sabbath River: In Search of a Lost Tribe of Israel,* which recounts his journeys to the remote corners of southwest China and northern Thailand in the company of the Jerusalem rabbi Eliyahu Avichail.[74] Avichail, founder and leader of Amishav (My People Return), a society dedicated to the finding and bringing back of the lost tribes, was also present. Indeed, the meeting had been convened after

Avichail approached the committee chair with evidence that he had "found the lost tribe of Menasseh in India." Like countless searchers before him, he had spent decades touring the globe in search of the lost tribes.[75] Finally, the gathering also included an anthropologist who was a specialist on the tribes.[76] All that was missing were Protestant missionaries and Jesuit globetrotters to render the audience a compilation of ten tribes investigators across the centuries. The discussion, however, did encompass the full trajectory of knowledge produced in the ten tribes' wake, as if all the knowledge accumulated over millennia had drained into the Jerusalem meeting room.

The twenty-eight-page minutes of the meeting shows the discussants arguing about how best to determine the location of the ten tribes, and how to uphold or reject Avichail's claim. Had the tribes undergone cultural, physical, and social transformations? Had they become "heathenized"? Was restoration of these Israelites to Judaism possible, and if so, how best to effect it? Finally, was reunion with these missing siblings a vital necessity?

The participants were skeptical and didn't seem to want to uphold the claim. After all, they reasoned, there are many claimants to ten tribes status all over the world. They feared a deluge of millions of requests to immigrate to Israel. The meeting was adjourned without a decision. But later on, amid some debate, several hundred Mizu were indeed brought to Israel. How simple it suddenly seems! Gone are conjecture and speculation. After debate, peoples are definitively ruled in, or out.

As is well known, during the 1980s and 1990s, the Jewish state successfully brought thousands of Ethiopians to live in Israel. A 1973 ruling had declared them "Children of the Tribe of Dan," drawing on sources going back to Zemah Gaon's tenth-century response to the Qayrawanis on the question of Eldad's identity. So, too, the Mennashites from India, many of whom ultimately landed in the settlements of the Gaza Strip, from which they were removed during the disengagement in 2005. Astonishingly, a headline at the time read, "A Lost Tribe Fears Being Lost Again." The story began, "Uprooted 2700 years ago, the Ten Tribes are being uprooted again"—and with breathtaking ease, a millennia-old story blotted out a much more present and surrounding uprootedness, that of the Palestinians.[77]

These ten tribers were not the only ones in the settlements. On April 6, 2003, the Israeli newspaper Ma'ariv reported that a delegation of rabbis and settlers had converted several hundred "Indians" in the Andes of Peru. The then chief Ashkenazi rabbi, Meir Lau, had sent a delegation of rabbis to the site where García, Montezinos, and Rocha had first found the ten tribes in the seventeenth century.[78] Thus, hundreds of Andeans were brought "home." More recent arrivals have since been sent, appropriately, to the senior settlement of Shavei

Shomron (Returnees to Samaria), not far from ancient Samaria, the original capital of the ten tribes—where it all began.

A well-known Talmudic proverb says: "He who loses one soul it is as if he has lost the whole world." Rearranged, there is a different truth in this phrase. Loss creates whole worlds.

The story of the ten lost tribes is ultimately a story of profound loss, the loss of a group of people, deported and disappeared. But the loss of the tribes is not finished. It is not a past event but a living loss, sustained and felt over millennia. With its multiple recordings, its inscription with theological, geographical, and ultimately political import, it is a story encoded with enduring meaning. It is not, however, only a story of loss. It is also a story of creation. Once declared lost, the ten tribes went on to create, time and again, the edges of the earth and the boundaries of the world; they have conjured into existence whole places, such as Arzareth and Sambatyon; charted paths of supposed migration across the face of the earth; built land bridges between Asia and Europe and the Americas; inscribed real places with meaning and rendered them intelligible. The ten tribes have provided centuries of world travelers with itineraries and meaning. Whole peoples have been imbued with meaning through reference to them. They have promised the hope of redemption and humanity's unity.

This book has been concerned with the history of this story, a history that, as we have seen, moved from despair to hope; from here-and-now hope to eschatology and messianism; from messianism to romanticism and adventure. Ultimately, it moved to political resolution. But overall, the element that has lent the story its enduring power, that has transcended history, is loss.

The profundity of this loss is reflected in the frequency with which some observers of the Holocaust—like Avigdor Shahan, whose young friends were murdered in their desperate flight from the Nazis across the Dneister River, their Sambatyon—invoked the lost tribes in the effort to explain their grief. By mid-December 1942, the Jews confined by the Nazis to the Warsaw ghetto had a fairly clear idea of what was going on in Treblinka, the camp to which Jews from Warsaw were sent. German evacuations of the ghetto were well under way, and earlier that month, 2,000 children had been taken away to be gassed. Historian Emanuel Ringelblum (1900–1944), who was also confined to the ghetto, meticulously documented the horrors around him. The children's parents feared the worst, but allowed themselves some slim hope. Ringelblum comments on the Jewish refusal to believe that so many of their number were being lost. He entitled his diary entry for December 15, 1942, "The Ten Tribes":

I believe that years after the war, when all the secrets of the [death]
camps will be revealed, miserable mothers will still be dreaming that
the children snatched out of their arms are somewhere in the depths
of Russia; that expeditions will be organized to search for the
thousands of the camps [where] the exterminated Jews [might be still
living]. In a period so distant from romanticism, a new legend will be
formed about the millions of Jews who were slaughtered, a legend
similar to that of the ten tribes.[79]

The loss of the tribes, this "huge tear that does not heal," has spoken to and
mobilized thousands of people across different times, places, and contexts,
animating them to create different worlds—temporal, human, and physical. It
is loss, then, that has, more than any other of its features, made the story of the
ten tribes a truly global story and its history truly a world history. But ever
nested within this profound loss and absence has been its mobilizing corollary:
the idea of restitution, redemption, and wholeness. I allow myself to end, then,
with the most hopeful vision that the possibility of finding the lost tribes ever
produced: Ben-Israel's promise of the restoration of peace to the world "and
concord, which is the only Mother of all good things."

Notes

INTRODUCTION

1. Shahan, *El 'Ever ha-Sambatyon*, 11.

2. Romanian and German armies murdered about 185,000 deported Ukrainian and Romanian Jews in Transnistria between September 1941 and March 1943.

3. Shahan, *El 'Ever ha-Sambatyon*, 12–13.

4. Neubauer, "Where Are the Ten Tribes?" I, II, III, IV.

5. Other languages provide other examples. For instance, in Hebrew, the word "never" is *le-'olam*, which literally means "to world." The word "ever" is *me-'olam*, which literally means "from world." In both cases the origin of the expression stems probably from the temporal qualities of the word "world." Thus, "world/'olam" in this case represents the ultimate most absolute (and somehow still indefinite) unit of time.

6. Rocha, *El origen de los indios*, 123.

7. Kingsborough, *Antiquities;* Goodkind, "Lord Kingsborough." See also Peñafiel, *Nombres Geograficos de Mexico.*

8. McLeod, *Epitome;* McLeod, *Korea.*

9. Grimaldi, *Manasseh in Scotland.*

10. Forster, *Monuments of Assyria.*

11. Wolff, *Missionary Journal;* Wolff, *Researches;* Wolff, *Travels.*

12. Rosen, *Oriental Memories*, 102.

13. Haga, *Sefer Ha-Berit Ha-Hadash.*

14. Rosen, *Oriental Memories.*

15. See, for example, Parfitt and Egorova, *Genetics;* Parfitt, "Constructing Black Jews."

16. Hyamson, "Lost Tribes," 641.

17. For a good survey in English of some of these groups, see Gonen, *Ends of the Earth*.

18. Koishi, *Nihonjin;* and particularly Matsumoto and Eidelberg, *Yamato Minzoku Yudayajin*. Matsumoto even argues that ten tribesmen escaping Asia were the founders of the Yamato state.

19. Anderson, *God's Covenant Race*.

20. On the Almohads and Berbers and the ten lost tribes, see Nebot, *Les Tribus Oubliées*, 32–34.

21. Margolis, "Finding the Lost Tribes." It will be impossible to provide references to all instances. For the best study of various versions of such claims, see Parfitt, *Lost Tribes of Israel*.

22. Kirsch, "Lost Tribes," 58. Kirsch ties the assigning of the "lost tribal identity" to discovered tribes to "the expansion of the world system," 65. The study of assigning lost tribal identity in such contexts started with Godbey, *Lost Tribes a Myth*. For a comprehensive bibliography, see Parfitt, *Lost Tribes of Israel*. See also Parfitt, "Hebrew in Colonial Discourse."

23. I borrow both terms and their definitions from Pratt's *Imperial Eyes*, 6–7.

24. Hyamson, "Lost Tribes," 640–641.

25. Lyman, "Postmodernism," 192.

26. Witsius, *Dekaphylon*. James Calvert (d. 1698), *Naphtali . . . Reditu Decem Tribuum* (Naphtali . . . The Return of the Ten Tribes), which also has a historical segment in it, is a few years earlier but is mostly focused on the theory that the Native Americans are the descendants of the tribes.

27. Muller, *After Calvin*, 176–188.

28. Witsius, *Dekaphylon*, 307.

29. Ibid., 330.

30. Ibid., 306.

31. Floyer, *Sibylline Oracles*, xiv. See also Floyer, *Prophecies*, 155–161, and elsewhere. On Floyer, see Hamilton, *Apocryphal Apocalypse*, 279–285.

32. The best and most comprehensive study of such an inflection of the ten tribes is Andrew Gow's *The Red Jews*, which focuses on late medieval and early modern Germany. The literature in Hebrew is vast; for a bibliography, see Vail, *Me-'Ever La-Sambatyon*.

33. Jacobovici and Halpern, *Quest for the Lost Tribes;* Cameron et al., *Lost Tomb of Jesus*.

34. Lee, *Lost Tribe;* see also Simons, *Exiled Times;* Blackwell, *Michael's Fire;* Aronin, *Lost Tribe*.

35. Somtow, *Aquila in the New World*.

36. McGrady, *Beyond the Black Ocean*. On McGrady, see Terrar, "Catholic Socialism."

37. Lindelof, *Trip to the North Pole*, 11.

38. Ibid., 197–198.

39. "Travels of Binyamin the Third," "The Portuguese Traveler Who Visited the Tribes of Simeon and Issacher," "How the Goat Led the Way to the Ten Tribes," and more are all cited in Vail, *Me-'Ever La-Sambatyon*, 66–70.

40. Bloch, *The Past Keeps Changing*, 32.

41. *History of Johnson County, Iowa*, 275.

42. Anxiety and *not* memory.

43. Yet the theological significance of the story of the lost tribes is mostly missing from the few analytical studies touching on the subject. See Kirsch, "Lost Tribes"; Lyman, "Lost Tribes of Israel"; and Lyman, "Postmodernism."

44. For a survey of all prophecies, see Neubauer, "Where Are the Ten Tribes?" I.

45. Hine, *Forty-Seven Identifications* (1871), 4.

46. Haga, *Sefer Ha-Berit Ha-Hadash*, I.

47. Simon, *Hope of Israel*, 364.

48. Yuval, "Myth of the Jewish Exile."

49. Ibid., 27.

50. Ibid., 33.

51. Ibid., 27.

52. Rutherford, *Israel-Britain*, 5.

53. Popkin, "Age of Reason."

54. See Idel, *Messianic Mystics*, 60–65; Schwartz, *Faith at the Crossroads*, 161.

55. Lyman, "Lost Tribes of Israel," 159.

56. Raz-Krakotzkin, "Galut be-toch Ribonut"; Raz-Krakotzkin, "A National Colonial Theology."

57. Ramaswamy, *Lost Land of Lemuria*, 18.

58. Ibid., 1–2.

59. Ibid., 7. In this, she follows George Bataille, who said that "sacred things are constituted through an operation of loss."

60. Ramaswamy, *Lost Land of Lemuria*, 8.

61. Wauchope, *Lost Tribes*, 6.

62. See http://www.varchive.org/ce/baalbek/gozan.htm.

63. "Fabulous geography" is a term she borrows from Joseph Conrad. Ramaswamy, *Lost Land of Lemuria*, 14.

64. Rusconi, "Introduction," in Columbus, *Book of Prophecies*, 26.

65. Eliade, *Sacred and Profane*, 20.

66. Wright, "Terrae Incognitae," 12.

67. Glacken, *Traces*, 35. See also Park's complaint in "Religion and Geography," 442.

68. May, *Kant's Concept of Geography*.

69. Park, *Sacred Worlds*, 11.

70. Shalev, "Sacred Geography." For instance, sacred geographers had a great of deal of interest in the location of the land of Ophir, which is mentioned in the Bible (1 Kings 9–10) as the source of the gold for Solomon's projects. Shalev, "Sacred Geography," 16–23.

71. Cited in Shalev, "Geographia Sacra," 182.

72. Haga, *Sefer Ha-Berit Ha-Hadash*, I.

73. Rabbi Juda Loew of Prague, *Netzah Israel*, 34, 68–71.

74. I am relying heavily here on André Neher's approach to this specific idea of Maharal's concerning new worlds, although Neher thinks more in terms of time and history rather than space and geography. See Neher, *Jewish Thought*, 142–144.

75. Moyn, "Amos Funkenstein," 646. See also Funkenstein, *Theology*.

76. Thorowgoodm *Digitus Dei*, title page. Gillis, *Islands of the Mind*, 121.

77. Ibid., 1.

78. Ramaswamy, *Lost Land of Lemuria*, 6–7, 15–16.

79. Dirlik, "Performing the World," 396. See also his "Confounding Metaphors."

80. See Nagel, *The View from Nowhere*.

81. I borrow this phrase from Carlo Ginzburg's *No Island Is an Island* ("The Old and the New World as It Is Seen from Nowhere," 1–24).

82. Seeing the world as the "ultimate frame of reference" is in Dirlik's "Performing the World," 396. This view also distinguishes this work from what is sometimes called "ecumenical history"—an all-inclusive world history.

CHAPTER 1

1. All dates and chronologies for Assyrian, Israelite, and Judahite kings, biblical prophets, and events are taken from Liverani, *Israel's History*.

2. See Becking, *Fall of Samaria;* Galil, *Yisrael ve-Ashur*.

3. Machinist, "Fall of Assyria," 179.

4. Finkelstein and Silberman, *Bible Unearthed*, 220.

5. For a discussion of these campaigns and their history, see Na'aman, "Ahab's Chariot Force"; Na'aman, "Jehu, Son of Omri."

6. Younger, "Deportations of the Israelites," 214–215. The Assyrians used different designations for the northern kingdom. This is discussed in Kelle, "What's in a Name?"

7. It is not even clear whether Shalmaneser V did indeed besiege Samaria. See Na'aman, "Historical Background."

8. Younger, "Deportations of the Israelites," 207.

9. Na'aman, "Rezin of Damascus."

10. Younger, "Deportations of the Israelites," 206.

11. Younger, "Deportations of the Israelites," 216, also discusses the difference in numbers.

12. Broshi and Finkelstein, "Population of Palestine."

13. Younger, "Deportations of the Israelites," 227.

14. Ibid., 224.

15. Cited in Na'aman, "Population Changes," 206. See also Na'aman and Zadok, "Sargon II's Deportations."

16. Na'aman, "Population Changes," 214.

17. Barmash, "Nexus of History," 218.

18. Tadmor, *Inscriptions*, 123.

19. Ibid., 47.

20. Ibid., 43, 45, 47, 67, 115.

21. Younger, "Deportations of the Israelites," 219; see also his n. 73. On this point, there is a consensus. However, while scholars of the period seem to agree on 157 deportations in the Near East during that period, there is no agreement on the number of deportees (ranging, according to estimates, from 1.5 to 4.5 million people). See Oded, *Mass Deportations*.

22. Younger, "Deportations of the Israelites," 221–223.

23. Ibid., 219.

24. Oded, *Mass Deportations*, 87–98. Ran Zadok, "Notes," identified names containing Israelite elements (such as the Yahwistic *yhw*) in some areas in Mesopotamia dating back to the period after the Assyrian campaigns.

25. Younger, "Deportations of the Israelites," 220.

26. Younger, "Israelites in Exile," 66.

27. A classic, but misled, perception of Assyria is A.T. Olmstead (1880–1945), *History of Assyria*. For an evaluation of Assyrian propaganda, see Hamilton, "The Past as Destiny," 217–222.

28. Oded, *War, Peace and Empire*, 163.

29. Oppenheim, "Neo-Assyrian and Neo-Babylonian Empires."

30. Grayson, "Histories and Historians."

31. See Fales, *Assyrian Royal Inscriptions*.

32. Oded, *War, Peace and Empire*, 120–131.

33. Ibid., 54–56.

34. Ibid., 102–106.

35. King, "The Eighth"; Moore and Lewis, *Birth of the Multinational*, 100–131.

36. Liverani, "Fall of the Assyrian Empire," 374.

37. See George, "Assyria"; and particularly Gitin, "Neo-Assyrian Empire"; Elat, "Phoenician Overland Trade"; Elat, "Economic Relations"; Na'aman, "Tiglath-pileser III's Campaigns."

38. Cifola, *Analysis*, 190.

39. Tadmor, *Inscriptions*, 97; see another list of universalistic titles in Cifola, *Analysis*, 157–158.

40. Tadmor, *Inscriptions*, 97. The term "four quarters of the earth" (the "whole world") was included in one of the titles of the Mesopotamian god Enlil. See Glassner, *Mesopotamian Chronicles*, 129.

41. Oded, *War, Peace and Empire*, 164.

42. Cited in Joannès, *Age of Empires*, 80.

43. Tadmor, *Inscriptions*, 195, 105.

44. Oded, *War, Peace and Empire*, 163–165.

45. Parker, *Mechanics of Empire*, 127–128.

46. Cifola, *Analysis*, 157.

47. See Vanderhooft, *Neo-Babylonian Empires*, 115–202.

48. Liverani, *Israel's History*, 158–159; Vanderhooft, *Neo-Babylonian Empires*, 123–135. Vanderhooft dedicates much room to a discussion concerning the dating of these prophecies, which is a major point of debate among scholars. It is clear that many of the oracles belong in a later period (early sixth century). However, earlier Assyrian realities

and events (such as the fall of Sidon in 701, lamented in Isaiah 23) strongly resonate in the oracles.

49. See Bredin, *Studies in the Book of Tobit*.

50. Vaux, *Nineveh and Persepolis*, 62–67; Bonomi, *Nineveh and Its Palaces*, 52–57, 79–80.

51. Howitt, *History of the Supernatural*, 276.

52. Rennell, *Geography System of Herodotus*, 512–535.

53. On the representation of the Assyrian Empire in Isaiah, see Machinist, "Assyria."

54. Oppenheim, "Neo-Assyrian and Neo-Babylonian Empires," 133.

55. Parker, *Mechanics of Empire*, 396.

56. A quick survey shows that variations on the term "end of the earth" occurs fifteen times in the biblical books, excluding the Psalms. The breakdown is five times in each prophet: Isaiah, Jeremiah, and Ezekiel.

57. Parker, "Garrisoning the Empire."

58. Parpola, "Assyrian Identity," 4.

59. Hamilton, "The Past as Destiny," 217.

60. The word *Aretz* is translated differently. The King James Version says, "Thou hadst removed it far unto all the ends of the earth." The Oxford Bible has: "you have extended all frontiers of the country."

61. See Gallagher, *Sennacherib's Campaign to Judah*, 22–90. Gallagher shows that the prophecies of Isaiah were delivered around the time of the invasion and not after.

62. See Na'aman, "Hezekiah"; Finkelstein and Silberman, *Bible Unearthed*, 251–264. Sennacherib, on the other hand, was apparently very embarrassed after this setback and labored hard to cover up his defeat in Palestine. See Laato, "Assyrian Propaganda," 215–226.

63. For a summary of this period, see Finkelstein and Silberman, *Bible Unearthed*, 149–296.

64. See Sweeney, *King Josiah of Judah*; Liverani, *Israel's History*, 171–182.

65. Finkelstein and Silberman, *Bible Unearthed*, 289–292.

66. Halpern, *First Historians*, 276.

67. For a summary of these events, see Liverani, *Israel's History*, 183–199.

68. Ibid., 363–368.

69. See Halpern, *First Historians*; Finkelstein and Silberman, *Bible Unearthed*, 283–298.

70. See, for example, Dever, *What Did the Biblical Writers Know*; Levin and Mazar, *ha-Pulmus 'al ha-Emet ha-Historit ba-Mikra*.

71. Na'aman, "Forced Participation"; Na'aman, "Tiglath-pileser III's Campaigns."

72. Younger, "Deportations of the Israelites," 221–222.

73. See a summary of these events in Finkelstein and Silberman, *Bible Unearthed*, 251–274.

74. On prophecies as foretelling, see McKenzie, *How to Read the Bible*, 67–90.

75. Peckham, *History and Prophecy*, 133–134.

76. I borrow the notion of "becoming lost" from Pamela Barmash's superbly researched essay, where she argues that the tribes were lost through the ways in which

their deportation was written and processed during the later period of the Second Temple. While I agree with her line of argument, I suggest that this moment of losing the tribes occurred much earlier, even before the Babylonian captivity, and that at work were theological and geographical considerations, so Barmash's choice of "memory" as the central category for her analysis of the transformation of the story, and "transfiguration of memory" as the main explanation for it are not directly applicable here. Barmash, "Nexus of History."

77. See Stuart Hall's seminal essay on this: "Cultural Identity and Diaspora."

78. See Liverani, *Israel's History*, 218–219.

79. Ibid., 214–230.

80. Hine, *Forty-Seven Identifications* (1871), 4.

81. Bassin, "Lost Ten Tribes [of] Anglo-Israel," 7.

82. Liverani, *Israel's History*, 218–221.

CHAPTER 2

1. The book of Esdras is mostly known as Fourth Esdras or 4 Ezra; I will stick to the Greek "Esdras" to avoid confusion with the canonical Ezra. See Bergren, "Christian Influence," 102–128. For basic details on the book's variations, see Nigosian, *Ancient Writings to Sacred Texts*, 198–199.

2. Baumgarten, "The Jewish People"; Gafni, *Land, Center and Diaspora*.

3. Josephus, *Works of Flavius Josephus*, 372.

4. This periodization follows Peter Schäfer's in *History of the Jews*.

5. See Jobes and Silva, *Invitation to the Septuagint*, 29–44.

6. One of these was *Oracula Sibyllina*, another Jewish apocalypse that mentions the coming "ten tribes, lost by the Assyrian[s]," who will look for their other Hebrew brethren.

7. See Acts 7:8, 26:7; James 1:1; Revelation 21:12; Luke 19:28, 22:30.

8. Daniel Boyarin, among others, questions this differentiation between Jews and Christians at these early stages of the postbiblical period. Boyarin, *Border Lines*, 1–13.

9. For the dating of this book, see Murphy, "2 Baruch."

10. Some such epistles have been compiled, for instance, in Wishnevitz, *Metsi'at 'aseret ha-shevatim*.

11. Hamilton, *Apocryphal Apocalypse*, 1.

12. For the dating of these passages, see Coggins and Knibb, *First and Second Books*, 101–105.

13. An interesting take on the various audiences of Esdras is in Esler, *First Christians*, 110–130.

14. On the origins of the messianic idea, see Sacchi, *Jewish Apocalyptic*, 150–167.

15. Gow, *The Red Jews*, 37–64.

16. Romm, *Edges of the Earth*, 3–5.

17. On the "man of the sea" and other apocalyptic visions, see Beale, "Problem of the Man from the Sea."

18. One should remember, of course, that it was in fact Sargon, Shalmaneser's successor, as explained in the previous chapter. This biblical confusion of the two Assyrian kings shall remain with us throughout.

19. Robinson, "Introduction," 86. See also VanderKam and Adler, *Jewish Apocalyptic Heritage*, 83–84.

20. This may explain why the word "Arzareth" almost never occurs in Hebrew texts.

21. Wright, "Note on the 'Arzareth' of 4 Esdr. xiii. 45."

22. Witsius, *Dekaphylon*, 368.

23. Anderson, *Alexander's Gate*, viii.

24. Westrem, "Against Gog and Magog," 56.

25. Anderson, *Alexander's Gate*, 3.

26. Romm, *Edges of the Earth*, 37.

27. Cited in ibid., 38.

28. Ibid., 39.

29. Robertson and Inglis, "The Global Animus," 43.

30. The book of Ezra was originally bound together with Nehemiah.

31. The same statement appears almost verbatim in the last words of 2 Chronicles to emphasize the chronological continuity between the narratives of exile and return.

32. Kuhrt, "Cyrus Cylinder." A translation of it appears in Edelman, *Origins*, 362–363.

33. For the Persian imperial policies relating to this particular case, see Edelman, *Origins*, 332–351.

34. For this episode and Ezra's role in it, see Liverani, *Israel's History*, 252–257.

35. For the image of Ezra and on the Persian Empire and the Torah, see Watts, *Persia and Torah*.

36. On Ethiopia as Cush in the Talmud, see Neubauer, *Géographie*, 410.

37. Babylonian Talmud, Megillah, 11a. The image is not unfounded. On Ptolemy's world map, the two seem to meet. This linkage between India and Ethiopia is unique to the Talmud at the time. See Mayerson, "A Confusion of Indias."

38. Romm, *Edges of the Earth*, 49–50.

39. Ibid., 57.

40. Ibid., 106.

41. Ibid., 82–94.

42. Allen, *Persian Empire*, 111–122.

43. See also the book of Esther, 3:12–15, 8:8–14, 9:29–31.

44. Josephus, *Works of Flavius Josephus*, 372.

45. On Ezra in Josephus, see Feldman, "Josephus' Portrait of Ezra." Feldman points out that Josephus adds details to the biblical story of Ezra's appointment by the Persian rulers. This says something about a lacuna in Josephus's treatment of the ten tribes being "left behind." If he already took the liberty to embellish on the biblical narrative (the issuing of epistles), why didn't he add more detail on the question of the tribes?

46. See again Yuval, "Myth of the Jewish Exile."

47. See Haran, "Early to Classical Prophecy."

48. Coggins and Knibb, *First and Second Books*, 268–269.

49. Severus, *Sacred History*, bk. II, ch. 11, in Schaff et al., trans., *Sulpitius Severus*.

50. Commodianus, *Commodiani Carmina*, 176. Commodianus is referring here to Esdras 13:40. On Commodianus and Esdras, see Bergren, "People Coming from the East." See also Robinson, "Introduction." Citing this verse, Richard Bauckham comments, "this is clearly no longer the real geography of the historical diaspora of the northern Israelites, but a mythical place beyond the known world." I would also stress that echoed here are real geographical considerations in placing this mythical place beyond Persia. See Bauckham, *Gospel Women*, 102.

51. Babylonian Talmud, Qiddushin, 72a. On these locations, see Neubauer, *Géographie*, 372–374.

52. Babylonian Talmud, Sanhedrin, 94a.

53. Moazami, "Millennialism," 1–16.

54. Anderson, *Alexander's Gate*, 62.

55. Midrash *Sifra*, ch. 8, 4. Cited also in Neubauer, "Where Are the Ten Tribes?" I:20.

56. Neubauer, "Where Are the Ten Tribes?" I:20.

57. Mishnah, Sanhedrin, 10:10.

58. Babylonian Talmud, Sanhedrin, 110b.

59. Midrash *Bereshith Rabba*, 73, 6. All Midrashim appear in Eisenstein, *Otsar Midrashim*.

60. Palestinian Talmud, Sanhedrin, 53b. This is Neubauer's translation with my emendments.

61. Midrash *Pesikta Rabbati*, 31. Biblical Riblah is in Babylon, but located also in Syria and therefore is an equivalent for Antiochia. This translation is from Braude, *Pesikta Rabbati*, 617.

62. Midrash *Lamentations Rabbah*, 2:5.

63. Midrash *Numbers Rabbah*, 16:25.

64. Neubauer, "Where Are the Ten Tribes?" I:20.

65. Etheridge, *The Targums; Targum Yonathan*; Exodus 34:10.

66. Midrash *'Eser Galuyot*, in Jellinek, *Bet ha-Midrash*, 113–116.

67. Neubauer, "Where Are the Ten Tribes?" IV:412; Friedlaender, "Jews of Arabia."

68. Jones, *Pliny*, 10:392–394. On Pliny's work as imperial project, see Murphy, *Pliny the Elder's Natural History*.

69. Josephus, *Works of Flavius Josephus*, 450.

70. Babylonian Talmud, Sanhedrin, 65a.

71. Another interpretation of 'Aqiva's martyrdom is in Boyarin, *Dying for God*, 107–108, and passim.

72. Feldman, *Jew and Gentile*, 158–161. However, see also Michael, "Jewish Sabbath"; Gandz, "Origin of the Planetary Week"; Zafran, "Saturn and the Jews"; Broughall, "Pattern of the Days"; Bentwich, "Graeco-Roman View of Jews"; Bruce, "Tacitus on Jewish History." There is also a highly relevant connection between Saturn and messianism. Kabbalah scholar Moshe Idel, has recently ventured to make precisely such connections. By way of introducing a new interpretation of the 17th-century "messiah" Sabbatai Zvi, and aiming to "broaden the pertinent contexts of the emergence and expansion of Sabbataianism," Idel points to the connection between the name

"Shabtai," and that of the planet Saturn (in Hebrew also Shabtai, "the Sabbath Planet"). Drawing on medieval traditions connecting Saturn, Jews, and the Sabbath (Saturn-day), Idel proposes that "astral mythology," and not only Jewish kabalistic tradition, be "taken into account" in the writing of the history of this Messianic movement. Taking his cue from redemptive qualities assigned to Saturn in Jewish astrological writings, Idel offers a combined reading of medieval and early modern astrological depictions of the star and depictions of Zvi, emphasizing among other things the melancholic quality supposedly "shared" by the planet and his Shabtai Zvi's namesake. Idel ventures that some aspects in Sabbataianism "restore some mythical traits of Greek themes lost over the centuries. See Idel, "Saturn and Sabbatai Tzevi," 199–201. See also, Goldish, *Sabbatean Prophets*.

73. Tacitus, *History of Tacitus*, 194–195.

74. Cited in Macey, *Patriarchs of Time*, 27.

75. Cited in ibid., 26.

76. Alexander, *Planet Saturn*, 29.

77. Cited in ibid., 54.

78. Ludolf, *New History of Ethiopia*, 45–46.

79. *Pesikta Rabbati*, 31:10. Translation is from Braude, *Pesikta Rabbati*, 617, with my minor corrections.

80. This verb, based on the name of the animal, never appears anywhere else.

81. Sacchi, *Jewish Apocalyptic*, 150.

CHAPTER 3

1. For the story of Dan, see Judges 1–3. For Samson's stories, see Judges 13–16.

2. For the Hebrew original, I am using the fifteenth-century collection of documents known as *Sefer Eldad ha-Dani*, in Epstein, *Kitve R. Avraham*, 1–211. The English translation of Eldad's story is from Adler, *Jewish Travellers*, 4–21. I will be using Adler's translation with my emendments. For the history of these documents, see Schloessinger, *Ritual of Eldad ha-Dani*, 1–9; and Wasserstein, "Eldad ha-Dani."

3. The Romarnos were one of the seven kingdoms in Ethiopia. See Krauss, "New Light."

4. In some peculiar cases, misreading Eldad's text produced new speculations about the ten tribes. For instance, Eldad mentions that the Tribes reside in the real place named "Najd" in Arabia ("The highlands of Najd [in] the region of Mecca"). However, because a word spelled similarly in Hebrew, "Najd" was often rendered "neged," which means "opposite," "against," or "facing." Thus, Eldad's "Najd in Mecca" was misread as "neged Mecca" and turned into a fictional place name: "Neged Mecca" ("Facing Mecca,"). This misreading led many to believe that the Ten Tribes were hidden somewhere in front of Mecca, ready to attack it. Adler himself mistranslates the sentence in the same way. See Adler, *Jewish Travellers*, 8.

5. Adler, *Jewish Travellers*, 7.

6. Ibid., 14.

7. Epstein, *Eldad ha-Dani*, 43.

8. Midrash, *Bereshith Rabba*.

9. Rabinowitz, "Eldad ha-Dani." "Assin" is how the Arabic place name al-Sin is pronounced.

10. For Islamic/Arabic and Chinese connections in this period, see Hourani, *Arab Seafaring*. For a translation of some classical sources, see Ahmad et al., *Arabic Classical Accounts*.

11. I have written extensively, perhaps too much, on this issue. See Ben-Dor, "Even unto China."

12. Eldad also wrote an epistle to the Jews of Spain. Neubauer, "Where Are the Ten Tribes?" II.

13. Cited in Neubauer, "Where Are the Ten Tribes?" II:186.

14. Cited in Neubauer, "Where Are the Ten Tribes?" II:187. Neubauer provides several additional examples of commentary following Saʿadya (II:186–190).

15. Cited in Epstein, *Eldad ha-Dani*, 7.

16. Carmoly et al., *Relation d'Eldad le Danite*; Carmoly, *Sipur Eldad ha-Dani*.

17. The citations are from Schloessinger, *Ritual of Eldad ha-Dani*, 2.

18. Neubauer, "Where Are the Ten Tribes?" II:109–110.

19. Adler, *Jewish Travellers*, 9.

20. Ibid., 17.

21. Ibid., 16.

22. Ibid., 17 Eldad is conflating two stories here, but this probably indicates that he was familiar with stories as they appeared in the written Midrash, which was redacted only decades before. Another possibility is that Eldad is reworking the Qurʾanic story concerning the children of Moses, "a nation guided in truth" (Qurʾan 7:159).

23. For a discussion, see Rabinowitz, "Eldad ha-Dani." Rabinowitz also raised the possibility that Eldad was a Chinese Jew. See also Adler's introduction to his translation, *Jewish Travellers*, 4–5. The most extensive study of Eldad's story is in Epstein, *Kitve R. Avraham*, 1–189.

24. Morag, "Eldad Haddani's Hebrew," 244–245.

25. The Himyarite kings were known to have converted to Judaism, but it is hard to determine what was meant by "conversion." On the rise of Himyar, see Bāfaqīh, *L'unification du Yémen antique*, 12–34. There are plenty of Arabic, Greek, and Syriac sources on the Jewish kings of Himyar. The most important studies of the Jews of Himyar are Israel Ben-Zeev's *Taʾrikh al-Yahud* and *ha-Yehudim ba-ʿArav*.

26. See, for example, Chaudhuri, *Trade and Civilisation*, 34–62.

27. Ben-Zeev, *ha-Yehudim ba-ʿArav*, 55–71.

28. For an account of these events based on these sources, see Smith, "Events in Arabia." See also Moberg, *Book of the Himyarites*, cxxxvi–cxli.

29. On Kaʿb as a storyteller, see Perlmann, "Another Kaʿb al-Ahbār Story"; and Halperin and Newby, "Two Castrated Bulls." For another interpretation of the man's career, see Ben-Dor, "Response to Kanan Makiya." Incidentally, or perhaps not, Kaʿb is also a somewhat disputed figure in Islamic tradition. While most Suni scholars accept him as a reliable authority, some maintain that he was a fraud and a swindler. McAuliffe, "Assessing the Israʾiliyyat."

30. Ben-Zeev, *ha-Yehudim ba-ʿArav*.

31. On the book itself, see Khoury, "Geschichte oder Fiktion." This book itself draws on many earlier traditions, many of them biblical, and draws on the connections between Ka'b and Wahb.

32. "Nisba Wlad Ham," in Ibn Hisham et al., *Kitāb al-Tijān*, 25–51. This section precedes the large chapter on the kings of Himyar, which begins on p. 51.

33. Adler, *Jewish Travellers*, 10.

34. "Malik Sa'b Dhu'l Qarnain," in Ibn Hisham et al., *Kitāb al-Tijān*, 81–93.

35. Gumilev coins this term in his study of the legendary Prester John. Gumilev, *Searches*, 4–6.

36. For an identification of some of the geographical names in Eldad's story, see Krauss, "New Light."

37. Adler, *Jewish Travellers*, 15.

38. The Gaons (Geonim), heads of the schools in Babylonia, were the last rabbinic figures who enjoyed indisputable authority. They, at least ostensibly, guided the entire Jewish world from Babylonia through an immense correspondence of questions and answers, known as the *responsa* literature. The institution of the Gaon collapsed in the eleventh century, but *responsa* is still the most vital element of Jewish legal life.

39. Adler, *Jewish Travellers*, 15, 17.

40. This section, which later became known as *The Ritual of Eldad ha-Dani*, was scrutinized by Max Schloessinger in 1908. Schloessinger, *Ritual of Eldad ha-Dani*, 9–104.

41. In fact, Christian theological anxiety about this was even stronger since Jesus, as we saw in the previous chapter, does command the apostle to preach to the "lost sheep of Israel."

42. All citations (and a few more) are in Schloessinger, *Ritual of Eldad ha-Dani*, 1–2.

43. Mishnah, Sanhedrin, 7:3.

44. Adler, *Jewish Travellers*, 16, 17, 18.

45. See, for example, Kadir, *Columbus*, 187–192.

46. Adair, *History of the American Indians*, 61.

47. Williams, *Hebrewisms of West Africa*, 1–24.

48. Adler, *Jewish Travellers*, 18–19, 20–21.

49. Cited in Corinaldi's collection of legal rulings, *Yahadut Etiopia*, 118 (for Radbaz), 243–254 (for Yosef). A shorter version of the collection in English is in Corinaldi, *Jewish Identity*.

50. See Kaplan, *Beta Israel;* Parfitt, *Operation Moses.*

51. See Beckingham and Hamilton, *Prester John;* see also Silverberg, *Realm of Prester John.*

52. Cited in Silverberg, *Realm of Prester John*, 7.

53. Grant, *Nestorians.*

54. Gumilev, *Searches*, 6–7.

55. Bar-Ilan, "Prester John," 291.

56. Ullendorff and Beckingham, *Hebrew Letters of Prester John*, 1.

57. Cited in Neubauer, "Where Are the Ten Tribes?" III:186.

58. Gow, *The Red Jews*, 33ff. I cannot do enough justice to the way in which Gow discusses at length the various sources for the tale and its reception.

59. Cited in Corinaldi, *Jewish Identity*, 99. For a survey of the various letters of Prester John and their Hebrew translations, see ibid., 97–101.

60. Ullendorff and Beckingham, *Hebrew Letters of Prester John*, 60.

61. See, for one example, Adler, *Itinerary of Benjamin of Tudela*, 52–53.

62. Ibid., 81–82.

63. Ibid., 30, 31, 40–41.

64. Ibid., 84.

65. Adler, *Jewish Travellers*, 11.

66. Adler tried to suggest that Benjamin's Cush is actually in Asia, commenting in his n. 166, "It should be remembered that *Cush* in ancient Jewish literature does not always signify Ethiopia, but also denotes parts of Arabia, especially those nearest to Abyssinia." However, I think that, in this particular case, Benjamin's Cush is indeed Ethiopia. His language suggests crossing the desert and he identifies Cush twice elsewhere as "the land of Cush, which is called al-Habash [Ethiopia]." Adler, *Itinerary of Benjamin of Tudela*, 96–97. Furthermore, the question is what constitutes "Ethiopia" in this context. Perhaps it is a greater Ethiopia that includes Arabian territories across the straits.

67. Adler, *Itinerary of Benjamin of Tudela*, 83–84.

68. Ibid., 98n168.

69. Ibid., 70. In contrast, in 1948 there were 55,000 Jews in Yemen and an additional 8,000 in the British-controlled port of Aden.

70. Ibid., 72.

71. Whitlocke, *Annals of the Universe*, 135.

72. See Scholem, *Sabbatai Sevi*, 332–353.

73. Rodinson, *Muhammad*, 193.

74. Ibid., 214. See also 249–254.

75. Ibid., 249–254.

76. Adler, *Itinerary of Benjamin of Tudela*, 1.

77. Montano, *Itinerarium Beniamini Tudelensis*.

78. Abulafia, "Seven Types of Ambiguity," 14.

79. Khadduri, *War and Peace*, 253–257.

80. For a brief and general summary of these events, see Jackson, "Mongol248s and Europe."

81. Schmieder, "Christians, Jews, Muslims," 274–277.

82. Cited in ibid., 280.

83. Paris, *Matthew Paris's English History*, 313.

84. Schmieder, "Christians, Jews, Muslims," 277.

85. Higgins, "Defining the Earth's Center."

86. Mandeville, *Mandeville's Travels*, 95.

87. Ibid., 211.

88. Ibid., 212.

89. Ibid., 210.

90. Idel, *Mystical Experience*, 2.

91. For one account of the battle, see Smith, "Ayn Jalut." For updated research, see Amitai-Preiss, *Mamluk-Ilkhanid War*.

92. Idel, *Messianic Mystics*, 58.

93. Ibid., 63.

94. Ibid.

95. Ibid., 81–82.

CHAPTER 4

1. David Reuveni's journal, entitled *Sipur David ha-Re'uveni* (Story of David the Reubenite), was preserved in manuscript form in the Bodleian Library at Oxford. The document was edited and published in Palestine by Aescoly in 1940 (Aescoly et al., *Sipur David ha-Re'uveni*). Aescoly published in the same book a collection of related documents and studies that are being used here as well. Aescoly also added a long essay on David, parts of which were previously published in English (Aeścoly, "David Reubeni,"). Lea Sestieri published an Italian translation and a scholarly edition of the manuscript with an appendix containing related documents (Sestieri, *David Reubeni*). In 1993, a facsimile of the 1940 edition was published with two new introductory articles dealing with the messianic image of David and with the history of the manuscript by Elias Lipiner and Moshe Idel (in separate pagination).

2. "Lettera di Ser Marco Foscari *orator* in corte," in Sestieri, *David Reubeni*, 203. For a study concerning the debates relating to David's identity as an imposter, focusing on questions of truth and authority in the early modern period, see Eliav-Feldon, "Invented Identities."

3. Aescoly et al., *Sipur David ha-Re'uveni*, 172.

4. The original runs as follows: "dicendo che per la via del mar Rosso cum le nave de Portagallo facilmente si potria satisfar a tal effecto... offerendosi andar in persona a far tal effetti, promettendo me se haverano il modo de artellarie, ehe tenirano tutti li machometani in guerra et che subiugerano la Meca." "Lettera di Ser Marco Foscari *orator* in corte," in Sestieri, *David Reubeni*, 203.

5. "Deposition fece Zuambatista Ramusio," in Aescoly et al., *Sipur David ha-Re'uveni*.

6. Adler, *Itinerary of Benjamin of Tudela*, 71–72.

7. Ramusio published the *Travels* only in 1559, but he had the manuscript years before. See Jackson, "Marco Polo and His 'Travels.'"

8. Marco Polo, *The Travels*, 87–107.

9. See a summary in Eliav-Feldon, "Invented Identities," 206–209.

10. Aescoly et al., *Sipur David ha-Re'uveni*, 1–26 (Hebrew pagination). See also, in the same volume, Aescoly, "David Reubeni," 38–39; and Eliav-Feldon, "Invented Identities," 210–211.

11. "Deposition fece Zuambatista Ramusio," in Aescoly et al., *Sipur David ha-Re'uveni*, 189.

12. Elias Lipiner, an expert on the Portuguese Inquisition, has brilliantly uncovered that, having been arrested while on a mission in 1532 to Emperor Karl V of the Holy Roman Empire, David was surrendered to Spain and burned at the stake in Llerena on September 8, 1538. Lipiner, "'Iyunim be-Farashat David Re-uveni u-Sholomo Molcho," in Aescoly et al., *Sipur David ha-Re'uveni*, xlv–lxvi. In the same essay, Lipiner also surveys the various theories about David's death prior to this discovery.

13. The larger context of the exchange between the two is discussed in depth by Benjamin Gampel, "A Letter." Gampel identifies this ha-Lorki with Joshua ben Joseph Al-Lorki, who converted during the 1410s, took the name of Gerónimo de Santa Fe, and is known in Jewish Iberian history as a formidable anti-Jewish polemicist. He was the personal physician of Pope Benedict XIII (1328–1423) and the "hero" of the infamous Disputation of Tortosa (1413–1414).

14. Lorki, *Igeret Yehosh'a a-Lorki*, 98.

15. The full sentence runs as follows: "'adayin tihyeh kayemet u-shelema ve-davar ze lo yavi le-hulshat ha-bitahon." Lorki, *Igeret Yehosh'a a-Lorki*, 99.

16. For a short discussion of the man and his writings, see Glatzer, "Pablo de Santa Maria."

17. See Bodian, "Men of the Nation."

18. For an account of the riots, see Wolff, "The 1391 Pogrom."

19. Netanyahu, *Don Isaac Abravanel*, 207.

20. Ibid., 230.

21. For the numbers of converts and expelled, see Kamen, "The Mediterranean."

22. Ibid., 33.

23. Netanyahu, *Don Isaac Abravanel*, 230.

24. In *Yeshu'ot Meshiho*, Abravanel dedicates a whole chapter to reaffirming the belief that the ten tribes had not disappeared, that they would fulfill the promise of return, and he struggles to explain Rabbi 'Aqiva's position that they would not.

25. Netanyahu, *Don Isaac Abravanel*, 231–232.

26. Yerushalmi, "Messianic Impulses," 468.

27. Aescoly mentions Abravanel's prognostications foretelling the coming of a messiah on three different dates close to the arrival of David as possible causes for the messianic response, but ignores altogether Abravanel's highly relevant ideas about the ten tribes. Aescoly et al., *Sipur David ha-Re'uveni*, 155–156 (Hebrew pagination).

28. Moshe Idel discusses David's military image and its impact on Hayyim Vital in his introduction to the 1993 edition. Idel, "Mavo," in Aescoly et al., *Sipur David ha-Re'uveni*, xix–xliii.

29. This should be termed "an era of mutual discovery"; Northrup, "Vasco da Gama and Africa."

30. See Beckingham, "Ethiopian Embassy to Europe"; "Achievements of Prester John."

31. "Obadiah's Letter to His Father 1488." Adler's translation is emended in consultation with the critical edition of the original letters in Bertinoro, *Me-Italyah li-Yerushalayim*, 74.

32. Adler, *Jewish Travellers*, 246–247, with my emendments based on the original in Bertinoro, *Me-Italyah li-Yerushalayim*, 86.

33. Neubauer, "Where Are the Ten Tribes?" III:196–201.

34. Kaplan, *Beta Israel*, 77–78.

35. Ibid., 81–82.

36. Ibid., 80.

37. Ibid., 79.

38. Cassuto, "Mi haya David ha-Re'uveni," 342–346.

39. Shohat, "Le-Farashat David ha-Re'uveni," 109.

40. See Faroqhi, *Pilgrims and Sultans*.

41. Azriel Shohat mentions, somewhat hesitantly, that in "Yemen [David] could have learned about the attempts of the famous Portuguese sailor Albuquerque to take over [the] Indian Ocean route in the beginning of the second decade of the Sixteenth Century." Shohat, "Le-Farashat David ha-Re'uveni," 109.

42. Hillelson, "David Reubeni's Route."

43. Spaulding, "The Nile," 132–133.

44. Aescoly et al., *Sipur David Ha-Re'uveni*, 172.

45. The main sentence runs as follows: "hominem assidue commeantium as ea loca et cursus illus frequntantium copiam habet. Ex quibus poterit certius omina haec intelligere." The full version of the letter is in Balau and Sadoleto, *VII Clementis Monumenta Saeculi XVI*, 28.

46. For a concise biography, see Ames, *Vasco da Gama*.

47. "Charisimo in Christo filiio nostre David Alnazarani Abbassiae et Aethiopiae Regi illustri," in Aescoly et al., *Sipur David ha-Re'uveni*, 176–178.

48. Thornton, "The Portuguese in Africa," 138.

49. See Lucena, *The Obedience of a King of Portugal*.

50. There was another mission that failed in 1486. See Russell-Wood, *The Portuguese Empire*, 12.

51. Beckingham, "Travels of Pero da Covilha," discusses the problems in Covilhan's itinerary. The name of this Covilhan appears in several different versions (Covilhã, Covilhão, Covilham and many others). I am following here the version used in the only comprehensive biography of Covilhan from 1898, by Ficalho, *Viagens de Pedro da Covilhan*. Admittedly, this version is also the easiest on the eye.

52. There are two translation of Alvares's narrative, "How Pedro de Covilham, a Portuguese, is in the country of the Prester, and how [he] came here, and why he was sent," in Alvares, *The Prester John of the Indies*, 369–376, from 1961. I am using here the earlier and fuller translation from 1881: Alvares, *Narrative of the Portuguese Embassy*. Alvares came to Ethiopia in the entourage of Ambassador Dom Rodrigo de Lima, who had been sent to Ethiopia in 1515.

53. Alvares, *Narrative of the Portuguese Embassy*, 178.

54. For a fictional work on the man, see Brandão, *Pedro da Covilhan*.

55. Ficalho, *Viagens de Pedro da Covilhan*, 58–59.

56. Beckingham, "Travels of Pero da Covilha," 16.

57. Ficalho, *Viagens de Pedro da Covilhan*, 180.

58. Alvares, *Narrative of the Portuguese Embassy*, 178.

59. Ibid., 304–307.

60. Ibid., 104.

61. Ibid., 350.

62. Beckingham, "Some Early Travels in Arabia," 167.

63. See García-Arenal, *A Man of Three Worlds*.

64. Eliav-Feldon, "Invented Identities."

65. Rogers, *Quest for Eastern Christians*, 20–21.

66. Russell-Wood, *The Portuguese Empire*, 21–21.

67. Ibid., 13–14.

68. Alvares, *Narrative of the Portuguese Embassy*, 171, 183, 239–240, 350–353, 390–393.

69. It wasn't printed until 1586, and is also known as *Itinera Mundi*, in its Latin rendition by Thomas Hyde.

70. Farissol, *Igeret Orhot 'Olam*, 1. I am using here the first edition of the text from Venice (1586) as well as Thomas Hyde's bilingual Hebrew/Latin edition from 1691. Hyde, *Igeret Orhot 'Olam, id est, Itinera Mundi, sic Dicta Nempe Cosmographia*, xx (hereafter, *Itinera mundi*).

71. Ruderman, *World of a Renaissance Jew*, 131–143.

72. Raz-Krakotzkin, *The Censor*.

73. Farissol, *Igeret Orhot 'Olam*, 2; Hyde, *Itinera mundi*, xx.

74. Farissol, *Igeret Orhot 'Olam*, title page.

75. Headley, "Sixteenth-Century Venetian Celebration."

76. Ruderman, *World of a Renaissance Jew*, 136.

77. Farissol, *Igeret Orhot 'Olam*, 15; Hyde, *Itinera Mundi*, 110.

78. Farissol, *Igeret Orhot 'Olam*, 16; Hyde, *Itinera Mundi*, 115.

79. Gans, *Sefer Tsemah David*, 48.

80. Rossi, *Sefer Me'or 'Enayim*, 189–195.

81. Gans, *Sefer Tsemah David*, 48–49. See also Neher, *Jewish Thought*, 145.

82. Neher, *Jewish Thought*, 135–147.

CHAPTER 5

1. Or 1648; dating is unclear.

2. On the history of Portuguese/Sephardic Jews in the early modern Atlantic world and in particular their connection to Brazil and to Amsterdam, see Israel, *The Dutch Republic;* and Israel, *Diasporas within a Diaspora*, 97–125.

3. For the background of the publication of the story in Amsterdam, see Méchoulan and Nahon, "Introduction," in Ben-Israel, *Hope of Israel* (1987), 1–97.

4. The original runs as follows: "yo soy Hebreo del Tribo de Levi mi dios es Adonay [Hebrew, My Lord] y todo lo demas es engaño." Ben-Israel, *Orígen de los Americanos*, 4. The book was published in 1650 in Spanish, Latin, and Hebrew. It was translated into English that year as well. Here, I am using the Spanish version of the book.

5. Ben-Israel, *Orígen de los Americanos*, 9.

6. Ibid., 10–12.

7. Hamilton, *Apocryphal Apocalypse*, 31–65.

8. Ibid., 216.

9. For an overview, see Kamen, *Spain's Road to Empire*, 3–150.

10. See Greenblatt, *Marvelous Possessions;* and Ryan, "Assimilating New Worlds."

11. For a history of the Catholic Church in colonial Latin America, see Greenleaf, *Roman Catholic Church*. See also González and González, *Christianity in Latin America*.

12. Romm, "Biblical History and the Americas." For a comprehensive study of all explorations, see Silverberg, *Golden Dream*.

13. Raleigh, *Discovery of the Large . . . Empire*.

14. For a brief account of Ponce de León, see Fernández-Armesto, *Pathfinders*, 193–194. On de Orellana, see Smith, *Explorers of the Amazon*, 39–89; and Silverberg, *Golden Dream*, 144–157.

15. Pagden, *Peoples and Empires*, 115–116.

16. Cited in Kadir, *Columbus*, 146.

17. Columbus, *Book of Prophecies*, 270–277.

18. Delaney, "Columbus's Ultimate Goal," 271.

19. Ibid., 287.

20. Rusconi, "Introduction," in Columbus, *Book of Prophecies*, 7.

21. Watts, "Prophecy and Discovery," 94.

22. Ibid., 102.

23. Yeager, "Siege of Jerusalem," 92 and n. 45.

24. Columbus, *Book of Prophecies*, 336–347; Isaiah 11 is quoted on 339. See the scholarly editor's comment on this issue on 27–28.

25. Kadir, *Columbus*, 137 and throughout.

26. Hamilton, *Apocryphal Apocalypse*, 28–30.

27. Kadir, *Columbus*, 140.

28. Ibid., 142.

29. Ibid., 179–192.

30. Columbus, *Select Letters*, 143, 163. See also Kadir, *Columbus*, 141.

31. Vespucci, *Mundus Novus*.

32. Columbus, *Select Letters*, 106, 108, 130. Flint suggests that the ten tribes were part of the "imaginative landscape" of Columbus as coming from the "end of east," as part of the medieval legacy that Columbus inherited. This makes sense, but there is no specific evidence for this in his writings. See Flint, *Imaginative Landscape*, 12–14.

33. Parfitt, *Lost Tribes of Israel*, 91–114.

34. Greenblatt, *Marvelous Possessions*, 12–13.

35. Quoted from Penn's 1682 diary in Weems, *Life of William Penn*, 174. On the topic of the Jewish Indian Theory, see Popkin, "Rise and Fall"; see also, for example, Sanders, *Lost Tribes*. For a brilliant discussion of political aspects of the theory, see Katz, "Israel in America."

36. Popkin, "Rise and Fall," 64.

37. Seed, "Are These Not Also Men?"

38. See, for example, Livingstone, *Preadamite Theory*.

39. Münster, "Asia wie es jetziger zeit nach den furnemsten Herrschaften beschriben ist" (Basel, 1550). The map was reproduced several times later as well.

40. For a study of the cosmography, see McLean, *Cosmographia of Sebastian Münster*.

41. Raz-Krakotzkin, *The Censor*, 23. On Christian Hebraism, see the classic Rosenthal, "The Rise of Christian Hebraism." For a more recent study, see Coudert and Shoulson, *Hebraica Veritas?*

42. McLean, *Cosmographia of Sebastian Münster*, 21.

43. Cosgrove, *Apollo's Eye*, 114.

44. Short, *Making Space*, 36.

45. Ibid., 54.

46. Trakulhun, "Widening of the World," 394.

47. Short, *Making Space*, 54.

48. Davidson, *The Idea of North*.

49. Cited in Gow, *The Red Jews*, 172. Hondius's maps of Asia, with all the uncertainties he ascribed to the north, did not include Arzareth.

50. Anderson, *Alexander's Gate*, 101–104. This raises the question, for which I do not have a clear answer, of why the ten tribes do not appear in Mercator's chart, and Gog and Magog do not appear in Ortelius's *Theater*. It is perhaps telling that the two legends do not appear on the same map.

51. King, *The Black Sea*, 26–29, 44–46.

52. Ibid., 34–35.

53. Ibid., 26.

54. For the fabulous qualities of the north, see Davidson, *The Idea of North*, 33–34, 50–67.

55. Johnson, "The Scythian," 250.

56. King, *The Black Sea*, 34–36.

57. Demaitre and Demaitre, "The Five Avatars," 315–316.

58. Gow, *The Red Jews*, 141–157.

59. Bouwsma, *John Calvin*, 12. See also McLean, *Cosmographia of Sebastian Münster*, 32–34. On Calvin's Basel years, see also 12–22.

60. Cited in Boer, *John Calvin*, 190–191.

61. Short, *Making Space*, 56.

62. For a comparison of Münster and Ortelius and their works, see ibid., 76–79.

63. Cosgrove, *Apollo's Eye*, 130.

64. Some of the stories have nothing to do with the ten tribes. I am here limiting myself only to those that are related to them.

65. On the Hephthalites in northern India, see Biswas, *Political History*. A huge collection of Chinese sources on them is in Yu, *Yanda Shi Yanjiu*. For Byzantine sources, see de Saint-Martin, *Les Huns Blancs*.

66. It seems that this variation was quite common although I admit that I did not find a sixteenth-century source. Gibbon, for instance, refers to them in the eighteenth century as "Nephthalites." Gibbon, *Decline and Fall*, 203. It may well be that Ortelius was the first to coin the term "Nephthalites." Godbey, ever hostile to "Jewish lies" and to

any attempt to base the ten tribes story on a real entity, complains that "the Jewish geographer Abram Ortelli" relies on "etymological fictions." Godbey, *Lost Tribes a Myth*, 381.

67. Melion, "Ad Ductum Itineris."

68. Montano, *Itinerarium Beniamini Tudelensis.*

69. The original, which the reader can see on the map, runs as follows: "4 Esdras. Arsareth. Hic 10 tribus seceßere et Totatorû siue Tartatorum loco Scythicæ substituerunt Vnde Gauthæ / seu Gauthay à summa Dei gloria aßerenda ibidicti sunt." Ortelius, *Theatrum Orbis Terrarum*, map opposite p. 105. The translation of the text is taken from Broecke, *Ortelius Atlas Maps*, 163.1.

70. Nuti, "The World Map," 44.

71. Harris, "Religious Position of Abraham Ortelius," 102. Harris also shows that Ortelius was quite open to including or conveying ideas that he may have not personally embraced.

72. Harris, "Religious Position of Abraham Ortelius," 137.

73. Ruland, "Survey of the Double-Page Maps," 85; Cosgrove, *Apollo's Eye*, 130.

74. Harris, "Religious Position of Abraham Ortelius," 89.

75. Petry, *Gender, Kabbalah, and the Reformation*, 1.

76. Wanley, *Wonders of the Little World*, 134.

77. Eco, *Foucault's Pendulum*, 457. See also 417–420. The Sambatyon features in another of Eco's novels, *Baudolino.*

78. Cited in Secret, *Postel Revisité*, 181n1.

79. Kuntz, *Guillaume Postel*, ix.

80. Bouwsma, *Concordia Mundi*, 298.

81. Dubois, *Mythologie des Origines.*

82. On Postel's concept of history, see Bouwsma, *Concordia Mundi*, 251–292.

83. Kuntz, *Guillaume Postel*, 146.

84. Secret, *Postel Revisité*, 177–178.

85. Postel: "Admirabilis Judaerum clausorum seu decem tribuum Israel, sub Turcarum et Ismaelitarum potentia redactarum historia, atque ipsa Ismaelitarum origo." An incipit by Postel as well as the headlines of each page of this unpublished essay are in Secret, *Bibliographie*, 116–117. Postel later returned to the subject of the origins of the Tartars, Turks, and Arabs.

86. Postel wrote this in his *De la Repvblique des Turcs*. Secret, *Postel Revisité*, 178.

87. Secret, *Postel Revisité*, 181; Davidson, *The Idea of North*, 34. On Postel as a geographer and cartographer, see Destombes, "Guillaume Postel, Cartographe."

88. Cited in Bouwsma, *Concordia Mundi*, 58.

89. See, for example, the connection between this song and the one sung by Deborah the prophetess in Judges 5.

90. Postel was very familiar with the Zohar and used it for all sorts of purposes, most notably for establishing his own messianic and prophetic aspirations. Petry, *Gender, Kabbalah, and the Reformation*, 31–45, 71–93.

91. Cited in Secret, *Postel Revisité*, 179.

92. Génebrard, *Chronographiae libri quatour*, 158–159.

93. For a succinct analysis and description of the significance of the Canaries in the global context, see Fernández-Armesto, *Pathfinders*, 126, 128–129, 164–168.

94. Abreu de Galindo, *Historia de la Conquista*, 24–25.

95. Ibid., 26.

96. Viera y Clavijo, *Noticias de la historia*, 120–121.

97. Abreu de Galindo, *Historia de la Conquista*, 26–27.

98. Ibid., 27–29.

99. On Christians, conversos, and Jews in the fifteenth century, see Nirenberg, "Enmity and Assimilation."

100. Gitlitz, "Hybrid Conversos," 1–2.

101. Silverblatt, *Modern Inquisitions*, 151.

102. Richard Popkin comments that the "rise and fall of the Jewish Indian theory is a measure of the changing roles of religion and science in accounting for the world," implying that the Jewish Indian theory was deserted as science produced more convincing evidence concerning the origins of the Indians and as scripture's binding power weakened (Popkin, "Rise and Fall," 81–82). Perhaps, rather, what we see is how science came to serve scripture in discussions about the ten tribes. "Scientific" argumentation became increasingly important when it came to proving or disproving certain theories about the ten tribes.

103. See, in this context, Pagden, *Fall of Natural Man*, 1–56.

104. Hamilton, *Apocryphal Apocalypse*, 209–211.

105. Durán, *Historia de las Indias*.

106. For details of Durán's life, see the introduction to *Historia de las Indias* by Ramírez, iii–xvi. See also Kadir, *Columbus*, 180.

107. Durán, *Historia de las Indias*, 3.

108. Ibid., 1–6.

109. Kadir, *Columbus*, 180–181.

110. On Montesinos and las Casas, see Vickery, *Bartolomé de Las Casas*, 44–49. A different approach to las Casas is Castro, *Another Face of Empire*, 54–62.

111. Ben-Israel, *Orígen de los Americanos*, 15–16.

112. Plato, *Timaeus*, 75.

113. Cook, "Ancient Wisdom."

114. For a summary of the Atlantic theory, see Wauchope, *Lost Tribes*, 28–49.

115. Acosta, *Historia Natural y Moral*, 70. I am consulting here the translation by Mangan et al. although I have made some major emendments. Acosta, *Natural and Moral History*, 69.

116. Brading, *First America*, 185.

117. Acosta, *Natural and Moral History*, 33–38.

118. Acosta, *Historia Natural y Moral*, 68–69; Acosta, *Natural and Moral History*, 67–68.

119. The original runs as follows: "Y cierto . . . que no ai Lengua en todas las Naciones de Asia, Africa, y Europa, y aun en el Mundo Nuevo . . . que tanto use de estas dos letras T.L. como la Mexicana." García, *Origen de los Indios*, 144.

120. Humboldt, *Personal Narrative of Travels*, 325.

121. Wauchope, *Lost Tribes*, 7–27.

122. García, *Origen de los Indios*, 100–112.

123. See Moreno, *Fray Juan de Torquemada*.

124. García, *Origen de los Indios*, 121. Cf. Brading, *First America*, 198.

125. García, *Origen de los Indios*, 35.

126. Nordenskjöld, "The Influence of the 'Travels of Marco Polo.'"

127. Owens, "Myth of Anian."

128. Maldonado's letter with drawings of the straits is found in Barrow, *Chronological History of Voyages*, app. 2, 24–45.

129. Ben-Israel, *Orígen de los Americanos*, 120.

130. García, *Origen de los Indios*, 185.

131. Rocha, *Tratado*, 1:xi. Rocha also published a book on the great comet of 1680–1681 (Kirch's Comet). See Johnson, "Periwigged Heralds." For a discussion of Rocha's origins, theories, and sources, see Franch, "Introduccion," *El origen de los indios*, 1–37.

132. Rocha, *Tratado*, 1:xii.

133. Ibid., 2:41–42.

134. Ibid., 2:41–78.

135. The original runs as follows: "fueron los Tultecas, que fueron tronco y rama de las diez tribus y mucos de ellos vinieron desde Arzaret, penetrando por dicho reino de Anian y pasando el estrecho del mismo nombre." Ibid., 1:80–81.

CHAPTER 6

1. See Goldman, *Hebrew and the Bible*, 15–23; Goldman, *God's Sacred Tongue*, 61–101.

2. Heylyn, *Cosmographie*, 8, 655–715; See also Heylyn, *Microcosmus*.

3. Bar-Yosef, *Holy Land*.

4. For a history of the English Bible in that period, see Nicolson, *God's Secretaries*. On the Bible and political thought in England at the time, see particularly Hill, *The English Bible*, 3–78.

5. Hill, *The English Bible*, 49.

6. Defoe, *Jure Divino*, 5:20–21.

7. Great Britain, Parliament, House of Commons, *History and Proceedings*, 155.

8. Hutton, *Charles the Second*. On the political crisis of the entire period, see Harris, *Revolution*.

9. Peyton, *Divine Catastrophe*, 37–38.

10. *A Collection of State Tracts*, 1:491.

11. Ridpath, *Parliamentary Right Maintain'd*, 8, 18–19.

12. Ridpath, ibid, 19. See also Acherley, *Britannic Constitution*, 15.

13. Thom, *Revolt of the Ten Tribes*, 44.

14. Erskine, *Equity and Wisdom*, 9–10. There is clearly a link here to the Scottish Enlightenment that is still in need of exploring.

15. *Fall of Britain* 9 (January 4, 1777): 52–53.

16. Keteltas, *God Arising and Pleading*, 12.

17. American Anti-Slavery Society, *Quarterly Anti-Slavery Magazine* 2 (Jan. 1836): 122.

18. Harper, *The Pro-Slavery Argument*, 295. See also Lowance, *A House Divided*, 83.

19. Junkin, *Political Fallacies*, 223–228.

20. Aughey, *Iron Furnace*, 35–36.

21. Defoe, *Danger of the Protestant Religion*, 8.

22. On Basnage and Jewish history, see Elukin, "Jacques Basnage."

23. Basnage, *History of the Jews*, 66.

24. Ibid., 161.

25. Hamilton, *Apocryphal Apocalypse*, 11–12, 204–248; Gow, *The Red Jews*, 130–176. The most detailed survey of the ten tribes and millenarianism is Parfitt, *Lost Tribes of Israel*, 66–90.

26. Hill, "Till the Conversion of the Jews," 13. See also Matar, "George Herbert, Henry Vaughan." For a general discussion on Jewish-Christian relations and messianism at that time, see Popkin, "Jewish-Christian Relations." For a different role of Jews in apocalyptic thinking, see Williamson, "Jewish Dimension."

27. Scholem, *Sabbatai Sevi*, 289–290.

28. On Serrarius during Sabbatai Zvi's times, see Goldish, *Sabbatean Prophets*, 150–153, 155.

29. Roth, *A Life*, 186.

30. Richard Cogley has examined most aspects of the English debate about the ten tribes. Cogely, "Some Other Kinde of Being."

31. On Ben-Israel and various prominent Christian scholars in Europe, see Roth, *A Life*, 140–175.

32. Wall, "Amsterdam Millenarian Petrus Serrarius," 76.

33. Roth, *A Life*, 181–184. For a fuller account of the dialogue between Ben-Israel and Christian millenarians, see Wall, "Amsterdam Millenarian Petrus Serrarius." See also Katz, "Menasseh ben Israel's Christian Connection."

34. Cogley, "Ancestry," 1–4.

35. Thorowgood, *Iewes in America*, 93.

36. Cogley, "Some Other Kinde of Being," 35–55. On Eliot, see Cogley, *John Eliot's Mission*.

37. Cogely, "Ancestry," 329–330.

38. Thorowgood, *Iewes in America*, 25. Cited also in Cogely, "Ancestry," 330.

39. See, for example, Katz, "Israel in America."

40. Witsius, *Dekaphylon*, 322–330.

41. Simon, *Hope of Israel*, 318.

42. For a summary of the mission to Cromwell and a collection of documents relating to it, see Wolf, *Menasseh Ben Israel's Mission*. See also Roth, *A Life*, 225–273. On the settlement of Jews in England, see Katz, *Philo-Semitism*.

43. On Vieira and Ben-Israel, see Méchoulan, "Menasseh Ben Israel"; Wall, "Amsterdam Millenarian Petrus Serrarius."

44. See Popkin, *Isaac La Peyrère*, 94–115.

45. Wall, "Amsterdam Millenarian Petrus Serrarius," 190.

46. Ben-Israel, *Conciliator.*

47. On Vossius, a friend of Ben-Israel, and the father of Conciliador's translator, and his irenism, see Rademaker, *Life and Work.*

48. Ben-Israel, *Hope of Israel* (1650), A5.

49. Ben-Israel, "To the Courteous Reader," *Hope of Israel* (1650), A12.

50. See the complete list in Ben-Israel, *Orígen de los Americanos*, xxxxix–liii; and in the English version of *Hope of Israel*, 1–3. On Dei Rossi and ha-Kohen, see Yerushalmi, *Zakhor*, 53–76.

51. Ben-Israel, "To the Courteous Reader," *Hope of Israel* (1650), A12.

52. Ben-Israel, *Hope of Israel* (1650), 40.

53. Ibid., 21.

54. Ibid., 36.

55. Ibid., 41.

56. I borrow the term "irenicon" from Adam Nicolson's *God's Secretaries*, 66.

57. Ben-Israel, *Hope of Israel* (1650), 83–84.

58. Thorowgood et al., *Digitus Dei*, title page.

59. David Katz exposes this best. See Katz, "Israel in America."

60. Kidd, *Forging of Races*, 61–63.

61. Crawford, *An Essay*, 3.

62. The song was printed on a leaflet of Trinity Church, Richmond, Virginia, and was sung "to the tune of Star in [the] East," on July 1, 1832. On Livermore, see Brekus, "Harriet Livermore."

63. Popkin, "Rise and Fall."

64. See Silverberg, *Mound Builders.*

65. Boudinot, *Star in the West*, 29–30.

66. Ibid., 117.

67. Simon, *Ten Tribes of Israel.*

68. Urban, *Gentleman's Magazine*, 537–538 (this specific issue was published in February 1837). On Kingsborough's search for the ten tribes, see Wauchope, *Lost Tribes*, 50–69; Goodkind, "Lord Kingsborough."

69. Kingsborough, *Antiquities*, 25–26.

70. Simon, *Ten Tribes of Israel*, 366–367.

71. Smith, *View of the Hebrews*. On Rafinesque, see Warren, *Constantine Samuel Rafinesque*. See also his own account of his global travels in Rafinesque, *A Life of Travels.*

72. Rafinesque, "The American Nations."

73. For a relevant evaluation of Mormonism, see Kidd, *Forging of Races*, 226–237.

74. Ibid., 228.

75. Cited in Brough, *Lost Tribes*, 65. On Pratt, see England, *Life and Thought.*

76. Cited in Brough, *Lost Tribes*, 50.

77. A recent example is the Australian geneticist Simon Southerton, a former active Mormon for thirty years. This time using DNA as evidence, Southerton offers a meticulous critique of the sacred Mormon texts in order to refute central Mormon claims about the migration to America. So far, his claims do not seem to have hurt Mormonism. Southerton, *Losing a Lost Tribe.*

78. See Olive, *The Lost Tribes.*

79. Brothers, *Revealed Knowledge;* Bar-Yosef, *Holy Land*, 51–60; Roth, *Nephew of the Almighty.*

80. See, for example, Festinger, *When Prophecy Fails.*

81. On Anglo-Israelism and race, see Kidd, *Forging of Races*, 203–218; Reisenauer, "British-Israel."

82. Baron, *History of the Ten "Lost" Tribes*, 7.

83. Bar-Yosef, *Holy Land*, 54–55.

84. Ibid., 45.

85. Ibid., 182–246. Given the huge body of Anglo-Israelist literature, I focus only on those aspects associated directly with debates about the significance of the ten lost tribes.

86. Brothers, "Farther Elucidation," 23 It is important to remember, though, that ideas about Britain as a "Chosen Nation," had been in circulation in England during the seventeenth century. See Hill, *English Bible*, 264–270.

87. Brothers, "Farther Elucidation," 24.

88. Ibid., 26.

89. Brothers, *Revealed Knowledge*, 48.

90. Basnage, *History of the Jews*, vi.

91. See Fletcher, *Of the Rus Commonwealth.* See also Cogely, "Some Other Kinde of Being."

92. See the detailed history of this treatise in Cogley, "Most Vile and Barbarous Nation."

93. Fletcher, "The Tartars," in Fletcher and Lee, *Israel Redux*, 2–3.

94. Cogley, "Most Vile and Barbarous Nation," 807.

95. Farley, *Scandinavian Influences*, 5.

96. Hultkrantz, "Swedish Research." See also Rudbeck, *Book of Birds.*

97. Ekman, "Gothic Patriotism," 57.

98. Kidd, *Forging of Races*, 172.

99. Olender, *Languages of Paradise*, 1–6.

100. On Rudbeck Sr., see King, *Finding Atlantis*, 4.

101. On Rudbeck Sr. and Christina, see ibid., 12–13, 20–21. On Ben-Israel and Christina, see Katz, "Menasseh ben Israel's Mission." On the queen, see Buckley, *Christina.*

102. Olender, *Languages of Paradise*, 2.

103. Ekman, "Gothic Patriotism," 60–62.

104. Rudbeck, *Specimen Usus Linguae Gothicae*, 83.

105. Ibid., 83–84.

106. Rudbeck, "Of the Origin of the Estonians, Finns, and Laplanders."

107. Pringle, *Master Plan.*

108. Oxonian, *Israel's Wanderings*, 3.

109. Burr, *Anglo-Saxon Riddle.*

110. Baron, *History of the Ten "Lost" Tribes*, 9. For an example, see Pritchett, *Enduring Empire of the British.*

111. Hine, *Seventeen Positive Identifications;* Hine, *The English Nation Identified;* Hine, *Forty-Seven Identifications of the British Nation.*

112. Poole, *Anglo-Israel* (1879); and Poole, *Anglo-Israel* (1889).

113. Hine, "Preface to the New Edition," *Forty-Seven Identifications* (1878), iii.

114. Whale, "Art of Conversation," 7.

115. Carpenter, *Biblical Companion.*

116. Carpenter, *Israelites Found,* 28. More than a century later, E. Raymond Capt did the same type of scholarship, basing his studies on Assyrian tablets. Capt, *Missing Links Discovered.*

117. Hine, *Forty-Seven Identifications* (1871), 10–11. A more geographically informed argument is found in Carpenter, *Israelites Found,* 40–44.

118. Oxonian, *Israel's Wanderings,* 4–5.

119. See Olender, *Languages of Paradise.*

120. Oxonian, *Israel's Wanderings,* 9–24.

121. Ibid., 45.

122. Ibid., 4.

123. Wild, *Lost Ten Tribes,* xv.

124. Oxonian, *Israel's Wanderings,* 130.

125. See, for example, Mackendrick, *Destiny of America;* Rutherford, *Anglo-Saxon Israel.* For one attempt to replicate the same relationship in England and Scotland, see Grimaldi, *Manasseh in Scotland.*

126. Collins, *"Lost" Ten Tribes of Israel.*

CONCLUSION

1. On that globality, see Nussbaum, *Global Eighteenth Century,* 1–20.

2. Ortelius, *An Epitome of Ortelius.*

3. Urban, *Gentleman's Magazine,* 671–675.

4. See the impressive list of their subscribers in Churchill, *Collection of Voyages,* 4–7.

5. This is similar to the rise of the philosophy of immanence as developed by Giordano Bruno (1548–1600) and Baruch Spinoza (1632–1677).

6. Milton, *Paradise Regained,* in *Poetical Works,* 610.

7. Pedro Lozano (1697–1752) summarized these positions in the early eighteenth century. Lozano, *Historia de la Conquista,* 363–377. See also, for all Spanish positions, *Isagoge Histórico Apologético,* 16–20, 59–154; Medina, *Los Aborígenes de Chile,* 65–66; Prince, *Origen de los Indios,* 79, 114–115, 136–138.

8. Ballantyne, "Empire," 122–123.

9. Beasley, *Empire,* 136.

10. Heber and Heber, *Life of Reginald Heber,* 112.

11. London Society for Promoting Christianity amongst the Jews, "Extract from the Report of the Committee of the London Society for Promoting Christianity amongst the Jews with Dr. Buchanan's Speech as to the State of the Jews in the East." Reprinted in Buchanan, *Works,* 36. For Buchanan's inquiries, see 144–152.

12. Pakenham, *Scramble for Africa*, xxii.

13. On search activity in India and Indochina, see Parfitt, *Lost Tribes of Israel*, 115–148.

14. Purchas, *Purchas His Pilgrimes* (1625), 1204.

15. Raleigh, *Works of Sir Walter Raleigh*, 216–270, 290–365.

16. Purchas, *Pvrchas his pilgrimage* (1613), 336.

17. Purchas, *Purchas His Pilgrimes* (1625), 120–122. Five years later, the interested reader could also consider the completely contradictory position of Giovanni Botero (1544–1617), an Italian political thinker who opined that the "Tartar Hordes" in the vicinity of the Straits of Anian "issued from those ten tribes of Israel." Botero, *Relations of the Most Famous Kingdomes*, 505.

18. Purchas, *Purchas His Pilgrimage* (1626), 559–562.

19. Montano, *Itinerarium Beniamini Tudelensis*; Hyde, *Igeret Orhot 'Olam, id est, Itinera Mundi*.

20. Churchill, *Collection of Voyages*, 81.

21. Lockman, *Travels of the Jesuits*, 28–34.

22. Rennell, *Geography System of Herodotus*, 1:512–535. Rennell's treatment was unique in using logic alongside biblical, ancient, and modern geography to show that the ten tribes were exiled sequentially in small groups and assimilated within the numerous peoples of Asia.

23. The text was first published in the nineteenth century by Neubauer. I am using here the admirable bilingual annotated edition of David Malkiel, "The Sambatyon."

24. In 1690, La Croix published his *Nouvelle Methode pour Apprendre Facilement la Geographie Universelle*, and Corneille published his *Dictionnaire Universel* in 1708. See Malkiel, "The Sambatyon," 176nn70–72. At about the same time of Lampronti, the great French philosopher Denis Diderot (1713–1784) also included a very short entry on Sambatyon in his famous *Encylopédie*. In this entry, Diderot wrote laconically that the "Flueve Sabbatique" is "a river that some authors claim exists in Palestine." It is evident that Diderot did not consult Lampronti or other sources. He mentioned only Josephus, Pliny, and Dom Augustin Calmet's *Catholic Encyclopedia*. See, Diderot, "Sabatique, Le Flueve."

25. This corresponds with Ruderman's discussion of Lampronti; he points out that Lampronti did not hesitate to subject his Jewish legal rulings to contemporary science even if science contradicted the Talmud. See Ruderman, *Jewish Thought*, 256–272.

26. Malkiel, "The Sambatyon," 171.

27. The original reads as follows:

Me se con tuto cio paresse strano as alcuno come possono restare occultante le predette dieci tribù dalla vista dei geografi doppo massime le moderne navigationi, riflettano di gratia come siasi potuto nascondere per quasi nove secoli nel mezzon delle Spagne il territorio de Las Batueças, nel regno di Leon, tra Salamanca a Placentia sino el tiempo del Re Filippo 2do. (Malkiel, "The Sambatyon," 170)

28. Münchhausen, *Münchhausen at the Pole*, 84.

29. Southey, *Letters from England*, 145.

30. Southey, *Selections*, 3:264.

31. *Blackbeard*, 148.

32. The earliest example is Vincent Leblanc, *World Surveyed*, 360–361. Another is the popular *Travels* of Scottish physician John Bell (1691–1780).

33. Benjamin ben Jonah, *Travels of Rabbi Benjamin*.

34. Pinkerton, *General Collection*, 7:4–24.

35. Livingstone, *Narrative of an Expedition*, 84.

36. Livingstone, *Zambezi Expedition*, 136.

37. Cited in Newman, *Imperial Footprints*, 84.

38. Aronin, *Lost Tribe*, published in 1924. See the introduction for contemporary books of fictional adventure.

39. Anderson, *Historical Account*, 196.

40. Wolff's zeal was infectious. The American preacher Harriet Livermore was converted to the cause after reading one of Wolff's sermons. Hoxie, "Harriet Livermore," 44.

41. The best biography of Wolff is probably Palmer, *Joseph Wolff*. See also Wolff's autobiography, *Missionary Journal*, 5–52.

42. The best illustration is Godbey's own account of Wolff: *Lost Tribes a Myth*, 16–20.

43. Wolff, *Researches*, 13.

44. Ibid., 138

45. Wolff, *Narrative*, 55.

46. Hopkirk, *Great Game*, 121–291.

47. Wolff, *Travels*, 330. This scene was told in numerous places. See, for example, Ripley and Dana, *Universal Library*, 516.

48. Samuel, *Remnant Found*, 107.

49. Ibid., 15–25.

50. Haga, *Sefer Ha-Berit Ha-Hadash*.

51. See Cohen, *History in Three Keys*; also Esherick, *Origins of the Boxer Uprising*.

52. Haga, *Sefer Ha-Berit Ha-Hadash*, 17–18.

53. Morgenstern, *Hastening Redemption*, 77–110.

54. On the Taiping Rebellion, see Spence, *God's Chinese Son*.

55. Haga, *Sefer Ha-Berit Ha-Hadash*, 10–11.

56. Ibid., 17.

57. Ibid., jacket copy.

58. Ramaswamy, *Lost Land of Lemuria*, 1.

59. See Parfitt and Trevisan Semi, *Judaising Movements*; Parfitt, *Operation Moses*; Parfitt, *Lost Tribes of Israel*.

60. Trevisan Semi, *Jacques Faitlovitch*, 11.

61. Ibid., particularly 1–46.

62. Kasdoi, *Shivtei Yaakov*, 1–45.

63. Ibid., 184.

64. For an English version of his work, see Ben-Zvi, *The Exiled and the Redeemed*.

65. Aescoly et al., *Yisrael*.

66. On Aescoly in this regard, see Gries, "Messiah Scribe."

67. Already in 1934, Faitlovitch had appealed to some leaders of the Zionist movement that Ethiopians be included in the Zionist project—a suggestion rejected because "the Ethiopians are Cushites [blacks] who converted to Judaism in the sixth century BCE."

68. Emanuel, *Sefer Mewaser Weomer*, 1–9 (English section).

69. Emanuel, "Introduction," in ibid., n.p.

70. Hurwitz, *Sefer Kol Mevaser*.

71. Emanuel, *Sefer Mewaser Weomer*, 6 (Hebrew section).

72. Cited in Hurwitz, *Sefer Kol Mevaser*, 1.

73. Committee for Immigration, Absorption, and the Diaspora, Israeli Knesset, Protocol No. 36, January 11, 2000.

74. Halkin, *Across the Sabbath River*.

75. For Avichail's general travels, see *Lost Tribes in Assyria;* Avichail, *Shivte Yisrael;* Avichail, *The Tribes of Israel.* On Menasseh in India, see Avichail, *Shinlung fate—Shevet Menashe.* On Rabbi Kook, see Avichail, *Avne Derekh.*

76. Vail, *Me-'Ever La-Sambatyon;* Weil, "Lost Israelites."

77. Hason, "Shevet Avud."

78. Livneh, "Coming Home."

79. Ringelblum, *Ksovim fun geto*, 44.

Bibliography

Abreu de Galindo, Juan de. *Historia de la Conquista de Las Siete Islas de Canaria.* Santa Cruz de Tenerife, Spain: Goya, 1977.

Abulafia, David. "Seven Types of Ambiguity, ca. 1100–1500," in *Medieval Frontiers: Concepts and Practices,* ed. David Abulafia and Nora Berend, 1–33. Aldershot, Hants, England: Ashgate, 2002.

Acherley, Roger. *The Britannic Constitution; or, The Fundamental Form of Government in Britain. Demonstrating, the Original Contract Entred into by King and People, According to the Primary Institutions Thereof, in This Nation. Wherein Is Proved, That the Placing on the Throne King William III. Was the Natural Fruit and Effect of the Original Constitution. And, That the Succession to This Crown, Establish'd in the Present Protestant Heirs Is De Jure, and Justify'd, by the Fundamental Laws of Great Britain. And Many Important Original Powers and Privileges, of Both Houses of Parliament, Are Exhibited.* London: Printed for A. Bettesworth [etc.], 1727.

Acosta, José de. *Historia Natural y Moral de las Indias: Publicada en Sevilla en 1590.* Madrid: R. Anglés, 1894.

———. *Natural and Moral History of the Indies: Chronicles of the New World Order,* trans. Jane E. Mangan, Walter Mignolo, and Frances M. López-Morillas. Durham, N.C.: Duke University Press, 2002.

Adair, James. *The History of the American Indians, Particularly Those Nations Adjoining to the Mississippi, East and West Florida, Georgia, South and North Carolina, and Virginia.* London: E. and C. Dilly, 1775.

Adler, Elkan Nathan. *Jewish Travellers.* London: Routledge, 1930.

Adler, Marcus N. *The Itinerary of Benjamin of Tudela: Critical Text, Translation and Commentary.* London: H. Frowde, 1907.

Aeščoly, A. Z. "David Reubeni in the Light of History," *The Jewish Quarterly Review*, New Series, Vol. 28, No. 1 (July, 1937): 1–45.

Aescoly, Aaron Zeev. Sipur David ha-Reʻuveni: ʻal-pi ketav-yad Oksford. Sifriyah hisṭoryografit, 1–2. Yerushalayim: ha-Ḥevrah ha-E.Y. le-hisṭoryah ve-etnografyah, be-siyuʻa Mosad Byaliḳ, 1940.

———. *Yisrael: Yediʻat ʻAmenu, Mahuto, Shevatav u-Leshonotav.* Jerusalem: R. Mas, 1952.

Aescoly, Aaron Zeev, Moshe Idel, and Elias Lipiner. *Sipur David ha-Reʻuveni: ʻal-pi ketav-yad Oksford.* Jerusalem: Mosad Byalik, 1993.

Ahmad, S. Maqbul, ʻUbayd Allah ibn ʻAbd Allah Ibn Khurradadhbih, and Sulayman al-Tajir. *Arabic Classical Accounts of India and China.* Shimla: Indian Institute of Advanced Study in association with Rddhi-India, Calcutta, 1989.

Albuquerque, Afonso de. *Comentários do Grande A. Dalboquerque Capitao Geral que foi das Indias Orientaes,* ed. Nicoláo Pagliarini. Lisboa, Portugal: n.p., 1774.

———. *The Commentaries of the Great Afonso Dalboquerque, Second Viceroy of India,* trans. Walter de Gray Birch. London: Printed for the Hakluyt Society, 1875.

Alcock, Susan, ed. *Empires: Perspectives from Archaeology and History.* New York: Cambridge University Press, 2001.

Alexander, A. F. O'D. *The Planet Saturn: A History of Observation, Theory, and Discovery.* London: Faber and Faber, 1962.

Allen, Lindsay. *The Persian Empire.* Chicago: University of Chicago Press, 2005.

Alvares, Francisco. *Narrative of the Portuguese Embassy to Abyssinia during the Years 1520–1527,* trans. Henry Edward John Stanley. London: Hakluyt Society, 1881.

———. *The Prester John of the Indies: A True Relation of the Lands of the Prester John, Being the Narrative of the Portuguese Embassy to Ethiopia in 1520,* trans. Francisco Alvares, Henry Edward John Stanley Stanley, C. F. Beckingham, and George Wynn Brereton Huntingford. Cambridge: Published for the Hakluyt Society at the University Press, 1961.

American Anti-Slavery Society. *Quarterly Anti-Slavery Magazine.* New York: American Anti-Slavery Society, 1835–1837.

Ames, Glenn Joseph. *Vasco da Gama: Renaissance Crusader.* New York: Pearson/Longman, 2005.

Amitai-Preiss, Reuven. *The Mamluk-Ilkhanid War.* Cambridge: Cambridge University Press, 1998.

Anderson, Alexander. *An Historical Account of the Circumnavigation of the Globe, and of the Progress of Discovery in the Pacific Ocean: From the Voyage of Magellan to the Death of Cook.* New York: Harper & Bros., 1837.

Anderson, Andrew Runni. "Alexander at the Caspian Gates." *Transactions and Proceedings of the American Philological Association* 59 (1928): 130–163.

———. *Alexander's Gate, Gog and Magog, and the Inclosed Nations.* Cambridge, Mass.: Medieval Academy of America, 1932.

———. "The Arabic History of Dulcarnain and the Ethiopian History of Alexander." *Speculum* 6.3 (July 1931): 434–445.

Anderson, James H. *God's Covenant Race, from Patriarchal Times to the Present: Selection of Addresses Uniting This Subject with the Divine Testimony of the Prophet Joseph Smith*. Salt Lake City, Utah: Deseret News Press, 1946.

Arkhipov, Andrei. *Po tu Storonu Sambationa: Etiudy o Russko-Evreiskikh Kul'turnykh Iazykovykh i Literaturnykh Kontaktakh, v X–XVI vekakh* (On the Other Side of the Sambation: Studies in Russo-Hebrew Linguistic and Cultural Contacts in the 10th–17th Centuries). Oakland, Calif.: Berkeley Slavic Specialties, 1995.

Armstrong, Herbert W. *The United States and Britain in Prophecy*. New York: Everest House, 1980.

Aronin, Ben. *The Lost Tribe: Being the Strange Adventures of Raphael Drale in Search of the Lost Tribes of Israel*. New York: Simons, 1924.

Asher, Adolf, and Leopold Zunz. *The Itinerary of Rabbi Benjamin of Tudela*. London: A. Asher, 1840.

Astren, Fred. *Karaite Judaism and Historical Understanding*. Columbia: University of South Carolina Press, 2004.

Aughey, John H. *The Iron Furnace; or, Slavery and Secession*. Philadelphia: W. S. & A. Martien, 1863.

Avichail, Eliyahu. *Avne Derekh: be-Mishnat Ha-Rav Kuk*. Jerusalem: Avihayil, 1978.

———. *The Lost Tribes in Assyria*. Jerusalem: Amishav, 1978.

———. *Shinlung fate—Shevet Menashe*. Jerusalem: n.p., 1990.

———. *Shivte Yisrael: Ha-ovdim Veha-nidahim*. Jerusalem: Amishav, 1986.

———. *Shivte Yisrael: Ha-ovdim Veha-nidahim*, 2nd ed. Jerusalem: Avihayil, 1998.

———. *The Tribes of Israel*. Jerusalem: Amishav, 1990.

A. Z. C. "Portugal in Quest of Prester John, Elaine Sanceau." *Geographical Journal* 103.1–2 (Jan.–Feb. 1944): 82–83.

Bāfaqīh, Muhammad. *L'unification du Yémen antique: La Lutte entre Saba, Himyar et le Hadramawt, du Ier au IIIème Siècle de l'ère Chrétienne*. Paris: Geuthner, 1990.

Balau, Pietro, and Jacopo Sadoleto, eds. *VII Clementis Monumenta Saeculi XVI*. Innsbruck, Austria: Libraria Academica Wagneriana, 1885.

Ballantyne, Tony. "Empire, Knowledge and Culture: From Proto-globalization to Modern Globalization," in *Globalization in World History*, ed. A. G. Hopkins, 115–140. New York: Norton, 2002.

Bar-Ilan, Meir. "Prester John: Fiction and History." *History of European Ideas* 20.1–3 (1995): 291–298.

Barmash, Pamela. "At the Nexus of History and Memory: The Ten Lost Tribes." *AJS Review* 29.2 (2005): 207–236.

Baron, David. *The History of the Ten "Lost" Tribes: Anglo-Israelism Examined*. London: Morgan & Scott, 1915.

Barrow, John. *A Chronological History of Voyages into the Arctic Regions: Undertaken Chiefly for the Purpose of Discovering a North-East, North-West, or Polar Passage between the Atlantic and Pacific*. London: J. Murray, 1818.

Bar-Yosef, Eitan. *The Holy Land in English Culture 1799–1917: Palestine and the Question of Orientalism*. Oxford: Clarendon, 2005.

Basnage, Jacques. *The History of the Jews, from Jesus Christ to the Present Time: Containing Their Antiquities, Their Religion, Their Rites, the Dispersion of the Ten Tribes in the East and the Persecutions This Nation Has Suffer'd in the West. Being a Supplement and Continuation of the History of Josephus*, trans. Thomas Taylor. London: T. Bever and B. Lintot [etc.], 1708.

Bassin, Elieser. "The Lost Ten Tribes [of] Anglo-Israel by a Jew." Lecture delivered in 1884; reprint, Hollywood, Calif.: Dr. Clem Davies' Ministry, 1940.

———. *The Modern Hebrew and the Hebrew Christian*. London: J. Nisbet, 1882.

Bataille, Georges, trans. Allan Stoekl. *Visions of Excess: Selected Writings 1927–1939*. Manchester: Manchester University Press, 1985.

Bauckham, Richard. *Gospel Women: Studies of the Named Women in the Gospels*. Grand Rapids, Mich.: Eerdmans, 2002.

Baumgarten, Albert. "The Jewish People in the Second Temple Period as an 'Imagined Community'?" in *Center and Diaspora: The Land of Israel and the Diaspora in the Second Temple, Mishna, and Talmud periods*, ed. Isaiah M. Gafni, 17–36. Jerusalem: Zalman Shazar, 2004 (in Hebrew).

Beale, Gregory K. "The Problem of the Man from the Sea in IV Ezra 13 and Its Relation to the Messianic Concept in John's Apocalypse." *Novum Testamentum* 25, fasc. 2 (Apr. 1983): 182–188.

Beasley, Edward. *Empire as the Triumph of Theory: Imperialism, Information, and the Colonial Society of 1868*. London: Routledge, 2005.

Beaver, Adam G. "A Holy Land for the Catholic Monarchy: Palestine in the Making of Modern Spain, 1469–1598." Ph.D. diss., Harvard University, 2008.

Becking, Bob. *The Fall of Samaria: An Historical and Archaeological Study*. Leiden: Brill, 1992.

Beckingham, C. F. "An Ethiopian Embassy to Europe c. 1310." *Journal of Semitic Studies* 34.2 (Autumn 1989): 337–346.

———. "Some Early Travels in Arabia." *Journal of the Royal Asiatic Society of Great Britain and Ireland* 3–4 (1949): 155–176.

———. "The Travels of Pero da Covilha and Their Significance." *Congresso Internacional de Historia dos Descobrimentos: Resumo* (1960): 3–16.

———. "The Achievements of Prester John," in C. F. Beckingham & Bernard Hamilton, eds., *Prester John, the Mongols, and the Ten Lost Tribes*, 1–22. Aldershot: Ashgate, 1996.

Beckingham, C. F., and Bernard Hamilton, eds. *Prester John, the Mongols and the Ten Lost Tribes*. Aldershot, England: Variorum, 1996.

Bell, John. *Travels from St. Petersburg in Russia, to Diverse Parts of Asia . . . by John Bell . . . in Two Volumes*. Dublin: Printed for Robert Bell, 1764.

Ben-Dor, Zvi. "An Arab-Jew in Rome: A History in Three Acts." Paper presented at the Middle East Studies Association meeting, Washington, D.C., November 24, 2008.

———. "'Even unto China': Displacement and Chinese Muslim Myths of Origin." *Bulletin of the Royal Institute for Inter-Faith Studies* (Winter 2002–2003): 93–114.

———. "A Response to Kanan Makiya's *The Rock*," in *Responses to Kanan Makiya's The Rock: A Tale of Seventh-Century Jerusalem*, ed. Daniel Terris and Sylvia Fuks Fried, 23–29. Brandeis, Mass.: Brandeis University Press, 2004.

Ben-Israel, Manasseh. *The Conciliator of R. Manasseh Ben Israel: A Reconcilement of the Apparent Contradictions in Holy Scripture, to Which Are Added Explanatory Notes, and Biographical Notices of the Quoted Authorities.* New York: Hermon, 1972.

———. *The Hope of Israel: Written by Menasseh Ben Israel, a Hebrew Divine, and Philosopher. Newly Extant, and Printed in Amsterdam, and Dedicated by the Author to the High Court, the Parliament of England, and to the Councell of State. Translated into English, and Published by Authority. In This Treatise Is Shewed the Place Wherein the Ten Tribes at This Present Are, Proved Partly by the Strange Relation of One Anthony Montezinus, a Jew, of What Befell Him As He Travelled Over the Mountaines Cordillære, with Divers Other Particulars About the Restoration of the Jewes, and the Time When,* trans. Moses Wall. London: by R.I. for Hannah Allen, at the Crown in Popes-head Alley, 1650.

———. *The Hope of Israel,* trans. Moses Wall, ed. Henry Méchoulan and Gérard Nahon. Oxford: Oxford University Press, 1987.

———. *Mikveh Yisra'el, Esto es, Esperança de Israel.* Amsterdam: Semuel Ben Israel Soeiro, 1650.

———. *Orígen de los Americanos . . . esto es, Esperanza de Israel.* 1650; reprint, Madrid: S. Perez Junquera, 1881.

Benjamin of Tudela *Sefer Masa'ot shel Rabbi Benyamin Me-Tudela,* trans. Marcus Nathan Adler. Jerusalem: HaUniversitah HaIvrit HaChug Le Historiah Shel Am Yisrael, 1966.

Benjamin ben Jonah. *Travels of Rabbi Benjamin, Son of Jonah, of Tudela: Through Europe, Asia, and Africa: from the Ancient Kingdom of Navarre, to the Frontiers of China. Faithfully Tr. from the Original Hebrew, and Enriched with a Dissertation, and Notes, Critical, Historical, and Geographical,* trans. B. Gerans. London: Printed for the Translator and sold by Messrs. Robson [etc.], 1783.

Bentley, Jerry. "Shapes of World History in Twentieth-Century Scholarship," in Michael P. Adas, ed., *Agricultural and Pastoral Societies in Ancient and Classical History,* 3–35. Philadelphia: Temple University Press, 2001.

Bentwich, Norman. "The Graeco-Roman View of Jews and Judaism in the Second Century." *Jewish Quarterly Review,* new ser., 23.4 (Apr. 1933): 337–348.

Ben-Zeev, Israel. *ha-Yehudim ba-'Arav: korot ha-Yehudim ba-hatsi ha-i 'Arav u-derom Erets Yisrael 'ad hofa'at ha-Islam ve-'ad Gerusham me-Rov Gelilot 'Arav.* Jerusalem: Ahïasaf, 1957.

———. *Ka'b al Ahbar seine Stellung im hadit und in der islamischen Legendenliteratur.* Gelnhausen: F. W. Kalbfleisch, 1933.

———. *Ta'rikh al-Yahud fi Bilad al'Arab fil-Jahiliya wa-Sadr al-Islam.* Misr (Cairo): Matba'a al-I'timad, 1927.

Ben-Zvi, Itzhak. *The Exiled and the Redeemed.* Philadelphia: Jewish Publication Society of America, 1963.

Berg, Johannes van den, and Ernestine G. E. van der Wall. *Jewish-Christian Relations in the Seventeenth Century: Studies and Documents.* Dordrecht: Kluwer Academic, 1988.

Bergren, Theodore A. "Christian Influence on the Transmission History of 4, 5, and 6 Ezra," in *The Jewish Apocalyptic Heritage in Early Christianity,* ed. James C. VanderKam and William Adler, 102–128. Assen, Netherlands: Van Gorcum, 1996.

Bergren, Theodore A. "The 'People Coming from the East' in 5 Ezra 1:38." *Journal of Biblical Literature* 108.4 (Winter 1989): 675–683.

Bertinoro, Obadiah, *Me-Ialyah li-Yerushalayim: igrota shel R. Ovadyah mi-Barenura me-Erets Yiśra'el: mahadurah biḳortit*, ed. Menachem Emanuele Artom, and Avraham DvidRamat Gan: Universtat Bar-Ilan, 1997.

Biswas, Atreyi. *The Political History of the Hunas in India.* New Delhi: Munshiram Manoharlal, 1973.

Blackbeard: A Page from the Colonial History of Philadelphia. New York: Harper, 1835.

Blackwell, Pam. *Michael's Fire.* Salt Lake City, Utah: Onyx, 2002.

Bloch, Chana. *The Past Keeps Changing: Poems.* Riverdale-on-Hudson, N.Y.: Sheep Meadow Press, 1992.

Boardman, John. *The Cambridge Ancient History*, vol. 3, pt. 2: *The Assyrian and Babylonian Empires and Other States of the Near East, from the Eighth to the Sixth Centuries B.C.* Cambridge: Cambridge University Press, 1991.

Bodian, Miriam. "'Men of the Nation': The Shaping of Converso Identity in Early Modern Europe," *Past and Present* 143 (May 1994): 48–76.

Boer, E. A. de. *John Calvin on the Visions of Ezekiel: Historical and Hermeneutical Studies in John Calvin's "Sermons Inédits," Especially on Ezek. 36–48.* Leiden: Brill, 2004.

Bonomi, Joseph. *Nineveh and Its Palaces: The Discoveries of Botta and Layard, Applied to the Elucidation of Holy Writ.* London: Office of the Illustrated London Library, 1852.

Botero, Giovanni. *Relations of the Most Famous Kingdomes and Common-Wealths Thorowout the World: Discoursing of Their Situations, Religions, Manners, Customes, Strengths, Languages, Greatnesse and Policies.* London: John Haviland, 1630.

Boudinot, Elias. *The Age of Revelation; or, The Age of Reason Shewn to Be an Age of Infidelity.* Philadelphia: Asbury Dickins, 1801.

———. *A Star in the West; or, A Humble Attempt to Discover the Long Lost Ten Tribes of Israel, Preparatory to Their Return to Their Beloved City, Jerusalem.* Trenton, N.J.: D. Fenton, S. Hutchinson, and J. Dunham, 1816.

Bouwsma, William James. *Concordia Mundi: The Career and Thought of Guillaume Postel, 1510–1581.* Cambridge, Mass.: Harvard University Press, 1957.

———. *John Calvin: A Sixteenth-Century Portrait.* New York: Oxford University Press, 1988.

Boyarin, Daniel. *Border Lines: The Partition of Judaeo-Christianity.* Philadelphia: University of Pennsylvania Press, 2004.

———. *Dying for God: Martyrdom and the Making of Christianity and Judaism.* Stanford, Calif.: Stanford University Press, 1999.

Brading, D. A. *The First America: The Spanish Monarchy, Creole Patriots, and the Liberal State, 1492–1867.* Cambridge: Cambridge University Press, 1991.

Brandão, Zephyrino Norberto Goncalves. *Pedro da Covilhan: Episodio Romantico do Seculo XV.* Lisboa, Portugal: Antiga Casa Bertrand–J. Bastos, 1897.

Braude, William G. *Pesikta Rabbati: Discourses for Feasts, Fasts, and Special Sabbaths.* New Haven, Conn.: Yale University Press, 1968.

Bredin, Mark. *Studies in the Book of Tobit: A Multidisciplinary Approach.* London: Clark, 2006.

Brekus, Catherine A. "Harriet Livermore, the Pilgrim Stranger: Female Preaching and Biblical Feminism in Early-Nineteenth-Century America." *Church History* 65.3 (1996): 389–404.

Broecke, M. P. R. van den. *Ortelius Atlas Maps: An Illustrated Guide*. Netherlands: HES, 1996.

Broecke, M. P. R. van den, P. C. J. van der Krogt, and Peter H. Meurer. *Abraham Ortelius and the First Atlas Essays Commemorating the Quadricentennial of His Death, 1598–1998*. Houten, Netherlands: HES, 1998.

Broshi, Magen, and Israel Finkelstein. "The Population of Palestine in Iron Age II." *Bulletin of the American Schools of Oriental Research* 287 (Aug. 1992): 47–60.

Brothers, Richard. "A Farther Elucidation of the XIIth Chapter of Daniel," in *Wrote in Confinement. An Exposition of the Trinity With a Farther Elucidation of the Twelfth Chapter of Daniel: One Letter to the King: and Two to Mr. Pitt, &c.*, 17–37. [London?]: n.p., 1796.

———. *A Revealed Knowledge, of the Prophecies & Times. Wrote Under the Direction of the Lord God, and Published by His Sacred Command: It Being the First Sign of Warning for the Benefit of All Nations. Containing, with Other Great and Remarkable Things, Not Revealed to Any Other Person on Earth, the Restoration of the Hebrews to Jerusalem, by the Year 1798: Under Their Revealed Prince and Prophet. Book the First*. London: G. Riebau's, 1794.

Brough, R. Clayton. *The Lost Tribes: History, Doctrine, Prophecies, and Theories about Israel's Lost Ten Tribes*. Bountiful, Utah: Horizon, 1979.

Broughall, M. S. "The Pattern of the Days in Ancient Rome." *Greece & Rome* 5.15 (May 1936): 160–176.

Brown, Samuel Albert. *The House of Israel; or, The Anglo-Saxon*. Portland, Oreg.: S. A. Brown by Boyer Print. & Advertising, 1925.

Bruce, F. F. "Tacitus on Jewish History." *Journal of Semitic Studies* 29 (1984): 33–44.

Buber, Salomon. *Midrash Ekhah Rabah: 'Al pi Ketav Yad Ha-Ganuz Be-Otsar Ha-Sefarim Be-Romi*. Tel Aviv: n.p., 1963.

Buchanan, Claudius. *The Works of the Rev. Claudius Buchanan, L.L.D*. New York: Whiting and Watson, 1812.

Buckley, Veronica. *Christina, Queen of Sweden: The Restless Life of a European Eccentric*. New York: Fourth Estate, 2004.

Burnett, Stephen G. *From Christian Hebraism to Jewish Studies: Johannes Buxtorf (1564– 1629) and Hebrew Learning in the Seventeenth Century*. Leiden: Brill, 1996.

Burr, William Henry. *The Anglo-Saxon Riddle; or, The Riddle of Our Origin, Present Grandeur, and Future Greatness . . . Also, Its Solution*. London: W. H. Guest, 1873.

Calvert, James. *Naphtali, seu, Colluctationes theologicæ cum tribus ingentibus dubiis viz De reditu decem tribuum, [De] conversione Judæorum, [De] mensuris sacris Ezekielis*. Londini: Typis Andræ Clark, impensis Ric. Lambert . . . & apud Jo. Martyn, 1672.

Calvin, Jean. *Calvin: Commentaries*, trans. Joseph Haroutunian. Grand Rapids, Mich.: Christian Classics Ethereal Library, 1990.

———. *Commentaries on the Book of the Prophet Jeremiah and the Lamentations*. Edinburgh: Calvin Translation Society, 1850.

Cameron, James, Simcha Jacobovici, Felix Golubev, Ric Esther Bienstock, Graeme Ball, and Ron White. *The Lost Tomb of Jesus.* Port Washington, N.Y.: Koch Vision, 2007.

Capt, E. Raymond. *Missing Links Discovered in Assyrian Tablets: Study of Assyrian Tables That Reveal the Fate of the Lost Tribes of Israel.* Thousand Oaks, Calif.: Artisan Sales, 1985.

"Captivity of the Tribes: Little People's Lesson," Sept. 18, 1898, *Little People's Lesson Pictures (LPLP),* The American Sunday-School Union, Philadelphia & NY (1896–1916).

Carew, Mairéad. *Tara and the Ark of the Covenant: A Search for the Ark of the Covenant by British-Israelites on the Hill of Tara (1899–1902).* Dublin: Discovery Programme/ Royal Irish Academy, 2003.

Carmoly, Eliakim. *Mevaseret Tsiyon: Igrot Al Aseret ha-Shevatim mi-tokh Kitve Yad.* 1840; reprint, Jerusalem: Kedem, 1971.

———. *Notice historique sur Benjamin de Tudèle.* N.p., 1852.

———. *Sipur Eldad ha-Dani: Odot Aseret ha-Shevatim u-Nehar Sambatyon.* Paris: Efrayim Hadamar, 1828.

Carmoly, Eliakim, et al. *Relation d'Eldad le Danite, voyageur du IXe siècle.* Paris: Ve Dondey-Dupré, 1838.

Carpenter, William. *The Biblical Companion; or, An Introduction to the Reading and Study of the Holy Scriptures: Comprising a Comprehensive Digest of the Principles and Details of Biblical Criticism, Interpretation, Theology, History, Natural Science, Etc.* London: Thomas Tegg, 1836.

———. *The Israelites Found in the Anglo-Saxons: The Ten Tribes Supposed to Have Been Lost, Traced from the Land of Their Captivity to Their Occupation of the Isles of the Sea: with an Exhibition of Those Traits of Character and National Characteristics Assigned to Israel in the Books of the Hebrew Prophets.* London: G. Kenning, 1874.

Cassuto, M. D. "Mi haya David ha-Re'uveni." *Tarbiz* 32 (1963): 339–358.

Castro, Daniel. *Another Face of Empire: Bartolomé de Las Casas, Indigenous Rights, and Ecclesiastical Imperialism.* Durham, N.C.: Duke University Press, 2007.

Chaudhuri, K. N. *Trade and Civilisation in the Indian Ocean: An Economic History from the Rise of Islam to 1750.* Cambridge: Cambridge University Press, 1985.

Church of Jesus Christ of Latter-day Saints. *The Book of Mormon: Another Testament of Jesus Christ; The Doctrine and Covenants of the Church of Jesus Christ of Latter-Day Saints; The Pearl of Great Price.* Salt Lake City, Utah: Church of Jesus Christ of Latter-day Saints, 1981.

Churchill, John. *A Collection of Voyages and Travels.* London: Printed for Awnsham and John Churchill, 1704–1732.

Cifola, Barbara. *Analysis of Variants in the Assyrian Royal Titulary from the Origins to Tiglath- Pileser III.* Naples, Italy: Istituto universitario orientale, 1995.

Cogan, Mordechai, and Israel Eph'al, eds. *Ah, Assyria: Studies in Assyrian History and Ancient Near Eastern Historiography Presented to Hayim Tadmor.* Jerusalem: Magnes Press, Hebrew University, 1991.

Coggins, R. J., and Michael A. Knibb. *The First and Second Books of Esdras.* Cambridge: Cambridge University Press, 1979.

Cogley, Richard W. "The Ancestry of the American Indians: Thomas Thorowgood's
   Iewes in America (1650) and Jews in America (1660)." *English Literary Renaissance*
   35.2 (2005): 304–330.

———. *John Eliot's Mission to the Indians before King Philip's War.* Cambridge, Mass.:
   Harvard University Press, 1999.

———. "'The Most Vile and Barbarous Nation of All the World': Giles Fletcher the
   Elder's *The Tartars; or, Ten Tribes* (ca. 1610)." *Renaissance Quarterly* 58.3 (2005):
   781–814.

———. "'Some Other Kinde of Being and Condition': The Controversy in Mid-
   Seventeenth-Century England over the Peopling of Ancient America." *Journal of the
   History of Ideas* 68.1 (Jan. 2007): 35–56.

Cohen, Paul A. *History in Three Keys: The Boxers as Event, Experience, and Myth.* New
   York: Columbia University Press, 1997.

*A Collection of State Tracts, Publish'd on the Occasion of the Late Revolution in 1688. And
   During the Reign of King William III . . . To Which Is Prefix'd, the History of the Dutch
   War in 1672. Translated from the French Copy Printed at Paris in 1682 . . . With a
   Table . . . and an Alphabetical Index.* London: 1705.

Collins, Steven M. *The "Lost" Ten Tribes of Israel—Found!* Boring, Oreg.: CPA Books, 1995.

Columbus, Christopher. *The Book of Prophecies Edited by Christopher Columbus,* ed.
   Roberto Rusconi. Berkeley: University of California Press, 1997.

———. *Select Letters of Christopher Columbus With Other Original Documents, Relating to
   His Four Voyages to the New World,* trans. Richard Henry Major and Diego Alvarez
   Chanca. London: Hakluyt Society, 1870.

Committee for Immigration, Absorption, and Diaspora, Israeli Knesset. Protocol
   No. 36. January 11, 2000.

Commodianus. *Commodiani Carmina,* ed. Bernhard Dombart. Vienna: apvd C. Geroldi
   filivm, 1887.

Cook, Harold J. "Ancient Wisdom, the Golden Age, and Atlantis: The New World in
   Sixteenth-Century Cosmography." *Terrae Incognitae* 10 (1978): 25–43.

Corinaldi, Michael. *Jewish Identity: The Case of Ethiopian Jewry.* Jerusalem: Mgness, 1998.

———. *Yahadut Etiopia: Zehut u-Masoret.* Jerusalem: Robin Mass, 1988.

Corneille, Thomas. *Dictionnaire Universel, Géographique et Historique.* Paris: J. B.
   Coignard, 1708.

Cosgrove, Denis E. *Apollo's Eye: A Cartographic Genealogy of the Earth in the Western
   Imagination.* Baltimore, Md.: Johns Hopkins University Press, 2001.

Coudert, Allison, and Jeffrey S. Shoulson. *Hebraica Veritas? Christian Hebraists and the
   Study of Judaism in Early Modern Europe.* Philadelphia: University of Pennsylvania
   Press, 2004.

Coulbeaux, Jean Baptiste. *Histoire Politique et Religieuse d'Abyssinie Depuis Les Temps Les
   Plus Reculés Jusqu'à l'Avenement de Ménélick II.* Paris: Geuthner, 1929.

Crawford, Charles. *An Essay on the Propagation of the Gospel In Which There Are
   Numerous Facts and Arguments Adduced to Prove That Many of the Indians in America
   Are Descended from the Ten Tribes.* Philadelphia: Printed and sold by James
   Humphreys, 1801.

Cumings, Bruce. *North Korea: Another Country.* New York: New Press, 2003.

Cúneo, Roberto Fabregat. "Estudio de un Prejuicio acerca de los Orígenes del Hombre Americano." *Revista Mexicana de Sociología* 24.3 (Sept.–Dec. 1962): 937–945.

Daston, Lorraine. "Introduction: The Coming into Being of Scientific Objects," in *Biographies of Scientific Objects,* ed. Lorraine Daston, 1–14. Chicago: University of Chicago Press, 2000.

Davidson, Peter. *The Idea of North: Topographics.* London: Reaktion, 2005.

Davis, Natalie Zemon. *Trickster Travels: A Sixteenth-Century Muslim between Worlds.* New York: Hill and Wang, 2006.

Defoe, Daniel. *The Danger of the Protestant Religion Consider'd, from the Present Prospect of a Religious War in Europe.* London: n.p., 1701.

———. *Jure Divino: A Satyr. In twelve books. By the author of The True-Born-Englishman.* London: n.p., 1706.

dei Rossi, Azariah ben Moses. *Sefer Me'or 'Enayim.* Jerusalem: Makor, 1969.

Delaney, Carol. "Columbus's Ultimate Goal: Jerusalem." *Comparative Studies in Society and History* 48 (2006): 260–292.

Demaitre, Edmund, and Ann Demaitre. "The Five Avatars of the Scythian." *History of European Ideas* 2.4 (1981): 315–337.

de Saint-Martin, Vivien. *Les Huns Blancs; ou, Ephthalites des Historiens Byzantins.* Paris: E. Thunot, 1849.

Destombes, Marcel. "Guillaume Postel, Cartographe." In *Guillaume Postel 1581–1981: Actes du colloque international d'Avranches 1981,* 361–371. Paris: Guy Trédaniel, 1985.

Dever, William G. *What Did the Biblical Writers Know, and When Did They Know It? What Archaeology Can Tell Us about the Reality of Ancient Israel.* Grand Rapids, Mich.: Eerdmans, 2001.

Diderot, Denis. "Sabatique, Le Flueve." in Diderot, Denis, and Jean Le Rond d'Alembert. *Encyclopédie, ou, Dictionnaire Raisonnédes Sciences, des Arts et des Métiers,* 457–458. A Paris: Chez Briasson, 1751.

Dirlik, Arif. "Confounding Metaphors, Inventions of the World: What Is World History For?" in *Writing World History 1800–2000,* ed. Benedikt Stuchtey and Eckhardt Fuchs, 91–131. Oxford: Oxford University Press, 2003.

———. "Performing the World: Reality and Representation in the Making of World Histor(ies)." *Journal of World History* 16.4 (2005): 391–410.

Dubois, Claude-Gilbert. *La Mythologie des Origines chez Guillaume Postel de la Naissance à La Nation.* Orléans, France: Paradigme, 1994.

Durán, Diego. *The Aztecs: The History of the Indies of New Spain.* New York: Orion, 1964.

———. *Historia de las Indias de Nueva-España y islas de Tierra Firme,* ed. José Fernando Ramírez and Gumesindo Mendoza. Mexico: J. M. Andrade y F. Escalante, 1867.

Eco, Umberto. *Baudolino.* New York: Harcourt, 2002.

———. *Foucault's Pendulum.* San Diego, Calif.: Harcourt Brace Jovanovich, 1989.

Edelman, Diana Vikander. *The Origins of the "Second" Temple: Persian Imperial Policy and the Rebuilding of Jerusalem.* London: Equinox, 2005.

Eisenstein, Judah David. *Otsar Midrashim.* New York: n.p., 1915.

Ekman, Ernst. "Gothic Patriotism and Olof Rudbeck." *Journal of Modern History* 34.1 (Mar. 1962): 52–63.

Elat, M. "The Economic Relations of the Neo-Assyrian Empire with Egypt." *Journal of the American Oriental Society* 98.1 (1977): 20–34.

———. "Phoenician Overland Trade within the Mesopotamian Empire," in *Ah, Assyria: Studies in Assyrian History and Ancient Near Eastern Historiography Presented to Hayim Tadmor*, ed. Mordechai Cogan and Israel Eph'al, 21–35. Jerusalem: Magnes, 1991.

Eliade, Mircea. *The Sacred and Profane: The Nature of Religion*. London: Harcourt Brace, 1959.

Eliav-Feldon, Miriam. "Invented Identities: Credulity in the Age of Prophecy and Exploration." *Journal of Early Modern History* 3.3 (Aug. 1999): 203–232.

Elukin, Jonathan M. "Jacques Basnage and *The History of the Jews:* Anti-Catholic Polemic and Historical Allegory in the Republic of Letters." *Journal of the History of Ideas* 53.4 (1992): 603–631.

Emanuel, Menahem Mendel. *Sefer Mewaser Weomer: Nehomas Menahem Kol be-Ito* (The Lost Tribes of Israel: A Call in Time and the Redemption of Israel). Jerusalem: Eretz-Israel Press, 1928.

England, Breck. *The Life and Thought of Orson Pratt*. Salt Lake City: University of Utah Press, 1985.

Epstein, Abraham. *Eldad ha-Dani seine berichte über die X Stämme und deren Ritus in Verschiedenen Versionen nach Handschriften und Alten Drucken*. Pressburg, Germany: Druck von Adolf Alkalay, 1891.

———. *Kitve R. Avraham Epshtein*. Jerusalem: Mosad Harav Kuk, 1949.

Erskine, John. *The Equity and Wisdom of Administration in Measures That Have Unhappily Occasioned the American Revolt, Tried by the Sacred Oracles*. Edinburgh: n.p., 1776.

Esherick, Joseph. *The Origins of the Boxer Uprising*. Berkeley: University of California Press, 1987.

Esler, Philip Francis. *The First Christians in Their Social Worlds: Social-Scientific Approaches to New Testament Interpretation*. London: Routledge, 1994.

Etheridge, J. W. *The Targums of Onkelos and Jonathan Ben Uzziel on the Pentateuch: With the Fragments of the Jerusalem Targum from the Chaldee*. London: Longman, Green, Longman, and Roberts, 1862.

Faierstein, Morris M., Hayyim Vital, and Isaac Judah Jehiel Safrin. *Jewish Mystical Autobiographies: Book of Visions and Book of Secrets*. New York: Paulist, 1999.

Fales, F. Mario, ed. *Assyrian Royal Inscriptions: New Horizons in Literary, Ideological, and Historical Analysis: Papers of Symposium Held in Cetona (Siena), June 26–28, 1980*. Rome: Istituto per l'Oriente, Centro per le antichità e la storia dell'arte del vicino Oriente, 1981.

Fall of Britain 9 (January 4, 1777).

Farissol, Abraham ben Mordecai. *Igeret Orhot 'Olam*. Venice: G. de Gara, 1586.

Farley, Frank Edgar. *Scandinavian Influences in the English Romantic Movement*. Boston: Ginn, 1903.

Faroqhi, Suraiya. *Pilgrims and Sultans: The Hajj under the Ottomans, 1517–1683*. London: Tauris, 1994.

Feldman, Louis H. *Jew and Gentile in the Ancient World: Attitudes and Interactions from Alexander to Justinian*. Princeton, N.J.: Princeton University Press, 1996.

———. "Josephus' Portrait of Ezra." *Vetus Testamentum* 43, fasc. 2. (Apr. 1993): 190–214.

Fernández-Armesto, Felipe. *Pathfinders: A Global History of Exploration*. New York: Norton, 2006.

Ficalho, Francisco Manuel de Melo. *Viagens de Pedro da Covilhan*. Lisboa, Portugal: A. M. Pereira, 1898.

Finkelstein, Israel, and Neil Asher Silberman. *The Bible Unearthed: Archaeology's New Vision of Ancient Israel and the Origin of Its Sacred Texts*. New York: Free Press, 2001.

Fitzgerald, Timothy. *Discourse on Civility and Barbarity*. New York: Oxford University Press, 2008.

Fletcher, Giles. *Of the Rus Commonwealth: Folger Documents of Tudor and Stuart Civilization*, ed. Albert J. Schmidt. Ithaca, N.Y.: Cornell University Press, 1966.

Fletcher, Giles, and Samuel Lee. *Israel Redux; or, The Restauration of Israel, Exhibited in Two Short Treatises. The First Contains an Essay Upon Some Probable Grounds, That the Present Tartars Near the Caspian Sea, Are the Posterity of the Ten Tribes of Israel*. London: S. Streater, 1677.

Flint, Valerie I. J. *The Imaginative Landscape of Christopher Columbus*. Princeton, N.J.: Princeton University Press, 1992.

Floyer, John. *The Prophecies of the Second Book of Esdras Amongst the Apocrypha, Explained: And Vindicated from the Objections Made against Them. To Which Are Added, a Comment on the Prophecies of Zachary and Micah: with Some Observations Concerning the Prophecies of Daniel and Malachi: Likewise the State of the Jews After the Return of the Two Tribes, Till the Resurrection of the Just . . . By Sir John Floyer, Knt.* London: Mich. Johnson, 1721.

———. *The Sibylline Oracles: Translated from the Best Greek Copies, and Compar'd with the Sacred Prophesies, Especially with Daniel and the Revelations and with so Much History As Plainly Shews, That Many of the Sibyls Predictions Are Exactly Fulfill'd: with Answers to the Objections Usually Made against Them*. London: R. Bruges, 1713.

Forster, Charles. *The Monuments of Assyria, Babylonia and Persia: With a New Key for the Recovery of the Ten Lost Tribes*. London: R. Bentley, 1859.

Frick, Frank S. "The Rechabites Reconsidered." *Journal of Biblical Literature* 90.3. (Sept. 1971): 279–287.

Friedlaender, Israel. "The Jews of Arabia and the Rechabites." *Jewish Quarterly Review*, new ser., 1.2 (Oct. 1910): 252–257.

Friedman, O. Michael. *Origins of the British Israelites: The Lost Tribes*. San Francisco, Calif.: Mellen Research University Press, 1993.

Funkenstein, Amos. *Theology and the Scientific Imagination from the Middle Ages to the Seventeenth Century*. Princeton, N.J.: Princeton University Press, 1986.

Gafni, Isaiah. *Land, Center and Diaspora: Jewish Constructs in Late Antiquity*. Sheffield, England: Sheffield Academic, 1997.

Gallagher, William R. *Sennacherib's Campaign to Judah: New Studies*. Leiden: Brill, 1999.

Galil, Gershon. *The Chronology of the Kings of Israel and Judah*, Leiden: Brill, 1996.

———. *Yisrael ve-Ashur* (Israel and Assyria). Tel Aviv: Zemorah-Bitan, 2001.

Gampel, Benjamin R. "A Letter to a Wayward Teacher: The Transformations of Sephardic Culture in Christian Iberia," in *Cultures of the Jews: A New History*, ed. David Biale, 389–448. New York: Schocken, 2002.

Gandz, Solomon. "The Origin of the Planetary Week; or, The Planetary Week in Hebrew Literature." *Proceedings of the American Academy for Jewish Research* 18 (1948–1949): 213–254.

Gans, David ben Solomon. *Sefer Tsemah David*, ed. Mordechai Breuer. Jerusalem: Magnes, 1982.

García, Gregorio. *Origen de los Indios del Nuevo Mundo*. 1607; segunda edicion, Madrid: n.p., 1729; facsimile edition Mexico: Fondo de Cultura Económica, 1981.

García-Arenal, Mercedes. *A Man of Three Worlds: Samuel Pallache, a Moroccan Jew in Catholic and Protestant Europe*. Baltimore, Md.: Johns Hopkins University Press, 2003.

Gelderblom, Arie-Jan, Jan L. de Jong, and M. van Vaeck, eds. *The Low Countries as a Crossroads of Religious Beliefs*. Leiden: Brill, 2004.

Génebrard, Gilbert. *Gilb. Genebrardi...Chronographiae libri quatour. Priores dvo svnt de rebvs veteris populi, & praecipuis quatour millim annorum gestis. Posteriores, è D. Arnaldi Pontaci Vasatensis episcopi Chronographia aucti, recentes historias reliquorum annorum complectuntur...Subiuncti sunt libri Hebraeorum chronologici eodum interprete*. Paris: Apud viduam Martini iuuenem, 1585.

George, A. R. "Assyria and the Western World," in *Assyria 1995: Proceedings of the 10th Anniversary Symposium of the Neo-Assyrian Text Corpus Project, Helsinki, September 7–11, 1995*, ed. Simo Parpola and R. M. Whiting, 69–76. Helsinki: The Project, 1997.

Gerber, Israel J. *The Heritage Seekers: American Blacks in Search of Jewish Identity*. Middle Village, N.Y.: Jonathan David, 1977.

Gibbon, Edward. *The Decline and Fall of the Roman Empire*. New York: Collier, 1899.

Gillis, John. *Islands of the Mind: How the Human Imagination Created the Atlantic World*. New York: Palgrave-Macmillan, 2004.

Ginzburg, Carlo. *No Island Is an Island: Four Glances at English Literature in a World Perspective*. New York: Columbia University Press, 2000.

———. "Style: Inclusion and Exclusion," in *Wooden Eyes: Nine Reflections on Distance*, 109–138. New York: Columbia University, Press, 2001.

Gitin, Seymour. "The Neo-Assyrian Empire and Its Western Periphery," in *Assyria 1995: Proceedings of the 10th Anniversary Symposium of the Neo-Assyrian Text Corpus Project, Helsinki, September 7–11, 1995*, ed. Simo Parpola and R. M. Whiting, 77–103. Helsinki: The Project, 1997.

Gitlitz, David M. "Hybrid Conversos in the 'Libro llamado el Alboraique.'" *Hispanic Review* 60.1 (Winter 1992): 1–17.

Glacken, Clarence J. *Traces on the Rhodian Shore: Nature and Culture in Western Thought from Ancient Times to the End of the Eighteenth Century*. Berkeley: University of California Press, 1967.

Glas, George. *The History of the Discovery and Conquest of the Canary Islands: Tr. from a Spanish Manuscript Lately Found in the Island of Palma. With an Enquiry into the Origin of the Ancient Inhabitants. To Which Is Added, A Description of the Canary Islands, Including the Modern History of the Inhabitants, and an Account of Their Manners, Customs, Trade, &c.* London: R. and J. Dodsley [etc.], 1764.

Glassner, Jean-Jacques. *Mesopotamian Chronicles.* Leiden: Brill, 2005.

Glatzer, Michael. "Pablo de Santa Maria on the Events of 1391." in Almog, S. *Antisemitism Through the Ages,* 127–137. Oxford, England: Pergamon Press, 1988.

Godbey, Allen. *The Lost Tribes a Myth: Suggestions towards Rewriting Hebrew History.* Durham, N.C.: Duke University Press, 1930.

Goldish, Matt. *The Sabbatean Prophets.* Cambridge, Mass.: Harvard University Press, 2004.

Goldman, Shalom. *God's Sacred Tongue: Hebrew & the American Imagination.* Chapel Hill: University of North Carolina Press, 2004.

———. *Hebrew and the Bible in America: The First Two Centuries.* Hanover, N.H.: University Press of New England, 1993.

Gonen, Rivka. *To the Ends of the Earth: The Quest for the Ten Lost Tribes of Israel.* Northvale, N.J.: Jason Aronson, 2002.

González, Ondina E., and Justo L. González. *Christianity in Latin America: A History.* Cambridge: Cambridge University Press, 2008.

Goodkind, Howard W. "Lord Kingsborough Lost His Fortune Trying to Prove the Maya Were Descendants of the Ten Lost Tribes." *British Archeological Review* 11.5 (1985): 54–65.

Gow, Andrew. *The Red Jews: Antisemitism in an Apocalyptic Age, 1200–1600.* Leiden: Brill, 1995.

Grant, Asahel. *The Nestorians; or, The Lost Tribes: Containing Evidence of Their Identity; an Account of Their Manners, Customs, and Ceremonies; Together with Sketches of Travel in Ancient Assyria, Armenia, Media, and Mesopotamia; and Illustrations of Scripture Prophecy.* London: J. Murray, 1841.

Grant, Asahel, and A. C. Lathrop. *Memoir of Asahel Grant, M.D.: Missionary to the Nestorians.* New York: M. W. Dodd, 1847.

Grayson, A. Kirk. "Histories and Historians in the Ancient Near East: Assyria and Babylonia." *Orientalia* 49 (1980): 140–149.

Great Britain. Parliament. House of Commons. *The History and Proceedings of the House of Commons from the Restoration to the Present Time: Containing the Most Remarkable Motions, Speeches,* vol. 2. London: n.p., 1742.

The Great Deliverance of the Whole House of Israel: What It Truly Is, by Whom It Shall Be Performed, and in What Year…In Answer to a Book Called The Hope of Israel, Written by a Learned Jew of Amsterdam Named Menasseh Ben Israel. London: Printed by M. S., 1652.

Greenblatt, Stephen. *Marvelous Possessions: The Wonder of the New World.* Chicago: University of Chicago Press, 1991.

Greenleaf, Richard E. *The Roman Catholic Church in Colonial Latin America.* New York: Knopf, 1971.

Gries, Zeev. "Messiah Scribe: A'aron Ze'ev Aescoli." *Peamim* 100 (Summer 2004): 147–157 (in Hebrew).

Grimaldi, Alexander Beaufort. *Manasseh in Scotland: A Biblical and Historical Study.* London: R. Banks & Son, 1916.

Gumilev, Lev. *Searches for an Imaginary Kingdom: The Legend of the Kingdom of Prester John.* Cambridge: Cambridge University Press, 1987.

Haga, Uziel. *Sefer Ha-Berit Ha-Hadash 'im Ha-Nahar Sambatyon bi-Medinat Hina.* Petrokov, Poland: Shlomovitz, 1906.

Haight, Sarah Rogers. *Letters from the Old World.* New York: Harpers and Brothers, 1840.

Halkin, Hillel. *Across the Sabbath River: In Search of a Lost Tribe of Israel.* Boston: Houghton Mifflin, 2002.

Hall, Stuart. "Cultural Identity and Diaspora," in *Identity: Community, Culture, Difference*, ed. Jonathan Rutherford, 222–237. London: Lawrence & Wishart, 1990.

Hallamish, Moshe, Yosef Rivlin, and Raphael Shuchat. *Ha-Gr'a u-Veit Midrasho.* Ramat Gan, Israel: Bar-Ilan University, 2003.

Halperin, David J., and Gordon D. Newby. "Two Castrated Bulls: A Study in the Haggadah of Ka'b Al-Ahbar." *Journal of the American Oriental Society* 102.4 (1982): 631–638.

Halpern, Baruch. *The First Historians: The Hebrew Bible and History.* San Francisco, Calif.: Harper & Row, 1988.

Hamilton, Alastair. *The Apocryphal Apocalypse: The Reception of the Second Book of Esdras (4 Ezra) from the Renaissance to the Enlightenment.* Oxford: Clarendon, 1999.

Hamilton, Mark W. "The Past as Destiny: Historical Visions in Sam'al and Judah under Assyrian Hegemony." *Harvard Theological Review* 91.3 (July 1998): 215–250.

Haran, Menahem. "From Early to Classical Prophecy: Continuity and Change." *Vetus Testamentum* 27, fasc. 4 (Oct. 1977): 385–397.

Harper, William, James Henry Hammond, William Gilmore Simms, and Thomas R. Dew. *The Pro-Slavery Argument, As Maintained by the Most Distinguished Writers of the Southern States Containing the Several Essays on the Subject.* Charleston, S.C.: Walker, Richards, 1852.

Harris, Jason. "The Practice of Community: Humanist Friendship during the Dutch Revolt." *Texas Studies in Literature and Language* 47.4 (2005): 299–325.

———. "The Religious Position of Abraham Ortelius," in *The Low Countries as a Crossroads of Religious Beliefs*, ed. Arie-Jan Gelderblom, Jan L. de Jong, and M. van Vaeck, 89–141. Leiden: Brill, 2004.

Harris, Tim. *Revolution: The Great Crisis of the British Monarchy, 1685–1720.* London: Allen Lane, 2006.

Hason, Nir. "Shevet Avud Mefahed la-Lechet le'Ibud." *Haaretz* (Aug. 25, 2004).

Hayes, John Haralson. *Amos, the Eighth-Century Prophet: His Times and His Preaching.* Nashville, Tenn.: Abingdon, 1988.

Headley, John M. "The Sixteenth-Century Venetian Celebration of the Earth's Total Habitability: The Issue of the Fully Habitable World for Renaissance Europe." *Journal of World History* 8.1 (1997): 1–27.

Heber, Reginald, and Amelia Shipley Heber. *The Life of Reginald Heber*. New York: Protestant Episcopal Press, 1830.

Heylyn, Peter. *Microcosmus: A Little Description of the Great World*. Oxford: Turner u.a, 1625.

———. *Cosmographie in Four Bookes: Containing the Chorographie and Historie of the Whole Vvorld, and All the Principall Kingdomes, Provinces, Seas and Isles Thereof*. London: Henry Seile, 1652.

Higgins, Iain Macleod. "Defining the Earth's Center in a Medieval 'Multi-Text': Jerusalem in *The Book of John Mandeville*," in *Text and Territory: Geographical Imagination in the European Middle Ages*, ed. Sylvia Tomasch and Sealy Gilles, 29–53. Philadelphia: University of Pennsylvania Press, 1998.

Hill, Christopher. *The English Bible and the Seventeenth-Century Revolution*. London: Allen Lane, 1993.

———. "Till the Conversion of the Jews," in *Millenarianism and Messianism in English Literature and Thought 1650–1800*, ed. Richard Henry Popkin, 12–36. Leiden: Brill, 1988.

Hillelson, S. "David Reubeni's Route in Africa." *Jewish Quarterly Review*, new ser., 28.3 (Jan. 1938): 289–291.

Hine, Edward. *The English Nation Identified with the Lost House of Israel by Twenty-Seven Identifications*. Manchester, England: J. Heywood; Birmingham, England: R. Davies, 1871.

———. *Forty-Seven Identifications of the Anglo-Saxons with the Lost Ten Tribes of Israel, Founded Upon Five Hundred Scripture Proofs*. New York: Huggins, 1878.

———. *Forty-Seven Identifications of the British Nation with the Lost Ten Tribes of Israel: Founded upon Five Hundred Scripture Proofs*. London: W. H. Guest, S. W. Partridge, 1874.

———. *Seventeen Positive Identifications of the English Nation with the Lost House of Israel*. London: G. J. Stevenson, 1870.

Hirschberg, H. Z. *Yisrael ba-Arav: Korot ha-Yehudim be-Himyar ve-Hig'az me-Hurban Bayit sheni ve-ad mas e ha-tselav*. Tel Aviv: Masadah, 1946.

History of Johnson County, Iowa, Containing a History of the County, and Its Townships, Cities and Villages from 1836 to 1882. Together with Biographical Sketches. N.p., 1883.

Hopkirk, Peter. *The Great Game: The Struggle for Empire in Central Asia*. New York: Kodansha International, 1992.

Hourani, George Fadlo. *Arab Seafaring in the Indian Ocean in Ancient and Early Medieval Times*. Princeton, N.J.: Princeton University Press, 1995.

Howitt, William. *The History of the Supernatural in All Ages and Nations, And in All Churches, Christian and Pagan: Demonstrating a Universal Faith*. London: Longman, Green, Longman, Roberts, & Green, 1863.

Hoxie, Elizabeth F. "Harriet Livermore: 'Vixen and Devotee.'" *New England Quarterly* 18.1 (Mar. 1945): 39–50.

Hudson, Charles. "James Adair as Anthropologist." *Ethnohistory* 24.4 (Autumn 1977): 311–328.

Hultkrantz, Åke. "Swedish Research on the Religion and Folklore of the Lapps." *Journal of the Royal Anthropological Institute of Great Britain and Ireland* 85.1–2 (1955): 81–99.

Humboldt, Alexander von. *Personal Narrative of Travels to the Equinoctial Regions of America, During the Years 1799–1804*, trans. Aimé Bonpland and Thomasina Ross. London: H. G. Bohn, 1852.

Hurwitz, Simon Hirsch. *Sefer Kol Mevaser: Makhil Yedi ot Nikhbadot mi-Metsi'ut ha-Iyim ha-Rhokot umi-Kol Perate Mekomot Aseret ha-Shevatim, u-Veno Mosheh.* Yerushalayim: Bi-Defus Salomon, 1922.

Hutton, Ronald. *Charles the Second, King of England, Scotland, and Ireland.* Oxford: Clarendon, 1989.

Hyamson, Albert M. "The Lost Tribes, and the Influence of the Search for Them on the Return of the Jews to England." *Jewish Quarterly Review* 15.4 (July 1903): 640–676.

Hyde, Thomas. *Igeret Orhot 'Olam, id est, Itinera Mundi, sic Dicta Nempe Cosmographia.* Oxford: e theatro Sheldoniano, impensis Henrici Bonwick, 1691.

Ibn Hisham, 'Abd al-Malik, et al. *Kitāb al-Tijān fi mulūk Himyar.* Haydarabad al-Dakkan, India: Matba'at Majlis Da'irat al-Ma'arif al-'Uthmaniyah, 1928.

Idel, Moshe. *Messianic Mystics.* New Haven, Conn.: Yale University Press, 1998.

———. *The Mystical Experience in Abraham Abulafia.* Albany: State University of New York Press, 1988.

———. "Saturn and Sabbatai Tzevi: A New Approach to Sabbateanism," in *Toward the Millennium: Messianic Expectations from the Bible to Waco,* ed. Peter Shafer and Mark Cohen, 173–202. Leiden: Brill, 1998.

Isagoge Histórico Apologético General de Todas Las Indias y Especial de la Provincia Sn. Vicente Ferrer de Chiapa y Goathemala de el orden de Predicadores; libro inédito hasta ahora, que, con motivo de la celebración del cuarto centenario del descubrimiento de América, ha mandado publicar el gobierno de la república de Guatemala. Madrid: Tip. de T. Minuesa de los Ríos, 1892.

Israel, Jonathan I. *Conflicts of Empires: Spain, the Low Countries and the Struggle for World Supremacy, 1585–1713.* London: Hambledon, 1997.

———. *Diasporas within a Diaspora: Jews, Crypto-Jews, and the World of Maritime Empires (1540–1740).* Leiden and Boston: Brill, 2002.

———. *The Dutch Republic and the Hispanic World, 1606–1661.* Oxford: Clarendon, 1982.

Israel, Jonathan I., and Stuart B. Schwartz. *The Expansion of Tolerance: Religion in Dutch Brazil (1624–1654).* Amsterdam: Amsterdam University Press, 2007.

Jackson, Peter. "Marco Polo and His 'Travels.'" *Bulletin of the School of Oriental and African Studies, University of London* 61.1 (1998): 82.

———. "The Mongols and Europe," in *The New Cambridge Medieval History,* vol. 5, ed. David Abulafia, 703–719. Cambridge: Cambridge University Press, 1999.

Jacobovici, Simcha, and Elliott Halpern. *Quest for the Lost Tribes.* New York: A&E Home Video, 1999.

Jellinek, Adolph. *Bet ha-Midrash: Midrashim Ketanim Yeshanim u-Ma'amarim Shonim.* Jerusalem: Sifre Vahrmann, 1967.

Joannès, Francis. *The Age of Empires: Mesopotamia in the First Millennium* BC. Edinburgh: Edinburgh University Press, 2000.

Jobes, Karen H., and Moisés Silva. *Invitation to the Septuagint*. Grand Rapids, Mich.: Baker Academic, 2000.

Johnson, Christopher. "'Periwigged Heralds': Epistemology and Intertextuality in Early American Cometography." *Journal of the History of Ideas* 65.3 (July 2004): 399–419.

Johnson, James William. "The Scythian: His Rise and Fall." *Journal of the History of Ideas* 20.2 (Apr. 1959): 250–257.

Jones, W. H. S., trans. *Pliny: Natural History*. Cambridge, Mass.: Harvard University Press, 1975.

Josephus, Flavius. *The Works of Flavius Josephus: Comprising the Antiquities of the Jews; a History of the Jewish Wars; and Life of Flavius Josephus*, trans. William Whiston. Philadelphia: Leary & Getz, 1856.

Junkin, George. *Political Fallacies: An Examination of the False Assumptions, and Refutation of the Sophistical Reasonings, Which Have Brought on This Civil War*. New York: Scribner, 1863.

Kadir, Djelal. *Columbus and the Ends of the Earth: Europe's Prophetic Rhetoric as Conquering Ideology*. Berkeley: University of California Press, 1992.

———. "To World, to Globalize: Comparative Literature's Crossroads." *Comparative Literature Studies* 41.1 (2004): 1–9.

Kamen, Henry. The Mediterranean and The Expulsion of Spanish Jews in 1492 *Past and Present* 119 (1988): 30–55.

Kamen, Henry Arthur Francis. *Spain's Road to Empire: The Making of a World Power, 1492–1763*. London: Allen Lane, 2002.

Kaplan, Steven. *The Beta Israel (Falasha) in Ethiopia from Earliest Times to the Twentieth Century*. New York: New York University Press, 1992.

Kaplan, Yosef, Richard H. Popkin, and Henry Méchoulan, eds. *Menasseh ben Israel and His World*. Leiden: Brill, 1989.

Kasdoi, Zevi. *Shivtei Yaakov u-netsure Yisrael: Homer le-Hakirah 'al Odot 'Aseret ha-Shevatim*. Haifa, Israel: N. Warhaftig, 1928.

Katz, David S. "Israel in America: The Wanderings of the Lost Ten Tribes from 'Mikveigh Yisrael' to Timothy McVeigh," in *The Jews and the Expansion of Europe to the West, 1450–1800*, ed. Paolo Bernardini and Norman Fiering, 107–122. New York: Berghahn Books, 2001.

———. "Menasseh ben Israel's Christian Connection: Henry Jessey and the Jews," in *Menasseh ben Israel and His World*, ed. Yosef Kaplan, Richard H. Popkin, and Henry Méchoulan, 117–138. Leiden: Brill, 1989.

———. "Menasseh ben Israel's Mission to Queen Christina of Sweden, 1651–1655." *Jewish Social Studies* 45 (1983): 57–72.

———. *Philo-Semitism and the Readmission of the Jews to England, 1603–1655*. Oxford: Clarendon, 1982.

Kelle, Brad E. "What's in a Name? Neo-Assyrian Designations for the Northern Kingdom and Their Implications for Israelite History and Biblical Interpretation." *Journal of Biblical Literature* 121.4 (2002): 639–666.

Keteltas, Abraham. *God Arising and Pleading His People's Cause; or, The American War in Favor of Liberty against the Measures and Arms of Great Britain.* Newburyport, Mass.: John Mycall, 1777.

Khadduri, Majid. *War and Peace in the Law of Islam.* Baltimore, Md.: Johns Hopkins University Press, 1955.

Khoury, Raif Georges. "Geschichte oder Fiktion. Zur erzählerischen Gattung der ältesten Bücher über Arabien," in *Story-telling in the Framework of Nonfictional Arabic Literature,* ed. Leder Stefan, 370–387. Wiesbaden, Germany: Harrassowitz, 1999.

———. *Wahb b. Munabbih.* Wiesbaden, Germany: Harrassowitz, 1972.

Kidd, Colin. *The Forging of Races: Race and Scripture in the Protestant Atlantic World, 1600–2000.* Cambridge: Cambridge University Press, 2006.

King, Charles. *The Black Sea: A History.* Oxford: Oxford University Press, 2004.

King, David. *Finding Atlantis: A True Story of Genius, Madness and an Extraordinary Quest for a Lost World.* New York: Harmony, 2005.

King, Philip J. "The Eighth: The Greatest of Centuries?" *Journal of Biblical Literature* 108.1 (Spring 1989): 3–15.

Kingsborough, Edward King. *Antiquities of Mexico: Comprising Fac-Similes of Ancient Mexican Paintings and Hieroglyphics.* London: A. Aglio, 1830–1848.

Kirsch, Stuart. "Lost Tribes: Indigenous People and the Social Imaginary." *Anthropological Quarterly* 70.2 (Apr. 1997): 58–67.

Knights, C. H. "The History of the Rechabites: An Initial Commentary." *Journal for the Study of Judaism in the Persian, Hellenistic and Roman Period* 28.4 (1997): 413–436.

———. "The Nabataeans and the Rechabites." *Journal of Semitic Studies* 38.2 (1993): 227–233.

———. "Towards a Critical Introduction to the History of the Rechabites." *Journal for the Study of Judaism in the Persian, Hellenistic and Roman Period* 26.3 (1995): 324–342.

Knoppers, Gary N. J., and Gordon McConville, eds. *Reconsidering Israel and Judah: Recent Studies on the Deuteronomistic History.* Winona Lake, Ind.: Eisenbrauns, 2000.

Knuteson, Knute. *The Ten Lost Tribes.* Spanish Fork, Utah: The Author, 1925.

Koeman, Cornelis. *The History of Abraham Ortelius and His Theatrum Orbis Terrarum.* New York: American Elsevier, 1964.

Koishi, Yutaka. *Nihonjin to Yudayajin no rengō o sekai ga osoreru riyū: ju buzoku no daiyogen.* Tokyo: Kōbunsha, 1987.

Krauss, S. "New Light on Geographical Information of Eldad Hadani and Benjamin of Tudela." *Tarbiz* 8 (1937): 208–232 (in Hebrew).

Kuhrt, A. "The Cyrus Cylinder and Achaemenid Imperial Policy." *Journal for the Study of the Old Testament* 25 (1983): 86–87.

Kuntz, Marion Leathers. *Guillaume Postel, Prophet of the Restitution of All Things: His Life and Thought.* The Hague: Nijhoff, 1981.

———. "Guillaume Postel and the Universal Monarchy: The State as a Work of Art," in *Guillaume Postel 1581–1981: Actes du colloque international d'Avranches 1981,* 233–256. Paris: Guy Trédaniel, 1985.

Laato, Antti. "Assyrian Propaganda and the Falsification of History in the Royal Inscriptions of Sennacherib." *Vetus Testamentum* 45, fasc. 2 (Apr. 1995): 198–226.

La Croix, A. Phérotée de. *Nouvelle Methode pour Apprendre Facilement la Geographie Universelle: contenant le traité de la sphere, la description du globe terrestre & celeste, les parties du monde divisées en leurs etats, empires, royaumes, republiques, provinces, &c.: le tout enrichy de Cartes avec les armoiries des provinces & de figures de diverses nations.* Lyon, France: Chez Jean-Baptiste Barbier, 1690.

Lampronti, Isaac Hezekiah ben Samuel. *Paḥad Yitsḥak.* Yerushalayim: Mosad ha-Rav Ḳuḳ, 1961.

Lasswell, Harold D., Daniel Lerner, and Hans Speier, eds. *Propaganda and Communication in World History,* vol. 1: *The Symbolic Instrument in Early Times.* Honolulu: University of Hawaii Press, 1979.

Lavezzo, Kathy. *Angels on the Edge of the World: Geography, Literature, and English Community, 1000–1534.* Ithaca, N.Y.: Cornell University Press, 2006.

Leblanc, Vincent. *The World Surveyed; or, The Famous Voyages & Travailes of Vincent le Blanc, or White, of Marseilles: Who from the Age of Fourteen Years, to Threescore and Eighteen, Travelled Through Most Parts of the World...Containing a More Exact Description of Several Parts of the World, Than Hath Hitherto Been Done by Any Other Authour.* London: Printed for John Starkey, 1660.

Lee, Mark. *The Lost Tribe.* New York: Picador, 1998.

Leket Hipus 'Aseret ha-Shevatim: Osef Ma'amarim u-Mehkarim be-'Inyan Hipus Aseret ha-Shevatim. Jerusalem: Yerid ha-sefarim, 1999.

Levine, Lee I., and Amihay Mazar. *ha-Pulmus 'al ha-Emet ha-Historit ba-Mikra* (The Controversy over the Historicity of the Bible). Jerusalem: Yad Ben Tsevi, 2001.

Lindelof, O. J. S. *A Trip to the North Pole; or, The Discovery of the Ten Tribes, as Found in the Arctic Ocean.* Salt Lake City, Utah: Tribune Printing, 1903.

Liverani, Mario. "The Fall of the Assyrian Empire: Ancient and Modern Interpretations," in *Empires: Perspectives from Archaeology and History,* ed. Susan Alcock, 374–391. New York: Cambridge University Press, 2001.

———. *Israel's History and the History of Israel,* trans. Chiara Peri and Philip R. Davies. Oakville, Conn.: Equinox, 2005.

Livermore, Harriet. *Millennial Tidings.* Philadelphia: The Author, 1831.

———. "Song Millennial." Trinity Church, Richmond, Virginia, July 1, 1832.

Livingstone, David. *Narrative of an Expedition to the Zambesi and Its Tributaries: And of the Discovery of the Lakes Shirwa and Nyassa, 1858–1864.* New York: Harper & Bros., 1866.

———. *The Zambezi Expedition of David Livingstone, 1858–1863.* London: Chatto & Windus, 1956.

Livingstone, David N. *The Preadamite Theory and the Marriage of Science and Religion.* Philadelphia: American Philosophical Society, 1992.

Livneh, Neri. "Coming Home." *Haaretz Friday* (July 19, 2002).

Lockman, John, ed. *Travels of the Jesuits, into Various Parts of the World: Particularly China and the East-Indies.* London: T. Piety, 1762.

Loew, Rabbi Juda of Prague (Maharaı). *Netzah Israel*. Jerusalem: Machon Jerusalem, 2004.

Longenecker, Bruce W. *2 Esdras*, Sheffield: Sheffield Academic Press, 1995.

Lorki, Yeshosu'a. *Igeret Yehosh'a a-Lorki*, in *Ozar Wikuhim: A Collection of Polemics and Disputations*, ed. Judah David Eisenstein, 98–104. 1928; reprint, Tel Aviv: n.p., 1969.

Lowance, Mason I. *A House Divided: The Antebellum Slavery Debates in America, 1776–1865*. Princeton, N.J.: Princeton University Press, 2003.

Lozano, Pedro. *Historia de la Conquista del Paraguay, Rio de la Plata y Tucuman*. Buenos Aires: Casa Editora Imprenta Popular, 1873.

Lucena, Vasco Fernandes de. *The Obedience of a King of Portugal*, trans. Francis Millet Rogers. Minneapolis: University of Minnesota Press, 1958.

Ludolf, Hiob. *New History of Ethiopia: Being a Full and Accurate Description of the Kingdom of Abessinia, Vulgarly, Though Erroneously Called the Empire of Prester John: in Four Books . . . Illustrated with Copper Plates*, trans. J. P. London: Samuel Smith, 1682.

Lyman, Stanford M. "The Lost Tribes of Israel as Problem in History and Sociology," in *Roads to Dystopia: Sociological Essays on the Postmodern Condition*, ed. Stanford M. Lyman, 159–187. Fayetteville: University of Arkansas Press, 2001.

———. "Postmodernism and Construction of Ethno-cultural Identity: The Jewish-Indian Theory and the Lost Tribes of Israel," in *Roads to Dystopia: Sociological Essays on the Postmodern Condition*, ed. Stanford M. Lyman, 189–203. Fayetteville: University of Arkansas Press, 2001.

Macey, Samuel L. *Patriarchs of Time: Dualism in Saturn-Cronus, Father Time, the Watchmaker God, and Father Christmas*. Athens: University of Georgia Press, 1987.

Machinist, Peter. "Assyria and Its Image in the First Isaiah." *Journal of the American Oriental Society* 103.4 (Oct. 1983): 719–737.

———. "The Fall of Assyria in Comparative Ancient Perspective," in *Assyria 1995: Proceedings of the 10th Anniversary Symposium of the Neo-Assyrian Text Corpus Project, Helsinki, September 7–11, 1995*, ed. Simo Parpola and R. M. Whiting, 179–196. Helsinki: The Project, 1997.

Mackendrick, William Gordon. *The Destiny of America, with an Appendix: Who Are the Japanese?* Boston: A. A. Beauchamp, 1921.

Malkiel, David. "The Sambatyon and the Ten Lost Tribes in *Pahad Yizhaq* by Isaac Lampronti." *Pe'amim* 94–95 (Winter–Spring 2003): 159–180.

Mandeville, John. *Mandeville's Travels*, ed. M. C. Seymour. New York: Oxford University Press, 1968.

Marcus, David. "Nineveh's 'Three Days' Walk' (Jonah 3:3): Another Interpretation," in *On the Way of Nineveh: Studies in Honor of George M. Landes*, ed. Stephen L. Cook and S. C. Winter, 42–53. Atlanta, Ga.: Scholars, 1999.

Margolis, David. "Finding the Lost Tribes: Traces of the Tribes Are Popping Up All Over." Available at: http://www.davidmargolis.com (accessed August 3, 2006).

Matar, Nabil I. "George Herbert, Henry Vaughan, and the Conversion of the Jews." *Studies in English Literature, 1500–1900* 30.1 (Winter 1990): 79–92.

Matsumoto, Michihiro, and J. Eidelberg. *Yamato Minzoku Yudayajin setsu no nazo o ou.* Tokyo: Tama Shuppan, 1992.

May, John A. *Kant's Concept of Geography: And Its Relation to Recent Geographical Thought.* Toronto: University of Toronto Press, 1970.

Mayerson, Philip. "A Confusion of Indias: Asian India and African India in the Byzantine *Sources.*" *Journal of the American Oriental Society* 113.2 (Apr.–June 1993): 169–174.

McAuliffe, Jane Dammen. "Assessing the Isra'iliyyat: An Exegetical Conundrum," in *Story-telling in the Framework of Nonfictional Arabic Literature,* ed. Leder Stefan, 346–376. Wiesbaden, Germany: Harrassowitz, 1999.

McGrady, Thomas. *Beyond the Black Ocean.* Chicago: Charles H. Kerr, 1901.

McKenzie, Steven L. *How to Read the Bible: History, Prophecy, Literature-Why Modern Readers Need to Know the Difference, and What It Means for Faith Today.* New York: Oxford University Press, 2005.

McLean, Matthew. *The Cosmographia of Sebastian Münster: Describing the World in the Reformation.* Aldershot, England: Ashgate, 2007.

McLeod, N. *Epitome of the Ancient History of Japan.* Nagasaki: Printed for the Author at the Rising Sun Office, 1879.

———. *Korea and the Ten Lost Tribes of Israel with Korean, Japanese, and Israelitish Illustrations.* Yokohama: n.p., 1879.

Méchoulan, Henry. "Menasseh Ben Israel and the World of the Non-Jew," in *Menasseh ben Israel and His World,* ed. Yosef Kaplan, Richard H. Popkin, and Henry Méchoulan, 83–97. Leiden: Brill, 1989.

Medina, José Toribio. *Los Aborígenes de Chile.* Santiago de Chile: Fondo Histórico y Bibliográfico José Toribio Medina, 1952.

Melion, Walter S. "Ad Ductum Itineris et Dispositionem Mansionum Ostendendam: Meditation, Vocation, and Sacred History in Abraham Ortelius's Parergon." *Journal of the Walters Art Gallery* 57 (1999): 49–72.

Michael, Hugh J. "The Jewish Sabbath in the Latin Classical Writers." *American Journal of Semitic Languages and Literatures* 40.2 (Jan. 1924): 117–124.

Milton, John. *The Poetical Works of John Milton: To Which Is Prefixed the Life of the Author,* ed. Egerton Brydges and J. M. W. Turner. London: William Tegg, 1848.

Moazami, Mahnaz. "Millennialism, Eschatology, and Messianic Figures in Iranian Tradition." *Journal of Millennial Studies* (Winter 2000): 1–16.

Moberg, Axel. *The Book of the Himyarites: Fragments of a Hitherto Unknown Syriac Work.* Lund: Gleerup, 1924.

Montano, Benito Arias. *Itinerarium Beniamini Tudelensis: in quo res memorabiles, quas ante quadrigentos annos totum ferè terrarum orbem notatis itineribus dimensus vel ipse vidit vel à fide dignis suae aetatis hominibus accepit, breuiter atque dilucidè describuntur.* Antwerp: ex officina Christophori Plantini, architypographi regij, 1575.

Moore, Karl, and David Lewis. *Birth of the Multinational: 2000 Years of Ancient Business History, from Ashur to Augustus.* Herndon, Va.: Copenhagen Business School Press, 1999.

Morag, Shlomo. "Eldad Haddani's Hebrew and the Problem of His Provenance." *Tarbiz* 66 (1997): 223–246 (in Hebrew).

Moreno Toscano, Alejandra. *Fray Juan de Torquemada y su Monarquía Indiana*. Xalapa, Mexico: Universidad Veracruzana, 1963.

Morgenstern, Arie. *Hastening Redemption: Messianism and the Resettlement of the Land of Israel*. New York: Oxford University Press, 2006.

Moyn, Samuel. "Amos Funkenstein on the Theological Origins of Historicism." *Journal of the History of Ideas* 64.4 (2003): 639–657.

Muller, Richard. *After Calvin: Studies in the Development of a Theological Tradition*. Oxford: Oxford University Press, 2003.

Münchhausen, Karl Friedrich Hieronymus von. *Münchhausen at the Pole; or, The Surprising and Wonderful Adventures of a Voyage of Discovery: Consisting of Some of the Most Marvellous Exploits Ever Performed by Man; Together with a Correct List of the Curiosities Brought Home and Deposited in the Museum and Tower of London*. London: J. Johnston, 1819.

Murphy, Frederick J. "2 Baruch and the Romans." *Journal of Biblical Literature* 104.4 (Dec. 1985): 663–669.

Murphy, Trevor Morgan. *Pliny the Elder's Natural History: The Empire in the Encyclopedia*. Oxford: Oxford University Press, 2004.

Na'aman, Nadav. "Ahab's Chariot Force at the Battle of Qarqar," in Na'aman, *Ancient Israel and Its Neighbors*, 1–12.

———. *Ancient Israel and Its Neighbors: Interaction and Counteraction*. Winona Lake, Ind.: Eisenbrauns, 2005.

———. "Forced Participation in Alliances in the Course of the Assyrian Campaigns to the West," in Na'aman, *Ancient Israel and Its Neighbors*, 16–39.

———. "Hezekiah and the Kings of Assyria," in Na'aman, *Ancient Israel and Its Neighbors*, 98–117.

———. "The Historical Background to the Conquest of Samaria (720 BCE)," in Na'aman, *Ancient Israel and Its Neighbors*, 76–93.

———. "Jehu, Son of Omri: Legitimizing a Loyal Vassal by His Lord," in Na'aman, *Ancient Israel and Its Neighbors*, 13–15.

———. "Population Changes in Palestine following Assyrian Deportations," in Na'aman, *Ancient Israel and Its Neighbors*, 200–219.

———. "Rezin of Damascus and the Land of Gilead," in Na'aman, *Ancient Israel and Its Neighbors*, 40–55.

———. "Tiglath-pileser III's Campaigns against Tyre and Israel (734–732 BCE)," in Na'aman, *Ancient Israel and Its Neighbors*, 56–67.

Na'aman, Nadav, and Ran Zadok. "Sargon II's Deportations to Israel and Philistia (716–708 B.C.)." *Journal of Cuneiform Studies* 40.1 (Spring 1988): 36–46.

Nagel, Thomas. *The View from Nowhere*. New York: Oxford University Press, 1986.

Nebot, Didier. *Les Tribus Oubliées d'Israël: l'Afrique Judéo-Berbére, des Origines aux Almohades: Essai Historique*. Paris: Romillat, 1999.

Neher, André. *Jewish Thought and the Scientific Revolution of the Sixteenth Century: David Gans (1541–1613) and His Times*. Oxford: Oxford University Press, 1986.

Netanyahu, B. *Don Isaac Abravanel, Statesman and Philosopher.* Philadelphia: Jewish Publication Society of America, 1968.

Neubauer, Adolf. "Where Are the Ten Tribes? I. Bible, Talmud, and Midrashic Literature." *Jewish Quarterly Review* 1.1 (Oct. 1888): 14–28.

———. "Where Are the Ten Tribes? II. Eldad the Danite." *Jewish Quarterly Review* 1.2 (Jan. 1889): 95–114.

———. "Where Are the Ten Tribes? III. Early Translators of the Bible and Commentators: Abraham Bar Hiyya, Benjamin of Tudela, Prester John, Obadiah of Bertinoro, Abraham Levi and His Contemporaries." *Jewish Quarterly Review* 1.3 (Apr. 1889): 185–201.

———. "Where Are the Ten Tribes? IV (Concluded)." *Jewish Quarterly Review* 1.4 (July 1889): 408–423.

Neubauer, Adolphe. *La Géographie du Talmud.* Hildesheim, Germany: G. Olms, 1967.

Neusner, Jacob. *Invitation to Midrash: The Workings of Rabbinic Bible Interpretation: A Teaching Book.* San Francisco, Calif.: Harper & Row, 1989.

———. *Lamentations Rabbah.* Atlanta, Ga.: Scholars, 1997.

———. *The Midrash Compilations of the Sixth and Seventh Centuries: An Introduction to the Rhetorical, Logical, and Topical Program.* Atlanta, Ga.: Scholars, 1989.

Newman, James L. *Imperial Footprints: Henry Morton Stanley's African Journeys.* Washington, D.C.: Brassey's, 2004.

Nicolson, Adam. *God's Secretaries: The Making of the King James Bible.* New York: HarperCollins, 2003.

Nigosian, Salomon A. *From Ancient Writings to Sacred Texts: The Old Testament and Apocrypha.* Baltimore, Md.: Johns Hopkins University Press, 2004.

Nirenberg, David. "Enmity and Assimilation: Jews, Christians, and Converts in Medieval Spain." *Common Knowledge* 9.1 (2003): 137–151.

Noah, Mordecai M. *Discourse on the Evidences of the American Indians Being the Descendants of the Lost Tribes of Israel: Delivered before the Mercantile Library Association, Clinton Hall.* New York: James Van Norden, 1837.

Nordenskjöld, Baron A. E. "The Influence of the 'Travels of Marco Polo' on Jacobo Gastaldi's Maps of Asia." *Geographical Journal* 13.4 (Apr. 1899): 396–406.

Northrup, David. "Vasco da Gama and Africa: An Era of Mutual Discovery, 1497–1800." *Journal of World History* 9.2 (1998): 189–211.

Nussbaum, Felicity. *The Global Eighteenth Century.* Baltimore, Md.: Johns Hopkins University Press, 2003.

Nuti, Lucia. "The World Map as an Emblem: Abraham Ortelius and the Stoic Contemplation." *Imago Mundi* 55 (2003): 38–55.

Oded, Bustenay. "History vis-à-vis Propaganda in the Assyrian Royal Inscriptions." *Vetus Testamentum* 48, fasc. 3 (July 1998): 423–425.

———. *Mass Deportations and Deportees in the Neo-Assyrian Empire.* Wiesbaden, Germany: Reichert, 1979.

———. *War, Peace and Empire: Justifications for War in Assyrian Inscriptions.* Wiesbaden, Germany: Reichart, 1992.

Olender, Maurice. *The Languages of Paradise: Race, Religion, and Philology in the Nineteenth Century.* Cambridge, Mass.: Harvard University Press, 1992.

Olive, Phyllis Carol. *The Lost Tribes of the Book of Mormon—the Rest of the Story: A Correlation between the Nephite Nation and the Mound Builders of the Eastern United States.* Springville, Utah: Bonneville, 2001.

Olmstead, A. T. *History of Assyria.* London: Scribner's, 1923.

Oppenheim, Leo A. "Neo-Assyrian and Neo-Babylonian Empires," in *Propaganda and Communication in World History,* vol. 1: *The Symbolic Instrument in Early Times,* ed. Harold D. Lasswell, Daniel Lerner, and Hans Speier, 111–144. Honolulu: University of Hawaii Press, 1979.

Ortelius, Abraham. *An Epitome of Ortelius His Theater of the Vvorld, Vvherein the Principal Regions of the Earth Are Descrived in Smalle Mappes. VVith a Brief Declaration Annexed to Ech Mappe. And Donne in More Exact Manner, Then Lyke Declarations in Latin, French, or Other Languages. It Is Also Amplyfied with New Mappes Wanting in the Latin Editions.* At London [i.e. Antwerp]: Printed by [typis H. Swingenij [for]] Iohn Norton, 1601.

———. *Theatrum Orbis Terrarum Abrahami Orteli Antverp: The Theatre of the Whole World.* London: Iohn Norton, 1606.

Owens, Robert R. "The Myth of Anian." *Journal of the History of Ideas* 36.1 (Jan.–Mar. 1975): 135–138.

Oxonian. *Israel's Wanderings; or, The Scüths, the Saxons, and the Kymry: A Connected Account Tracing the Lost Tribes of Israel into the British Isles.* London: British Israel Identity, 1881.

Pagden, Anthony. *The Fall of Natural Man: The American Indian and the Origins of Comparative Ethnology.* Cambridge: Cambridge University Press, 1982.

———. *Peoples and Empires: A Short History of European Migration, Exploration, and Conquest, from Greece to the Present.* New York: Modern Library, 2001.

Paine, Thomas. *The Age of Reason: Being an Investigation of True and Fabulous Theology.* Paris: Printed by Barrois, 1794.

Pakenham, Thomas. *The Scramble for Africa, 1876–1912.* New York: Random House, 1991.

Palmer, Hurley Pring. *Joseph Wolff: His Romantic Life and Travels.* London: Heath, Cranton, 1935.

Parfitt, Tudor. "Constructing Black Jews: Genetic Tests and the Lemba—the 'Black Jews' of South Africa." *Developing World Bioethics* 3.2 (2003): 112–118.

———. "Hebrew in Colonial Discourse." *Journal of Modern Jewish Studies* 2.2 (October 2003): 159–173.

———. *Journey to the Vanished City: The Search for a Lost Tribe of Israel.* New York: St. Martin's, 1993.

———. *The Lost Ark of the Covenant: Solving the 2,500 Year Old Mystery of the Fabled Biblical Ark.* New York: HarperOne, 2008.

———. *The Lost Tribes of Israel.* London: Weidenfeld & Nicolson, 2002.

———. *Operation Moses: The Untold Story of the Secret Exodus of the Falasha Jews from Ethiopia.* New York: Stein and Day, 1985.

Parfitt, Tudor, and Yulia Egorova. *Genetics, Mass Media and Identity: A Case Study of the Genetic Research on the Lemba and Bene Israel.* London: Routledge, 2006.

Parfitt, Tudor, and Emanuela Trevisan Semi. *Judaising Movements: Studies in the Margins of Judaism*. London: RoutledgeCurzon, 2002.

Paris, Matthew. *Matthew Paris's English History: From the Year 1235 to 1273*, trans. J. A. Giles and William Rishanger. London: H. G. Bohn, 1852.

Park, Chris. "Religion and Geography," in *Routledge Companion to the Study of Religion*, ed. J. Hinnells, 439–455. London: Routledge, 2004.

———. *Sacred Worlds: An Introduction to Geography and Religion*. London: Routledge, 1994.

Parker, Bradley J. "Garrisoning the Empire: Aspects of the Construction and Maintenance of Forts on the Assyrian Frontier." *Iraq* 59 (1997): 77–87.

———. *The Mechanics of Empire: The Northern Frontier of Assyria as a Case Study in Imperial Dynamics*. Helsinki: Neo-Assyrian Text Corpus Project, 2000.

Parpola, Simo. "Assyrian Identity in Ancient Times and Today." *Journal of Assyrian Academic Studies* 18.2 (2004): 5–49.

Parpola, Simo, and R. M. Whiting, eds. *Assyria 1995: Proceedings of the 10th Anniversary Symposium of the Neo-Assyrian Text Corpus Project, Helsinki, September 7–11, 1995*. Helsinki: The Project, 1997.

Peckham, Brian. *History and Prophecy: The Development of Late Judean Literary Traditions*. Garden City, N.Y.: Doubleday, 1993.

Peñafiel, Antonio. *Nombres Geograficos de Mexico: Cataloga Alfabetico de Los Nombres de Lugar Pertenecientes al Idioma*. Ciudad de Mexico: Secretario de Fomento, 1885.

Perlmann, Moshe. "Another Ka'b al-Ahbar Story." *Jewish Quarterly Review*, new ser., 45.1 (July 1954): 48–58.

Petry, Yvonne. *Gender, Kabbalah, and the Reformation: The Mystical Theology of Guillaume Postel, 1510–1581*. Leiden: Brill, 2004.

Peyton, Edward. *The Divine Catastrophe of the Kingly Family of the House of Stuarts; or, A Short History of the Rise, Reigne, and Ruine Thereof. Wherein the Most Secret and Chamber Abominations of the Two Last Kings Are Discovered, Divine Justice in King Charles His Overthrow Vindicated, and the Parliaments Proceedings against Him Clearly Justified*. London: T. Warner, 1731.

Pinkerton, John. *A General Collection of the Best and Most Interesting Voyages and Travels in All Parts of the World, Many of Which Are Now First Translated into English. Digested on a New Plan*. London: Longman, Hurst, Rees, and Orme [etc.], 1808.

Plato. *Timaeus*, trans. Benjamin Jowett. Champaign, Ill.: Project Gutenberg, 1990.

Polliack, Meira. *Karaite Judaism: A Guide to Its History and Literary Sources*. Leiden: Brill, 2003.

Polo, Marco. *The Travels of Marco Polo*, trans. Ronald Latham. London: Penguin, 1972.

Poole, William H. *Anglo-Israel; or, The British Nation the Lost Tribes of Israel*. Toronto: Bengough Bros., 1879.

———. *Anglo-Israel; or, The Saxon Race Proved to Be the Lost Tribes of Israel*. Detroit, Mich.: Winn, 1889.

Popkin, Richard H. "The Age of Reason versus the Age of Revelation: Two Critics of Tom Paine: David Levi and Elias Boudinot: Essays Honoring Alfred Owen

Aldridge," in *Deism, Masonry, and the Enlightenment*, ed. J. A. Leo Lemay, 158–170. Newark: University of Delaware Press, 1987.

———. "David Levi, Anglo-Jewish Theologian." *Jewish Quarterly Review*, new ser., 87.1–2 (July–Oct. 1996): 79–101.

———. *Isaac La Peyrère (1596–1676): His Life, Work, and Influence*. Leiden: Brill, 1987.

———. "Jewish-Christian Relations in the Sixteenth and Seventeenth Centuries: The Conception of the Messiah." *Jewish History* 6.1–2 (Mar. 1992): 163–177.

———. "The Rise and Fall of the Jewish Indian Theory," in *Menasseh ben Israel and His World*, ed. Yosef Kaplan, Richard H. Popkin, and Henry Méchoulan, and, 63–82. Leiden: Brill, 1989.

Post-angel; or, Universal Entertainment (London) 4.4 (April 1701).

Pratt, Mary Louise. *Imperial Eyes: Travel Writing and Transculturation*. London: Routledge, 1992.

Prince, Carlos. *I. Origen de los Indios de América. II. Origen y civilization de los Indígenas del Perú*. Lima, Peru: Impreso en casa del autor, 1915.

Pringle, Heather Anne. *The Master Plan: Himmler's Scholars and the Holocaust*. New York: Hyperion, 2006.

Pritchett, Percy Hugh. *The Enduring Empire of the British: An Account of the Remarkable Unconscious Testimony of Several Historians Never Before Used in British-Israel Evidence, Which Is Shown to Exactly Fit in with the Picture Scripture Draws of the Scattered, Outcast, Wandering, Lost Ten-Tribed Israel Led to the British Isles, and Destined to Ultimately Become a Blessing to the Whole World*. London: Covenant, 1928.

Purchas, Samuel. *Pvrchas his pilgrimage; or, Relations of the world and the religions obserued in all ages and places discouered, from the Creation vnto this present: bin foure partes: this first containeth a theologicall and geographicall historie of Asia, Africa, and America, with the ilands adiacent: declaring the ancient religions before the floud, the heathnish, Jewish, and Saracenicall in all ages since* . . . London: Printed by W. Stansby for H. Fetherstone, 1613.

——— *Purchas His Pilgrimes In Fiue Bookes. The First, Contayning the Voyages and Peregrinations Made by Ancient Kings, Patriarkes, Apostles, Philosophers, and Others, to and Thorow the Remoter Parts of the Knowne World: Enquiries Also of Languages and Religions, Especially of the Moderne Diuersified Professions of Christianitie. The Second, a Description of All the Circum-Nauigations of the Globe. The Third, Nauigations and Voyages of English-Men, Alongst the Coasts of Africa . . . The Fourth, English Voyages Beyond the East Indies, to the Ilands of Iapan, China, Cauchinchina, the Philippinæ [32] with Others . . . The Fifth, Nauigations, Voyages, Traffiques, Discoueries, of the English Nation in the Easterne Parts of the World . . . The First Part*. London: Printed by William Stansby for Henrie Fetherstone, 1625.

———. *Purchas His Pilgrimage; or, Relations of the World and the Religions Observed in All Ages and Places Discovered, from the Creation Vnto This Present. Contayning a Theologicall and Geographicall Historie of Asia, Africa, and America, with the Ilands Adiacent. Declaring the Ancient Religions Before the Floud, the Heathenis, Iewish, and Saracenicall in All Ages Since*. London: Printed by William Stansby for Henrie

Fetherstone, and are to be sold at his shop in Pauls Church-yard at the signe of the Rose, 1625.

Rabinowitz, Louis. "Eldad ha-Dani and China." *Jewish Quarterly Review*, new ser., 36.3 (Jan. 1946): 231–238.

Rademaker, C. S. M. *Life and Work of Gerardus Joannes Vossius (1577–1649)*. Assen, Netherlands: Van Gorcum, 1981.

Rafinesque, C. S. "The American Nations and Tribes Are Not Jews." *Atlantic Journal and Friend of Knowledge* 1.3 (Autumn 1832): 98–99.

———. *A Life of Travels and Researches in North America and South Europe; or, Outlines of the Life, Travels and Researches of C. S. Rafinesque...Containing His Travels in North America and the South of Europe; the Atlantic Ocean, Mediterranean, Sicily, Azores, &c., from 1802 to 1835, with Sketches of His Scientific and Historical Researches &c.* Philadelphia: Printed for the Author by F. Turner, 1836.

Raleigh, Walter. *The Discovery of the Large, Rich, and Beautiful Empire of Guiana, With a Relation of the Great and Golden City of Manoa (Which the Spaniards Call El Dorado) Etc. Performed in the Year 1595.* New York: B. Franklin, 1970.

———. *The Works of Sir Walter Ralegh, Kt., Now First Collected. To Which Are Prefixed the Lives of the Author.* New York: B. Franklin, 1965.

Ramaswamy, Sumathi. *The Lost Land of Lemuria: Fabulous Geographies, Catastrophic Histories.* Berkeley: University of California Press, 2004.

Randles W. G. L. "South-East Africa as Shown on Selected Printed Maps of the Sixteenth Century." *Imago Mundi* 13 (1956): 69–88.

Raz-Krakotzkin, Amnon. *The Censor, the Editor, and the Text: The Catholic Church and the Shaping of the Jewish Canon in the Sixteenth Century.* Philadelphia: University of Pennsylvania Press, 2007.

———. "Galut be-toch Ribonut: le-Bikoret Shelilat ha-Galut" (Exile within Sovereignty: Toward a Critique of the Negation of Exile in Israeli Culture), pts. 1 and 2. *Theory and Criticism* 4–5 (1993–1994): 6–23 and 113–132.

———. "A National Colonial Theology: Religion, Orientalism, and Construction of the Secular in Zionist Discourse." *Tel Aviver Yahrbuch* (2000): 304–318.

Reisenauer, Eric Michael. "British-Israel: Racial Identity in Imperial Britain, 1870–1920." Ph.D. diss., Loyola University of Chicago, 1997.

Rennell, James. "Concerning the Disposal of the Ten Tribes of the Jews, which were Carried into Captivity to Nineveh: Commonly Called the First Captivity," in Rennell, James, *The Geography System of Herodotus Examined and Explained, by a Comparison with Those of Other Ancient Authors, and with Modern Geography,* 512–535. London: C. J. G. & F. Rivington, 1830.

Rey, Charles Fernand. *The Romance of the Portuguese in Abyssinia: An Account of the Adventurous Journeys of the Portuguese to the Empire of Prester John, Their Assistance to Ethiopia in Its Struggle against Islam and Their Subsequent Efforts to Impose Their Own Influence and Religion, 1490–1633.* New York: Negro Universities Press, 1929.

Ridpath, George. *Parliamentary Right Maintain'd; or, The Hanover Succession Justified. Wherein the Hereditary Right to the Crown of England Asserted, &c. Is Consider'd, in III Parts.* [London]: n.p., 1714.

Ringelblum, Emanuel. *Ksovim fun geto*. Warsaw, Poland: Idisz Buch, 1961.

Ripley, George, and Charles A. Dana. *A Universal Library: The New American Cyclopaedia*. New York: Appleton, 1863.

Robertson, Roland, and David Inglis. "Beyond the Gates of the Polis: Reconfiguring Sociology's Ancient Inheritance." *Journal of Classical Sociology* 4.2 (2004): 165–189.

———. "The Global Animus: In the Tracks of World Consciousness." *Globalizations* 1.1 (2004): 38–49.

Robinson, J. Armitage. "Introduction to the Story of Zosimus," in *Texts and Studies, Contributions to Biblical and Patristic Literature*, ed. J Armitage Robinson, 86–91. Cambridge: Cambridge University Press, 1891.

Rocha, Diego Andrés. *El origen de los indios*, ed. José Alcina Franch. Madrid: Historia, 1988.

———. *Tratado Único y Singular del Origen de los Indios del Perú, Méjico, Santa Fé y Chile*. 1681; reprint, Madrid: n.p., 1891.

Rodinson, Maxime. *Muhammad*. London: Penguin, 1996.

Rogers, Francis Millet. *The Quest for Eastern Christians*. Minneapolis: University of Minnesota Press, 1962.

Romm, James S. "Biblical History and the Americas: The Legend of Solomon's Ophir, 1492–1591," in *The Jews and the Expansion of Europe to the West, 1450 to 1800*, ed. Paolo Bernardini and Norman Fiering, 27–46. New York: Berghahn Books, 2001.

———. *The Edges of the Earth in Ancient Thought: Geography, Exploration, and Fiction*. Princeton, N.J.: Princeton University Press, 1992.

Rosen, Friedrich. *Oriental Memories of a German Diplomatist*. London: Methuen, 1930.

Rosenthal, Frank. "The Rise of Christian Hebraism in the Sixteenth Century." *Historia Judaica* 7 (1945): 167–191.

Roth, Cecil. *A Life of Menasseh Ben Israel: Rabbi, Printer, and Diplomat*. New York: Arno, 1975.

———. *The Nephew of the Almighty: An Experimental Account of the Life and Aftermath of Richard Brothers*. London: E. Goldston, 1933.

Rudbeck, Olof. *Olavi Rudbeck filii Atlantica illustrata: sive illustrium, nobilium, principum atque regum insula, ubi et prisci Hesperidum horti*. Upsalis: Wernerianis, 1732.

Rudbeck, Olof. *Olof Rudbeck's Book of Birds: A Facsimile of the Original Watercolours (c. 1693–1710) of Olof Rudbeck the Younger in the Leufsta Collection in Uppsala University Library*, ed. Björn Löwendahl. Stockholm: Björck & Börjesson, 1986.

Rudbeck, Olof [Olavi Rudbecki fil]. *Specimen Usus Linguae Gothicae, in Eruendis Atque Illustrandis Obscurissimis Quibusvis Sacrae Scripturae locis: addita analogia linguae gothicae cum sinica, nec non finnonicae cum ungarica*. Uppsala, Sweden: Joh. Henr. Werner, 1717.

Rudbeck the Younger, Olof. "Of the Origin of the Estonians, Finns, and Laplanders" (1727, *Acta Literaria Suecia*), translated in *Acta Germanica; or, The Literary Memoirs of Germany, &c.: Being a Choice Collection of What Is Most Valuable . . . Not Only in the Several Literary Acts, Publish'd in Different Parts of Germany, and the North . . . but Likewise in the Several Academical Theses . . . in the Several Faculties, at the Universities*

All Over Germany, &c. Done from the Latin and High-Dutch, by a Society of Gentlemen . . . Illustrated with Copper-Plates, ed. Godfrey Smith, 306–309. N.p., 1743.

Ruderman, David B. *Jewish Thought and Scientific Discovery in Early Modern Europe.* Detroit, Mich.: Wayne State University Press, 2001.

———. *The World of a Renaissance Jew: The Life and Thought of Abraham Ben Mordecai Farissol.* Cincinnati, Ohio: Hebrew Union College Press, 1981.

Ruland, Harold L. "A Survey of the Double-Page Maps in Thirty-Five Editions of the 'Cosmographia Universalis' 1544–1628 of Sebastian Münster and in His Editions of Ptolemy's 'Geographia' 1540–1552." *Imago Mundi* 16 (1962): 84–97.

Russell-Wood, A. J. R. *The Portuguese Empire, 1415–1808: A World on the Move.* Baltimore, Md.: Johns Hopkins University Press, 1998.

Rutherford, Adam. *Anglo-Saxon Israel, or Israel-Britain: An Explanation of the Origin, Function and Destiny of the Norse-Anglo-Celto-Saxon Race in the British Empire, U.S.A., Holland, Scandinavia and Iceland.* London: The Author, 1939.

———. *Israel-Britain or Anglo-Saxon Israel: An Explanation of the Origin, Function and Destiny of the Anglo-Saxon Race in the British Empire and the U.S.A.* London: Rutherford, 1934.

Ryan, Michael T. "Assimilating New Worlds in the Sixteenth and Seventeenth Centuries." *Comparative Studies in Society and History* 23.4 (Oct. 1981): 519–538.

Sacchi, Paolo. *Jewish Apocalyptic and Its History.* Sheffield, England: Sheffield Academic, 1990.

Samuel, Jacob. *The Remnant Found; or, The Place of Israel's Hiding Discovered. Being a Summary of Proofs, Showing That the Jews of Daghistan of the Caspian Sea Are the Remnant of the Ten Tribes: The Result of Personal Investigation During a Missionary Tour of Eight Months in Georgia, by Permission of the Russian Government in the Years 1837 and 1838.* London: J. Hatchard and Son, 1841.

Sanceau, Elaine. *The Land of Prester John: A Chronicle of Portuguese Exploration.* New York: Knopf, 1944.

Sanders, Ronald. *Lost Tribes and Promised Lands: The Origins of American Racism.* New York: HarperPerennial, 1992.

Sarna, Jonathan D. *Jacksonian Jew: The Two Worlds of Mordecai Noah.* New York: Holmes & Meier, 1981.

Schäfer, Peter. *The History of the Jews in the Greco-Roman World.* London: Routledge, 2003.

Schaff, Philip, et al., trans. *Sulpitius Severus, Vincent of Lerins, John Cassian.* Peabody, Mass.: Hendrickson, 1994.

Scherb, Victor I. "Assimilating Giants: The Appropriation of Gog and Magog in Medieval and Early Modern England." *Journal of Medieval and Early Modern Studies* 32.1 (2002): 59–84.

Schloessinger, Max. *The Ritual of Eldad ha-Dani Reconstructed and Ed. from Manuscripts and a Genizah Fragment.* Leipzig, Germany: R. Haupt, 1908.

Schmieder, Felicitas. "Christians, Jews, Muslims—and Mongols: Fitting a Foreign People into the Western Christian Apocalyptic Scenario." *Medieval Encounters* 12.2 (Oct. 2006): 274–295.

Scholem, Gershom. *Sabbatai Sevi: The Mystical Messiah, 1626–1676*. Princeton, N.J.: Princeton University Press, 1973.

———. *Zohar = The Book of Splendor: Basic Readings from the Kabbalah*. New York: Schocken, 1995.

Schroeder, Christoph O. *History, Justice, and the Agency of God: A Hermeneutical and Exegetical Investigation on Isaiah and Psalms*. Leiden: Brill, 2001.

Schur, Nathan. *History of the Karaites*. Frankfurt am Main, Germany: Peter Lang, 1992.

Schwartz, Dov. *Faith at the Crossroads: A Theological Profile of Religious Zionism*. Leiden: Brill, 2002.

Secret, François. *Bibliographie des manuscrits de Guillaume Postel*. Geneva, Switzerland: Droz, 1970.

———. *Postel Revisité: Nouvelles Recherches sur Guillaume Postel et son Milieu*. Milan, Italy: Arché, 1998.

Seed, Patricia. "'Are These Not Also Men?' The Indians' Humanity and Capacity for Spanish Civilisation." *Journal of Latin American Studies* 25.3 (Oct. 1993): 629–652.

———. *Ceremonies of Possession in Europe's Conquest of the New World, 1492–1640*. Cambridge: Cambridge University Press, 1995.

Sestieri, Lea. *David Reubeni: un ebreo d'Arabia in missione segreta nell'Europa del '500*. Genoa, Italy: Marietti, 1991.

Shahan, Avigdor. *El 'Ever ha-Sambatyon: Masa' be-'Ikvot 'Aseret ha-Shevatim* (Towards the Sambatyon: A Journey in the Footsteps of the Ten Tribes). Tel Aviv: HaKibbutz ha-Meuhad, 2003.

Shalev, Zur. "Geographia Sacra: Cartography, Religion, and Scholarship in the Sixteenth and Seventeenth Centuries." Ph.D. diss., Princeton University, 2004.

———. "Sacred Geography, Antiquarianism and Visual Erudition: Benito Arias Montano and the Maps in the Antwerp Polyglot Bible." *Imago Mundi* 55 (2003): 56–80.

Shohat, Azriel. "Le-Farashat David ha-Re'uveni." *Zion* 35 (1970): 96–116.

Short, John R. *Making Space: Revisioning the World, 1475–1600*. Syracuse, N.Y.: Syracuse University Press, 2004.

Sicker, Martin. *Between Rome and Jerusalem: 300 Years of Roman-Judaean Relations*. Westport, Conn.: Praeger, 2001.

Silverberg, Robert. *The Golden Dream: Seekers of El Dorado*. Athens: Ohio University Press, 1996.

———. *Mound Builders of Ancient America: The Archaeology of a Myth*. Greenwich, Conn.: New York Graphic Society, 1968.

———. *The Realm of Prester John*. Athens: Ohio University Press, 1996.

Silverblatt, Irene M. *Modern Inquisitions: Peru and the Colonial Origins of the Civilized World*. Durham, N.C.: Duke University Press, 2004.

Simon, Barbara Anne. *The Hope of Israel: Presumptive Evidence That the Aborigines of the Western Hemisphere Are Descended from the Ten Missing Tribes of Israel*. London: R. B. Seeley, 1829.

———. *The Ten Tribes of Israel Historically Identified with the Aborigines of the Western Hemisphere*. London: R. B. Seeley and W. Burnside, 1836.

Simon, Marcel. *Verus Israel: A Study of the Relations between Christians and Jews in the Roman Empire, 135–425*. New York: Oxford University Press, 1986.

Simons, Jake. *The Exiled Times of a Tibetan Jew*. Edinburgh: Polygon, 2005.

Smith, Anthony. *Explorers of the Amazon*. Chicago: University of Chicago Press, 1994.

Smith, Ethan. *View of the Hebrews; or, The Tribes of Israel in America*. Poultney, Vt.: Smith & Shute, 1823.

Smith, John Masson, Jr. "'Ayn Jalut: Mamluk Success or Mongol Failure?" *Harvard Journal of Asiatic Studies* 44.2 (Dec. 1984): 307–345.

Smith, Joseph. *The Book of Mormon: An Account Written by the Hand of Mormon upon Plates Taken from the Plates of Nephi*. Salt Lake City, Utah: Church of Jesus Christ of Latter-day Saints, 1981.

Smith, Richard. *Chinese Maps: Images of All under Heaven*. New York: Oxford University Press, 1996.

Smith, Sidney. "Events in Arabia in the 6th Century A.D." *Bulletin of the School of Oriental and African Studies* 16.3 (1954): 425–468.

Southerton, Simon G. *Losing a Lost Tribe: Native Americans, DNA, and the Mormon Church*. Salt Lake City, Utah: Signature, 2004.

Southey, Robert. *Letters from England*. London: Longman, Hurst, Rees, Orme, and Brown, 1814.

———. *Selections from the Letters of Robert Southey*. London: Longman, Brown, Green, and Longmans, 1856.

Spaulding, Jay. "The Nile: Histories, Cultures, Myths." *Journal of African History* 42.1 (2001): 132–133.

Spence, Jonathan D. *God's Chinese Son: The Taiping Heavenly Kingdom of Hong Xiuquan*. New York: Norton, 1996.

Sucharitkul, Somtow. *Aquila in the New World*. New York: Wildpres, 2000.

Sweeney, Marvin A. *King Josiah of Judah: The Lost Messiah of Israel*. New York: Oxford University Press, 2001.

Tacitus, Cornelius. *The History of Tacitus*, trans. Alfred John Church and William Jackson Brodribb. London: Macmillan, 1876.

Tadmor, Hayim. "History and Ideology in the Assyrian Royal Inscriptions," in *Assyrian Royal Inscriptions: New Horizons in Literary, Ideological, and Historical Analysis: Papers of Symposium Held in Cetona (Siena), June 26–28, 1980*, ed. F. Mario Fales, 13–33. Rome: Istituto per l'Oriente, Centro per le antichità e la storia dell'arte del vicino Oriente, 1981.

———. *The Inscriptions of Tiglath-pileser III, King of Assyria: Critical Edition, with Introductions, Translations, and Commentary*. Jerusalem: Israel Academy of Sciences and Humanities, 1994.

Taylor, Edward. *Primitive Culture: Researches into the Development of Mythology, Philosophy, Religion, Language, Art, and Custom*. New York: Brentano's, 1924.

Terrar, Toby. "Catholic Socialism: The Reverend Thomas McGrady." *Dialectical Anthropology* 7.3 (Jan. 1983): 209–235.

Theodor, Julius, and Chanoch Albeck. *Midrash Bereshit Rabba*. Jerusalem: Wahrmann, 1965.

Thom, William. *The Revolt of the Ten Tribes: A Sermon Preached in the Church of Govan, on the Forenoon of the Public Fast, December 12th, 1776. By William Thom.* Glasgow: Robert Chapman and Alexander Duncan, 1778.

Thornton, John K. "The Portuguese in Africa," in *Portuguese Oceanic Expansion, 1400–1800*, ed. Francisco Bethencourt and Diogo Ramada Curto, 138–160. Cambridge: Cambridge University Press, 2007.

Thorowgood, Thomas. *Iewes in America; or, Probabilities That the Americans Are of That Race With the Removall of Some Contrary Reasonings, and Earnest Desires for Effectuall Endeavours to Make Them Christian.* London: Printed by W.H. for Tho. Slater,, 1650.

Thorowgood, Thomas, John Dury, and Manasseh ben Israel. *Digitus Dei: New Discoveryes with Sure Arguments to Prove That the Jews (a Nation) or People Lost in the World for the Space of Near 200 Years, Inhabite Now in America; How They Came Thither; Their Manners, Customs, Rites and Ceremonies; the Unparallel'd Cruelty of the Spaniard to Them; and That the Americans Are of That Race. Manifested by Reason and Scripture, Which Foretell the Calling of the Jewes; and the Restitution of Them into Their Own Land, and the Bringing Back of the Ten Tribes from All the Ends and Corners of the Earth, and That Great Battell to Be Fought. With the Removall of Some Contrary Reasonings, and an Earnest Desire for Effectuall Endeavours to Make Them Christians. Whereunto Is Added an Epistolicall Discourse of Mr. John Dury, with the History of Ant. Monterinos, Attested by Manasseh Ben Israell, a Chief Rabby. By Tho. Thorowgood, B.D.* London: Thomas Slater, 1652.

Thorowgood, Thomas, and John Eliot. *Iews in America; or, Probabilities, That Those Indians Are Judaical, Made More Probable by Some Additionals to the Former Conjectures. An Accurate Discourse Is Premised of Mr. John Elliot, (Who First Preached the Gospel to the Natives in Their Own Language) Touching Their Origination, and His Vindication of the Planters.* London: H. Brome, 1660.

Trakulhun, Sven. "The Widening of the World and the Realm of History: Early European Approaches to the Beginnings of Siamese History, c. 1500–1700." *Renaissance Studies* 17.3 (2003): 392–417.

Trevisan Semi, Emanuela. *Jacques Faitlovitch and the Jews of Ethiopia.* London: Vallentine Mitchell, 2007.

2 Baruch: The Book of the Apocalypse of Baruch the Son of Neriah, trans. R. H. Charles, in *The Apocrypha and Pseudepigrapha of the Old Testament in English.* Oxford: Oxford University Press, 1913.

Ullendorff, Edward, and C. F. Beckingham. *The Hebrew Letters of Prester John.* Oxford: Oxford University Press, 1982.

Urban, Sylvanus. *The Gentleman's Magazine and Historical Review (1857 January–June).* London: Henry and Parker, 1857.

Vail, Shalvah. *Me-'Ever La-Sambatyon: Ha-Mitos shel 'Aseret Ha-Shevatim Ha-Avudim* (Beyond the Sambatyon: The Myth of the Ten Lost Tribes). Tel Aviv: Bet haTefutsot, 1991.

Vanderhooft, David Stephen. *The Neo-Babylonian Empires and Babylon in the Latter Prophets.* Atlanta, Ga.: Harvard Semitic Museum Monographs, Scholars Press, 1999.

VanderKam, James C., and William Adler. *The Jewish Apocalyptic Heritage in Early Christianity.* Assen, Netherlands: Van Gorcum, 1996.

Vaux, W. S. W. *Nineveh and Persepolis: An Historical Sketch of Ancient Assyria and Persia, with an Account of the Recent Researches in Those Countries.* London: A. Hall, Virtue, 1850.

Vespucci, Amerigo. *Mundus Novus: Letter to Lorenzo Pietro Di Medici,* trans. George Tyler Northrup. Princeton, N.J.: Princeton University Press, 1916.

Vickery, Paul S. *Bartolomé de Las Casas: Great Prophet of the Americas.* New York: Paulist, 2006.

Viera y Clavijo, José de. *Noticias de la historia general de las Islas de Canaria contienen la descripcion geografica de todas. Una idea del origen, caracter, usos y costumbres de sus antiguos habitantes: de los descubrimientos, y conquistas que sobre ellas hicieron los Europeos: de su gobierno eclesiastico, político y militar: del establecimiento, y succesion de su primera nobleza: de sus varones ilustres por dignidades, empleos, armas, letras, y santidad: de sus fabricas, producciones naturales, y comercio, con los principales sucesos de los ultimos siglos.* Madrid: Blas Román, 1772.

Vieira, Padre António. *Esperanças de Portugal, quinto império do mundo: primeira e segunda vida de El-Rei Dom Joã o quarto, escritas por Gonçalves Bandarra.* Lisboa: Editorial Nova Ática, (n.d.)

Vital, Hayyim ben Joseph. *Sefer ha-Hezyonot: Darkhe Hayim.* Jerusalem: Shuvi Nafshi, 2001.

Wall, Ernestine G. E. van der. "The Amsterdam Millenarian Petrus Serrarius (1600–1669) and the Anglo-Dutch Circle of Philo-Judaists," in *Jewish-Christian Relations in the Seventeenth Century,* ed. J. van den Berg and E. G. E. van den der Wall, 73–94. Leiden: Kluwer, 1988.

———. "Petrus Serrarius and Menasseh Ben Israel: Christian Millenarianism and Jewish Messianism in Seventeenth-Century Amsterdam," in *Menasseh ben Israel and His World,* ed. Yosef Kaplan, Richard H. Popkin, and Henry Méchoulan, 164–190. Leiden: Brill, 1989.

Wanley, Nathaniel. *The Wonders of the Little World; or, A General History of Man. In Six Books. Wherin by Many Thousands of Examples Is Shewed What Man Hath Been from the First Ages of the World to These Times...Collected from the Writings of... Historians, Philosophers...and Others.* London: T. Basset [etc.], 1678.

Warren, Leonard. *Constantine Samuel Rafinesque: A Voice in the American Wilderness.* Lexington: University Press of Kentucky, 2004.

Wasserstein, David. "Eldad ha-Dani and Prester John," in *Prester John, the Mongols and the Ten Lost Tribes,* ed. C. F. Beckingham and Bernard Hamilton, 213–236. Aldershot, England: Variorum, 1996.

Watts, James W. *Persia and Torah: The Theory of Imperial Authorization of the Pentateuch.* Atlanta, Ga.: Society of Biblical Literature, 2001.

Watts, John D. W. *Vision and Prophecy in Amos.* Macon, Ga.: Mercer University Press, 1997.

Watts, Pauline Moffitt. "Prophecy and Discovery: On the Spiritual Origins of Christopher Columbus's 'Enterprise of the Indies.'" *American Historical Review* 90.1 (Feb. 1985): 73–102.

Wauchope, Robert. *Lost Tribes & Sunken Continents: Myth and Method in the Study of American Indians*. Chicago: University of Chicago Press, 1962.

Weems, M. L. *The Life of William Penn, The Settler of Pennsylvania, the Founder of Philadelphia, and One of the First Lawgivers in the Colonies, Now the United States, in 1682*. Philadelphia: U. Hunt, 1829.

Weil, Shalva. "Lost Israelites from the Indo-Burmese Borderlands: Re-Traditionalisation and Conversion among the Shinlung or Bene Menasseh." *Anthropologist* 6.3 (2004): 219–233.

Westrem, Scott D. "Against Gog and Magog," in *Text and Territory: Geographical Imagination in the European Middle Ages*, ed. Sylvia Tomasch and Sealy Gilles, 54–58. Philadelphia: University of Pennsylvania Press, 1998.

Whale, George. "The Art of Conversation." *Gentleman's Magazine* (Jan. 1891): 7–21.

Whitlocke, Bulstrode. *Annals of the Universe: Containing an Account of the Most Memorable Actions, Affairs, and Occurrences Which Have Happen'd in the World, but Especially in Europe, from the Year 1660 Where Mr. Whitlock Leaves Off, to the Year 1680: in Two Decades, with an Index to the Whole: Being a Continuation of the Said Mr. Whitlock's Memorials*. London: Printed for William Carter, 1709.

Wigen, Karen, and Martin Lewis. *The Myth of Continents: A Critique of Metageography*. Berkeley: University California Press, 1997.

Wild, Joseph. *The Lost Ten Tribes*. London: Robert Banks, 1879.

Williams, Joseph J. *Hebrewisms of West Africa: From Nile to Niger with the Jews*. New York: L. MacVeagh, Dial Press, 1930.

Williamson, Arthur H. "The Jewish Dimension of the Scottish Apocalypse," in *Menasseh ben Israel and His World*, ed. Yosef Kaplan, Richard H. Popkin, and Henry Méchoulan, 7–30. Leiden: Brill, 1989.

Wishnevitz, David Aharon. *Metsi'at 'aseret ha-shevatim*. N.p., 1900.

Witsius, Herman. *Dekaphylon: Sive De Decem Tribubus Israelis*, in *Hermanni Witsii Aegyptiaca, et Dekaphylon. Sive, de Aegyptiacorum Sacrorum Cum Hebraicis Collatione Libri Tres. et Liber Singularis. Accessit Diatribe De Legione Fulminatrice Christianorum, sub Imperatore Marco Aurelio Antonino*, 236–330. Amsterdam: Excudit Gerardus Borstius, 1683.

Wolf, Lucien. *Menasseh Ben Israel's Mission to Oliver Cromwell: Being a Reprint of the Pamphlets Published by Menasseh Ben Israel to Promote the Re-Admission of the Jews to England, 1649–1656*. London: Macmillan, 1901.

Wolff, Joseph. *Missionary Journal and Memoir of the Rev. Joseph Wolff, Written by Himself*, ed. John Bayford. London: J. Duncan, 1824.

———. *Narrative of a Mission to Bokhara*. New York: Harper & Bros., 1845.

———. *Researches and Missionary Labours among the Jews, Mohammedans, and Other Sects*. London: J. Nisbet, 1835.

———. *Travels and Adventures of the Rev. Joseph Wolff Late Missionary to the Jews and Muhammadans in Persia, Bokhara, Cashmeer, etc.* London: Saunders, Otley, 1860–1861.

Wolff, Philippe. "The 1391 Pogrom in Spain: Social Crisis or Not?" *Past and Present* 50 (1971): 4–18.

Worsley, Israel. *A View of the American Indians: Their General Character, Customs, Language, Public Festivals, Religious Rites, and Traditions: Shewing Them to Be the Descendants of the Ten Tribes of Israel; the Language of Prophecy Concerning Them, and the Course by Which They Travelled from Media into America*. London: Printed for the Author, 1828.

Wright, John K. "Terrae Incognitae: The Place of Imagination in Geography." *Annals of the Association of American Geographers* 37.1 (Mar. 1947): 1–15.

Wright, William A. "Note on the 'Arzareth' of 4 Esdr. xiii. 45." *Journal of Philology* 3 (1871): 113–114.

Yamauchi, Edwin M. "The Reconstruction of Jewish Communities during the Persian Empire." *Journal of the Historical Society* 4.1 (Jan. 2004): 1–25.

Yeager, Suzanne. "The Siege of Jerusalem and Biblical Exegesis: Writing about Romans in Fourteenth-Century England." *Chaucer Review* 39.1 (2004): 70–102.

Yerushalmi, Yosef Hayim. *Zakhor, Jewish History and Jewish Memory*. Seattle: University of Washington Press, 1982.

———. "Messianic Impulses in Joseph ha-Kohen," in Bernard Dov Cooperman, *Jewish Thought in the Sixteenth Century*, 460–487. [Cambridge, Mass.]: Harvard University Center for Jewish Studies, 1983.

Younger, Lawson K., Jr. "The Deportations of the Israelites." *Journal of Biblical Literature* 117.2 (Summer 1998): 201–227.

———. "Israelites in Exile: Their Names Appear at All Levels of Assyrian Sources." *Biblical Archeology Review* (Nov.–Dec. 2003): 36–44 and 65–66.

Yu, Taishan. *Yanda Shi Yanjiu*. Jinan, China: Qilu shushe, 1986.

Yuval, Israel. "The Myth of the Jewish Exile from the Land of Israel: A Demonstration of Irenic Scholarship." *Common Knowledge* 12.1 (Winter 2006): 16–33.

———. *Shene Goyim bevitnekh: Yehudim ve-Notsrim, Dimuyim Hadadiyim* (Two Nations in Your Womb: Jews and Christians, Mutual Perceptions). Tel Aviv: Am Oved, 2000.

———. *Two Nations in Your Womb: Perceptions of Jews and Christians in Late Antiquity and the Middle Ages*. Berkeley: University of California Press, 2006.

Zadok, Ran. "Notes on the Early History of the Israelites and Judeans in Mesopotamia." *Orientalia* 51 (1982): 391–393.

Zafran, Eric. "Saturn and the Jews." *Journal of the Warburg and Courtauld Institutes* 42 (1979): 16–27.

Index